CU01261054

Hermeneutics, Scriptural Politics, and Human Rights

Also by Bas de Gaay Fortman

God and the Goods (1998)

Also by M. A. Mohamed Salih

Interpreting Islamic Political Parties (2009)
African Parliaments between Government and Governance (2006)

Hermeneutics, Scriptural Politics, and Human Rights

Between Text and Context

Edited by Bas de Gaay Fortman,
Kurt Martens, and M. A. Mohamed Salih

palgrave
macmillan

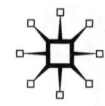

HERMENEUTICS, SCRIPTURAL POLITICS, AND HUMAN RIGHTS
Copyright © Bas de Gaay Fortman, Kurt Martens, and M. A. Mohamed Salih, 2009.

All rights reserved.

First published in 2009 by PALGRAVE MACMILLAN® in the United States—a division of St. Martin's Press LLC, 175 Fifth Avenue, New York, NY 10010.

Where this book is distributed in the UK, Europe, and the rest of the world, this is by Palgrave Macmillan, a division of Macmillan Publishers Limited, registered in England, company number 785998, of Houndmills, Basingstoke, Hampshire RG21 6XS.

Palgrave Macmillan is the global academic imprint of the above companies and has companies and representatives throughout the world.

Palgrave® and Macmillan® are registered trademarks in the United States, the United Kingdom, Europe and other countries.

ISBN: 978-0-230-62223-4

Library of Congress Cataloging-in-Publication Data is available from the Library of Congress.

A catalogue record of the book is available from the British Library.

Design by Scribe Inc.

First edition: March 2010

10 9 8 7 6 5 4 3 2 1

Printed in the United States of America.

Contents

List of Abbreviations and Acronyms	vii
Contributors	ix
Preface	xiii
Introduction M. A. Mohamed Salih, Bas de Gaay Fortman, and Kurt Martens	1

Part I   Hermeneutics, Communities of Readers, and Context

1	Religious Identity, Differences, and Human Rights: The Crucial Role of Hermeneutics M. A. Mohamed Salih and Bas de Gaay Fortman	21
2	Islamic Texts, Democracy, and the Rule of Law: Toward a Hermeneutics of Conciliation Salman Haq	37
3	Interpretation in Canon Law: Faith or Reason? Phillip J. Brown	53
4	Judicial Textualism: An Analysis of Textualism as Applied to the United States Constitution Herman Philipse	69
5	Arbitrary Readings? Christianity and Islam as Capricious Hermeneutic Communities Karel Steenbrink	81
6	Changing Hermeneutics in Reading and Understanding the Bible: The Case of the Gospel of Mark Geert van Oyen	99

Part II   Hermeneutics, Religious Freedom, and Exclusion

7	The Qur'an and Religious Freedom: The Issue of Apostasy Ali Mirmoosavi	125

8	*Dignitatis Humanae*: A Hermeneutic Perspective on Religious Freedom as Interpreted by the Roman Catholic Church Kurt Martens	143
9	Strangers and Residents: The Hermeneutic Challenge of Non-Jewish Minorities in Israel Deborah Weissman	163
10	Religious Texts as Models for Exclusion: Scriptural Interpretation and Ethnic Politics in Northern Nigeria Niels Kastfelt	185
11	In the Name of Allah: Jihad from a Shi'a Hermeneutic Perspective Seyed Sadegh Haghighat	205
12	Views on Women in Early Christianity: Incarnational Hermeneutics in Tertullian and Augustine Willemien Otten	219
13	Women's Rights and the Interpretation of Islamic Texts: The Practice of Female Genital Mutilation Isatou Touray	237
References		253
Index		271

Abbreviations and Acronyms

AICs	African Institutes Churches
BJP	Bharata Janata Party
FGM	Female Genital Mutilation
ICCI	Inter-religious Coordinating Council in Israel
ICCJ	International Council of Christians and Jews
ICCO	Inter-Church Organisation for Development Co-operation
IESCO	Islamic Educational, Scientific and Cultural Organization
LCCN	Lutheran Church of Christ in Nigeria
MK	Mark (Gospel according to)
MUI	Majelis Ulama Indonesia
OIC	Organization of the Islamic Conference
OSCE	Organization for Security and Cooperation
PBUH	Peace be upon him
SCC	Supreme Constitutional Court (Egypt)
SIS	Sisters In Islam
UDHR	Universal Declaration of Human Rights of 1948
UNOCI	United Nations Operation in Côte d'Ivoire
WCC	World Council of Churches
WLUML	Women Living Under Muslim Laws
ZCC	Zimbabwe Council of Churches

Contributors

Phillip Brown is Assistant Professor at the School of Canon Law at the Catholic University of America. He is a former Dean of the School of Theology and Associate Professor of Canon Law at St. Mary's Seminary and University in Baltimore, Maryland; a priest of the Diocese of Bismarck, North Dakota, and a member of the Society of St. Sulpice. He received his J.C.D. *summa cum laude* from the Pontifical Gregorian University in 1999 upon the successful defense of his dissertation *Canon 17 CIC 1983 and the Hermeneutical Principles of Bernard Lonergan.*

Bas de Gaay Fortman is Professor and Chair in Political Economy of Human Rights at the Utrecht University School of Law in the Netherlands. In 1966, he received his PhD based on a dissertation titled *Theory of Competition Policy. A Confrontation of Economic, Political and Legal Principles* (Amsterdam: North Holland Publishing Company). He has previously taught at the Institute of Social Studies in The Hague (1972–2002), the University of Zambia (1967–1971) and the Free University Amsterdam (1965–1967). He has published extensively in the fields of economic order, political economy, human rights and the rule of law, and conflict and religion, including *God and the Goods* (coauthor, Geneva: World Council of Churches Publications 1998) and *The Life and Times of Religion and Human Rights* (with M. A. Mohamed Salih, in Walter van Beek et al. [eds.], *Meeting Culture*, Maastricht: Shaker Publishing 2003), and "Moses and all the Prophets. A Constructive Critique on Ecumenical Response to Economic Injustice," in Frans Bouwen (ed.), *60 years: The Ecumenical Movement at the Crossroads*, Kampen (NL: Kok 2008). He is involved in the International Summer School in Law and Religion at the University of Siena (Italy) and in the Canon Law Faculty of the Catholic University Louvain (Msgr. Willy Onclin Chair in Comparative Canon Law 2003/2004).

Seyed Sadegh Haghighat is a faculty member of the Department of Political Science at Mofid University in Qom, Iran. He graduated in political theory from Tarbiat Modares (TM) University in Tehran, and studied at the Islamic Seminaries in Qom between 1981 and 2004. His PhD thesis on *Distribution of Power in Shi'a Political Thought* focused on Shi'a jurisprudence. Among his many publications is *Six Theories about the Islamic Revolution's*

Victory (ed.), translated in English and Arabic (Tehran: Alhoda, 2000). Most of his publications are available at www.s-haghighat.ir

Niels Kastfelt was Director of the Centre of African Studies at the University of Copenhagen. His main field of research is religion and society in Nigeria on which he has published widely. His major publications are *Religion and Politics in Nigeria. A Study in Middle Belt Christianity* (London 1994), *Scriptural Politics. The Bible and the Koran as Political Models in the Middle East and Africa* (London 2003) and*Religion and African Civil Wars* (London 2005). He is currently completing a book on *The New Way of the Bachama. Christianity, History and Hope in Northern Nigeria*.

Salman Haq is currently a Legal Officer with the United Nations Operation in Côte d'Ivoire (UNOCI). He has previously held positions with the Canadian Bar Association's International Development Program and with the Democratization Department of the Organization for Security and Cooperation (OSCE) in Belgrade, Serbia. Raised to the Bar in Ontario, Canada in 2004 he practiced litigation law with McCarthy Tétrault in Toronto. Salman Haq has a JD in Law and an MA and BSc (Honors) in Economics. His research focuses on the rule of law, good governance, and international development in developing and postconflict countries. As a young Muslim born in Canada, he also writes on the relationship between Islamic law and universal human rights.

Kurt Martens is Associate Professor at the School of Canon Law at the Catholic University of America in Washington DC. At the Catholic University of Louvain, he completed his PhD/J.C.D. in 2004. Before joining the Catholic University of America in the fall of 2005, he was member of the junior academic staff of the Faculty of Canon Law of the Catholic University Leuven (Belgium) from 1997 until 2005. During the 2002–2003 academic year, he was visiting professor at the *Institut de droit canonique* of the *Université Marc Bloch* in Strasbourg (France). During the 2004–2005 academic year, he taught at the Radboud University in Nijmegen (the Netherlands). He was visiting professor at the Faculty of Canon Law of St. Paul University in Ottawa (Canada), where he taught in English and in French (2005). He is editor of the periodical *Law, Religion and Society* (published in Brussels, Belgium by Larcier) and he is an associate editor of *The Jurist*. He is also involved in the International Summer School in Law and Religion at the University of Siena (Italy).

Sayed Ali Mir Moosavi is a faculty member of the Department of Political Science at Mofid University in Qom, Iran. He completed his PhD in 2002. Dr. Mirmoosavi followed Islamic and Shi'a studies including jurisprudence, theology, and philosophy at the Islamic seminaries in Qom. Together with Dr. Haghighat he published a comparative book about the foundations of Human rights in Islam and other schools of thought in

2001 (in Farsi). In fall 2005, he published his book on Islam, *Tradition and the Modern State* (also in Farsi). Other publications include articles on human rights and political theory in Islam and the West.

Willemien Otten is Professor of Theology and History of Christianity at the University of Chicago Divinity School. At the University of Amsterdam, she completed her PhD in 1989 on a dissertation titled *The Anthropology of Johannes Scottus Eriugena*. Raised as a Protestant, she previously taught in the United States at Loyola University of Chicago (1990–1994) and Boston College (1994–1997), both Jesuit universities, before joining Utrecht University in 1997 as Professor of Church History. There she was Dean of Theology between 2003 and 2007. She is currently involved as coeditor with Karla Pollmann (University of St. Andrews) in a multivolume project on the reception of Augustine between 430 and 2000, to appear with Oxford University Press.

Geert van Oyen is Professor of Exegesis of the New Testament at Louvain-La-Neuve, Belgium. He previously taught at Utrecht University (1999–2008) where he also functioned as Dean of the School of Divinity. Among his many publications is a major treatise on "The Mark Code" (2006).

Herman Philipse is Professor at Utrecht University. Having read both law and philosophy, he has taught at the universities of Louvain, Leiden, Oxford, Paris IV and Cologne. He writes on modern philosophy and epistemology. Among his many publications is *Heidegger's Philosophy of Being: A Critical Interpretation* (Princeton: Princeton University Press, 1998).

Mohamed Abdelrahim (M.A) Mohamed Salih is professor of politics of development at both The Institute of Social Studies and The Hague and the Department of Political Science, Leiden University, The Netherlands. *African Parliaments between Government and Governance* (Palgrave Macmillan: New York, 2005); and *Interpreting Islamic Political Parties* (Palgrave Macmillan: New York, forthcoming September 2009).

Karel Steenbrink is Professor Emeritus in Intercultural Theology, Utrecht University. He completed his PhD in 1974. He studied Christian and Islamic theology at the Radboud University Nijmegen and the Darussalam College of Gontor, Indonesia. From 1981 to 1988, he taught the Western tradition in Islamic studies at the State Academy of Islamic Studies in Jakarta and Yogyakarta, Indonesia. He was a visiting professor at the Institute of Islamic Studies of McGill University (Montreal, Canada) in 1992–1993. He has widely published on Islam and Christianity in Indonesia and more recently also on Qur'an interpretation.

Isatou Touray is Executive Director of Gamcotrap, a women's rights organization working on sexual and reproductive health and rights of women. Until her current job, she was the Deputy Director General and

Principal Management Trainer and Coordinator of the Gender Program at the Management Development Institute. She is also the National Coordinator of the Women and Law Project, of Women Living Under Muslim Laws (WLUML) Gambian Chapter. She is a member of the planning committee organizing a global movement for equality and justice in the Muslim family.

Deborah Weissman is President of the International Council of Christians and Jews (ICCJ). She is a Jewish educator with a deep interest and involvement in inter-religious dialogue and education. Her many publications include "Jewish religious education as peace education: from crisis to opportunity," in Robert Jackson and Satoko Fujiwara (eds.), *Peace Education and Religious Plurality: International Perspectives*, Routledge (2008), and "Towards a Humanistic Hermeneutic of Jewish Texts" in Anantanand Rambachan, A. Rashied Omar, and M. Thomas Thangaraj (eds.), *Hermeneutical Explorations in Dialogue: Essays in Honor of Hans Ucko*, Indian Society for Promoting Christian Knowledge (2007).

Preface

Post September 11 has confronted the world with frightful consequences of a scripturally conjured *Jihadism*. The Utrecht University School of Law together with the School of Divinity invited a select group of scholars to engage in a joint hermeneutic endeavor. The aim was to understand the intricacies of text interpretation in a world full of manipulation of religious and legal texts for political purposes. The papers presented on the conference probed the need for continuous reexamination and reformulation of jurisprudential precepts and the interpretations of religious scriptures that form their foundation. The participants were theologians, jurists, anthropologists, and political scientists from all over the world. Their spiritual background was diverse: secular as well as religious, Islamic as well as Jewish, Protestant as well as Roman Catholic Christians.

This volume builds on that conference, focused as it was on hermeneutics, scriptural politics, and human rights. Following intensive academic discussion and review, the participants rewrote their papers, bringing them in line with recent insights. Additionally, as editors we have approached other scholars whose work deals with hermeneutics, scriptural politics and human rights. The result is the chapters of this volume, which are unique for their focus on the intricacies of text interpretation from an interdisciplinary academic orientation, ushering in interfaith experiences on human rights and the questions surrounding multiculturalism while linking the past to the present.

We are greatly indebted to Laura Hils of the University of Cincinnati for the invaluable editorial assistance. As editors, we are grateful to Ms. Leslie O'Brien and Mr. Erik Hoff of Goldenwest Editing in California, USA, for English editing the manuscript before submission. Thanks also to the Board of Utrecht University, the Netherlands Ministry of Foreign Affairs, the Inter-Church Organisation for Development Co-operation (ICCO) and the Catholic Development Organization (Cordaid) for supporting the activities that lead to the conception and preparation of this book.

Bas de Gaay Fortman, Kurt Martens, and
M. A. Mohamed Salih The Hague, June 2009

Introduction

*M. A. Mohamed Salih, Bas de Gaay Fortman,
and Kurt Martens*

This book provides an analysis of the reemergence of hermeneutics and the political interpretation of scriptural texts in post-September 11, 2001, with special emphasis on Christianity, Islam, and Judaism. Three relevant domains of hermeneutics and scriptural politics inform the contents of this book: human rights, democracy and law, and exploration of how scriptures and percepts have been reinvented and reinterpreted in order to respond to contemporary, social, and political concerns.

At a larger synthesis, the book examines the role of religion in contemporary politics and society and how it influences the nature of state and citizens relationships, particularly in situations where scriptural politics is used or abused to advance models of social and political organization incompatible with concerns with social justice and human rights. Likewise, it probes the antithetical nature of individual autonomous reasoning, the emancipative potential of scriptural politics and its capacity as a mobilizing force for collective action.

Therefore, the introduction is organized to reflect four sections and a conclusion that correspond to the book contents: (1) Hermeneutics: Religious and Secular, (2) Human Rights, Religion, and Scriptural Politics, (3) Religious Identity and Scriptural Politics and (4) the Structure of the Book, and (5) Conclusions. Put together, this volume engages the current debate on hermeneutics and its mediation between scriptures and action whether religious, political or social, violent or peaceful, supportive or abusive of human rights.

The book is divided into two overlapping parts traversing its grounding on hermeneutics, scriptural politics, and human rights. These are Part I: Hermeneutics, Communities of Readers, and Context and Part II: Hermeneutics religious Freedom and Exclusion.

Part I explores questions pertaining to religious identity and multiculturalism, democracy and human rights between scripture (text) and context, textualism and its changing role and understanding of religious and secular hermeneutics. In Part II, we give more emphasis to concrete human rights issues in respect to religious freedom, women's rights, scriptural politics in the case of women and minorities and the uses and abuses of the scriptures as instruments for inclusion or exclusion.

Hermeneutics: Religious and Secular

Without entering into competing definitions of what hermeneutics is or is not, we are content that hermeneutics is the theory of interpretation applied to written monuments whether religious or secular (Jeanrond 1991, 1). In keeping with this premise, this volume focuses on hermeneutics and scriptural politics with particular reference to freedom of religion, the protection of minorities, us-them divides, women's rights, democracy and the rule of law. This broad definition of hermeneutics also explains why we have, for example, slated a chapter on the American Constitution following Levine's contention that, "a body of literature has emerged comparing constitutional textual analysis to Biblical hermeneutics." In his view, this scholarship has been based on the recognition that, like the Constitution, the Bible (for some believers) functions as an authoritative legal text that must be interpreted in order to "serve as the foundation for a living community" (Levin 1998, 511–12). Other scholars of hermeneutics also lamented on this, which gives us greater comfort in dealing with the American Constitution as monumental text, while the rest of the authors have dealt with philosophical, theological, biblical, Qur'anic, political, and canon legal practices.

For example, does the principle of freedom of speech justify slur? Should not all human rights be interpreted and understood in the context of respect for human dignity as intended by the founding fathers and mothers? To be sure, while the transformation of scriptural hermeneutics into meaning, and meaning into political or social action for the good of society cannot be disregarded, the abuse of scriptural hermeneutics and their employment as instruments of hate can produce disastrous consequences.

By-and-large, the analyses contained in this volume come closer to the work of Richard Ernstein on *Beyond Objectivism and relativism: Science, Hermeneutics, and Praxis*, whereby the analysis of praxis (or theory of practice), discourse, and political judgment are intimately related (Ernstein 1983, 44). This conception is ultimately tied to, but critical of, the possibility of attempting to create a commonly negotiable interpretation of scriptures as "written monuments." Within this perspective the debate that engulfed what Phillips calls the hermeneutics of recollection (the conviction that there is a message in religion which we need to heed) or the hermeneutics of suspicion (rejection of the existence of a divine reality in religion or treating religion as a product of illusion devout of social reality) come to life (Phillips 2001, 1). The theme contrasting these two types of hermeneutics is well treated in both critical hermeneutics and religious studies where hermeneutics has gained prominence in respect to the significance of religious interpretations in contemporary world affairs (Ormiston and Schrift 1990).

Scriptural politics is about religion and the protection of faith, as well as the assertion that the creation of a collective or rather a universal identity (see Salih and Fortman's chapter in this book) is possible in the face of or vis-à-vis real or imagined enemies, competitors, or even collaborators. In today's multicultural, multireligious societies, the potential use and abuse of hermeneutics and scriptural politics is as real as the chapters contained in this book explain.

Human Rights, Religion, and Scriptural Politics

Historically, human rights have their antecedents in the enlightenment and the rationalistic doctrine of natural rights, which recognized individuals as subjects endowed with rights with two implications: (1) the state is a protector of natural rights by entering into a social contract with citizens and (2) the state no longer derives its sovereignty from the divine but from the requirement that it should protect the natural rights of its citizens (right to life, liberty, property, security, etc.) The Universal Declaration of Human Rights (1) recognizes the inherent dignity and the equal and inalienable rights of all members of the human family as the foundation of freedom, justice, and peace in the world; (2) is a general standard for achievement for all peoples and all nations; and (3) states that all human beings are born free and equal in dignity and rights (Nowak 2003). From this perspective, we are content with the contention that human rights refer to certain core rights that include rights to life, liberty, and security of the person; and against arbitrary imprisonment, slavery, torture, and genocide. Beyond these, there is the rule of law (e.g., the right to a fair trial); political rights to democratic rule and political participation; economic rights for just and favorable remuneration sufficient for an existence worthy of human dignity, and health care; and rights of communities (self-determination.) These enumerated rights are said to belong to everyone regardless of race, color, sex, language, religion, birth, and social status, and without distinction on the basis of the political, jurisdictional or international status of the country or territory to which a person belongs (Beitz 2003, 36). These existential rights, argues Nowak, are an essential manifestation of human dignity around which a host of other human rights evolve (Nowak 2003, 9).

The relationship between human rights and religion is complex. Religion "draws on wellsprings of mystery, fear (of the unknown and death), hope, morality, exaltation," argues Gustafson (Gustafson and Juviler 1999, 9). It can help validate or repudiate human rights for all. Essentially, Christianity, Judaism, and Islam espouse certain elements of the "golden rule" (Nowak 2003, 9), but some of their militant believers are inclined to view themselves as the sole guardians of truth, a position that can tempt them to intolerance even against whatever they define as deviant, either within their own faith or at the boundaries (Gustafson and Juviler 1999, 7). Fundamentalist and at times militant interpretations of the scriptures could be misguided, intolerant, deviate from the true path of religion, inflict harm, and even abuse the human rights of their opponents using what they perceive as the authenticity of the religious text as a source of admonition.

Evidently, while in some respects religion has been an aspiration for the respect of human rights, in others, religious institutions violated the human rights of some of their believers or those of other religions. In this volume, the cases involving the position of women in early Christianity, the use of the Qur'an as justification of the violation of the human rights of opposing ethnic groups in Nigeria or the practice of female genital mutilation (FGM) in Gambia are provided. Some religious institutions in Islam, Christianity, and Judaism justify the denial of minority human rights with references to the scriptures. The phrase "religious persecution" is broadly used to refer to incidences where a minority religious group such as the Shi'a in Pakistan, Muslims in Thailand, or Christians in China or the denial of places of worship to those who profess faiths other than Islam in Saudi Arabia (Boyle and Sheen 1997).

Scriptures themselves do not abuse human rights; the manner in which they are interpreted in, for example, conflict situation between two adversaries (groups, communities of believers or states) can ignite bellicose feelings and engender conflicts. Contradictions have often risen from questions pertaining to the contradictory stands of some religious institutions as individuals guaranteed by the universal human rights, including women's rights, minority rights, capital punishment, abortion, freedom of religion and same-sex unions (Kalscheur 2007). Although the book does not deal with these aspects and their scriptural comments, put in context, it reveals the delicate relationship between religion and human rights in context informed by the hermeneutics of religion, its level of fixity, determinism, or moderation.

The relationship between religion, ideology, and human rights tends to be uneasy. Among other things, this relates to ways and means of interpreting divine or holy texts. Yet, to proclaim one principle as the decisive hermeneutic factor or ushering in the only truth, will work neither in theory nor in practice. In this volume, hermeneutics barely refers to the theory and methodology of interpreting texts or suggesting that it is possible to determine a universally valid interpretation of the scriptures on the basis of an analysis of understanding (Dilthy and Frithjof 1996, 230) beyond text and context. Because this volume is an attempt to articulate hermeneutics within Christianity, Islam, and Judaism and across as well as beyond them, any meaningful analysis will seek understanding rather than determinism.

To be sure, as there is no single universally valid interpretation even within the same religion and its various denominations, there is likewise no universally valid interpretation in different religions. Differences of interpretation bear the insignia of different ways of how scriptures are used as sources for ordering human affairs or subscribing what value systems should become supreme in this process.

Rarely in human history have religious texts been so deeply at the heart of global debate as they are today. Behind the events of September 11 were individuals identifying themselves as Muslims with the intent to do God's will. Since texts from the Qur'an were cited to justify mass murder, September 11 raised worldwide interest in interpretation of the holy scriptures and religious traditions, particularly the relationship between religious texts, politics, and the contents of interpreting them. Undoubtedly, perceptions and discourses about *the other* are partially rooted in hermeneutics and literal interpretations of holy texts. The popular entrenched perception that Islam would always remain bound to a literal interpretation of "violent" texts in the Qur'an without regard to context is misleading. Hermeneutics of suspicion stands at the roots of intolerance or lack of understanding and thus masks the modern guise of Orientalism (Said 1978). Such hermeneutics denies the fact that Muslims, Christians, and Jews or believers in any other religion for that matter, are not uniform and in reality belong to a broad array of believers, ranging from the secular to the moderate to the militant.

Notably, however, like the Qur'an, the Bible is also full of texts that tend to be classified as brutal. Such texts number 1,400 or so, more at any rate than in the Qur'an. An example is Exodus 32:27–28, where Moses orders in the name of God that every man of Israel put "his sword by his side, and go in and out from gate to gate throughout the camp, and slay every man his brother, and every man his companion, and every man his neighbor," which was an order followed to such an extent that "there fell of the people that day about three thousand men." Even within its context—idolatry—it remains precarious to construct a meaningful contemporary message from such a text. Besides, some classifications of texts are as problematic as their interpretation of secular principles of peace and justice rest on obvious misunderstandings. One striking example is Jesus' admonition, "Think not that I come to send peace on earth: I came not to bring peace, but a sword" (Matthew 10:34). Jesus did not advocate violence. Rather, he told his disciples that they would *encounter* animosity. A genuine hermeneutic issue arises when several verses in monumental texts apparently contradict each other, which exonerates the need for acknowledging that texts have a historical context, and more so world religions as such, which can be misleading when interpreted and acted upon outside that context.

For example, the question arises whether certain Islamic *Fiqh* precepts concerning women, non-Muslims, and freedom of religion do represent the real message of the original sources of Islam. Indeed, there is no way to escape the discipline of interpretation, which involves reconstructing the historical contexts of a text in order to infer the underlying spirit of message and meaning. In other words, as an Iranian colleague in a paper on Shi'a *Fiqh* and Universal Human Rights puts it, "the text may not speak for itself, as there is no text without a context" (Fatemi 2007). Thus, to understand the text one needs to understand and even reconstruct the context if the interpretation poses threats to the human dignity of those subjected to the implications of the hermeneutics that justifies inhumane treatment (e.g., the Islamic punishment by amputation of limbs for theft and stoning of women to death for committing adultery or using *shura* and consultative councils as a substitute for citizens exercising their preferences in free and fair elections).

The search for an open truth preoccupies the authors of the chapters that make up the content of this book, while lamenting on the implication of situations where truth is considered closed (i.e., not open to interpretation or negotiation) and exclusive, indeed a source of divides on the basis of us versus them. However, in the discursive narrative that mediates truth and subject, right precludes the imposition of one's own truth upon others. History has shown that there have been many instances where individuals or groups espoused the monopoly of the truth under pretext claims that an exclusive right to believe is absolute, leading to an extremist interpretation of Holy scriptures. Such understandings have often created internally insurmountable cleavages, eventually contributing to their demise.

The question that follows is what is the source of tension between certain elements of religion and human rights? We are reminded by Dalactoura that "the debate in the twentieth century regarding the foundations of knowledge, truth and moral values, is especially pertinent to the notion of human rights" (Dalactoura 1998, 9).

However, in the age of political correctness it might not be possible to ameliorate Gadamer's contention that being conscious of one's own prejudice is not necessarily unjustified and erroneous or that these prejudices inevitably distort the truth. Prejudices are biases of our openness to the world. They are simply conditions whereby what we encounter says something to us (Gadamer 1975) or about us. From this expansive perspective, understanding prejudice (not accepting it) is at the heart of a hermeneutics of recollection while obviously hermeneutics of suspicion accepts prejudicial claims based on social position, economic class, race, or status.

Those who justify violence against what they perceive as threats to their religious beliefs often claim monopoly of an exclusive truth that privileges themselves while demeaning others. The diversity of the religious and social backgrounds of authors of this book makes it unique in that they express their views on the need for an inclusive truth with reference to orthodox Judaism, Islam (both Sunni and Shi'a), and Christianity (both Catholic and Protestant). They offer a powerful critique of the human conditions with regard to the use and abuse of hermeneutics as an instrument of scriptural politics and its ramification for society.

Religious Identity and Scriptural Politics

Religious identity according to Giessen (quoted in Otten and Salemink) is one of three types of collective identity: 1) primordial (kinship, ethnicity, race, etc.); 2) tradition (language, costume, shared codes of conduct, and cultural traits); and 3) universal (professing a special sense of salvation, which implies tension between the reality of "the beyond" conveyed by the sacred, the elevated, and the transcendent and that of the earthly world, which is in need of transformation) (Otten and Salemink 2004, 6). These three archetypical codes of identity give recourse to the tension between three different types of foundation of identity: nature, tradition, and revelation or salvation, argue Otten and Salemink (2004, 6). Evidently, it is not only that European Christianity has confronted this tension within Europe, it was more so when missionaries set out to evangelize among indigenous peoples. The all-embracing primordial identities and traditions of the indigenous peoples have in most cases either existed side by side with or been integrated into Christianity. Peggy Brock (2005, 107) exposes the coexistence of the primordial, the traditional, and the universal among the indigenous peoples worldwide. While the missionaries vied to expand their version of Christianity, itself a product of a long interaction of their own collective identities; and Christianity, the universal collective identity, is only one of them. James Treat calls this "Native and Christian" with special reference to indigenous peoples' religious identity in the United States and Canada (Treat 1996).

The tensions between the primordial, tradition, and the universal identities, we argue, are not specific to Christianity and Judaism but are common to all religions, including Islam. Kastfelt illustrates that the presence of a universal Muslim identity in northern Nigeria has not prevented Muslims from using the Qur'an in order to justify the resonance of their ethnic superiority vis-à-vis the opposing groups. In this way, Islam is used to justify both primordial and collective identity and tradition (see Kastfelt in this volume). Likewise, Touray shows that Islam is used to justify the horrible tradition of Female Genital Mutilation (FGM) (also in this volume). Issues of how believers can act on interpretation could also be illustrated by Ayatollah Khomeini's fatwa urging Muslims to kill Salman Rushdie for publishing his novel *The Satanic Verses* (1988) and scenes of angry Muslim demonstrators denouncing the Danish cartoonist Jyllands-Posten (2005) for publishing cartoons depicting prophet Muhammed in such a manner that Muslims felt the cartoons are offensive to their religion. The clash of interpretations raged within the realm of freedom of expression and Muslims' contention that these were cases of Western insults to their religion.[1]

Obviously, the tensions between collective identities founded on "biological belonging," common tradition, or universal religious values exist within various religious denominations, geographies, and cultures, and between religions; and in both cases can contribute to the richness of religious experiences or misunderstandings often culminating in conflicts and hostility. On the one hand, religious collective identity is like any other identity; on the other hand, it is different in the sense that it claims the possibility of offering salvation, revelation, and redemption. It is also a potent source for mobilization, and as we have mentioned earlier, for good or for bad.

Scriptures enter the domain of politics through the formation of collective identities, which become important markers of faith and the faithful intent to produce and reproduce conditions favorable to their existence vis-à-vis their real or perceived adversaries. From this perspective, scripture becomes politicized when the religious establishment or institutions claim that religious reason should ultimately provide the identity marker as well as a prescription of how collective and individual lives should be conducted. Scriptural politics in this sense is about a quest to instill particular religious values and beliefs with the deliberate intent to form a distinct religious identity, leading or contributing to a distinct religiously informed way of life. It is a powerful step toward regulating all or specific facets of humanity or the politicization of religion at worst.

In Chapter 1 of this book, Salih and Fortman argue that scriptural politics is about conferring meaning and legitimacy to religious, social, or political acts considered important for producing and reproducing faith and several other religious and secular goals and objectives. In particular, they explain how in religion, as an exercise in universal identity formation, certain moral and ethical elements of the scripture offer competing regimes of truth, whereby their interpretation becomes a crucial source of religious identity formation. This means that framing, construction, and reconstruction are meant to produce one or more of the following postulates that define the role of scriptural politics in society: mobilization and manipulation of support; representation, identity formation, and construction; social visibility in the public sphere; assertion of rights; reinforcement or subversion of real or perceived hegemony; and protection of a way of life.

In short, hermeneutics, scriptural politics, and human rights is about scriptures or texts, and their interpretation in the context of universal human rights. It deals with the role of scriptural politics in informing the potency of religious identity, its formation, uses, and abuses. In this sense, scriptural politics is not merely about religion and the protection of faith, but also about the assertion that the creation of a collective or rather a universal identity is possible in the face of or vis-à-vis real or imagined enemies or competitors. In today's multicultural, multireligious societies, the potential use and abuse of hermeneutics and scriptural politics is as real as the chapters contained in this book explain.

Structure of the Book

This book is divided into two parts of distinct yet overlapping subthemes: Part I on hermeneutics, law, and communities of readers deals particularly with religious and secular scriptures, textualism, and the changing nature of hermeneutics in reading and understanding the Bible. As we have mentioned earlier in this introduction, the American Constitution is introduced as monumental text linking the domains of constitutional hermeneutics, which leads to its alleviation by civil rights activists and rights lawyers alike to the symbolic status of a sacred text. Part II on hermeneutics, religion, and human rights has emphasis on religious freedom, scriptural interpretation in the intensification of ethnic violence in Nigeria, and scriptural views on women's rights from early Christianity and contemporary Islam in Gambia. We take these in turn.

Part I of the book engages the current debate on the implications of religious text and the variety of scriptural politics and contexts. It responds to our contention that critical hermeneutics reinvokes polity in the interpretation of religious and written monuments. Arguing that hermeneutics is about critical reinvocation of questions of polity, agency, and structure, an attempt is made to resolve the tension between what Davey calls the hermeneutics of suspicion and the hermeneutics of conversation (or hermeneutic community of polity and experience, which simultaneously grounds and transcends the individual; Davey 2004). Fortman and Salih set the scene for exposing the political nature of critical hermeneutics by arguing that following September 11, critical hermeneutics has become akin to scriptural politics where religious, theological, and jurisprudential hermeneutics are used or abused across the religious divide. In this heightened milieu, where interpretation has become an instrument for acting upon the religious text, denying or granting rights to others, they argue that two fundamental questions tend to dominate religious discursive narratives and their interpretations: What duties and which rights are conferred by God applicable to all humans as the creation of God and regardless of their faith? And the second question is whether humans are sufficiently qualified to put into the words of God the possibility of faulting the mercy of God for political, social, or economic gains.

Salman Haq's chapter, "Islamic Texts, Democracy, and the Rule of Law: Toward a Hermeneutics of Conciliation" addresses one of the major debate points in contemporary Islamic global polity and how it projects itself or is being projected by the West. The question in Western percepts is whether an Islamic theocracy can tolerate a democracy, whereby democracy in Muslim states is taken to connote the rule of law. Haq argues that Muslims' responses to democracy are diverse and dependent on the strain of political Islam they profess (moderate or militant), and concludes that while Islam may be compatible with both democracy and the rule of law, much depends on the choice of interpretation of religious scriptures. The chapter signifies the critical role of hermeneutics as mediator of text and context and therefore features as a central argument on scriptural politics.

The question of faith and reason has dominated the debate on canon law pertaining to the reference point in interpretation. In "Canon Law: Faith or Reason," Brown outlines three reference points in analyzing, understanding, and interpreting canon law: a genitive element, the temporal matrix, and the locus of meaning. If we translate these three reference points into conception, promulgation, and mediation, the questions raised are surely about what is to be interpreted. The following questions are raised therein by the author: Does the meaning of a law exist in its text or somewhere else? (Örsy 1980, 24) Can the meaning be found in canonical tradition, the "mind of the legislator," a consensus of scholars, the "sense of the community" (Coriden 1982, 24), or the *Weltanschauung*? (Kneal 1982, 29) Can it have the same existence in such different locations? Or, must we speak of the relationship between the "locus of meaning" and the "locus of understanding"? Brown concludes that ultimately we arrive at understanding through reasoning, but reason must start somewhere. Reason explicates and confirms what has first been perceived, which is the ultimate objective.

In the end, knowledge is a relationship between perceived and perceiver, subject and object, subject and subject. The meaning and understanding of ecclesiastical laws is, therefore, an intersubjective reality, and should be recognized as such.

The United States Constitution comes under the analytical rigor of Philipse, with particular focus on judicial textualism (a normative doctrine of method according to which judicial interpretation of statutes should aim at establishing the *original* meaning of the text). Although Philipse deals with a secular text (the American Constitution), the questions he raises are to some extent similar to those Brown discussed, in respect to issues pertaining to interpretation of canon law. Philipse poses the question as follows: how does "textualism" fare in the judicial interpretation of statute law and, especially, of the U.S. Constitution? He is concerned with the *kind* of textualism that is defensible as a methodology for interpretation by judges, arguing that a sophisticated "applicative" version of textualism would have to be substituted for a simple version. Yet, he acknowledges that even a sophisticated version of textualism cannot be a self-sufficient philosophy of interpretation, because apart from the rules of textualism or originalism, there are many other rules that judges must heed in interpreting statutes. Philipse resolves the tension between simple and sophisticated applicative textualism by arguing that scientific methodology of statutory interpretation by judges is possible. Yet this "science of interpretation" is complex and allows for flexibility and diversity of opinion, because there is no algorithm for determining the specific weights that have to be assigned to the different *topoi* of interpretation in particular trade-offs. Another conclusion is that if the only defensible version of textualism in the judicial interpretation of the American Constitution is super-sophisticated applicative textualism, the difference with the doctrine of the Living Constitution is at most a minor one, concerning the weight that one assigns to the textualist *topos* among many other *topoi* of interpretation. Debates polarized by controversies are not the hallmark or exclusive monopoly of religious texts alone as Philipse succinctly demonstrated; secular constitutions can equally invite polemics based on conviction and context. The role of critical hermeneutics in this endeavor is crucial.

Building on Clifford Geertz's seminal work *The Interpretation of Cultures*, Steenbrink compares Islamic and Christian communities in Indonesia, focusing on the process of reinterpretation by comparing them with each other and with the primal traditions of illiterate cultures. He also elucidates the contemporary issues and debates confronting modern Islam and Christianity (economy, marriage, death penalty, homosexuality, religious freedom, and interreligious communication). Steenbrink argues that the overall processes of interpretation in both religions frequently, but not always, take the scriptures and traditions into consideration for discussing modern issues. However, the outcome of those discussions is often quite uncertain and involves ambiguity and even arbitrariness. The religions may fluidly adopt strict texts or interpret freely to the extent that they may look as if they abandoned the original text. Essentially, upon closer examination of reinterpretation in Indonesian Islam and Christianity, a simple return to the past or a reinvention of a pure and true tradition is not possible. Global religions work through this mixture of modernization and reinterpretation of old texts. The variety of case studies introduced by Steenbrink allows him to conclude that the world religions have flexibility in the application of classical texts to modern times. However, they may also seem arbitrary to outsiders. The situation becomes even more complex when we take into consideration the methods of individual or collective decision making, whether for private use or as an authority for a religious community.

In his chapter "Changing Hermeneutics in Reading and Understanding the Bible: The Case of the Gospel of Mark," van Oyen explores the Gospel of Mark, with the main objective of explaining the preliminary hermeneutic work that has to be done before reading the Bible. He illustrates how the new hermeneutic insights in biblical criticism can easily and successfully be interwoven with an interpretation of this gospel. Van Oyen introduces the reader to what he calls the Markan Code in order to contribute to a better understanding of how the Bible can function as a living text in the contemporary world. It is a Markan Code because, in his view, the content of the gospel is not free of obligation. The point is that it challenges its readers to make choices and decisions, because if the reader does not decide to unlock its meaning, it is incomplete. Thus, the *reading* process is ultimately a *learning* process. The readers, according to van Oyen, unravel the secrets of the Gospel of Mark to the extent that they are able to respond affirmatively to certain insights from the narrative. Van Oyen's point of departure is the plurality of meanings that can be derived from the text, in this case the Gospel of Mark. His conclusion is colorful and expansive: people now have liberty to explore the Bible and see where it inspires new perspectives, which involve a wider variety of interpretive approaches than has hitherto been the norm. By regaining an important position in individuals' lives and society at large, the Bible can contribute to some of the most complex issues of today, such as multiculturalism or specific ethical dilemmas. Yet, this is possible only if the Bible is treated as an open book not exploited by a select few, but available for everyone to read—as a sacred, a novel, a history, or an inspirational book.

Part II of this volume is dedicated to religious hermeneutics and certain major issues in respect of human rights' implementation: religious freedom, minorities, "religious" violence and women's rights. Understanding the real or perceived religious divide with regard to these historic as well as contemporary issues is both timely and urgent. It is timely because Muslims, Christians, and Jews no longer live apart, at least not in terms of politico-economic interdependence and geographic proximity. It is urgent because contemporary religious hermeneutics is capable of shaping the relationships among believers of different religions.

The two opening chapters of Part II are on religious freedom in Islam and Christianity respectively. Considering the diverse interpretations of Islamic scriptures, Mirmoosavi argues that it is difficult to determine one unequivocal view of Islam on the issue of religious freedom. Some Qur'anic verses reject compulsion in religion, while others denounce apostasy. Referring to the Shar'ia condemnation of apostasy as punishable by death or several civil sanctions, Mirmoosavi asks a number of important questions: Does outlawing apostasy, he laments, reflect the whole view of Islam? Or, can the Qur'anic texts be interpreted in a way that is not incompatible with religious freedom? How can we rethink Shar'ia to bring about a compromise between Islam and religious freedom? Mirmoosavi concludes that even though traditional interpretations may prevail, pragmatic necessities must repeal and frustrate these. The point is that freedom of religion was not compatible with past Islamic society where citizenship was based on religious belief. Thus, the juridical decrees on punishment of apostasy, which conflict with freedom of religion, reflect the conditions of past society.

While Mirmoosavi explains how religious freedom is expressed in the Qur'an, Martens pays attention to religious freedom from a hermeneutic perspective of the Roman Catholic Church. He examines the dialectics of absolute truth as "possessed" by an authoritative body such as the Roman Catholic Church and religious liberty on the part of individual human beings, focusing on renewed interest in religious liberty since the Second Vatican Council (1962–1965). Martens then ponders the question whether the council's document *Dignitatis Humanae* represents a renewed understanding, or a new interpretation of the same teaching? Or is the teaching of Vatican II on religious liberty a rupture with the past? He concludes that the teaching of the Roman Catholic Church has not considerably changed, but that renewed interpretation of the role of the state, in view of changes in society, and the rise of multicultural society has led to this fine-tuning.

Four chapters in Part II articulate the thorny issues of women, minorities, and "religious" violence, dealing with women in Islam and Christianity, with jihad in Islam, and with non-Jewish minorities in Israel. Weissman turns to the hermeneutic challenge of non-Jewish minorities in Israel from the viewpoint of interpreting classical Jewish texts. The starting point of her premise is that although Israel is a secular state, diverse political actors influence policy, especially the religious settlers and their opponents, both motivated by religious texts and the contending means of interpretation.

According to Weissman, even here the classical sources do bear some relevance on the complexities of the contemporary situation. The texts used to interpret the position of the non-Jews in the Land of Israel predate both Islam and Christianity. Based on the above considerations, argues Weissman, there are several questions that come to mind; for example, how does tradition look at non-Jews? In particular, how does it look at non-Jews living in the Land of Israel? Does the tradition offer a way to combine traditional religious commitments with modern democratic values? From the core perspective taken in this volume, Weissman's questions are crucially important not only in respect of Jewish hermeneutics, but also with regard to religious hermeneutics in general. Her conclusions are equally important, particularly the suggestion that traditional Jewish commentaries on non-Jewish residence in Israel can inform a modern worldview if we build on the notion that all of us are *gerim toshavim* (resident strangers), certainly with respect to the divine dresence. Indeed, mutual recognition of alienation-exile-refugee status will go a long way in helping to solve the Israeli-Palestinian conflict. Weissman also proposes that the Palestinians will be able to achieve the status of first-class citizens when the Jewish-democratic state clarifies their status and, in so doing, broadens the biblical notion of *ezrach*, acknowledging that there is need for a new understanding when women achieved suffrage. The expansion of the concept, in Weissman's view, can be realized through a Jewish hermeneutics that would eventually include the non-Jewish minorities living within the State of Israel to complete their legal full-fledged citizenship when a new understanding of their status in the Jewish state is developed.

Kastfelt explores the use of religious texts as political models facilitating ethnic identity construction. His empirical focus is on Northern Nigeria where political turmoil involves confrontations between Christians and Muslims. A general introduction on the characteristics of religious texts as models for exclusion is applied particularly to biblical paradigms as conceptualized by Paul Gifford. The case Kastfelt uses to illustrate converging trajectories of African Christianity, ethnicity, and politics concerns the creation of a new political community by the Bachama tribe. Biblical interpretation served here toward self-identification as a chosen people, the identification of prophetic leaders and moral justification of their ethnic political activism. Kastfelt relates these phenomena to a general trend in Nigerian politics, namely the transformation of ethnic conflicts into religious conflicts between Christianity and Islam.

Haghighat tackles the crucial issue of *jihad*, in radical-political circles interpreted as an Islamic license to be exempted from state-citizens' relationships pertaining to the rule of law, while engaging in "religious" violence. Jihad, he contends, must be interpreted within the specific context of the ancient state-tribe relations during the time of the revelation of Holy scripture. First and foremost is inner jihad, implying a struggle to find oneself at peace with God. Outer jihad is by nature defensive. Offensive jihad was allowed only in the time of the prophet Mohamed and even then directed at anti-Muslim polities, not secular ones.

Otten explores religious views on women in early Christianity, focusing on international hermeneutics in Tertullian and Augustine. She maintains that the unfolding of time and the need to hold on to the present-ness of the incarnation by appropriating the past in responsible fashion is ultimately what separates Augustine from Tertullian's eschatological and pragmatic approach to marriage. In response to Brooten, she argues that Augustine's conception of time rather than nature defines his view of marriage. Inherent in this incarnational view of time, she purports, is the idea that it allows for change, hope, and redemption. Yet Otten observes that the study of early Christian hermeneutics is both useful and delicate. This hermeneutics is significant, in her view, because it forces us to read and interpret early Christian theological texts in a way that includes women without isolating them. In essence, this method magnifies women's position. The contemporary relevance of Otten is directly related to *feminist* hermeneutics, whereby female and male theologians may fruitfully and jointly develop a keen eye for the incarnational focus of the church *fathers*.

Finally, Touray draws parallels between interpretations of the Qur'an, which incorporated the dominant patriarchal values regulating gender relations in ancient Arabia and traditional African practices such as female genital mutilation (FGM), early marriage and gender-based violence, which both at the community level and at the household level are features of many African cultures. The alliances between harmful traditional values and misconceived ideas about Islam, according to Touray, have privileged interpretations, which undermined women's rights. Touray laments, "as a Muslim, my shared faith gives me a shared meaning. However, as a feminist, I do not necessarily share the same interpretations on all ritualistic and doctrinal issues. Rather, I believe that women's rights must be seen in light of the diversity and individuality of women, not from a homogenous perspective." After explaining various competing perspectives on women's sexuality, Touray concludes that feminist interpretations represent a new way of understanding the text, without necessarily changing that text itself.

The dialectics of religions, politics, and human rights have often degenerated into rigid debates on the basis of predetermined positions. Yet, between text and context the authors of this volume appear to find the constructive space to contribute to creative insights conducive to conciliation in theory and practice.

Conclusions

In particular, this volume traverses the study of religion and politics in respect to five major issues relevant to the current debate on hermeneutics and its mediation between scriptures and action whether political or social, violent or peaceful, supportive or abusive of human rights.

Hermeneutics and scriptural interpretation in the domains of religion and human rights: Indeed, interpretation without regard to context and the hermeneutics that support it for the conflation of ethics and law, pose serious questions in respect of human rights issues directly related to the protection of human dignity of each and every human being. This appears to apply to all world religions. However, the contention that "every human being is sacred is, in my view, inescapably religious—and the idea of human rights is, therefore, ineliminably religious," as pronounced by Michael Perry is very controversial within every religion and between religions (1998, 12). Both collectively and individually, the chapters have shown that despite the recognition that human rights stem from the attributes of human beings, religious identity as a collective universal identity of a set of believers is amenable to diversity from within. Hermeneutics and scriptural interpretation and counterinterpretation, as the chapters show is derived from the tensions between attributes that are considered universally human and attributes that are considered religiously or culturally specific. In a sense the debate, turf conflicts and competing claims within religion are as diverse and complex as their claims with other religions and secularists. While the message and meaning of the religious verse (as we have seen earlier), constitute an embodiment of human dignity, dignity as described by Ignatieff as agency "expresses itself in political and civil freedom, in the exercise of human choice and collective deliberation." In effect, international human rights covenants and declarations seek to re-create for the international society of states the norms that govern the relationship between citizen and state in a democratic polity, to make all human beings citizens rather than subjects of the states they give obedience to (Ignatieff 2001).

Scriptural hermeneutics and the universally acknowledged nondiscrimination principle, for example, articles 1 and 2 of the Universal Declaration of Human Rights: The debate on universalism and relativism in human rights is well treaded and therefore there is no need to rehash it here (Bell, Nathan, and Peleg 2001; Gustafson and Juviler 1999; An-Na'im 1995; Berting et al. 1990). The contention between religion and the modern conception of human rights, (despite their claim of universality), constitute a domain of competing and at times contrasting views view vis-à-vis the debate on universality versus relativism. In other words, relativism invokes either bygone historical realities or realities reminiscent of the early life of religion, but projected by some religious establishments as at odds with the times of human rights. Due to their historical depth, which goes back to millennia, the times of all religions are unambiguous about the absence, even the abuse of human rights in the stark socioeconomic and political realities that contributed to their emergence. Orentlicher summarizes the relativists' position as follows: "Moral claims derive their meaning and legitimacy from the (particular) cultural tradition in which they are embedded" (2003, 141). In the relativists' view, argues Orentlicher, "What we call universal human rights is, in fact, an expression above all of Western values derived from the Enlightenment. Understood in this light, the human rights idea is at best misguided in its core claim that it embodies universal values—and at worst a blend of moral hubris and cultural imperialism." In our view, the counter critique of relativism centers on two points: (1) Cultural and religious relativists deny the objectivism and this is more so in the case of religion. In other words, with all their claims of universality, (2) religions have constantly adapted the messages of their times and life either to the changing global reality or to the realities of the societies and new geographical areas to which they have expanded.

Within this perspective, a focus on women's rights questions whether some patriarchal values embedded in Holy scripture should still govern religious interpretations and social expectations. It also questions whether the religious scripture should be used as the only source conferring or denying human rights to (political) minorities such as the Palestinian living in Israel or the occupied territories (see Weissman in this book). The wider implications of applying a hierarchy of human rights provider with the religious scriptures at its apex could also have far reaching implications for instance, for women. As Isatou Touray (in this volume) laments, it can be discerned in all communities where patriarchal norms and expectations dominate, and where the religious text is interpreted from a vantage point of men or otherwise male superiority over women.

Third, *religious freedom and apostasy focus on the nature of truth in relation to democracy, freedom of religion, and changing contexts of reading and interpreting the scriptures.* Even though conventional hermeneutics are justified by their believers as the upholders of the truth, the interpretations hold true to their religious beliefs, practice, and reason. Their aim is to invoke the authenticity of the religious text as a call for reconciling jurisprudence and religious faith. In such situations, freedom of religion is made subservient to divine rule (Boyle and Sheen 1997; Patrick and Long 1999). The reverse is also true, whereby secular states ban religious activities in fear that it is divisive or that the religious establishment is outspoken or loyal only to God instead of to government.[2]

In conclusion, this book brings together pertinent insights on the relationship between text and context. In particular, the chapters offer a powerful critique of the notion of isolating hermeneutics, textual interpretations and religious practice as distinct entities. Scriptural interpretations of religious or otherwise monumental texts play a pivotal role in informing and transforming religious identity, give new meanings to human rights in both secular and religious sense as well as the codes of conduct that inform the believer's action in multicultural and multireligious situations. On the other hand, politicized scripture and hermeneutics, as this book illustrates, transcend religion and mobilize forces of division and intolerance. It is from this perspective that we sought to offer a cross-religious account of the current possibilities and pitfalls of hermeneutics and scriptural politics in the domain of religious identity and human rights.

Notes

1. For more on these two incidences refer to Chakravorty (1995) and Maodoodi (2006).
2. In the specific case of ex-socialist countries see Anderson (2003).

Part I

Hermeneutics, Communities of Readers, and Context

1

Religious Identity, Differences, and Human Rights

The Crucial Role of Hermeneutics

M. A. Mohamed Salih and Bas de Gaay Fortman

Introduction

The aftermath of September 11, an event behind which were an ideology and individuals identifying themselves with Islam, produced two striking, almost contradictory trends that shaped the role of religion and culture in human interactions: (1) it elevated the debate on the coexistence of religions and cultures to new heights and (2) it signaled the return to culture and with it the return to religious identity, in a profound way. In the midst of democratization, modern governance, and the rule of law, the return to culture under the guise of religious conservatism (both Islamic and Christian) is puzzling, especially since the emergence of a global ethics has led to solidarity across cultural and religious divides.

At the same time, however, voices capable of creating simple contrasts between good and evil or civilization and barbarism created and dominated an increasingly polarized world. This is particularly apparent in the realm of ideologized religion, which resists universalistic solutions to complex political and social problems. The return of politicized religion, be it in symbolic or activist form, has reignited the importance of scriptural interpretation. Concurrently and increasingly, the dominant view of human rights texts is seen as weaponry in an ideological contest. Many people adhere to the universality of the texts in a rigid way that leaves no room for contextual interpretation.

In light of the events and trends described above, it is clear that hermeneutics is subject to manipulation because people act on the interpretations of religion. It is impossible to remove religious practice or theory from the realities people endure in the real world. When used as an instrument of the good, religion can deliver unprecedented justice, liberty, and freedom. From this perspective, our world needs religion as a spiritual source for what is just and right. Conversely, when used as an instrument of power and manipulation, it has been less respectful of human well-being and further removed from enhancing the common good. From that perspective, our world needs human rights laws as a system of protecting human dignity against any abuse of power. In other words, religion (in the wider sense of transcendental views on good and evil) and human rights need each other.

Religious Identity, Its Scope, and Differences

It is not difficult to compare and contrast religious identity; identity politics and contending identities generate markers to distinguish them from others. Generally, identity politics is informed by and informs collective memories of injustice or shared experiences of prosecution and fear. Groups often perceive those factors as a challenge to their unique heritage, values, and beliefs. Religious identity originates from the values of a community of believers and by feelings of real or imagined oppression or stigmatization can heighten that identity. As a result, religious identity may manifest itself in different forms of extremism as a way to counter oppression. However, in both religion and politics, identity can also develop into cooperation, solidarity and compassion within a community of believers. This sense of social welfare may also extend to groups outside the community when positive attitudes toward each other develop over the course of living together.

Given the general treatment of moral and ethical considerations as competing regimes of truth, the construction of religious texts is crucial to identity formation. Since there are currently fewer church, mosque, synagogue, and temple-goers than on the eve of the twentieth century, meaning construction becomes part of the following:

- Mobilization or manipulation of support
- Representation/identity formation and construction
- Social visibility in the public sphere
- Assertion of rights
- Reinforcement or subversion of real or perceived hegemony
- Protection of a way of life

Below is a review of the first three of these six postulates since they are instructive in defining this discussion. Later sections of this chapter include the others.

Mobilization/Manipulation of Support

Islamists in Pakistan provide one example of this trend. They were able to mobilize and manipulate religious support to establish the state of Pakistan, and the early leadership portrayed it as an Islamic community. Like other communities, the state of Pakistan is divided within (Shi'a and Sunni) and without (Muslims and minority Christians and Hindus). The perforation of the Islamic community into Islamic sects and brotherhoods allied to different political parties produced its own momentum, which at times contributed to violence. It is not difficult to show that Islam has been misused in order to violate the rights of others to worship in peace. Attacks of political-religious opponents during times of heightened political tensions have become a norm.

Similarly, the mobilization and manipulation of Catholicism and Protestantism throughout the history of divided Ireland has caused much misery. In the process, people from both sides of the community lived in fear of sectarian killings (which finally ended in peaceful settlement). In Northern Ireland, like in other similar situations, freedom of expression against injustice and calls for the return of reason became the first casualties of faith-based conflicts.

Representation, Identity Formation, and Construction

In peace and in conflict, representation has several manifestations, either democratic or ascribed. Representation by those considered the bearers of high moral ground feeds into identity formation and construction when a religious community confronts external pressure. In addition to the immediate assertion of differences vis-à-vis the other, religion can also be used (or abused) as an ideological instrument capable of laying claim to the religious nature of society and the state. Religion creates internal harmony within the confines of its community. However, if not interpreted or projected peacefully, religion reinforces conflicts that are informed by collective memories of persecution and threats of extinction. Since September 11, minority Muslims in Europe, the United States of America, Thailand, and the Philippines faced discrimination similar to that experienced by the Copts in Egypt and the Christians in India, Iraq, and South Sudan, to mention a few examples.

Visibility in the Public Sphere

Public visibility is about the dominant symbols that shape the sphere. The turban, veil, the cross, the crescent, the Star of David, the minarets, the mosque, the temple, the synagogue and the church are all examples. The visibility of these symbols is equally important as the deeper role they play to connect a community of believers to their God. According to Hindus, the sixteenth century Ayodhya Muslim mosque in Uttar Pradesh, India, is the site where the god Ram, an incarnation of Vishnu, was born. In 1992, politicians who sought to conflate Hinduism and the Indian state ignited 200,000 Bharatiya Janata Party (BJP) militants. They stormed the mosque and reduced it to rubble. Some 1,400 people, mostly Muslim, but also some Christians, died. The Hindu nationalists' idea to build a temple in place of a mosque was not only a correction to what they perceived as historical injustice; it also represented a struggle over whose symbols dominated the public sphere. Similarly, in Nigeria in June 2004, fighting broke out in the town of Numan after Muslims apparently refused to stop building a mosque near the home of the chief of a local Christian tribe. Christians said the mosque was an affront to them because its minaret was taller than the chief's palace.

The debate on whether to permit Muslim women to wear a scarf in school provides another example of contestation in the public sphere. This controversy developed in France, among other places. Since October 2004, France began expelling Muslim girls wearing headscarves in public schools in defiance of a new law that bans conspicuous religious symbols. There are numerous other examples where a community of believers attributes certain characteristics to people of another faith, which is only explicable in terms of religious misunderstanding. That process often occurs through misinterpretation of the scripture in order to support a particular nationalist, ethnic, or political viewpoint. In the three cases illustrated in this chapter, the contending groups used interpretations from religious and nonreligious sources. When expressed in the public sphere, political or religious identity becomes a source of authenticity for one's values and ideals. When political and religious identities are not distinguished, the two can become the same, a condition common to all religions. In those situations, religious identity portends that the attitudes, behavior, and moral ethics of the faithful are different from other religions because that particular community is authentic (Taylor 1989; Laclua 1994; Gutmann 1994; Martin 1994; Frishman, Otten and Rouwhorst 2004; Poulton and Taji-Farouki 1997; Brenner 1993; Chakrabarti 1993; Salih 2004).

Unfortunately, the best examples of the interplay between identity politics and religious come from extreme examples where conflict is an expected outcome. A clash of ideals often results in violent or subtle conflicts that poison social relations between believers of different faiths. On the other hand, when one seeks a particular identity in such a way that cooperation and solidarity rather than opposition and discord become defining elements perceived as necessary for the group's survival, one finds religious identity vis-à-vis the other, articulated vividly.

Identity and difference can resonate vis-à-vis the other. This is true in the domain of politics or religion. Conversely, violent religious conflicts are potent instruments for identity formation in ways that defy well-established norms of coexistence. The horrors that haunt many victims of religious conflicts, for instance in the former Yugoslavia (Bosnia Herzegovina and Kosovo), are unspeakable atrocities committed by neighbors, who before the war shared compassion, respect, and cooperation. One of the main outcomes of religious conflict is human rights abuse. These abuses are often committed in the name of protecting religion, in spite of the fact that religious difference is not the sole cause of conflict.

Ironically, secular, or to be more precise, political terms often explain the interpretation of religious ideals to justify human rights abuse in conflict situations. Conflicts create their own internal dynamics of human rights abuse. This includes curtailing the freedom of expression of those who oppose the war from within a particular community of believers. In recent wars, even those in which religions played a significant role, such as the war in South Sudan, violence against women has been rampant. Rape was a weapon of war in order to humiliate and undermine the dignity of the opposing faction. Other cases show torture, inhumane confinement and other abuses against prisoners of war. Such practices occur in secular states as well as in those that declare themselves religious. In both cases, one finds many textual interpretations that justify the actions of the perpetrators.

Equality, Difference, Religious Identity, and Human Rights

All human beings are born equal in dignity and rights and the Universal Declaration of Human Rights of 1948 (UDHR) affirms this in article 1. One may view this opening statement as a confession—a "secular" *ius divinum*—that postulates the transcendent character of human rights. Thus, UDHR views human equality with respect to dignity, a term that implies the uniqueness of the individual. In other words, *different people* are equal in rights: different but equal, equal but different. Various disciplines, particularly in feminist human rights literature studied the implications of this assertion. Emphasis lies in the distinction between equality and sameness. This distinction also refers to treatment of people—similarly rather than the same (Abeyesekera 1995, 30). Obviously, then, our equal rights comprise the freedom to identify differently from others. This includes identification with a distinct religion, even one that is different from that of the mainstream public-political community to which we belong. In Europe, this principle first appeared in the Peace of Westphalia (1648) after atrocious religious wars. In spite of that agreement, religious strife did not disappear. There is still an urgent need to protect the freedom of worship.

The international venture for the realization of human rights that started with the foundation of the United Nations and based on Franklin D. Roosevelt's four freedoms,[1] encompasses the freedom of worship. Yet, after sixty years of efforts to implement those freedoms, the whole enterprise still faces serious criticism. Amartya Sen, in respect of culture and human rights, categorizes the criticism in three major ways: legitimacy, coherence, and what he calls the cultural critique. As these points directly confront the transcendental question of human rights, it is important here to review them individually.

First, the *legitimacy* critique, although the term "legality critique" is preferred in this chapter, what Sen refers to is the view that there are no prelegislation rights. "Human beings in nature are ... no more born with human rights than they are born fully clothed" (Sen 1999, 228). The point is that the idea of inalienable human rights needs a convincing source other than enactment in positive law. Clearly, in this respect, religions or other types of encompassing world views must help to substantiate the "confession" that human beings are born equal in rights.

Second, in the *coherence* critique Sen refers to human rights as rights without remedies. Hence, they would be unconnected to normal "legal" rights. The present counter to this is that the realization of rights is never automatic: rights are always action-oriented. Although human rights should trump other rights in view of their transcendental nature, they tend to be even more action-oriented. Particularly in societies where the local, legal, and political processes have yet to embed internationally recognized human rights, the recognition of human rights becomes a struggle that requires inspiration and motivation. Again, here, now the role of religion seems crucial.

Third, in the *cultural* critique Sen refers to cultural *relativism* and asks: are the ethics underlying human rights truly universal? Clearly, it is not enough to dismiss this question with a simple reference to *juridical* universality. The issue is how each specific culture might provide the spiritual conviction that the global human rights project requires. Thus, the challenge becomes to diversify universal human rights in ventures connected with specific cultural contexts. Although this process presents many obstacles, it also provides many opportunities. One example is the Arab Charter on Human Rights that came into force on March 15, 2008, after ratification by seven Arab states.

Although the necessity of embedding human rights in a context of religion and culture is obvious, the Universal Declaration itself makes no mention of religion as a possible basis for such fundamental rights. While there was an attempt by the Dutch delegate, Father Beaufort OP, to amend the preamble with a reference to "man's divine origin and his eternal destiny," they rejected it as contrary to the universal nature of the declaration. Indeed, Father Beaufort's formula would have been out of place. The Universal Declaration stems from a secular religion (*religio* in the classical sense of "binding"), which arose from two centuries of Enlightenment thinking. Its starting point lies in the fundamental freedoms of the individual, which require protection against the power of the Sovereign (the state). Although the text does refer in the final articles to the community, and the duties of individuals with respect to the community, the UDHR remains centered on the individual. For the Saudi Arabian delegate, however, the fact that the declaration began and ended with the human being, without any reference to God, was sufficient reason to abstain.

In the period following the adoption of the Declaration, many interpreted the human rights project as a juridical challenge to legislate and to create procedural provisions for individual and state complaints. Human rights violations would be denounced everywhere based on an intrinsically neutral attitude toward the culture, regime, and level of prosperity in each country concerned. From the start, however, religion played its part in this project in two ways. First, as previously mentioned, freedom of worship (or nonworship) is one of the fundamental human freedoms. Second, religion, with all its beliefs and institutions, also falls under the universal norms of the declaration. Those who wish to discriminate against, or even kill others for religious reasons, are in serious conflict with human rights. The assassin of Israeli Prime Minister Rabin said, he was acting on "God's orders." So did the September 11 perpetrators who killed thousands of citizens, among whom were hundreds of Muslims. Evidently, resistance to rights for everyone, such as the right to life, may stem from religious convictions. The enactment of *apostasy* as a serious crime is indicative of a general attitude that considers a particular religion above human rights (van Krieken 1993). Conversely, generalized statements on the superiority of human rights to religion can provoke violent reactions. In light of these statements, it seems prudent to review the three remaining postulates of meaning construction now (see above for the first three).

- Assertion of rights
- Reinforcement or subversion of real or perceived hegemony
- Protection of a way of life

Assertion of Rights

Religion is a potent force in the struggle for rights, particularly when the rights of its own adherence are in jeopardy. The aim of such struggles is to protect spaces of worship, citizenship rights, and to render harmless intrusions by other religious and nonreligious institutions, including the state. The struggle for the assertion of rights to freedom of religion and expression of beliefs is often waged against states or other religions or secular ideologies (for example, communism) that contrive to constrain or prevent a religious community from expressing its beliefs. There is a plethora of literature on these subjects and insufficient room for them here. The assertion of religious rights has further been enhanced by article 1 of the Declaration on the Elimination of All Forms of Intolerance Based on Religion or Belief, which purports the following:

> 1) Everyone shall have the right to freedom of thought, conscience and religion. This right shall include freedom to have a religion or whatever belief of his choice, and freedom, either individually or in community with others and in public or private, to manifest his religion or belief in worship, observance, practice and teaching. 2) No one shall be subject to coercion which would impair his freedom to have a religion or belief of his choice. 3) Freedom to manifest one's religion or belief may be subject only to such limitations as are prescribed by law and are necessary to protect public safety, order, health or morals or the fundamental rights and freedoms of others.[2]

However, religion is not insular and it has always been involved in social justice struggles taking different and at times controversial sides, for example, civil rights, abortion, and the death penalty, to mention but a few contested topics. These struggles, as Yinger (1946) explains, give religion a place in the struggle for power with the tacit objective of using that power to influence events that affect the faithful rights and restore dignity to humanity (Yinger 1946). From religious social movements to liberation theology and the struggle of the underground churches in China, Shi'a in Pakistan, and Muslims in Thailand, the struggle for religious communities for the assertion of rights is all-absorbing. It takes at least two prominent forms the spiritual such as prayers and the practical whereby it assumes a political dimension (Yinger 1946). William P. Marshall (2000) explains the notion that religion is politics with reference to four compelling factors: "1) Religion may become involved in expressly partisan activity; 2) religion may assume a prominent role in public policy debates removed from the furtherance of a partisan political agenda; 3) religion has its political aspects even when it is not explicitly involved in the political controversies of the day; and 4) religion is political even when passive because it comprises part of the social fabric from which political choices are made" (Marshall 2000, 2).

In a sense, while religion aspires to create a universal collective identity, it is not immune from confronting deviant voices from within while aspiring to achieve the over arching goals that maintain its existence as a functioning institution. As a system of ideas, Marshall (2000) laments that "Religion competes with other religions and other ideologies to hold on to its adherents and sway others to its convictions by the power and force of its arguments. Like other ideologies, it is in a constant struggle for the hearts and minds of the citizenry. This struggle goes beyond the search for converts. Even when religion is not seeking to bring new members into its fold, it, like other systems of ideas, is interested in persuading others as to the merits of its values and beliefs."

Beyond the theological debate, there is also the practical engagement of religious institutions in such issues where the assertion of rights, some consider as a divine devotion, which requires the intervention of the believers to transform reality or prevent actions and behavioral patterns incompatible with its messages and meaning from happening.

In such situations of religious struggle for the assertion of rights or against persecution, hermeneutics give way to scriptural politics whereby the believers consider it their responsibility to answer a divine call and restore the authenticity of religion. Assertion of rights cannot, therefore be separated from the domains of religion, politics, and human rights whether scripted in religious or secular hermeneutics.

Reinforcement or Subversion of Real or Perceived Hegemony

The relationship between religion and politics, indeed the relationship between religion and power or the ability of religious institutions to speak to power is an ancient theme, which occupied much, and rightly so, of the hermeneutics of religion. The promise of all religions to live up to their call for filling the earth with justice and respect for human dignity is practiced to a greater or lesser extent. Many historic upheavals had a religious character and many wars were fought in the name of religion. In the Palestinian-Israeli conflict over the Holy Land, India-Pakistan conflict over Kashmir, the sectarian violence between Shi'a and Sunni Muslims in Iraq and the Northern Ireland conflict to name a few, religion is considered an important element of the struggle.

Abul Ala Maududi reinterpreted the objectives of jihad or holy war in the modern world to mean the struggle for national liberation whereby all states and governments anywhere on the face of the earth opposed to the ideology and program of Islam, regardless of the country or the Nation that rules it should be destroyed (A'la Maududi n.d., 9). As Sadegh Haghighat (in this book) illustrates, jihad has acquired a new interpretation in the contemporary Shi'a hermeneutic perspective, outlining three types of jihad: fundamentalist, traditionalist, and modernist. While fundamentalist jihad comes closer to Abul Ala Maudidi's revolutionary approach, traditionalists adopt the concept of the greater (inner) jihad rather than the lesser (outer) one. The "inner jihad" essentially refers to all the struggles that a Muslim could go through while adhering to the religion such as overcoming selfish motives, desires, emotions, and the tendency to grant primacy to earthly pleasures and rewards. On the other hand, modernist interpreters believe that while "jihad" might refer to an active war against an oppressive regime, such a war is only against that regime itself, not innocent people nor regimes who do not want to engage in war. In Haghighat's words, "Modernists consider jihad to be the most misunderstood aspect of their religion by non-Muslims. Islamic modernism seeks to make Islam relevant and responsive in the context of modern society."

In contrast to these Islamic views about jihad, there is also liberation theology's attempt to invoke the concept of "preferential option for the poor" whereas according to Thomas L. Schubeck (1995), solidarity with the poor urges the church to denounce "grave injustices stemming from mechanisms of oppression" (Schubeck 1995; Boff 1988: 24–25). They considered the daily life of the poor as an inspiration of an empowering and liberating faith, also of course, recognizing the suffering of Christ in the suffering of the poor. The Catholic Church in Latin America advanced a liberating social thought "starting from the lived faith of the poor, where theologians assume that God is present within the suffering of the poor and speaks to them" (Levi 1989; Lynch 1991; Boff 1988: 24–25; McGovern 1990).

Despite differences in assessing the success or failure of liberation theology, it used religion to subvert what the Catholic Church in Latin America perceived as the suffering of the poor. There are those who use religious texts as a scripture of struggle to subvert the hegemonic exploitative power structures dominated by the wealthy and unyielding (Kliever 1987; Schubeck 1995).

Contrasting jihad as reinterpreted by Abul Ala Maududi and a plethora of extremist Muslim thinkers, movements and liberation theology or, the position of women in early Christianity (see Otten in this book) or the position of non-Jewish citizens in Israel (see Weissman's chapter in this book) may be a means of contrasting the various ways religion can be used to reinforce or subvert real, or perceived hegemonic discourses. In both cases, the relationship between text and context, the nature of collective identities religion can engender and the scriptural politics that produces and reproduces these religions could be far-reaching and unrelenting.

Protection and Reproducing a Way of Life

Whether real or socially constructed, religion plays an important role in peoples' lives and, Durkheim is more eloquent in describing how religion is a unified system of beliefs and practices relative to sacred things. That is to say, taboos set apart and forbidden by beliefs and practices symbolically unite people into a moral community and also unite them with all those who adhere to these beliefs and practices (Durkheim 1915). It creates a moral community bonded by certain beliefs and sometimes morals, which pursues a distinctive way of life. In a sense, protecting one's religion or acting on one's religion is common to people who pay more attention than others do or, those who heed the call to protect or assert its supremacy over other religions and systems of belief. Historically, the inquisition (trying and convicting heretics and other offenders against the canon law) was a way of protecting religious purity deviance. In Islam, blasphemy edicts or fatwa against irreverence or defamation of God and the Prophet Muhammad are a way of maintaining the sanctity of religion against heretics and nonbelievers. Therefore, the restriction of religious freedom, dawa in Islam and evangelism in Christianity, are deliberate institutionalized means to convert to their respective religions.

As an aside, this case reveals the difficulty in determining the exact position in the liberal rule of law with respect to the hijab. In Canada, for example, one would strongly suspect that any regulation banning the wearing of the veil would violate the constitutional rights of freedom of expression and freedom of religion—both hallmarks of the liberal rule of law. Many Westerners, however, associate the hijab with repression and social exclusion of Muslim women and consequently, see it as incompatible with a substantive conception of the rule of law. Nevertheless, setting aside the question of whether prohibiting the wearing of the veil is truly consistent with a liberal conception of the rule of law, the fact remains that the Supreme Constitutional Court (SCC) was able to fashion its own interpretation of Shar'ia that is arguably consistent with both Islam and in particular, substantive conception of the rule of law.

The hijab issue is controversial because it goes beyond the hijab to encompass wider concerns with women's rights and to whether the hijab is part of a self-chosen Muslim identity or, coercive confirmation with tradition rather than a universal Muslim collective identity or a preservation of a Muslim way of life. "Women's rights are human rights" runs the slogan of the international women's movement. No religion today perceives women as inhuman. Yet, there are two reasons why the slogan is understandable. First, those who may enjoy theoretical acceptance tend to encounter massive practical denials. Generally, societies regard women as the bearers of culture. That is why they often face severe opposition when they seek recognition and realization of their human rights. This trend particularly applies when women challenge cultural stereotypes and religious practices. Second, human rights constitute the only universally recognized moral discourse. Consequently, a possible way to assert women's rights is through their foundation in universally accepted human rights norms. The hijab issue could straddle this connection if scriptural politics, visibility in the public space, and profiling a religious phase in a multicultural setting do not intervene in what some might interpret within the broader slogan "women's rights are human rights."

Religious Scripture and Practice: The Crucial Role of Hermeneutics

Despite attempts to promote the human rights project as a civil religion, its moral foundations remain subject to continuous discussion. Religion provides people with a transcendental basis for morally justifiable behavior. Moral standards are set and remain unalterable from a reality beyond direct human experience. Does this mean that respect for human rights is inherent in all religions? Practice shows it is not. First, the religious message itself may contain inhuman elements. This applies particularly to situations in which, apart from the religious core of the message, its cultural setting, too, is authorized and absolutized. In those situations, religion may sanctify a whole people or caste and will come into conflict with the principle of human equality. Generally, the basis of such faith is tradition and interpretation rather than the holy scriptures themselves. Hence, in respect to human rights realization there is an urgent need to reexamine the foundations of interpretation.

Two fundamental questions tend to dominate religious discursive narratives and their interpretations. First, what duties and rights come from God and are applicable to all humans regardless of their faith? The boundaries set forth by scripture challenge interpretation; in the second, hermeneutics, or, the science of interpretations has its own rationality and internal logic. Between the two, there is an ambiguous terrain where a less essentialist position would render respect for differences and observe the needs of human dignity.

Hermeneutics, or the art of understanding texts (both religious and secular), requires special attention during this time when the interpretation of sacred scripture has reentered the political fray of divergent religious claims and counterclaims. Political determinations of meaning and message, replete with laws, ethics, and norms, inform ways of life. Scriptures are symbolic models from which society obtains rigid precepts of guidance. As a starting point for further analysis, dialogue, and debate, scriptural hermeneutics can fall under three levels of interpretation:

1. *Social analysis.* This level of analysis situates hermeneutics of religious scriptures within a given social-historical context. It magnifies forms of domination or servitude conferred on the scripture to serve, maintain, or subvert reality.
2. *Meaning construction.* This level has an ideological dent specifically formed to mask or reveal reality, according to the perceived needs of the moment. This includes confrontational or reconciliatory messages and meanings. Hermeneutics assumes reason, acquired from the study of scriptures or rational justification of spiritual truth.
3. *Interpretative explications.* This level goes beyond formal scriptural hermeneutics to justify action. Hence, it transforms interpretation into meaning and meaning into political or social instruments for contesting both reality and truths held by others. The impossibility of human reason vis-à-vis the divinity of scriptures often creates tensions between rationalist and empiricist, as a criterion of truth, on one hand, and fanatic belief of scripture's divinity on the other.

In some religious views, there is resistance to subjecting hermeneutics to social analysis. This opposition reflects the attitude that religious scripture is divine, timeless, and beyond the scope of human ability to determine what God has revealed. Thus, fundamentalists object to any interpretation based on contextual social analysis that might reveal ranges of truth not captured by the spiritual scripture. However, in the scriptures, truth is not exhaustible and can appear in different manifestations depending on the interpreter.

In today's world, meaning construction has acquired new dimensions informed (or ill informed) by the return of scriptural hermeneutics to the first decade of the twenty-first century. Scriptural hermeneutics was once thought a relic of the seventeenth and eighteenth centuries, when the debate on God's moral law was at its highest. The return of scriptural hermeneutics in contemporary political debate is understandable, but its coincidence with the return of liberalism must be surprising to many secularists. The dual return of scriptural hermeneutics and liberalism ushers in a new era of contestation between various grains of liberalism. It also empowers spiritualism by creating the necessary space for some Qur'anic and biblical scholars to reincarnate conservative hermeneutics. The radical Imams' movement, not only in a Western country such as The Netherlands, but also in many Muslim countries, and the rise of Islamic fundamentalism alongside conservative Bible scholars in the United States, are clear indications of the paradoxical situation where conservative hermeneutics is born out of diverse shades of anticriticism (including reactionary criticism that God is the author of the scripture regardless of religion).

Interpretative explication is the oldest type of scriptural hermeneutics, and probably also the most used and abused form. It is an area where varying theological, philosophical, and sociological strands of thought clash. The use of scriptural hermeneutics to justify jihad, apartheid, slavery, killing, or excluding Jews, Muslims, or Christians is a common theme throughout human history. There is an urgent need for scholars of different religions to analyze and discuss concrete cases jointly that concern such matters as the right to life, bodily integrity and women's rights, to mention just a few divisive issues.

Conclusions

In its relation to society, religion has a dual character. It is precisely because religion transcends the daily concerns of the individual that it has to meet higher demands of integrity. However, it tends to lose credibility through ideologization and institutionalization. Religious identity then, needs protection and to become embedded in environments conducive to human rights. Church, mosque, temple and synagogue all must show respect for human rights. It is impossible to accomplish the global project for universal responsibility for one another's freedom and well-being without constant moral injections. Through their transcendental orientation, human beings learn to rise above their immediate interests and needs. Conversely, religion attains concrete relevance through its response to pragmatic human challenges.

This chapter discussed the untapped possibilities of religious faith that would ensure respect for human rights, sanctity of the human soul, and means to provide space to make decisions from the perspective of human difference. It introduced situations where religion has been the guardian of human rights, and explained incidents where religious interpretations have projected an image of cruelty and disrespect for justice and liberty. Hermeneutics is a tool easy to use or abuse because people act on the interpretations of religion. The transformation of scriptural politics into meaning, and meaning into political or social action for the good of society is welcome. However, we must guard against the abuse of scriptural hermeneutics as instruments of hate. It would be erroneous to argue that religious identities are not subject to change or that identities do not fall along a continuum of religious ideals. Changes in society, though, tend to occur more quickly than changes in religious teachings. Therefore, the power and practice of interpretation in some religions has not been able to keep pace with social changes. This reality invokes the ever-present question of whether the divinity of the scripture can be subject to liberal interrogation. When religion fails to contribute to human well-being, including basic freedoms and human rights, reinterpretation becomes divine responsibility to improve the human lot.

"Yes, we need God," Roger Garaudy concluded in his *Avons nous besoin de Dieu?* "God, whose presence in us manifests itself through the continual possibility of not surrendering blindly and passively to the spirits of this time but of taking active responsibility for the continuation of creation and life."[3] *Responsibility* is the keyword. Religion without any sense of responsibility is doomed. The basic principle of *universal responsibility*, which forms the foundation of the secular human rights project, might push religion toward a process of revitalization. Injecting religion with the notion of universal responsibility for the dignity of life will have to occur at the grass roots level. There are some signs that such a development is already taking place. If religion does not respond to those efforts, it will lose its meaning in the lives of people. If it does respond, religion will remain relevant in a world still characterized by systemic violations of basic human dignity.

Notes

1. Freedom of speech, freedom of worship, freedom from want, and freedom from fear.
2. UN, Declaration on the Elimination of All Forms of Intolerance and of Discrimination Based on Religion or Belief Proclaimed by General Assembly resolution 36/55 of November 25, 1981.
3. "Oui, nous avons besoin de Dieu ... dont la présence en nous se manifeste par la possibilité permanente de ne pas s'abandonner, aveugle et passif, aux dérives de ce courant, et de prendre la responsabilité de participer au pilotage de la création continuée de la vie" (Garaudy 1993, 201).

2

Islamic Texts, Democracy, and the Rule of Law

Toward a Hermeneutics of Conciliation

Salman Haq

The relationship between Islam and the West has been the subject of unprecedented scrutiny in the past few years. Since September 11, the international geopolitical news headlines have been dominated by stories from or about the Muslim world including the subsequent invasion of Afghanistan, the U.S.-led war in Iraq, Iran's purported nuclear ambitions, political instability in Pakistan, genocide in Sudan, and Israel's battles with Hamas in both Gaza and Lebanon. Right or wrong, many commentators linked these immediate events with broader questions about whether Islam is compatible with democracy and the rule of law.

It is clear that in recent years no other religion has received as much attention in this context as Islam, making it a particularly useful way to engage in the issue. Thus, the specific purpose of this chapter is to use Islam as an example to address the question of whether a theocratic religion can tolerate a democracy.[1] When most people talk about democracy in Muslim states, they are usually discussing democracy *and* the rule of law. As a result, this chapter also explores whether Islam is compatible with the rule of law.

The rest of the chapter is as follows. It begins with two seemingly obvious, but critical questions: what is democracy, and what is the rule of law? While most of us have a good idea of what both ideas are, they are in fact contested concepts. Both democracy and the rule of law can be conceived narrowly or broadly, and what definitions we use go a long way to determining whether Islam could ever be consistent with either concept. The second half of the chapter explores various historical elements of Islam and concludes that while Islam may be compatible with both democracy and the rule of law, much depends on the interpretation of religious scriptures.

The Rule of Law

The rule of law is not a precisely defined phrase, and this lack of clarity has spawned an impressive array of research that attempts to classify various definitions of the rule of law into particular categories such as formal and informal, ends-based and institutional-based, preliberal and liberal; and minimalist and expansionist. For some, the term has become so muddled that it has lost any real meaning or useful purpose (Toope 2003; Belton 2005, 5).[2]

For the purposes of this chapter, a useful classification is to divide the rule of law into two broad conceptions: substantive and procedural. The "substantive" rule of law herein defined is, rule according to some particular set of laws that are valued for their content, such as guarantees of basic human rights. The second conception, the "procedural" rule of law, is rule according to any laws generated by some legislative process, even if they are "bad" laws. The purpose of this rather simplistic classification is to underlie the importance of holding Islam up to a somewhat definable standard when assessing its compatibility with the rule of law. To understand the differences between these two conceptions properly, brief history is required.

Although talk of the rule of law may be a recent phenomenon in geopolitical circles, the concept is not new—and at its core, not conceptually difficult or complicated. Elements of the rule of law date back at least as far as the ancient Greeks (Tamanaha n.d.). Credit for developing the modern definition of the rule of law typically goes to Albert Venn Dicey, a British jurist and constitutional theorist (Dicey 1982). He wrote that the rule of law comprised three principles. First, *equality before the law*—all people are equal before the law, and that all, particularly government officials, must face the same laws and in the same courts as ordinary people. Second—*government bound by law*: authorities may not punish or interfere with any person unless authorized by the law. Put another way, the law must authorize all government action. Third, *individual rights* should be protected through *ordinary law*, and not rest on special, constitutional guarantees.[3]

Dicey's first two principles are the foundation for a *formal, minimalist*, or *procedural* conception of the rule of law. In addition to these two elements, which focus on restraints on government action, such a conception of rule of law requires the following (Peerenboom 2004): laws must be public and readily accessible. They must also be more than "on the books";

they must be effectively enforceable and applied fairly. Laws must also be clear, consistent, and stable; once adopted, enforcement must be predictable, free from arbitrariness, corruption, cronyism, and patronage.

The main advantage of a formal definition of the rule of law is that it is very clear and relatively objective once the formal criteria are chosen. Once standards are explicit, it is usually not difficult to observe the degree to which countries meet the standards or not. On the other hand, such a definition for the rule of law contains no assessment for whether laws are just or even efficient; the focus is on the creation and application of rules rather than with their contents.

These criticisms led to more *substantive* definitions of the rule of law. This conception is not concerned with the formal rules, except to the extent that they advance a particular substantive goal of the legal system. Unlike the formal approach, which tends to avoid value judgments, the substantive view necessarily includes elements of political morality such as particular economic arrangements (free-market capitalism or central planning), forms of government (democratic, socialist, authoritarian) or conceptions of human rights (libertarian, social welfare, communitarian, liberal; Peerenboom 2005, 4).

For example, Ronald Dworkin, an American legal philosopher, often cited for advancing an individual rights perspective on the rule of law wrote that such a rights-based conception: "assumes that citizens have moral rights and duties with respect to one another, and political rights against the state as a whole. It insists that these moral and political rights be recognized in positive law, so that they may be enforced *upon the demand of individual citizens* through courts or other judicial institutions ... The rule of law on this conception is the ideal of rule by an accurate public conception of individual rights" (Dworkin 1978, 262).

Obviously, the main advantage of the substantive version of the rule of law is the explicit equation of the rule of law with something good and desirable. On the other hand, substantive conceptions are necessarily subjective and therefore draw competing ideas of justice and morality. "If the rule of law is the rule of *good* law," says legal philosopher Joseph Raz, "then to explain its nature is to propound a complete social philosophy. But if so the term lacks any useful definition" (Raz 1977, 195–96).

In theory, whether the rule of law means something more or less formal or substantive is not a question of better or worse. Different conceptions have different advantages and disadvantages, and serve different purposes. Clearly, however, the procedural and substantive conceptions of the rule of law set up significantly different standards when determining whether Islam is compatible with the rule of law.

Democracy

As with the rule of law, democracy is not an easily definable term. Democracy comes from the Greek words *demos* ("people") and *kratos* ("power" or "rule"). Thus, a strict or minimalist conception of democracy would appear satisfactory through free and fair elections. However, when Western leaders typically talk of democracy, they are usually talking about much more.[4] In fact, as shown below, a full-fledged democracy would appear to subsume the substantive definition of the rule of law, making the two virtually indistinguishable from each other.[5]

An expansive version of democracy has much in common with the idea of good governance, which now often subsumes democracy as a goal by the international development community. In general, governance is a broad term that "encompasses the values, rules, institutions, and processes through which people and organizations attempt to work towards common objectives, make decisions, generate authority and legitimacy, and exercise power" (CIDA 2006b). More specifically, the characteristics of *good* governance include participation, transparency, responsiveness, accountability, equality, inclusiveness, and efficiency. Increasingly, the view of good governance is providing the enabling environment for achieving a wide array of development goals.

The procedural conception of the rule of law enters into the framework of good governance since it, too, emphasizes notions of equality, predictability, and stability. Furthermore, the rule of law is seen as either conceptually indistinct from democracy or, at the very least, critical to its sustainability. For example, if electoral rules do not apply equally, fairly and consistently, or if voting procedures were not publicly accessible and openly debated, then an election cannot be considered fair. Similarly, disputes over voting irregularities would need hearings by independent courts with judges who can render decisions free from political interference.

To go even further, however, a robust and sustainable democracy appears to require a commitment to the substantive conception of the rule of law. For example, in order to ensure full participation in a democracy, civil and political rights—such as freedom of thought or freedom of association—need protecting. Enabling legislation, such as beneficial tax rules for nongovernmental organizations or civic education, promotes substantive participation. Transparency in government is encouraged by a strong and independent media, which may require particular legislation or regulations, such as access to information rules. A responsive government is likely to require some sharing of power with other levels of government, particularly at the local level. Parliamentary scrutiny and legally enforceable standards assure accountability and efficiency. Anti-discrimination councils or human rights bodies may protect equality and inclusiveness. All this suggests that, at least in theory, good governance, embodied by democratic principles, links inextricably to the rule of *good* law.

The little empirical evidence that exists on this point further supports the fact that a narrow conception of democracy is conceptually different from the rule of law. Peerenboom notes that countries such as Singapore, Hong Kong, Oman, Qatar, Bahrain, and Kuwait all score high on rule of law indices, but low on democracy measures (Peerenboom 2005, 63–65). Conversely, a political system marked by free and fair elections does not necessarily translate into a legal system that ensures equality before the law and a government bound by law. In fact, as author and journalist Fareed Zakaria argues, protection of individual rights (often seen as a cornerstone of democracy) may be more the result of liberalism than democracy (Zakaria 1997). It happens that in the West, democracy meant *liberal* democracy—a political system marked by not only free and fair elections (the democratic part), but also by a substantive conception of the rule of law including the separation of powers as well as the protection of basic liberties of speech, assembly, religion, and property (the liberal part). These freedoms, one might term constitutional liberalism, are completely distinct from democracy. Liberalism may have coincided with democracy, but this chapter admits no clear links between the former and the latter. In terms of quantitative evidence, for example, economists Rigobon and Rodrik (2005) found that greater rule of law produces more democracy and vice versa, but the effects are not strong (Rigobon and Rodrik 2005, 533). In sum, the evidence suggests that a narrow conception of the rule of law need not necessarily march in lock step with democracy, even if the two tend to be mutually reinforcing (Peerenboom 2005, 63; Gurr 1986).[6]

Islamic Theocracy and Democracy

As discussed above, a substantive conception of democracy—one that goes beyond the notion of majority rule—quickly subsumes the principles of the rule of law. As such, this section deals solely with whether Islam is compatible with a narrow conception of democracy, that is, with a system of government that simply gives effect to the will of the people.

In contrast to the democratic ideal of the "rule of people," a theocracy is a form of government in which divine power governs an earthly human state. At first glance, then, it would appear that there is little room for democracy and theocracy to coexist. If a theocracy means that God's rules are paramount, what role could there be for the people to govern themselves according to their own needs and desires?

According to classical Islamic jurists, a government bound by Islamic law, or Shar'ia, was the best form of government because in such a system, human beings would have fettered authority over other human beings. The concept of a democracy creates difficulties in Islam because a democracy means that the rule of man trumps the rule of God. Nevertheless, as shown below, while there may be no way to reconcile Islamic theocratic principles with democracy fully, the assumption that the two are completely incompatible is false. In fact, as el Fadl argues, there is much in the broad traditions of Islamic thought to support the democratic ideal (El Fadl 2003, 8).

To begin with, while the Qur'an did not specify a particular form of government, it did identify some political and social values, such as mercy and compassion in social interaction, and social cooperation and mutual assistance in pursuit of justice. For the purposes of this section, one of the key values was the establishment of consultative and nonautocratic methods of governance (El Fadl 2003, 9). It would be logical, then, to assume that Muslims should choose the form of government that is most suitable to protecting these values.

Beyond such general statements, however, there is still the specific burden that Islam faces in reconciling the rule of man with the rule of God. After all, in an Islamic state, one concept of God is as the sovereign lawmaker. What does this mean, in practice? In order to carry out God's law, it is clear that human beings must give, at some point "effect to the Qur'an according to their limited personal judgments and opinions" (El Fadl 2003, 16). In other words, regardless of the supremacy of God's law, human interpretation of God's law is a necessity. To argue otherwise is to "pretend that human agents could possibly have perfect and unfettered access to the will of God and also that human beings could possibly become the mere executors of divine will, without inserting their own human subjectivities in the process" (El Fadl 2003, 16). The fact that God is sovereign and that God created humans cannot be used as an excuse to escape the undeniable fact that humans have been left with considerable responsibility to apply God's law. It would also be rather naïve to assume that, on occasion, humans would never exploit the notion of God's sovereignty to marginalize others.[7] It is this seemingly obvious point that opens the door for overlaps between democracy and Islamic theocracy.

At the time when the Prophet Mohammed received the Qur'an, there was no debate about who would interpret and apply God's law. The Prophet occupies an obviously special place in Islam, and clearly, He would bear the honor and responsibility to govern his people in an Islamic manner. However, the Prophet did not name a successor; in fact, he intentionally left the choice of leadership after his death to the Muslim nation as a whole (El Fadl 2003, 18).

The subsequent leaders of the Muslim nation were Caliphs, which means "successors" or "deputies." Although there was some possibility of calling the ruler the Caliph of God, they rejected it because unlike the relationship between the Prophet and God, there was no special relationship between the Caliph and God. The Caliph did not enjoy any of the authority that God or the Prophet maintained. The Caliph may have been the historical successor of the Prophet, but he was not necessarily the moral successor. According to Muslim jurists, the Caliph is "Chosen to apply the laws expounded by the Prophet and recognized by the Nation, and he, in all he does, is the Nation's trustee and representative; and it (the Nation) is behind him, correcting him and reminding him . . . and removing him and replacing him when he does what calls for his removal" (El Fadl 2003, 20).

In this sense, the ruler is the people's duly delegated agent charged with the obligation of implementing God's law. This opened the door for others to interpret and apply God's law. Despite the temptation to link the involvement of others to the notion of a representative government, however, there are two key points to remember. First, the role that others might play in assisting the Caliph would relate to the compliance of God's law, not to the fulfillment of the will of the people. Second and furthermore, since God's law was not always discernable, the Caliph was legally presumed to be making plausible interpretations of His will; as a result, most Sunni jurists therefore argued that a ruler is not removable from power unless he commits a clear, visible, and major infraction against God (El Fadl 2003, 22).

However, Muslim jurists did not completely sever the connection between the ruler and the people. In Sunni theory, the basis of the Caliph's power is on a contract between him and the people. Unfortunately, there is little historical information about the terms of this contract. Typically, though, jurists would include a list of terms that included an obligation to apply God's law and the obligation to protect Muslims and the territory of Islam; in return, the ruler enjoyed the people's support and obedience. It is unclear how strict this contract was, whether it was negotiable, and whether the terms were more implicit or explicit.

Most relevant for the present purposes is the question of who would have the power to choose and remove the ruler. Although there is disagreement among scholars about the size of the group, there is little evidence to suggest that it constitutes the public at large. Most jurists suggest that the group consists of those who possess the necessary "power" or "strength" to insure the obedience or the consent of the public. The likely candidates would be a certain number of the notables of society or the prominent jurists, who formed a socially and professionally recognized class of experts. The overwhelming majority of Muslim jurists do not suggest that the purpose of the Caliph's contract is to represent the will of the people.

The contract requires the consent of the people because the premise is a cooperative relationship between the governed and the ruler, with the sole purpose of guarding and protecting Islam and Shar'ia.

Nevertheless, it is not such a significant step to interpret "power" or "strength" as, for example, sufficient age to cast a vote in an election. Keeping in mind the context of early Islamic societies is one where the majority of people were illiterate; one could argue that the power to choose the ruler resides in those who have the ability to make reasonably rational choices, which today would include the general populace.[8] In short, it is not farfetched to equate the idea of a group of people choosing an Islamic leader with the idea of representative democracy. Furthermore, the power of this group should not be underestimated even if the group's purpose was to ensure compliance with God's law and not to give effect to their own wishes. As noted above, Shar'ia itself does not contain a large number of very specific rulings,[9] leaving a great deal of interpretative work to the ruler and, therefore, presumably a great deal of power in the hands of the people who choose him.

Further support for the concept of public involvement in decision making lies in the idea of a consultative government in Islam. The Qur'an instructs the Prophet to consult regularly with Muslims on significant matters, and it indicates that a society that conducts its affairs through some form of deliberative process is praiseworthy in the eyes of God (El Fadl 2003, 34). There are many historical reports indicating that the Prophet regularly consulted with his companions regarding the affairs of the state. The concept of the *shura* (consultative deliberations) after the Prophet's death has become a symbol of participatory politics and legitimacy (El Fadl 2003, 35). Although the precise nature of *shura* is not clear, most certainly it did not refer to the mere act of the ruler soliciting the opinions of some notables in society. In fact, the term seemed to signify the opposite of autocracy, government by force, or oppression. For some Muslim jurists, the concept of the *shura* became the same as the previously discussed group that chose the ruler. Most experts argue that the ruler had a mandatory duty to follow the group's opinions, although some say the ruler should attempt to attain consensus.

In summary, the ideas of the Caliph's contract, the group vested with the power to choose the Caliph, and the *shura* all point to at least some minimal involvement of the people, even if the evidence does not suggest full participation. Instead of a ruling autocrat capable of speaking on God's behalf, the authority resides to a council-like body empowered with the voice of God. Nevertheless, it is not absurd to suggest that there are elements here that broadly support the democratic ideal, at least with respect to political participation. The next section explores whether similar links lie between Islam and the rule of law. In some sense, this is the other critical part of the equation, because, as discussed earlier, a sustainable and robust democracy appears to require a commitment to the rule of law.

Faith and Procedural Law

A government bound by law means that it respects a process that protects legal values; a government of laws means that it is bound only to provide the full effect as to Islamic rules, irrespective of how those rules are applied or enforced.[10] The question, then, is whether Shar'ia is consistent with even this *limited* version of secular law. As with the discussion concerning the compatibility of Islam with democratic principles, the answer lies in the choice of interpretation. As el Fadl (2003) notes, it is quite possible for a government to faithfully implement the main technical rules of Shar'ia but otherwise flout the rule of law (28). For example, under the guise of protecting individuals from slander, the government could punish many forms of political and social criticism. To ensure public modesty, it could pass arbitrary laws banning public assembly. In general, there is very limited historical understanding of the notion of procedural fairness in Shar'ia. There is some sense that administrative practices of the state cannot be in violation of Shar'ia, but it is not clear exactly how far the government could go under the guise of guarding or properly fulfilling the purposes of Shar'ia. This may be because, in Islam the state's rule-making discretion only involve rules with temporal weight. What is clear is that Muslim rulers typically consulted with Islamic jurists on administrative practices and used their moral weight to thwart tyrannous measures. As time went on, however, the jurists' power waned. As el Fadl notes, "Modernity [has] turned [jurists] from 'vociferous spokesmen of the masses' into salaried State functionaries that play a primarily conservative and legitimist role for the ruling regimes in the Islamic world . . . The State has acquired a formidable power that only serves to further engrain the practice of authoritarianism in various Islamic States" (2003, 34).

In sum, what little we know about the restraint of government power in Islam reveals a significant role for jurists in curbing arbitrary government discretion. History reveals that the issue was not lost on early Islamic societies, although it would appear farfetched to suggest that the specific elements of a procedural rule of law reveal themselves in Shar'ia.

El Fadl (2003) himself adopts a different approach; one that he admits will require a "serious paradigm shift in Islamic thinking" (42). He argues that justice and whatever is necessary to achieve justice, is the very essence of God and Islam. God describes God's self as inherently just. He goes on to say that the overriding goal for Muslims is to pursue the fulfillment of justice through the adherence to the need for *mercy*: "mercy is a state in which the individual is able to be just with himself or herself, and with others, by giving each their due" (El Fadl 2003, 42). In order to achieve mercy, humans must "know another" and engage in a "purposeful moral discourse" (El Fadl 2003, 43–44). This opens the door to the concept of individual rights in Islam.

The source of protected rights in Islam comes from considering the five basic values or necessities promoted by Shar'ia: religion, life, intellect, lineage or honor, and property. However, these values did not obtain a holistic approach but rather a more instrumental use. For example, the prohibition against murder in Islamic law served the basic value of life; the law against apostasy protected the value of religion, and so on. The juristic tradition treated these five values in a way that reduced them to technical legalistic objectives. However, there is no reason why they could not form the "foundation for a systematic theory of individual rights in the modern age" (El Fadl 2003, 47).

In fact, there is ample evidence that Muslim jurists did come up with a number of individual rights, even if such rights developed without an overarching theory of rights. For example, jurists developed the idea of presumption of innocence in all criminal and civil proceedings, and they argued that the accuser always carried the burden of proof. Muslim jurists also condemned the use of torture and opposed the use of coerced confessions in all legal and political matters (El Fadl 2003, 47).

Islamic juristic tradition also holds that there are two types of rights—the rights of God and the rights of people. Only God can judge people on the violation of the rights of God, whereas only the people may forgive violations of the rights of the people. The rights of God are few and include things like the requirement of fasting during the holy month of Ramadan and praying five times a day. All other rights are by default the rights of people. Contrary to what one might believe a limited role given the supremacy of God in Islam, this suggests that there is a significant role for the judgment of humans by other humans. More to the point, this paradigm means that the interpretation and enforcement of a majority of rights in Islam falls to humans, and not God. This does not in any way diminish God's supremacy. In fact, "The right entitlements of human beings are simply a basic component of recognizing the direct accountability of individual agents to God, and not to other human beings" (el Fadl 2003, 56–57).

All this suggests is that Islam and the rule of law are mutually compatible in theory. However, theory and practice are entirely different, as evidenced by the paucity of Muslim countries around the world that managed to be democratic and follow the rule of law principles.[11] In order to lend some credibility to the theoretical possibility, it is necessary to find concrete examples. The remainder of this chapter examines how Egypt's Supreme Constitutional Court (SCC) interpreted a constitutional provision requiring that Shar'ia be the sole source of legislation (Lombardi and Brown 2006). The SCC's approach to Islamic interpretation suggests that even a liberal conception of the rule of law could be consistent with Islam.

Article 2 of Egypt's 1971 Constitution proclaimed that "the principles of the Islamic shar'ia are a chief source of legislation."[12] In 1980, the article was amended to say that the Islamic Shar'ia was *the* chief source of legislation, a small but significant change. Of course, article 2 did not explain what it meant by the term "the principles of the Islamic shar'ia," and it fell to the SCC to establish how it would interpret this critical passage. As discussed earlier, there was no one fixed method of interpretation in Islamic law. Therefore, the SCC had to decide to use one of the more common approaches, or, alternatively, come up with its own. In order to understand how the SCC ultimately decided, it is necessary to consider some basic Islamic legal theory.

Under classical Islamic legal theory, equally competent Muslim scholars could disagree on the interpretation of Shar'ia, God's law and the body of commands that God wants people to obey. If there were competing, equally valid interpretations (*fiqh*), classical theory said that the state could choose any of the valid interpretations. Furthermore, the state was not required to employ a scholar to derive a ruling for every situation that it wished to control. Ideally, though, it was supposed to consult with scholars to ensure that the laws it enacted were consistent with the chosen interpretation (Lombardi and Brown 2006, 396).

In classical Islamic theory, there were two principal ways of developing *fiqh*—*ijtihad* and *taqlid*. As discussed below, although *ijtihad* was the preferred technique—and one that would seemingly encourage a more purposive and liberal approach to Shar'ia—*taqlid* was relied upon more heavily (Lombardi and Brown 2006, 396). *Ijtihad* first required looking at the Qur'an and *hadith*, the stories of the Prophet's words and deeds. As it turns out, only a small number of scriptural commands were considered certain with respect to both their authenticity and meaning. In cases where the Qur'an and the *hadith* were not clear, *ijtihad* said that classical jurists would be able to look at previously established scriptural commands, examining the "interest" or "benefit" that the command promoted, and making an analogy on that basis. Each scriptural rule of Shar'ia was to promote the five important interests or benefits: religion, life, intellect, lineage or honor, and property. The problem is that using this somewhat purposive method of establishing new rules was of "contingent validity." As Lombardi and Brown (2006, 401) note, a rule derived in this way "ceased to be applicable whenever circumstances changed so dramatically that it no longer promoted effectively the goals that it was supposed to serve."

Over time, Islamic jurists abandoned *ijtihad* in favor of *taqlid*, the second method of developing *fiqh*. *Taqlid* did not look at juristic reason or employ a purposive approach. Instead, it developed rulings based on precedents from early masters of orthodox "guilds" of jurists. Early on, the dominant thought was that only state laws developed by an exceptionally trained jurist were legitimate. Later, it began to be accepted that a ruler could ensure legitimacy of law by simply ensuring that the laws did not require Muslims to perform acts deemed forbidden, and that the laws did not cause general harm to society by impeding the goals that Islamic jurists accepted as goals of the law (Lombardi and Brown 2006, 405).[13]

Over the course of the twentieth century, three competing modern approaches to Islamic legal interpretation began to predominate. First, the neotraditional approach asserted that only classically trained scholars have authority to interpret Shar'ia. For example, although the guilds of law had collapsed as effective teaching and licensing institutions in the nineteenth century, graduates from government-controlled institutions such as the prestigious al-Azhar University in Cairo were a class of special scholars that could approve state laws (Lombardi and Brown 2006, 407). The SCC, however, refused to follow this neotraditional approach, and instead employed elements from the two other modern approaches: utilitarian neo*ijtihad* and comparative neo*taqlid*.

Neo*ijtihad* followed classical *ijtihad* by first looking at universally accepted rules found in the scriptures. However, apart from rules deemed certain with respect to authenticity and meaning, the state would develop laws by adopting a utilitarian method. The only requirement under that method was that Islamic laws do "no harm and no retribution." Neo*ijtihad* suggested that an Islamic state must order people to act in a way that reason suggests will advance human welfare. As Lombardi and Brown note, this "utilitarian method of identifying Islamic norms and developing Islamic legislation left tremendous discretion in the hands of rulers or their legal advisors, who would have to determine whether a proposed statute was 'Islamic' largely on the basis of subjective conclusions about utility" (2006, 411).

The third modern approach to Islamic legal interpretation was neo*taqlid*. As with *taqlid*, neo*taqlid* derives from precedent and tradition. Where it differed was the standard to which precedent applied. Neo*taqlid* required looking not at the most recent custom, but at those legal principles implicitly respected by Muslims at all times during history. Once again, neo*taqlid* left legislators and/or judges with significant discretion to establish laws that advanced what they considered just or socially beneficial.

It was not until 1993 that the SCC issued a detailed opinion describing a theory of Islamic law and the basic outlines of its approach to Islamic legal interpretation. As discussed below, the SCC was able to use a combination of modern interpretative techniques to justify its philosophy of legal liberalism, which strongly protected negative liberties in the areas of economic regulation and human rights (Lombardi and Brown 2006, 417). Most important for the purposes of this chapter is the SCC's use of Islamic legal interpretation to develop a liberal implementation of Shar'ia.

The SCC interpreted article 2 to require the state to develop laws that meet two criteria: (1) they must be consistent with universally applicable scriptural rules of Islamic Shar'ia and (2) they must advance the goals of Shar'ia. With respect to the universally applicable rules, the SCC follows the modernist approach and only searches for those principles that are certain. Not surprisingly, then, the SCC found few rules that met this high standard. Concerning identifying the goals of Shar'ia, the SCC follows the classical tradition and looks to the key interests or benefits that Shar'ia promotes. However, along with these specific goals, the SCC also considers general goals—laws must simply not harm society. In this way, even if a law does not seem to meet a specific goal, it might very well promote some general goal that is just or socially beneficial. Working from this standpoint, the SCC argued for interpretations of Islamic law that are much more generous to women than the interpretations proposed by classical jurists. For example, the SCC upheld as Islamic legislation that husbands are required to pay alimony, legislation that provides women with a right to retroactive child support, and legislation that provides Egyptian women with the right to dissolve their marriage for *harm* if their husbands take a second wife (Lombardi and Brown 2006, 425).

In 1996, the SCC upheld a ministerial regulation that forbade schoolgirls from wearing the veil in public schools without written permission from their parents. In upholding the legislation, the court first found that there was no unambiguous Islamic scripture setting out exactly what parts of a woman must be covered. The SCC next turned to whether the regulation promoted specific or general goals. With respect to specific goals, it found that the purpose of veiling was to promote modesty, but concluded that unveiled faces do not promote lewd behavior. With respect to general goals, the SCC said that a ban on women covering their faces did not harm society, and that veiling created other indirect social costs, such as the inability for women to work and engage in public activities (Lombardi and Brown 2006, 428–29).

Conclusion

The current state of governance in many Muslim countries caused many observers in the West to question whether a country run according to Islamic law and principles could ever be compatible with democracy and the rule of law. In the view espoused here, the tentative answer is, "it depends." Pragmatically, it depends on what hermeneutic path Muslim countries choose to follow.

There is certainly enough evidence to suggest that political participation in governance is not a foreign concept in Islam. The supremacy of God in Islam is paramount, but such statements find their way into the speeches of Western leaders and into the constitutions of Western countries as well. For example, at the outset of Canada's Charter of Rights and Freedoms, the preamble says that "Canada is founded upon the principles that recognize the supremacy of God and the rule of law."[14] With respect to the rule of law, we have little historical evidence of a Diceyan rule of law. From a substantive point of view, there is also good reason to believe that one of the basic principles of Islam is justice and the protection of individual rights.

When autocratic and repressive regimes in the Muslim world denounce democracy and the rule of law as "imperialistic" or "Western," they only use a conveniently false tool to salvage their own system of government, one that could not possibly be consistent with the principles of equality, dignity and justice that are the basis of Islam, as found in the Qur'an and the Hadith.

Notes

1. The issues discussed here dominated the discussions of a session of the Public Law Committee of the International Bar Association at its annual meeting in Singapore, October 2007. Starting from the question whether a theocracy can tolerate democracy, the session looked particularly at the rule of law, its application, and impact on a regional and global basis.
2. Belton notes that the rule of law "concept emerges looking like the proverbial blind man's elephant—a trunk to one person, a tail to another."
3. This third principle is generally ignored when talking about rule of law in the context of the compatibility between religion and democracy. As an aside, however, it is quite controversial. For example, it rules out the notion of a written constitution as the source of legal power or authority. Specifically, Dicey believed that the common law foundation of the English system provided better protection to the individual than could a written constitution.
4. Why is democracy so important? Democracy is considered the best form of government that embodies the characteristics of good governance. For

example, free and fair elections—the hallmark of democracy—provide for greater political participation, increasing the chances that national development goals will reflect broad societal aspirations and priorities. Similarly, a democratic government is more likely to be accountable since it is more responsive to popular concerns and more transparent in its decision making. Democracy provides the only long-term, peaceful basis for managing competing ethnic, religious, and cultural interests in a way that minimizes the risk of conflict, one of the primary causes of underdevelopment.

5. For example, the right to freedom of expression could be considered a basic element of both democracy and the rule of law.
6. Ted Gurr argues that the protection of human rights is more likely in democracies because democratic governments "compromise in conflict and participation and responsiveness in relations between rulers and ruled, traits that are inconsistent with reliance on repressiveness as an instrument of influence or power."
7. Beyond the physical necessity of requiring human beings to interpret God's law, it is also possible (and in fact likely, given the paucity of specific directions) that God did not seek to regulate all human affairs as long as they observe certain minimal standards of moral conduct and that such standards included the preservation and promotion of human dignity and well-being.
8. This is not meant to imply that the ability to vote should require some basic level of wealth or education, an argument that some authoritarian leaders in developing countries use as justification for denying their citizens the right to elect their leaders.
9. As El Fadl notes, there was no singular authority conclusively and authoritatively defining Shar'ia law. The remarkable diversity of opinions and approaches within Islamic legal practices has formed a barrier against the formation of a central church that could rule in God's name.
10. Such a distinction, of course, exists not only in the context of Islamic governments, but all governments.
11. For example, with respect to the narrower definitions of democracy—free and fair elections—there are relatively few. Indonesia, the world's most populous Muslim country, stands out as one important example.
12. The full text of Article 2 reads as follows: "Islam is the state's official religion and it is a foundational source of legislation: (a) It is not permissible to enact a law that contradicts the fixed rulings of Islamic law; (b) It is not permissible to enact a law that contradicts the principles of democracy; (c) It is not permissible to enact a law that contradicts the basic rights and liberties mentioned in this constitution."
13. This extremely wide latitude, for example, was used by the Ottomans to justify the enactment of a wide range of state law.
14. Part I of the *Constitution Act, 1982*, Schedule B to the *Canada Act 1982* (U.K.), 1982, c. 11.

3

Interpretation in Canon Law

Faith or Reason?

Phillip J. Brown

There have been a number of new theories of canonical interpretation proposed in recent years, especially during what may be called the "intercodal" period (between the announcement in 1959 that the 1917 Code of Canon Law would be revised and promulgation of the new code in 1983; Moneta 1970; Canon Law Society of America 1982; Örsy 1979; Örsy 1992; Torfs 1995). Canonical interpretation involves the following considerations: its genitive element, the temporal matrix of interpretation, and the locus of meaning. The genitive element means the process of creating a law; the temporal matrix of interpretation refers to the point or points in time when a law has a particular meaning; and the locus of meaning is the "place" where the meaning resides (i.e., the object of understanding).

The genitive element represents a continuum from the recognition of the need for a law to promulgation. Looking backward, the sources of a law can be many and varied. Though promulgated by a single legislator, many people may be involved in assessing the need for a law and formulating its text. Meaning is also understood at various times and in various contexts. The meaning of a law develops throughout the genitive period and may be considered fixed only at promulgation, depending on the kind of meaning one intends. In any event, it is thereafter understood during casual reading by a layman, in a classroom of canon law students, during consideration by an academic or other expert, or when applied by an official interpreter, such as a judge or administrative official.

The variety of potential meanings raises numerous questions. What is the meaning at a given point in time? Is it static, fixed as at promulgation? Or, is it dynamic? (Moneta 1970, 33–44; Coriden 1982, 24; Örsy 1992, 64) Is the moment of promulgation crucial, or is it the "moment of mediation," when the law is being interpreted more important? (Moneta 1970, 38, 43–44) Does the meaning of a law exist in its text or somewhere else? (Örsy 1980, 45) Can the meaning be found in canonical tradition, the "mind of the legislator," in a consensus of scholars, the "sense of the community," (Coriden 1982, 24) or the *Weltanschauung*? (Kneal 1982, 29) Can it have the same existence in such different "locations"? Or, must we speak of the relationship between the "locus of meaning" and the "locus of understanding"?

Canonical tradition answers these questions by explaining that the meaning of a law is the intent of the legislator at the time of promulgation. The 1983 Code (particularly Canon 17), grounded in *Lumen gentium*, quite clearly adopts this traditional standard. New theories challenge that conceptualization, however. The philosopher and theologian Bernard Lonergan, for example, suggests a valuable hermeneutical method for interpreting church laws, consistent with Canon 17, based on reason and grounded in faith. This chapter will examine the essential principles of Lonergan's method, and will propose their application to canonical interpretation. In section 2, this chapter will fully examine traditional interpretive doctrine. Section 3 will introduce Lonergan's method and examine its applications to the interpretation of canon law. Finally, this chapter will conclude that reason grounded in faith is necessary for accurate canonical interpretation.

Traditional Interpretive Doctrine

First, within traditional canonical interpretive theory is the principle that the meaning of a law is a product of the intention of the legislator. Coming to understand that meaning is, therefore, the proper object of interpretation. If the text of a law is clear, then the legislator intended that meaning.[1] If the text of a law is not entirely clear, then the interpreter may look to other sources to determine the law's meaning.[2] A premier commentator of the pre-Vatican II era, Gommarus Michiels, called this the primary rule of interpretation.[3] An interpreter must consider the collective meaning of the words in order to construct the meaning of the entire law. The interpreter cannot do this by arbitrarily fitting individual meanings together. Rather, it is vital to consider each word of the text, as well as the overall context of the law. If a law cannot be understood through the text and context, either the interpreter lacks the capacity to understand the law, or there is a shortcoming in the written expression of the law.

Only when the meaning of a law cannot be determined from the verbal formula alone can the interpreter seek out other sources. Michiels referred to parallel places, such as the ends and circumstances of the law and the mind of the legislator, as secondary rules of interpretation. Even utilizing those rules, however, the objective is still to determine the proper meaning of the words in order to understand the intention of the legislator. According to Michiels, the "proper" meaning of the words is first the juridical meaning of all words that have one. If a word does not have a special juridical meaning, then the common meaning, the meaning as commonly understood and as reflected in dictionaries, should be consulted.[4] Finally, the etymological meaning, or even an "improper meaning," can be appropriate if it is shown that a particular word in the law has a meaning other than its common usage.

Since resorting to secondary sources is allowed only when the meaning of a law remains unclear after examining the text, usually there is no need to examine in detail the secondary sources that Canon 17 of the 1983 Code allows an interpreter to consult. While the 1917 Code restricted parallel places to other parts of the code itself, the 1983 Code permits recourse to other parallel usages when there is a sound basis for doing so. For example, an interpreter may consult the words from a Vatican II document to analyze a provision of the 1983 Code that carries out the document's teachings. With regard to "parallel places," there must be legislative evidence that demonstrates the relevance of any information gleaned from secondary sources. If no such evidence is present, secondary sources cannot serve as the basis for interpretation.

The application of traditional canonical doctrine, then, suggests a series of questions that interpreters might ask themselves when seeking to understand an ecclesiastical law:

1. Is the meaning intended by the legislator immediately clear from the text? If so, what is that meaning?
   a. Do I understand the meaning the legislator intended for the text right away? Do the words make sense in the text and context?
   b. If I do not understand all the words, what is the proper meaning of the words I do not understand?
2. Do any words have a special juridical meaning?
3. For those that do not, what is their usual meaning?
4. Do they lack any well-known meaning?
5. What is their etymological meaning, then?
6. Is it possible that any of the words have an "improper" meaning, in either common or juridical usage?
7. After considering all these possibilities, are there still individual words whose "proper" meaning remains obscure and doubtful to me and, if so, why? Is it my own lack of understanding, or is it something in the nature of the word that no one understands?

8. If the meaning of a law remains doubtful and obscure after considering the proper meaning of the words in text and context, why is this so?
   a. Is it because I lack something? Do I have enough training and experience to understand this law as intended by the legislator? Have I expended sufficient effort to arrive at the meaning intended by the legislator? Am I accepting the evidence, neither entertaining doubts where other trained canonists would have none, nor accepting conjecture rather than positive, extrinsic evidence from the legislator as to the meaning intended, either to sustain doubts or to attribute a meaning the law does not in fact express?
   b. Or does the verbal expression lack something?

By answering these questions, interpreters can reach a true understanding of the law. Whenever an interpreter cannot determine the meaning of a law, however, the first and foremost inquiry should be "Is it me, or is it something in the law?"

Lonergan's Hermeneutics

The Psychological, Theological, and Philosophical Basis for Lonergan's Method

Lonergan developed his hermeneutical principles in relation to theological and scriptural texts. However, they are also part of a larger effort to develop a general interpretive method that is applicable to all fields of human knowledge. This general applicability renders Lonergan's method particularly apt for canonical interpretation, especially considering its close affinity with traditional and widely accepted principles of canonical interpretation (Lonergan 1972, 364–65).

Lonergan's hermeneutical principles are one aspect of his transcendental method, which he derived from an analysis of the insights of St. Thomas Aquinas as applied to the context of twentieth-century science, philosophy, and psychology. His transcendental method is the result of an acute analysis of the human process of knowing, which necessarily involves considerations of epistemology and cognitional theory. Lonergan's method responds to Kantian doubts about the possibility of human knowing and the possibility of knowledge being "objective." Unlike Kant, Lonergan concludes that objectivity is possible, when based on authentic subjectivity. He called his method "transcendental" in part because it affirms the possibility of transcending personal subjective experience to reach objective knowledge of external realities. Lonergan's approach is especially appropriate for an era that often succumbs to Kantian doubts about the possibility of real communication, objective knowledge, or even the existence of objective sources of knowledge. These doubts even affect those who work in the domain of canon law.

Lonergan preoccupied himself with understanding the processes of human comprehension. He analyzed those processes by utilizing the discoveries of modern psychology and other scientific insights. Lonergan also applied the processes of human understanding to the insights of St. Thomas. Theologically, Lonergan embraces Aquinas's view that the human mind is an image of the Blessed Trinity, and that human understanding occurs in accordance with the processions of the Trinity. Psychologically, Lonergan's approach reflects the basic pattern of human cognitive operations that occur in every act of perception and understanding. Those operations, and the elements of Lonergan's transcendental method, include experience, understanding, judgment, and decision. These terms are to spark the inquirer's interest so that he or she probes deeper to reach an understanding of the full breadth and depth of the inquiry embarked upon.

Lonergan also shared Descartes' conviction that understanding complex concepts depends on the slow and steady accumulation of simple insights. As a result, Lonergan first set out to explore human cognition through simple examples. He sought to explain the process of experiencing, understanding, judging, and deciding at a basic level. According to Lonergan and Descartes, those simple insights lead to complex understanding and profound insights. Eventually, they culminate with the full breadth, if not the full majesty, of human understanding. Lonergan's transcendental method, therefore, propels conscious intentionality and promotes the subject to higher levels of awareness—from the experiential to the intellectual, from the intellectual to the rational, and from the rational to the existential (1972, 34–35). His method raises the subject to full consciousness and directs us to our goals: "The drive to understand is satisfied when understanding is reached, but it is dissatisfied with every incomplete attainment and so it is the source of ever further questions. The drive to truth compels rationality to assent when evidence is sufficient, but refuses assent and demands doubt whenever evidence is insufficient" (Lonergan 1972, 35).

When Lonergan speaks of "transcendence," he means a self-transcendence achieved through conscious intentionality. The first step toward conscious intentionality is attending to the data of sense and consciousness (1972, 35). Next, one apprehends a hypothetical world through inquiry and understanding. Finally, reflection and judgment lead to that which exists independently of us. Once the external reality is acknowledged, it can be understood. Lonergan rejects a Kantian worldview that denies the meaningfulness of objective reality. Instead, he affirms the capacity of human beings to apprehend and understand objective existence that is independent of the observing subject.

The underlying debate over the nature and possibility of intersubjective understanding and communication is beyond the scope of this chapter. The concern here is how to understand laws properly before they are applied. The proper application of laws is not, strictly speaking, the art of interpretation, but the art of jurisprudence, which nevertheless relies on the art of sound interpretation of the abstract meaning of laws. Understanding a law must rely on the same perceptual and mental processes involved in any act of perception and understanding outlined in Lonergan's transcendental method. It is time, then, to study the elements of that method more closely.

Lonergan's Method

According to Lonergan, method is "a normative pattern of recurrent and related operations yielding cumulative and progressive results" (Lonergan 1972, 4). For a canonist, this sounds very much like the process of jurisprudence itself. That is, the ways in which law, knowledge of the law, philosophies of law, and efforts to assure that law serves its underlying purposes, develop.

The "operations" of an interpretive method include seeing, hearing, touching, smelling, tasting, inquiring, imagining, understanding, conceiving, formulating, reflecting, marshaling and weighing the evidence, judging, deliberating, evaluating, deciding, speaking, and writing (Lonergan 1972, 6). The process of understanding begins with sensory experience, and proceeds through inquiry, to the processes of perception, imagination, and conceptualization. The operations involved in the process of understanding are transitive, not only in a grammatical sense but also in a psychological sense. Through the operations, one becomes aware of the focus of concern. In other words, the object becomes present to the subject. That presence is a psychological event that becomes the basis of the mental image ("word" in Thomistic terms). The mental image, then, becomes the object of understanding and interpretation insofar as it leads to the meaning of reality that is independent of the inquirer.

All of the operations referred to by Lonergan are both conscious and intentional. Intentional operations involve, in Lonergan's discourse, (1) experiencing one's experiencing, understanding, judging, and deciding; (2) understanding the unity and relations of one's experienced experiencing, understanding, judging, deciding; (3) affirming the reality of one's experienced and understood experiencing, understanding, judging, deciding; and (4) deciding to operate in accord with the norms immanent in the spontaneous relatedness of one's experienced, understood, and affirmed experiencing, understanding, judging, and deciding (Lonergan 1972, 14–15). In other words, Lonergan advocates that the ability to interpret accurately, meaningfully, and deeply requires that one becomes more consciously aware of what he or she is experiencing at any given moment, especially with regard to acts of interpretation and understanding. This more profound experience of experience itself and of understanding will lead to an awareness that it is necessary to make judgments about what one is experiencing oneself if it is to lead to genuine understanding. Making such judgments requires that one decide among the possible understandings that experience presents to one's own consciousness: which understanding represents most accurately and meaningfully what is true with respect to what one is experiencing, interpreting, and understanding?

The assumption that there is unity to truth is the premise for coming to such an understanding. This unity of all truth, and apprehension of the broader unity of what is true, is what Lonergan means by the "universal viewpoint." Thus, understanding any particular thing requires understanding its relationship to that broader unity, and it becomes necessary to act in accordance with what one has come to understand is true.

Thus, the object of all inquiry is objective truth. However, it is possible to know objective truth only through subjective experience, since the subject experiences, understands, affirms, judges, and decides. An accurate grasp of reality, then, depends on the authenticity of the inquirer. The inquirer, in this case the interpreter, must truly attend to what is experienced and understood as it is, not as distorted by preconceptions, desires, or some false concept that does not correspond to objective reality. The inquirer must then decide whether the objective truth has significance for his or her life, the present circumstances of the community, or the future.

Lonergan offers four transcendental precepts to guide the entire process of inquiry: be attentive, be intelligent, be reasonable, and be responsible.

1. *Be attentive.* The inquirer must attend to the data and all of the questions it raises and answers. If necessary, the inquirer must also enlarge the body of data to consider the controlling questions and answers fully, until he or she reaches a point of diminishing returns and the relevant data are exhausted.
2. *Be intelligent.* The inquirer must weigh and measure the data and become conscious of the operations involved in coming to understand the data. The inquirer must also engage in a self-correcting process of

learning that eliminates every false conception, every prejudice, and every desire that interferes with understanding the data.
3. *Be reasonable.* The inquirer cannot accept a distorted conception of the data and object of inquiry because that would represent a misunderstanding or even a flight from understanding. Further, the inquirer cannot accept an incomplete account of the relevant data but must accept nothing less than the truth as one's final conclusion.
4. *Be responsible.* The inquirer's final analysis should not misrepresent the facts or deny the full implications of the inquiry. The inquirer is also responsible for further action that will proceed from the inquiry.

A single maxim summarizes well the four precepts discussed above: be authentic. Through authentic subjectivity the inquirer will arrive at the truth as best it can be known. That truth will concern reality and not imaginary ideas of things that have no basis in objective reality. This objective truth is the only sound basis for human living and interaction. In the field of canon law, objective truth is the only just basis for ordering the human community and for developing honest, accurate, and appropriate interpretations of the laws that contribute to that order. If an interpreter embraces an unrelenting and immutable devotion to truth, then, as Lonergan says, he or she will have a rock on which to build:

> Let me repeat the precise nature of that rock. Any theory, description, account of our conscious and intentional operations is bound to be incomplete and to admit further clarifications and extensions. But all such clarifications and extensions are to be derived from the conscious and intentional operations themselves. They as given in consciousness are the rock; they confirm every exact account; they refute every inexact or incomplete account. The rock, then, is the subject in his conscious, unobjectified attentiveness, intelligence, reasonableness, responsibility. The point to the labor of objectifying the subject and his conscious operations is that thereby one begins to learn what these are and that they are. (Lonergan 1972, 20–21)

Lonergan's Method and Canon Law

According to Lonergan, *correspondence* is a key concept in the process of understanding objective truth through subjective experience. To be authentic, reliable, and meaningful, subjective understanding must correspond to the objective truth of what is perceived, apprehended, and understood. The whole process of understanding consists in large part of testing and verifying such correspondence. This is the critical juncture between Lonergan's thought and canonical interpretation, and highlights the crucial importance of understanding the source of the meaning of laws.

The true objective of canonical interpretation should first be to achieve a correspondence between the interpreter's understanding of a law and the meaning intended by the legislator. The legislator and interpreter have an undeniable, insuperable relationship, for the legislator invests a law with meaning, and the duty of the interpreter is to perceive, apprehend, and understand that meaning. Some deny that this is possible. Lonergan, however, elaborates throughout his writings precisely why and how that is possible. His approach contributes to a more dependable understanding of laws in large part because he affirms that it is possible to reach the meaning of a text intended by its author, or in the case of canonical texts, the meaning intended by the legislator.

The 1983 Code, in particular Canon 17, suggests a hermeneutical approach to interpretation of canon law (see also Kowal 2000). Canon 17 CIC 1983 provides that ecclesiastical laws are to be understood "according to the proper meaning of the words considered in their text and context." If the meaning remains doubtful and obscure after doing so, there is recourse "to parallel places, if any, to the purpose and circumstances of the law, and the mind of the legislator." These statements accord with both the predominant traditional approach to hermeneutics and with Lonergan's method.

Lonergan distinguishes three elements of interpretation: expression, simple interpretation, and reflective interpretation (1978, 562). He then assigns a letter symbol to each stage of the process of expression and a letter with prime number to each stage in the interpretive process. Hence,

> an expression is a verbal flow governed by a practical insight (F) that depends upon a principal insight (A) to be communicated, upon a grasp (B) of the anticipated audience's habitual intellectual development (C), and upon a grasp (D) of the deficiencies in insight (E) that have to be overcome if the insight (A) is to be communicated.
>
> By an interpretation will be meant a second expression addressed to a different audience. Hence, since it is an expression, it will be guided by a practical insight (F1), that depends upon a principal insight (A1) to be communicated, upon a grasp (B1) of the anticipated audience's habitual intellectual development (C1), and upon a grasp (D1) of the deficiencies in insight (E1) that have to be overcome if the principal insight (A1) is to be communicated.
>
> In the simple interpretation, the principal insight (A1) to be communicated purports to coincide with the principal insight (A) of the original expression. Hence, differences between the practical insights (F) and (F1) depend directly upon differences between the habitual insights (B) and (B1), (D) and (D1), and remotely upon differences between the habitual developments (C) and (C1), and the deficiencies (E) and (E1). (Lonergan 1978, 562)

The importance Lonergan places on correspondence between an original expression and later understanding and interpretation is readily apparent. An expression is a consciously intended act, and its meaning is that intended by the one making the expression. Interpretation, then, should flow toward understanding that intention.

Laws are the written expressions of the legislator, and as such are susceptible to interpretation. Although different texts require specific interpretations according to their specific nature, there are nonetheless interpretive principles applicable to any text regardless of its origin and nature. This is particularly true when the author is a single known individual. In canon law, the notion that the text of a law is the product of a single individual is a consequence of the concept of promulgation, even if the text itself is in fact the product of a collaborative effort. When promulgated, it becomes the text of the legislator, bearing the meaning he or she intended.

In reviewing Lonergan's hermeneutical principles for the interpretation of written texts, bear in mind the way these principles may apply to the interpretation of written ecclesiastical laws. First, Lonergan holds that "hermeneutics" means principles of interpretation, and "exegesis" is the application of those principles to a given task. He points out, however, that not every text is in need of exegesis:

> In general, the more a text is systematic in conception and execution, the less does it stand in need of any exegesis. So Euclid's Elements were composed about twenty-three centuries ago. One has to study to come to understand them, and that labor may be greatly reduced by a competent teacher. But while there is a task of coming to understand Euclid, there is no task of interpreting Euclid. The correct understanding is unique; incorrect understanding can be shown to be mistaken; and so, while there have been endless commentators on the clear and simple gospels, there exists little or no exegetical literature on Euclid. (Lonergan 1978, 153–54)

The texts of ecclesiastical laws fall somewhere in between the systematic conceptions and executions of Euclid's *Elements* and the simple, yet profoundly rich and symbolic writing of the gospels. No one can deny the effort to make legal texts systematic in conception and execution, nor that legal texts come into being in response to concrete facts, circumstances, and needs that provide a context for deriving precise meanings. Efforts to determine the meaning that the promulgator of a canonical text intended it to have are far more precise than efforts to determine the precise meaning of biblical texts.

For Lonergan the interpretation of a text involves three exegetical operations: (1) understanding the text, (2) judging how correct one's understanding of the text is, and (3) stating one's judgment of the correct understanding of the text (Lonergan 1978, 155). The first operation, understanding the text, has four main dimensions: (1) understanding the object to which the text refers, (2) understanding the words employed in the text, (3) understanding the author, and (4) arriving there through a process of learning (Lonergan 1978, 155). Based on this analysis, it is clear that the object of understanding a canonical text is to determine the meaning intended by its author, that is the legislator.

In order to comprehend fully the four dimensions of understanding a text stated above, Lonergan sets forth a process that includes six distinct elements: (1) understanding the object of interpretation, (2) understanding the words, (3) understanding the author, (4) understanding oneself, (5) judging the correctness of one's interpretation, and (6) stating the meaning (Lonergan 1978, 156–73). Canon 17 of the 1983 Code, on the other hand, requires that a text is approached through the second element, understanding the words. Despite that difference, the ultimate object of understanding for Lonergan is the same as that of an ecclesiastical law: the meanings "intended by the author of the text." A written text is an intentional entity created to reflect and communicate the author's meaning:

> It is a unity that is unfolded through parts, sections, chapters, paragraphs, sentences, words. We can grasp the unity, the whole, only through the parts. At the same time the parts are determined in their meaning by the whole which each part partially reveals. Such is the hermeneutic circle. Logically it is a circle. But coming to understand is not a logical deduction. It is a self-correcting process of learning that spirals into the meaning of the whole by using each new part to fill out and qualify and correct the understanding reached in reading the earlier parts. (Lonergan 1978, 159)

The hermeneutic circle Lonergan speaks of proceeds according to various principles and "rules":

> Rules of hermeneutics or exegesis list the points worth considering in one's efforts to arrive at an understanding of the text. Such are an analysis of the composition of the text, the determination of the author's purpose, knowledge of the people for whom he wrote, of the occasion on which he wrote, of the nature of the linguistic, grammatical, stylistic means he employed. However, the main point about all such rules is that one does not understand the text because one has observed the rules but, on the contrary, one observes the rules in order to arrive at an understanding of the text. Observing the rules can be no more than mere pedantry that leads to an understanding of nothing of any moment or to missing the point entirely. The essential observance is to note one's every failure to understand clearly and exactly and to

sustain one's reading and rereading until one's inventiveness or good luck have eliminated one's failures in comprehension. (Lonergan 1978 159–60)

In his discussion of hermeneutics, Lonergan distinguishes between scientific and literary interpretations. By "scientific" Lonergan is not referring to algebraic, mathematical, chemical, or other formulae. Rather, he is referring to verbal expressions that state insights subject to scientific collaboration and control. Literary interpretation, on the other hand, "offers the images and associations from which a reader can reach the insights and form the judgments that the interpreter believes to correspond to the content of the original expression" (Lonergan 1978, 586). The key difference between scientific and literary interpretations is that a scientific interpretation is consonant with scientific collaboration and control, whereas a literary interpretation represents the interpreter's opinion of the meaning and is free from methodical scientific collaboration and control. Legal interpretations, except those by the highest authority, are always subject to an assessment of their accuracy by some higher authority. As a result, legal interpretations develop through a process similar to scientific collaboration and control. The proper term for this process is jurisprudence.

Lonergan posits five canons for a methodical hermeneutics, which are applicable to canonical interpretation. Those canons are (1) relevance, (2) explanation, (3) successive approximations, (4) parsimony, and (5) residues. The canon of relevance presumes the interpreter begins from a universal viewpoint and that the interpretation conveys some differentiation of the protean notion of being. The universal viewpoint is a product of the dynamic structure of human cognitional activity and is the potential totality of all viewpoints. By "protean notion of being" Lonergan means the varied nature of existence and its ability to assume different forms. The universal viewpoint proceeds from being and the notion of being itself to a particular differentiation of that notion and that reality. That is, from one perspective understanding proceeds from the unity of all truth and the unity of all being to an understanding of some particular truth as related to the unity of all truth. From another perspective, an apprehension of the unity of all truth proceeds from one's understanding of the relevance of any particular datum to some larger relationship of meaning, which represents a particular differentiation of the whole of the unity of all truth:

> Being is (or is thought to be) whatever is (or is thought to be) grasped intelligently and affirmed reasonably. There is then a universe of meanings and its four dimensions are the full range of possible combinations of

1) experience and lack of experience,
2) insights and lack of insights,
3) judgments and of failures to judge, and
4) the various orientations of the polymorphic consciousness of man.

(Lonergan 1978, 567)

The universal viewpoint is, therefore, universal not by abstractness but by potential completeness. It attains its inclusiveness, not by stripping objects of their peculiarities, but by envisaging subjects in their necessities. There are no interpretations without interpreters. There are no interpreters without polymorphic unities of empirical, intelligent, and rational consciousness. There are no expressions for interpretation without other similar unities of consciousness. Nor has the work of interpreting anything more than a material determinant in the spatially ordered set of marks in documents and monuments. If the interpreter assigns any meaning to the marks, then the experiential component in the meaning will derive from his experience. The intellectual component will derive from his intelligence; the rational component will derive from his critical reflection on the critical reflection of another. Such are the underlying necessities and from them spring the potential completeness that makes the universal viewpoint universal (Lonergan 1978, 566–67).

Beginning from the universal viewpoint eliminates the relativity of the interpreter to his prospective audience and the relativity of both interpreter and audience to different places, times, and schools of thought. Placing the meaning of interpretation within the protean notion of being therefore secures a common field for all possible interpretations, provides for the possibility of an exact statement of the differences between opposed interpretations, and creates a reasonable hope that further appeals to the available data will eliminate any differences (Lonergan 1978, 587). The appeal to data and the relevance of data (rather than to unsubstantiated opinion) can overcome a tendency toward relativism in interpretation and ground interpretations in concrete fact. The canon of relevance demands that the basis of interpretive conclusions be data relevant to the inquiry undertaken. For the interpretation of church laws, this necessarily means data that relates to the intention of the legislator.

The canon of explanation requires that the interpreter's differentiation of the protean notion of being be explanatory, not merely descriptive. The contents and contexts of all relevant data and interpretations must relate not to us, but to one another. Descriptive interpretations may be correct, but they cannot avoid the problem of relativity. Relativity, in turn, excludes the possibility of scientific collaboration and control. An explanatory differentiation, therefore, involves three elements: (1) the genetic sequence in which insights are gradually accumulated; (2) the dialectical alternatives in which accumulated insights are formulated, with positions inviting further development and counterpositions shifting ground to avoid the kind of reversal they would otherwise demand; and (3) the possibility of the differentiation and specialization of modes of expression that comes with advances in culture and effective education. Thus, in order to seek understanding and to engage in discourse regarding what is understood, it is necessary to express positions that represent what one understands at any given moment.

The canon of successive approximations is based on the reality that the totality of documents and prior interpretations cannot be interpreted scientifically by a single interpreter or even by a single generation of interpreters. There must be a division of labor, and the labor must be cumulative. There is no assumption that at any particular time, perfect justice is achieved or perfectly just laws have been formulated. Rather, at any given time an existing formulation or interpretation is nothing more than the best approximation toward justice or the best expression of a just law that is possible at a particular time and place. Progress occurs because successive interpretations constantly build upon past insights and past examples of justice.

The canon of parsimony functions negatively to exclude whatever is unverifiable. Its positive function, however, invokes critical reflection. A relativist who fails to distinguish between the formally and virtually unconditioned will demand a complete explanation of everything before passing judgment on anything. A moderate realist, however, can rely on intermediate certitudes that arrive on the long road to complete explanation. When sufficient evidence is not available for detailed conclusions, there may still be enough evidence for less ambitious pronouncements. When it is not possible to substantiate positive conclusions completely, a number of negative conclusions may be possible that will provide the context for a more successful future inquiry. To the extent that the universal viewpoint is reached, radical surprises are excluded. To the extent that extrapolation comes from past meanings, relevant insights do not require genius but simply the thoroughness of painstaking and intelligent analysis. To the extent that the gap between original meaning and the resources available for expressing that meaning is closed, it is possible to form a more adequate expression. That is, language is always inadequate to express fully and accurately what is understood. There is always a certain gap between what is understood and the ability of language to express it. To the extent that this gap can be closed through the evolution and development of language and linguistic devices, it may become possible to get closer to arriving at the origin of ideas in the initial, transforming stresses and strains of linguistic usage.

The canon of residues recognizes that statistically insignificant phenomena that do not fit the overall pattern inevitably occur. This is true in physics, and Lonergan believed it to be true in any field that requires interpretation as well. The statistical insignificance of such phenomena renders them incapable of calling into question the basic validity of the perceived and verified pattern. The canon of residues counsels not to reject otherwise sound conclusions simply because of the occurrence of such residues.

Conclusion

Although Lonergan's method is highly rational, it is grounded in faith and follows St. Thomas Aquinas who believed that human reason is an image of the processions of the Blessed Trinity (Lonergan 1997, 191).[5] When asked if canon law involves faith or reason, one can reasonably answer "both." Canon law and canonical interpretation involve reason grounded in faith. In matters of faith there is often the temptation to understand so that one may believe, not realizing that one must first believe in order to understand. As St. Augustine once said, "unless you believe you shall not understand."[6] Ultimately, we arrive at understanding through reasoning, but reason must start somewhere. Reason explicates and confirms what has first been perceived, which is ultimately objective. Knowledge is ultimately a relationship between perceived and perceiver, subject and object, subject and subject. The meaning and understanding of ecclesiastical laws is, therefore, an intersubjective reality, and should be recognized as such.

Notes

1. "(1) Cum iuxta dicta, determinata verbalis formula sit uniuscuiusque legis elementum constitutivum, (quippe cum ipsa circumscribatur determinata legislatoris voluntas), recte ponitur tamquam regula primaria et principalis, quod praeprimis inspicienda sunt elementa instrinseca ipsius formulae verbalis, ac proinde quod ante omnia investiganda est et regulariter tamquam vera admittenda illa legis significatio, quae elucet ex ipsa verborum formula, sensu proprio, seu prout sonant, intellecta" (Michiels 1949, 515).
2. Ibid.
3. Ibid.
4. "Secundum propriam eorum significationem, praeprimis juridicam, quae si deficiat, usualem, vel denique naturalem" (Michiels 1949, 520). (Citing for cfr Barbosa, *l.c.*, Axioma 222, num. 4 et 7.)

5. See in particular pp. 206–8, citing *Summa theologiae* 1, q. 13, a. 11 c.; q. 14, a. 3. c. and aa. 2, 4; q. 27, a. 1 ad 2m, and a. 2 ad 2m; and q. 34, a. 2, ad 1m; and *Summa contra Gentiles*, 4, c. 11, §§ 1–11 and 17. See also Lonergan (1997) "*Verbum*: Definition and Understanding", in *Verbum: Word and Idea in Aquinas*, pp. 12–13, citing Summa theologiae 1, q. 93, a. 6 c: "... nec in ipsa rationali creatura invenitur Dei imago, nisi secundum mentem" ["nor is there found an image of God in the rational creature except in the mind"].
6. Augustine cites here Is. 7:9 in the Septuagint.

4

Judicial Textualism

An Analysis of Textualism as Applied to the United States Constitution[1]

Herman Philipse

Introduction

Textualism is a normative doctrine of method according to which judicial interpretation of statutes should aim at establishing the *original* meaning of the text. The term applies particularly with respect to the Constitution of the United States of America. Justice Antonin Scalia of the United States Supreme Court is one of the most notable proponents of textualism or originalism. According to Justice Scalia's major thesis in "A Matter of Interpretation" (Scalia 1997; Dworkin 2006),[2] textualism is necessary to avoid judicial liberty of interpretation, which is undesirable because it infringes on the separation of powers in a modern democracy. If, under the pretext of interpreting laws, justices of the Supreme Court in fact revise the Constitution and promulgate new laws, they are usurping the power exclusively assigned to the legislature (Weizer 2004).[3] For this reason, the Supreme Court, and indeed all courts, should adopt textualism or originalism in order to establish the *original* meaning of a statutory *text*.[4]

According to that approach, establishing the original meaning of the legal text is the sole objective of statutory interpretation. Justice Scalia's views are, indeed, representative of this approach, characterized as simple textualism. Both in the United States and in Europe, however, the vast majority of judges reject a simple methodology of textualism, so that the issue of textualism is a central controversy in the philosophy of law.

The objective of this chapter is to investigate how textualism fares in the judicial interpretation of statute law and, especially, of the U.S. Constitution. The main concern is with the *kind* of textualism that is defensible as a methodology for interpretation by judges. The chapter puts forth the argument that we have to substitute a sophisticated "applicative" version of textualism for a simple version. Even this sophisticated version cannot be a self-sufficient philosophy of interpretation because there are many other rules that judges must heed in interpreting statutes, apart from the rules of textualism or originalism. It follows that the difference between a tenable sophisticated version of textualism as a methodology of judicial interpretation and the so-called doctrine of the Living Constitution is one of degree and emphasis only (Brisbin 1997, 1998; Koby 1999).

The Living Constitution

Before broaching the major issue of textualism in judicial interpretation, it is necessary first to comment briefly on the theory of the Living Constitution, which stands in opposition to simple textualism. It is not difficult to sketch the global form of a justifying explanation of judicial interpretative freedom with regard to the American Constitution. The Founding Fathers were living at the very end of what one might call an essentially static world. Since the time of the Roman Empire, the average income per capita had not risen significantly, and changes in social relations could occur only within narrow margins. Naturally, then, the Founding Fathers conceived of the Constitution as a bulwark against change, and made it difficult to amend the text. According to article V, amending the Constitution not only requires a majority of two-thirds in both houses of Congress, but also ratification by three-fourths of the states. No wonder then, that only twenty-seven amendments have been adopted since 1787, two of which cancel each other out.[5]

In the nineteenth and twentieth centuries, however, the industrial revolution and the development of ever-new technologies produced economic and social changes completely beyond the imagination of the Founding Fathers. These changes created new social and political problems and often provided the wealth needed for solving them. With the abolition of slavery, the sacrosanct status of property suffered by the need for social justice and environmental protection. The decrease in child mortality enabled women to emancipate themselves from their subordinate roles, because fewer children per woman could sustain population levels. The severe restrictions upon federal powers and the relative moral and legal autonomy of the states as laid down in the Constitution became anachronistic because of modern means of transport and communication.

Generally, Americans perceive these social transformations as social progress, but only some of them are in amendments to the Constitution, such as the abolition of slavery (Amendment XIII). Most American judges feel that, given the near impossibility of amending the Constitution and given the vast economic and social changes since 1787, it is perfectly legitimate to interpret the text of the Constitution freely in order to adapt it to our present moral convictions, at least if these convictions are widely shared within the population. As Chief Justice John Marshall once observed, precisely because the Constitution was "intended to endure for ages to come," it has "to be adapted to the various *crises* [sic] of human affairs" (Pelikan, 2004, 8). Evidently, this is the general form of an argument in favor of the doctrine of The Living Constitution, and the widespread adherence to this type of argument is a causal factor that explains the practice of modernizing interpretations of the Constitution. According to this argument, the American Constitution is not merely the text of a historical document agreed upon in 1787. Rather it includes the living and evolving practice of interpreting this text in order to apply it to ever-new situations, which the founding fathers could not foresee (Amar 2005).[6]

What Is Textualism? Historical and Applicative Interpretations

Justice Scalia's essay "A Matter of Interpretation" is illustrative of simple textualism. According to this essay, the objective of textualism or originalism as a method of statutory interpretation is to establish the "original meaning of the text" of statutes or the Constitution (38). One should construe this meaning reasonably and not strictly (23). When interpreting texts a judge should not look for, or use: (a) the intent(ion) of the legislature (16–23), (b) presumptions and rules of construction that load the dice for or against a particular result (25–29), (c) legislative history (29–37), or (d) what the text "ought to mean in terms of the needs and goals of our present day society" (22, 38–47).

Whereas some textualists use the terms "textualism" and "originalism" as equivalents, legal philosophers usually distinguish between two types of originalism, namely textualism and intentionalism, as two different methodologies for establishing the original meaning of texts. Whereas textualism focuses on texts, their contexts, and the ordinary meaning of words at the time of production, intentionalism also allows other evidence for establishing the original meaning of a text, such as legislative history as an indication of the intent of the legislature. As argued below, the distinction between textualism and intentionalism is spurious in the case of individual speakers or authors, if one adopts a philosophically sound view of the factors that compose the "intention of an author."

In the case of texts produced by institutions such as legislatures, however, the notion of an "intention" is more problematic, since the final text is typically a product of compromises between many players, who may have very different intentions. Moreover, in the case of statutes, most members of the legislature will not have read the bills, let alone the committee reports on these bills, when voting, so that very often there simply is no such thing as, for example, "the intention of the majority of both houses of Congress." Clearly, it should be the law that governs, and not these divergent or nonexisting intentions of individual members of Congress (29–37). If "the intent of the law" has a legitimate role in the interpretation of statutes at all, it cannot be the subjective intention of legislators but only the objectified intent, that is "the intent that a reasonable person would gather from the text of the law, placed along the remainder of the *corpus iuris*" (17).

The doctrine of textualism, so construed, remains unsatisfactory in at least two respects. First, its positive statement about the objective of statutory interpretation is incomplete because it treats the original meaning of the text as if that is the *sole* objective of statutory interpretation. Whereas this may be true for a legal historian, who has purely scholarly or epistemic objectives, it cannot be true for a judge, who has to decide a case. The legal historian might conclude that statutory texts, taken in their original meaning, are full of gaps in the sense that they do not contain solutions for many cases, which the legislature did not foresee. However, the judge may not, as Justice Scalia says, "render a candid and humble judgment of 'Undecided'" (137). Because the judge has to decide upon a particular case, he has to fill in the gaps, and typically, it takes "interpretation" in those cases where the original meaning of the text is not at all plain or does not imply a decision for the case at issue.

It follows that one must distinguish between two very different types of interpretation, defined by different types of objectives, which this chapter terms 'scholarly' (or historical) interpretations and 'applicative' interpretations, respectively. Applicative interpretations are used in order to apply a text—mostly a normative text invested with some kind of authority—to a particular case or situation and, typically, to reach some kind of decision, legal, moral or otherwise. A scholarly or historical interpretation, on the other hand, merely aims at acquiring knowledge about the meaning of unclear passages in a text.[7] Textualism is the proper doctrine of interpretation in scholarly domains, such as the history of science or the history of philosophy. But in the applicative domain of judicial interpretation of statutes and the Constitution, textualism can be an adequate methodology only if one adds at least one other objective apart from establishing the original meaning of texts: the objective of reaching a satisfactory decision in the particular case at issue. So let us revise the definition of textualism for statutory interpretation. According to applicative textualism, statutory interpretation has *two* objectives: (1) to establish the original meaning of the legal text and (2) to enable the judge to take a decision in the particular case at issue. Since he stresses objective 1 only, textualism as defined by Justice Scalia may be called *simple* textualism.

It is precisely if there is tension between these two objectives, that is, if the original meaning of the legal text does not permit us to reach a decision in the case at issue, that interpretation is needed most. Clearly, it is in these situations that judges feel inclined to invoke other factors than "the original meaning of the text," such as (a) legislative intention, (b) rules of construction, (c) legislative history, or (d) considerations about the *ratio legis* or what the law ought to mean. Nevertheless, according to simple textualism, judges may not use these other factors at all. With regard to legislative intentions, for example, Justice Scalia quotes approvingly the remark of Justice Holmes as quoted by Justice Jackson: "We do not inquire what the legislature meant; we ask only what the statute means" (23). Concerning the appeal to legislative history, he says, "We did not use to do it, and we should do it no more" (37).

We may conclude that simple textualism is a splendid doctrine of interpretation when interpretation and application are relatively easy, because the original meaning of the statutory text implies a decision for the case at issue. However, when the original meaning of the text is unclear and/or does not enable us to reach a decision, requiring interpretation, this form of textualism is not of much help.[8]

This brings up the second unsatisfactory aspect of simple textualism. The argument to the effect that in interpreting statutes judges should not use extra-textual factors such as (a) legislative intention or (c) legislative history at all is obviously fallacious. The premise underlying that argument is as follows: since such use is illegitimate in some cases, namely in cases in which legislative intention or history is invoked *to set aside* a *clear* legal text, then the use of legislative intention or history is *always* illegitimate, even if it is merely used as evidence for establishing what a text means and what it implies for a particular case. But it simply does not follow from the premise that, generally speaking, legislative intention or history should not be used *contra legem*, that they should not be used at all. On the contrary, recourse to factors (a)–(d) may be indispensable when the original meaning of the statutory text is unclear, or when it does not enable us to reach a decision in the case at issue. It is a major and interesting challenge for applicative textualism to distinguish between legitimate and illegitimate uses of factors (a) – (d), a challenge that is beyond the intellectual horizon of simple textualism.

Judicial Interpretation

As we have seen, simple textualism will not do in the domain of judicial interpretation, since here the genre of interpretations is applicative, so simple textualism should be replaced by applicative textualism. However, can applicative textualism be vindicated as the optimal methodology for statutory interpretation? To what extent does a defensible version of applicative textualism differ from its official rival, the doctrine of the Living Constitution? Despite its critics, there are good specific arguments for the doctrine of the Living Constitution, derived from the nature of the American Constitution and of the political system as a whole. This section discusses two points. First, whether a democratic argument can adequately support a textualist interpretation in cases of judicial review of statutes and second, whether textualism can be a comprehensive theory of interpretation in the domain of judicial review.

Justice Scalia's central argument for applicative textualism in judicial interpretation of statutes and constitutions is an *argument from authority*. In modern democracies, which pay heed to the principle of the separation of powers, judges simply do not have the authority to promulgate new laws. If, under the guise of an "interpretation," the courts in fact create new statutes, they are usurping the legislative powers uniquely assigned to "the people and their representatives" (133).

The question is, can one rely on this democratic *argument from authority* for defending a textualist interpretation of the Constitution in cases of judicial review of statutes? Undeniably, this democratic *argument from authority* (more precisely: from *lack of authority*) has some power, although one should admit that there is no sharp distinction between "applying a statute" and "creating a new statute under the guise of an interpretation." Moreover, the legislature is able to rectify judicial interpretations of laws by promulgating new statutes, or, in principle, by amending the Constitution. In other words, nontextualist interpretations of laws do not fatally infringe on the principle of the separation of powers in a democracy.

Furthermore, most constitutions explicitly assign the power to apply and interpret the constitution, laws, and treatises valid in a country to the judiciary. For example, article III, section 2, of the Constitution of the United States assigns to the courts judicial power regarding "all Cases, in Law and Equity, arising under this Constitution, the Laws of the United States, and Treaties made, or which shall be made, under their Authority." Of course, the framers of constitutions realize that this craft of interpretation necessarily includes the filling of gaps in statutes and in the Constitution itself, and the type of stretched interpretation (by analogy, for example) that is often needed in order to apply articles to cases of which the legislature had never thought. Therefore, the democratic system of government itself has some built-in interpretive freedom.

If the issue is whether the Supreme Court should declare a law passed by a state legislature or by Congress unconstitutional and therefore void, one cannot say that the court should interpret the Constitution textually because otherwise "it would usurp legislative powers uniquely assigned to the people and their representatives." In cases of judicial review of statutes, a textualist interpretation of the Constitution may imply precisely that statutes promulgated by "the people and their representatives" will be annulled by the judiciary. Whereas they would not face annulment based on a nontextualist interpretation of the Constitution. Too often, a defense of textualism in the domain of judicial interpretation is merely a pretext for promoting a conservative or even reactionary stance on issues of judicial review.[9]

Some of the well-known examples of judicial annulment of statutes may prove illustrative. In 1923, the Supreme Court decided in *Adkins v. Children's Hospital* that a minimum-wage law for women enacted by Congress for the District of Columbia violated the right of freedom to contract on the part of the employer and the employee. Some years later, in *Coppage v. Kansas*, the Supreme Court held unconstitutional on similar grounds a Kansas law forbidding an employer to require an employee to enter into a so-called 'yellow-dog' contract, that is, a contract that required as a condition of employment that the employee promise not to join a labor union during the period of his employment. As William Rehnquist wrote in his book *The Supreme Court*, "the laws the Court was thus setting aside were the response of legislators in countless states to keenly perceived and prominently publicized problems of the day" (Rehnquist 2001, 112–14). It was only after President Roosevelt had threatened to "pack" the court that the Supreme Court discontinued invalidating New Deal legislation.

Another area where textualism can promote a reactionary stance in cases of judicial review is environmental legislation. According to the so-called "Takings Clause" of the Fifth Amendment, no "private property shall be taken for public use, without just compensation." In September 2002, Judge Douglas H. Ginsburg gave a notorious speech to the Cato Institute, a conservative libertarian club. He bemoaned what he called an absence of fidelity to the text of the Constitution, urging that the courts should return to their pre-New Deal interpretations. With regard to the Takings Clause, this would mean that property owners should receive complete compensation from states or the federal government when environmental and other regulations reduce the value of their property. Clearly, if this type of textualist interpretation of the Takings Clause applied as Ginsburg urges it should, no state or local government would dare to adopt any environmental regulations, since the costs would be staggering (Schwarz 2004, 2–3).[10]

Of course, such cases do not refute the doctrine of textualism with regard to judicial interpretation of the Constitution. The textualist might answer simply that judges do not have the authority to change the Constitution and therefore should be textualists, because the legislative power to amend the Constitution is assigned uniquely to Congress. However, the current argument is merely that the democratic argument from authority falls short of vindicating textualism with regard to the Constitution in cases of judicial review, since in these cases the textualist interpretation of the Constitution is typically used in order to annul laws that have been adopted by democratically elected legislatures. We may conclude, then, that this argument from authority is invalid in itself with regard to cases of judicial review.

Herein lies the main issue, the issue of whether applicative textualism can be a comprehensive methodology for judicial interpretation of statutes and of the Constitution. It appears that it cannot, since there are rules of judicial interpretation that any court must apply even though, in principle they cannot be incorporated in a textualist or originalist methodology. One example of such is the rule of *stare decisis*.[11] One might reply that this rule is external to any doctrine of interpretation, because it is not a rule of interpretation at all. If one decides to apply the rule of *stare decisis*, one does not interpret the relevant statute or constitutional provision, but rather decides not to interpret it anew. This reply oversimplifies the complexity of judicial decision making. In order to decide whether the rule of *stare decisis* applies with regard to a specific case, one must investigate whether this case sufficiently resembles an earlier case that involved a particular interpretation of a statute. In addition, in order to establish that the resemblance is legally relevant, one has to use the statute in question as a criterion of relevance. In other words, interpretation of the statute and the decision to apply the rule of *stare decisis* intertwine, because what one decides is that the earlier interpretation of the statute also covers this new case.

Another example of a rule that cannot be incorporated into applicative textualism or originalism is the maxim that the totality of laws and treaties of a country at a given time must be interpreted as a consistent system. This *maxim of holism*, as one might call it, implies that *later* amendments to the Constitution might influence the interpretation of *earlier* articles or amendments, and that *later* statutes might change the proper meaning of *earlier* statutes, so that it is incompatible with textualism or originalism. The *maxim of holism* also implies that ambiguities in *previously* enacted laws should be resolved in such a fashion that they are consistent with *newly* promulgated laws. One might even say that in principle, a newly enacted law has preference over an older law of the same level if the two are incompatible. Otherwise, it would be impossible to repeal an older law by a new law, or an older amendment to the Constitution by a newer amendment, as happened in the case of the eighteenth amendment concerning intoxicating liquors, later repealed by the twenty-first amendment. Clearly, then, the *maxim of holism* is incompatible with textualism or originalism.

Concerning judicial interpretation of statutes and of the Constitution, the conclusion that even applicative textualism cannot be a comprehensive philosophy of interpretation is evident. Rather, textualism is but one methodological *topos* among others, and a comprehensive philosophy of interpretation has to list all relevant *topoi*, such as *stare decisis*, the maxim of holism, and many others. Typically, in deciding which of several possible interpretations one should prefer in a specific case, one uses a trade-off between these *topoi*, assigning a different weight to each of them. This situation resembles theory choice in the empirical sciences, employing a number of different criteria for theoretical excellence, such as explanatory depth, simplicity, empirical adequacy, fertility for further research, consistency, coherence with established theories, and so on. As in the philosophy of science, a simplistic once-and-for-all methodology for the choice between rival views in judicial interpretation is impossible.

What this reduces to now is a methodology of "Super-Sophisticated Applicative Textualism." This philosophy may still differ somewhat from the doctrine of The Living Constitution in that it assigns *more weight* to the *topos* of textualism, but that is a difference of degree only. For example, one might hold that in the United States, it is not up to the Supreme Court to declare capital punishment unconstitutional by subsuming it under the "Cruelty" clause in the eighth amendment, because it is clear from the text of the fifth and the fourteenth amendments that the use of the death penalty is explicitly contemplated in the Constitution (cf. p. 46).[12] Accordingly, the decision to change the Constitution on this point falls to Congress, and a two-thirds majority of both houses is required. The specific weight that the "Super-Sophisticated Applicative" textualist attributes to the *topos* of textualism will differ from case to case, and between different legal domains. In penal law, for example, the *topos* has a greater weight than in civil law, because *nulla poena, nullum crimen, sine previa lege poenali*.

We may conclude that a scientific methodology of statutory interpretation by judges is possible. Yet this science of interpretation is complex and allows for flexibility and diversity of opinion, because there is no algorithm for determining the specific weights assigned to the different *topoi* of interpretation in particular trade-offs. We should also conclude that if the only defensible version of textualism in the judicial interpretation of the United States Constitution is Super-Sophisticated Applicative Textualism, the difference with the doctrine of the Living Constitution is at most a minor one, concerning the weight that one assigns to the textualist *topos* among many other *topoi* of interpretation.

Notes

1. This chapter was modified from Philipse, H. (2007) "Antonin Scalia's Textualism in Philosophy, Theology, and Judicial Interpretation of the Constitution," *Utrecht Law Review*, 3(2). A first draft of that article was written for a colloquium on interpretation at the occasion of a visit of Justice Antonin Scalia to the University of Leiden, The Netherlands, on September 10, 2004. Justice Scalia's own talk at this colloquium was devoted to an attempted refutation of my first draft, and I am very grateful for his generous criticisms. I also profited from comments by Justice Floris Bakels (Hoge Raad, The Netherlands), Professor Paul Cliteur (University of Leiden), Professor John Cottingham (University of Reading), Professor Willem Drees (U. of Leiden), Professor Hanjo Glock (U. of Reading, now München), Professor Dirk-Martin Grube (University of Utrecht), Dr. Peter Hacker (St. John's College, Oxford), the late Professor Oswald Hanfling (emeritus, Open University, GB), Dr. John Hyman (Queen's College, Oxford), Professor Hans Nieuwenhuis (U. of Leiden), Professor Hans Oberdiek (Swarthmore College, PA), Professor John Oberdiek (Rutgers University), Professor Joseph Raz (Balliol College, Oxford), and by the doctorate students of my seminar on analytic philosophy.
2. Scalia's textualism is endorsed by conservative judges such as Judge Alito.
3. I shall not dwell in this chapter on the differences between judicial interpretation of statutes and of the Constitution, focusing mainly on the latter.
4. Scalia uses the terms "Textualism" and "originalism" as equivalents. Usually, however, Textualism is considered one type of originalism, the other type being intentionalism.
5. Amendment XVIII, prohibiting the manufacture of intoxicating liquors, was repealed by Amendment XXI.
6. The very title of Amar's book, *America's Constitution: A Biography*, suggests that the Constitution is a living document, not one with a fixed textual meaning at birth.
7. Of course, more sophisticated distinctions between types of interpretations can be made, but that is not necessary for the purposes of this argument. For example, one might define "performative interpretations" as interpretations of plays aimed at staging old plays for a present-day audience, and one might distinguish between scholarly interpretations of unclear passages and scholarly interpretations of the point of a text as a whole.
8. In order to be somewhat more precise, we should distinguish between two different situations: (a) the legal text, as interpreted textually, does not imply any decision for the case at issue. Here, Textualism falls short of being a satisfactory doctrine of legal interpretation. (b) The text, as interpreted textually,

does indeed imply a decision, but that decision is considered to be unjust and counterproductive according to a broad consensus in present-day society. In the latter case, Textualism might be considered a sufficient doctrine of interpretation, for it now says: let's accept that "summa ius, summa iniuria" and leave it to the legislature to do something about it. And if, as happens very often, especially in the multi-party states of the European Continent, the legislature fails to produce the relevant legislation because of political stalemates within coalitions, the Textualist will conclude that the legislature is at fault, and not the judiciary. However, this option is at great cost to the system as a whole, and in most European countries, there is a consensus that in such cases, the judiciary should try modestly and cautiously to develop new rules required by society

9. In the two-party system of the United States, where the powers of the Republican Party are restricted mainly by a liberal judiciary, the defense of Textualism serves as a conservative instrument to limit the influence of courts. Similarly, the French revolutionaries of 1789 argued that judges are nothing but "la bouche de la loi" (the mouthpiece of the statute law), because they wanted to curb the influence of a conservative "noblesse de robe" (judiciary). Of course, judges cannot but develop statutes by interpretation, because the legislature is not able to anticipate all possible legal problems. In the multi-party systems of Continental Western Europe, the courts are much less politicized, and it is generally accepted that the judiciary is allowed to develop indispensable new rules, especially when the legislature fails to enact statutes because of persistent stalemates with coalitions.

10. Justice Ginsburg is a Reagan appointee to the federal court of appeals in Washington, DC. Reagan nominated him for the Supreme Court after the Senate rejected Robert Bork, but was forced to withdraw the nomination because Ginsburg had smoked marijuana with students at Harvard.

11. Stare decisis is the policy of the court to stand by precedent. It comes from Latin and means, "to stand by things decided."

12. Amendment VIII reads, "Excessive bail shall not be required, nor excessive fines imposed, nor cruel and unusual punishments inflicted." A plausible argument in this example would not be Scalia's originalist argument (p. 145), that "cruel" in this amendment *means* "what we consider cruel today," that is, at the time the mendment was promulgated. For "cruel" just means "cruel," and I agree with Dworkin (2006, 120–23) that the *extension* of the predicate "cruel" might shift over time because of changing moral sensibilities. One should apply the maxim of holism and rely on an interpretation of the Constitution *as a whole*, that is, on the impact of Amendments V and XIV on the interpretation of Amendment VIII. However, Scalia's naive textualism cannot allow that later amendments (such as XIV) influence the interpretation of earlier amendments (such as VIII).

5

Arbitrary Readings?

Christianity and Islam as Capricious Hermeneutic Communities

Karel Steenbrink

Hinduism, Buddhism, Judaism, Christianity, and Islam have been the keepers of a precious corpus of texts for many centuries. In most cases, they were oral traditions prior to written codification. The religious communities added chains of interpretations to the scripture, which sometimes also gained a high status. In Judaism, the *Talmud* gained nearly divine status. So have the sayings of the Prophet and his Companions, *hadith* in Islam, as well as the church fathers of Early Christianity. Nevertheless, history continues and the great religions rightly are hermeneutic communities. In every time, they start a new interpretation of the old texts. That is the common method of renewal. Clifford Geertz saw it in Moroccan Islam, where he observed a peculiar mixture of radical fundamentalism and determined modernism, as seen with so many modern movements: "Stepping backward in order better to leap is an established principle in cultural change; our own Reformation was made that way" (Geertz 1968, 69). It often looks as if some believers take the step backward only for the leap itself. What begins as a rediscovery of the scriptures may develop into a deification of them. Upon closer examination, a simple return to the past or a reinvention of a pure and true tradition is not possible. The global religions work through this mixture of modernization and reinterpretation of old texts.

This chapter will also give some general considerations about the process of reinterpretation by comparing Islam and Christianity with each other and with the primal traditions of illiterate cultures. It will then proceed to discuss some concrete issues of modern Islam and Christianity (economy, marriage, death penalty, homosexuality, religious freedom and interreligious communication). Furthermore, the chapter provides general conclusions, which relate to the Indonesian debates of the last decades, because of the personal experiences and involvement of this author. The overall process is clear and undisputed: the two religions often, but not always, take their scripture and tradition into consideration for the discussion of modern issues. However, the outcome of those discussions is often quite uncertain and involves ambiguity and even arbitrariness. The religions may follow strict texts, but also may apply free interpretation that looks as if they abandoned the original text. Because of the nature of this contribution as an extended, rewritten conference chapter, it will not present an overall, elaborated general theory. Rather, it will sometimes present one-sided viewpoints to stimulate further discussion within that other hermeneutic community, the academic world and its related circles.

Illiterate Societies as the Victims of the "McWorld" of Global Religions: Are Languages Rescued through the Translation of Sacred Texts?

Around 1910 the young Dutch missionary Joan Duyverman, working in the Indonesian region of Minahasa, described the process of preaching Christianity in terms of traditional agricultural practice of shifting cultivation. A few acres of a rich and varied tropical forest were burned down and rice was planted. After one or two years of harvest, the soil became exhausted and the farmers moved to another piece of forest, leaving the barren soil to wait for new plants. In most cases, elephant grass would grow, up to nine feet high and nearly impenetrable because of its razor-sharp leaves. From a great variety of plants and trees, a monoculture had grown. This was for many centuries the case in societies of shifting culture. Nowadays it happens more often and on a larger scale because of clearing land for plantations. In this way, large parts of the Amazon forest of Brazil and the forests of Malaysia and Indonesian Borneo had to make way for large grass fields or rubber and oil palm plantations. Instead of the rich variety, monocultures rose because "too much has been taken from them" (Duyverman 2005).

Is this also what happened religiously through centuries of missionary imperialism? In retrospect, the pious missionary Duyverman judged that Christianity had killed the rich Minahasa cultural and religious tradition, but had not given much more than basic teachings about a triune God, sin of man, and salvation through the cross of Christ in return. For all the festive happenings about birth, adulthood, marriage, death, and the life cycles of nature from planting to harvest, the great religion of Christianity mutilated and even crippled Minahasa society. Christianity outlawed the old traditions and gave little substance back to a society fond of festivals and ceremonies.

If we examine the religious statistics of the world, we see that the 'big five' currently control more than 90 percent of humankind. Christianity tops the list, Islam is second, followed by Hinduism, the Chinese mix of Taoism and Confucianism is fourth, and Buddhism concludes the list. In fact, many religious movements have protested against economic globalization (Wilfred 1991). In the view espoused in this chapter, the religious protestors often forget that they are also representatives of global institutions. Although many empires and economic systems rose and fell throughout history, "the world religions have survived. They are the longest lasting of civilization's primary institutions" (Hefner 1993, 34). They have brought freedom and enlightenment to many people, but also oppression.

One must acknowledge that the global religions did not simply destroy local religious traditions. Through massive translation projects, they also rescued the backbone of many cultural traditions, namely the local languages. In countries like India and Indonesia, and in many regions of Africa and Latin America, generations of missionaries and local staff studied languages and published grammars and dictionaries in order to translate the Bible. Recently, the *Summer School of Linguistics* and the related *Wycliff Bible Translators* performed this work. Often, translation has become the single major effort for the preservation and continuation of local languages. Thus, the new translation of the sacred text was not merely part of a movement that sought to replace earlier religious traditions; it was also a contribution to the conservation of a small tradition. The same is true for the various products of Islamic learning translated in local languages. Global Islam, however, was never as keen on its expression in local languages as contemporary Christianity (Sanneh 1989).

Usually the new Christian and Muslim communities accepted many pre-Christian and pre-Islamic traditions. This process is termed contextual theology in liberal or even mainstream Protestantism or, enculturation in Catholic missionary strategies. In Arabic and Muslim law, it is true *adat* or customary rules, strengthened by concepts like *maslaha* (public interest, profit of a community as a positive legal concept in Maliki ruling) or *istihsān* (preference or common sense as a criterion in Hanafi Islamic law; Schacht 1964, 60–61). Notwithstanding the overwhelming victory of the global religions over the smaller players in the religious market and the danger of impoverishment of religious life, a rich variety of religious practices still exists. In part, this is because of the continuation of the smaller groups within the global religions.

Therefore it is possible to conclude that the "big five religions" gained supremacy in the religious market. In many regions of the world, those religions reduced and sometimes even annihilated the vitality of local traditions. The translation of the Bible into the languages of other cultures, however, has also been instrumental in preserving those languages. In addition to other elements from those traditions, language serves as the backbone for many cultural and ethnic communities.

Internal Dynamics within Scriptures: Between Old and New within Christian and Muslim Traditions

There is a frequent and seemingly reasonable comparison between religious texts and law in terminology and in practical use. Christianity accepts the full text of Hebrew scripture as valid. Matthew 5:17 uses this terminology: "Do not think that I have come to abolish the Law of the Prophets; I have not come to abolish them but to fulfill them." This was done in a very subtle way in the verses on divorce in Matthew 19: 3–9, where Jesus says, "Haven't you read that at the beginning the Creator made them male and female and said: For this reason a man will leave his father and mother and be united to his wife, and the two will become one flesh? So they are no longer two, but one. Therefore what God has joined together, let man not separate." The audience then answered in a way that must be familiar to Muslims as well: because Moses made the earlier law more flexible by permitting divorce, the earlier law has been abrogated. This is similar to the traditional Muslim doctrine of *naskh*, where a later ruling within scripture abrogates the earlier ruling. Jesus, however, followed the doctrine of Mahmoud Taha and Abdullahi an-Na'im while stressing that the earlier ruling was the better one. In fact, this debate on divorce was not only on divorce per se, but was also a defense of the right of women against arbitrary divorce by men.

Religious texts are not like modern law because they show an internal variety. Various interpretations exist and the faithful may select his or her interpretation. One criterion is the sequence of revelation, but even here, various options remain available. Additionally, classical or basic religious texts are never a closed corpus. This is certainly true in the case of Buddhism, Hinduism, and Chinese religions. In Islam and Christianity, there is also some elasticity. The text itself and its first context, the first generations of readers cannot be separated entirely. In Islam, the immense corpus of *hadith* opens many doors for interpretation. In Christianity, the corpus of church fathers serves as secondary foundational texts. Therefore, the comparison with positive law is not true for many cases. Scriptural texts are diverse and have various origins. They are not consistent like most modern laws. In this way, they offer a broad opportunity for selection and reinterpretation.

Policy of Negation or Liberation: Option for the Secular

The most drastic strategy for a so-called modernization of ethics is the radical separation of contemporary practical rules from classic texts. According to this interpretation, sacred scripture is only for rituals and for doctrine about God, but not for economy, social ethics, or discussion of practical matters. This is the position of people like the individual working under the pseudonym of Ibn al Warraq and his *Institute for the Secularisation of Islamic Society*.[1] It is also the position of the Utrecht lecturer in Islamic Studies, Dr. Ghassan Ascha, who wrote several works on the position of women in Muslim law. He considered a total secularization of family law the only viable way for modern Muslims. According to him, every reinterpretation of sacred texts would be a waste of time. Ascha's position was summarized by Ibn Warraq:

> The Reformists cannot win on these terms, whatever mental gymnastics the reformists perform, they cannot escape the fact that Islam is deeply anti-feminist. Islam is the fundamental cause of the repression of Muslim women and remains the major obstacle to the evolution of their position. Islam has always considered women as creatures inferior in every way: physically, intellectually, and morally. This negative vision is divinely sanctioned in the Qur'an, corroborated by the *hadith* and perpetuated by the commentaries of the theologians, the custodians of Muslim dogma and ignorance. (Warraq 1995, 293; Ascha 1989, 11)[2]

Like many other modern Muslims, Ascha shares the conviction that Islam must be divided into sections on belief and rituals to remain valid. The social prescripts, on the other hand, should be exempted from the whole. Social prescripts relate to concrete conditions of time and place and therefore cannot be the same in all times and places. In most Muslim countries (like secular Syria where Ascha was educated), those prescripts are no longer valid or even relevant. Therefore, it is time to remove them from the body of Islamic truths and values. In addition, the prescripts about family and marriage, which still rule this field of social life in most Muslim countries, should be adapted to modern times and exempted from the religious body that rules them (Ascha 1996, 30).

The secular options discussed above would involve a reduction of the realm of religion. It would also segment modern society, since different rules would be valid for different sectors of life. Every aspect of society, such as art, sports, science, entertainment, and politics brings a set of values and rules of its own. Religion, therefore, is reducible to a specific sector. The religious sector would encompass the absolute, knowledge of the ultimate and unknowable, and knowledge about preexistence and life after death. Whatever we think of this different position, secularism is a widespread position in modern times, whether it is absolute and radical or relative and mild.

A universal strategy for adaptation of classical scripture to modern times is the division between religious and secular law. In this way, religion still relates to divinity, while for the secular it is ruled that "you know better about the practical things" (cf. Qur'an 22:46 "Do they not travel through the land, so that their hearts [and mind] may thus learn wisdom and their ears may thus learn to hear?").

Surprising Strategy of Selection: Debates on Economics

Christianity, and developments within the Jewish tradition, have been very relaxed in their position toward the Hebrew Bible. Most people no longer consider many sections valid. Not only have the detailed rulings on rituals and blood sacrifices in the temple been lifted, but also has the ban on interest. Exodus 22:25 clearly states "If you lend money to one of my people among you who is needy, do not be like a money lender; charge him no interest." Although it is ambiguous, the text in Luke 6:34–35 has also been used to defend the ban on interest. "And if you lend to those from whom you expect repayment, what credit is that to you? Even sinners lend to sinners, expecting to be repaid in full. But love your enemies, do good to them and lend to them without expecting to get anything." The ban on interest only ended during a complex historical process in the fifteenth through the sixteenth centuries. In that time, a growing economy in the cities provided the Jews an opportunity to act as moneylenders in European towns. The Jews could not own farmland or hold most jobs in the towns because the craft guilds prohibited Jewish members. Therefore, later medieval councils allowed them to work in the money business and to charge "modest interest" (Fourth Council of Lateran, 1215).

In Christianity, the urban theologian John Calvin, who was educated in Paris and worked in Geneva, was the first to defend the use of interest openly, at least for lending money to the wealthy. The combination of hard work and an ascetic lifestyle developed into the Reformed or Protestant basis of capitalism for a scholar like Max Weber. The debates during the last centuries focused on the differences between usury and interest.

They combined sound economic thinking with the moral duty to take care of the poor.

Another interesting position toward the Bible concerns the old Jewish economic ruling of a jubilee year. This practice fell away for a long time, but recently regained importance. A jubilee year, according to Leviticus 25 and 27 occurs once every fifty years (after a cycle of 7 × 7 years). It includes (1) rest of the soil; (2) reversion of landed property to its original owner by poverty to sell it; and (3) the manumission of those people whom, through poverty or otherwise, had become the slaves of their brethren. During the recent debate on the debt of developing countries, the old text resurfaced through the concept of the jubilee year. The history of these debates show how classical texts periodically become obsolete, then receive new attention and reinterpretation, and even new moral authority. The hermeneutic communities that use the texts employ several arguments for a renewal of the texts. Primarily, they argue that the authority of sacred texts is different from economic theories or from mere moral appeals. This is the mechanism of the great religions, especially in the field of practical rules and concrete problems of life.

As with the historical Christian and Jewish ban on interest, economic morality was a very important aspect of the early message of Islam. In the 1960s and 70s, some scholars even built their vision of the appeal of Muhammad totally on the socioeconomic significance of the ethics preached by Muhammad. For William Montgomery Watt, the central issue in the early message of the Qur'an was the transition of tribal ethics, which were concentrated on collective safety, unity and excellence of the tribe, to the individualistic urban life of Mecca. Tribal solidarity was a matter of life and death (see Watt 1953, 1956, 1961). The philosophy of tribal life in the desert, therefore, emphasized social ethics that focused on the unity and excellence of the tribe. In the new economy of urban Mecca, however, the successful and rich did not assume responsibility toward the poor based on tribal solidarity. Rather, as a consequence of their position as human beings, created by God, they were responsible to God for what they did with their fortune in this life. This is the message of many of the early prophetic passages of the Qur'an. They should not be read as moral philosophy nor as economic law, but as sociopolitical pamphlets, written with anger and power. To quote one of the most powerful chapters or surah 100:

> Surah 100 *Al-`Adiyat*, The Chargers
> In the Name of God, the Merciful, the Compassionate
> By the (steeds) that run, with panting (breath),
> And strike sparks of fire,
> And push home the charge in the morning,

And raise the dust in clouds the while,
And penetrate forthwith into the midst (of the foe) en masse;
Truly Man is, to his Lord, ungrateful,
And to that (fact) he bears witness (by his deeds),
And violent is he in his love of wealth.
Does he not know,—when that which is in the graves is scattered abroad,
And that which is (locked up) in (human) breasts is made manifest—
That their Lord had been Well-acquainted with them, (even to) that day?

Rhyme divides the three parts of this surah. Still, the style of words suggests that the surah also is a unity (Mir 1986, 1993). The first five lines after the opening formula evoke the apocalyptic conditions of the Day of Judgment (Neuwirth 1993). Like in the Apocalypse of St. John, the horses are a sign of war and destruction. In the Jewish Bible horses are also used for war, and camels for trade (cf. Ex. 15:1; Dt. 17:16; 1 Kings 4:26; Ap. 9:17). The second section introduces a man (a specific person or man in general?) who is wealthy and attached to his richness because he does not realize that everything in this world is transient. Therefore, the last verses go back to the opening scene of the apocalyptic horses[3] and remind (this) human being that on the Last Day, he or she will lose everything and will stand before God.

Scholars of Islam debate whether the concept of God as Creator or God as Lord of the Day of Judgment should receive priority. Both themes are in nearly all revelations of the early Meccan periods. This debate, however, is misleading because neither creation of the world nor the date and procedures of its end are the central topic of these revelations. In both, we find ethical and sociopolitical declarations about the way this world and this society should function (Bell 1969, 102–4; Steenbrink 1998; Bewley 1989).

Later developments in Islam gave more emphasis to the ban on usury or interest (Ar. *Rib?*). Qur'an 3:130 is one of the passages forbidding usury: "O ye who believe. Devour not usury, doubled and multiplied; but fear Allah, that ye may really prosper" (similar verses are 30:39; 2:275–80; 4:161). This ban has a long history. During the first generations of the Islamic movement, many people found loopholes to achieve the effect of charging interest, while still avoiding the precise letter of the ban. A widespread method was to ask for payment early and deliver goods late. The chapter on business transactions in the earliest standard book of Islamic Law, the *Muwatta* by Imam Malik bin Anas (712–795 CE) reproaches those who employ such tricks. To give just one example: "Malik said it was not proper for a man to sell a slave-girl to another man for one hundred dinars on credit and then to buy her back for more than the original price or on a credit term longer than the original term for which he sold her" (Bewley 1989, 247).

The original concern for the poor, as found in the prophetic texts of the Qur'an disappeared in the *Muwatta*. The text is often pure legal thinking, law-is-law and should be obeyed. The letter of the text should be maintained. Legal constructions that avoid the spirit of the law gain acceptance sometimes, sometimes not.

In modern time, we find new themes. The revival, or even rise of the system for the first time in history, of interest-free Islamic banking since the 1970s must be seen as a protest against global domination by western institutions like the International Monetary Fund (IMF), the World Bank, and other large banks. The Organization of the Islamic Conference (OIC) and fundamentalist Muslims in countries like Egypt, Malaysia, and Indonesia support interest-free banking because of pride and a desire to be free from Western influence. This new system looks more like a proud declaration of independence than a true concern for the poor. In this case, the specific application of an Islamic ruling may be an identity marker, as is often the case with the style of clothing or Muslim food. Islamic fashion is not (only) taken as a sign of modesty or defense of chastity and decency, but is used as a sign to show one's Muslim identity. Likewise, one may keep halal not simply for one's health or obedience to God's command but also to emphasize social belonging.

In this way, the old texts gain a new social and political meaning. The "Islamic system" is part of the much larger national system and, therefore, is a pious fringe of a much more complex society. In summary, the precise text of scripture is only one element in the decision about practical and moral issues. The conclusion of the process of interpretation and selection, or even exclusion, is unpredictable.

Glimpses of the Monogamy-Polygamy Debate

The sides in the polygamy debate take up quite different positions. Although monogamy was a Christian ruling from the beginning of Christianity, some independent African churches recently recalled the polygamous life of the patriarchs Abraham, Isaac, and Jacob. In some independent Christian Nigerian churches, this produced a permit for polygamy. These views also caused a heated debate in the World Council of Churches (WCC) in Harare in 1998, when they rejected the Celestial Church of Christ's membership because it permitted polygamy. Densen Mafinyani, general secretary of the Zimbabwe Council of Churches (ZCC) criticized the decision severely. He stated, "the WCC is intellectually refined and theologically advanced but it is out of touch with real people." The Zimbabwe Council of Churches, which hosted the meeting of the WCC, accepts African Institutes

Churches (AICs) who admit polygamous clergy. Frans Verstraelen, professor emeritus of Utrecht University, has worked in Zimbabwe and defended this viewpoint. "Polygamy in the African mindset can reflect status and is not something wrong or evil. And if the ZCC accepts the AIC, it is probably because it has a better idea of what is acceptable in the African context than someone from, say Sweden."[4]

This case adds a new dimension to the work of hermeneutic communities. Changes not only occur throughout the course of history, but also throughout different cultures. The most oft-quoted verse on the issue of monogamy is from Matthew 19:4–6. "Haven't you read that at the beginning the Creator made them male and female, and said: For this reason a man will leave his father and the two will become one flesh? So they are no longer two, but one. Therefore what God has joined together, let man not separate." This quote, however, does not concern monogamy. Rather, it addresses the ruling on divorce in the Hebrew Bible, revoked by Jesus. It may sound contradictory that in modern Christian practice (at least in most mainstream Protestant churches), divorce is discouraged, but also reluctantly accepted and divorcees have the opportunity to remarry. Unlike divorce, the Hebrew Bible accepts polygamy as more common and it was never overtly abolished by Jesus. Despite that fact, the greater global Christian tradition has not accepted the ZCC's lenient position. The Celestial Church of Christ, one of Nigeria's largest churches, remains outside the WCC.

In the Qur'an the best known and most important verses on polygamy are in 4:3: "If you fear that ye shall not be able to deal justly with the orphans, marry women of your choice, two or three or four: but if ye fear that you shall not be able to deal justly (with them), then only one, or (a captive) that your right hands possess, that will be more suitable, to prevent you from doing injustice" (Mt. 19).

Like in the case of Matthew 19, quoted above, it is clear that the basic subject of discussion is not polygamy. Rather, the real issue is the care for orphans. According to tradition, this verse pertains to the lost battle of Uhud in Medina. However, the occasion is not important here because the care for orphans is the emphasis of this verse. As a solution, the Qur'an suggests that men marry more women. The problem of polygamous relationships appears openly in the above verse. The possibility that Muslims will not be able to treat their wives with equal fairness is the central concern. If that is the case, then take only one wife. Modern Muslims extrapolate this verse as support for monogamy, since no one will be able to treat several women with the same amount of love and tenderness. In quite a few countries with Muslim majorities, modern laws have put restrictions on polygamy. These include administrative regulations (special permission from Islamic courts is required for polygamy) and restriction to specific cases (naked women, disabled, etc.). In addition, the entire Muslim world has abolished slavery by law so the remark about the possibility to take a slave as a wife is no longer relevant.

More Strategies of Selection: Changing Context versus Remaining Value (Modern Vatican Resistance against the Death Penalty and Muslim Theology on Violence)

In recent years the *evangelium vitae*, the Gospel of (protection of human) Life as an absolute value, has been an important issue in Vatican thinking, especially with Pope John Paul II. It has led to strict prohibition of abortion and euthanasia. It also strongly influenced the outspoken position of the Roman Catholic Church in its condemnation of the death penalty. In short, the most recent *Catechism of the Catholic Church* states that societies had few means to defend themselves against dangerous persons in former times. In some cases, therefore, the death penalty was appropriate. Nowadays most societies have better instruments, such as safe prisons. Therefore, the death penalty is no longer a proper method of punishment.

The traditional teaching of the church does not exclude, presupposing full ascertainment of the identity and responsibility of the offender, recourse to the death penalty when it is the only practicable means to defend the lives of human beings effectively against an aggressor. If, instead, bloodless means are sufficient to defend against the aggressor and to protect the safety of persons, public authority should limit itself to such means, because they better correspond to the concrete conditions of the common good and are more in conformity to the dignity of the human person. Today, in fact, given the means at the state's disposal to repress crime effectively by rendering inoffensive the one who has committed it, without depriving him definitively of the possibility of redeeming himself, cases of absolute necessity for suppression of the offender "today ... are very rare, if not practically non-existent" (Pope John Paul II, *Evangelium vitae* 56).

Why is there reference to the social change in the case of death penalty, but not in the judgment about euthanasia and abortion where modern medical science has made it necessary to think differently about these topics?[5] For the latter issues, the wording of the biblical command "thou shalt not kill" is taken to be absolute (of the Ten Commandments, it is fifth in the Catholic, and sixth in the Protestant tradition). In the case of capital punishment, however, the Bible does not absolutely forbid the death penalty, even though the wording is more reserved than in the history of Christianity. The historical emphasis on "an eye for an eye and a tooth for a tooth" (Exodus 21:24) was replaced with Matthew 5:39: "But I tell you, do not resist an evil person. If someone strikes you on the right cheek, turn to him the other also." Perhaps the most radical follower of this message was Mahatma Gandhi, who mobilized a massive anti-British nationalist movement in twentieth century South Africa and India based on this text.

The fact that the teachings of Jesus resonate with the Qur'an is less widely known. Surah 5:45 reads: "We ordained therein for them [the Jews in the Torah]: 'Life for life, eye for eye, nose for nose, ear for ear, tooth for tooth, wounds equal for equal.' But if any one remits the retaliation by way of charity, it is an act of atonement for himself." Muhammad Asad, a former Jew and converted Muslim, reflects on this verse: "This, read in conjunction with the following verses [about Jesus criticizing the Jews] would seem to be an allusion to the time-bound quality of the Mosaic Law. Alternatively, the above admonition may have been part of the original teachings of the Torah which may have been subsequently corrupted or deliberately abandoned by its followers" (Asad 1993, 153).

There is a strong mystical tradition in Islam that serves as a corrective toward violent talk about *jihad*. The first meaning of *jihad* is "effort, serious action, endeavor." This meaning is also present in the word for religious specialist, the scholar who is entitled to start new interpretations and who is the executor of *ijtihad*. The two words share the same three basic consonants: *j.h.d.* In the twelfth century, the mystical tradition discussed the "small *jihad*," which is the physical war against the enemies of the Muslim community. More importantly, however, the mystical tradition also discussed the more difficult "greater *jihad*," which is the internal struggle of the faithful against their own passions, emotions, and greed. It is simple to interpret that discussion as an extension of the philosophy that forgiveness is better than revenge and that love should replace hatred; both concepts are well represented in authentic scriptural traditions.

Indonesian Muslim Debate on Mixed Islamic-Christian Marriages

In Islamic law, commonly women inherit only half the portion men receive. According to Qur'an 4:11, the male shall receive "a portion equal to that of two females." In Indonesia, however, a law mandating equal inheritance between the genders overrules this verse. The argument behind that practice is that the Qur'an started from a zero portion for women in the pre-Islamic period of Arabia and increased it to at least half of that of men, because the Qur'an could not immediately improve the poor situation for women. In Indonesia, women traditionally received the same portion as men, and that method of distribution should continue. The law Religious Courts Lay (1989) and the related Codification (or Compilation) of Islamic Law of 1991, continued the equal position of women based on a style of reinterpretation called "re-actualization" or "contextualization" (Sulastomo 1995).

Another situation that involves gender equality is the mixed marriage between Muslims and "people of the book" or, Jews and Christians. No Muslim woman may marry a non-Muslim man, but Qur'an 5:5 states that Muslim men may marry Jewish or Christian women: "This day are (all) things good and pure made lawful unto you. The food of the People of the Book is lawful unto you and yours is lawful unto them. (Lawful unto you in marriage) are (not only) chaste women who are believers, but chaste women among the People of the Book, revealed before your time,—when ye give them their due dowers, and desire chastity, not lewdness, nor secret intrigues."

Notwithstanding this clear permit, the Majelis Ulama Indonesia (MUI) formed a different decision in this matter in 1980. It believed that another text provided a stronger basis for belief. The text it followed prohibited marriage between a Muslim and an unbeliever, then placed Christians and Jews on one line with the unbelievers. This was a strong decision of the MUI after a new marriage law passed in 1974 had opened the possibility of marriage between Muslims and people of other religions. The 1974 law only stipulated that "marriage should take place according to the religious law of the partners." The *fatwa* of 1980 does not have the power of law, because in theory the Majelis Ulama Indonesia is just one private body among others that issue fatwas. Muslims are free to follow it or not.

The Indonesian administration in the 1980s and 90s slowly began following the MUI decision starting with local offices of the Ministry of Religion in Jakarta who refused to celebrate marriage between any Muslim and a partner from another faith. The Jakarta initiative followed in other places. Since the mid-1990s, no mixed marriage between any Muslim and someone of other faiths is legal, at least not in Indonesia itself where the civil registration does not accept mixed couples. For those couples who do not want to commit a formal lie and temporarily change religion for the sake of the civil administration, their only option is to contract a marriage in a foreign country, then proceed through a legalization process in Indonesia.

Why was scripture reinterpreted in an elastic and contextual way for the issue of inheritance, while a hard line was taken against the issue of mixed marriages, even though that view goes against the majority of global Islam? Other than some arbitrary and political arguments, it is difficult to find any support for this capricious style of decision. The most evident political argument against mixed marriages is the fear Indonesian Muslims have about the so-called "Christianization" of their country. Formerly, there were hardly any Christians in the country. Now, the number has increased to about three percent in the island of Java (3.6 million out of 120 million), many of them converted nominally to Islam. Notwithstanding the still small percentage of Christians, this conversion has become a political issue. Some hard-line Muslims proposed the death penalty for apostasy. This is impossible in modern Indonesia, however, and even throughout Islamic history, it only emerges in exceptional circumstances, always with more political than religious fervor (Mudzhar 1993, 85–87; Pompe 1988; IDEM 1991).

The Difficult Debate on Homosexuality

Scriptural texts about, or rather against, homosexuality are few but severe. Genesis 19 of the Hebrew Bible conveys the story of the wicked cities of Sodom and Gomorrah. Angels that arrive to warn the only pious man, Lot, are attacked by (male) inhabitants of the two cities who want to have sex with Lot's visitors. Unlike most people, Lot takes the obligation of hospitality higher than the honor and physical integrity of his daughters and he suggests to his compatriots that they should take his two virgin daughters instead of his visitors. After the destruction of the evil cities, Lot remains alone with his two daughters. They see no possibility to find another man besides their father and decide to make him drunk, then seduce him into sexual intercourse so they can become pregnant and bear children. This odd story ends in 19:37–38 with the conclusion that their children are the ancestors of the Moabites and the Ammonites. This story, at least the section after the destruction of the evil towns, is clearly some kind of gossip or thematic story to blame traditional southern enemies of the Jewish people. We must question whether we should also accept the first section of the story from a similar viewpoint. The other texts from the Hebrew Bible that discuss homosexuality, Leviticus 18:22 and 20:13, are very short.

The best known text in Christian scripture is Romans 1:26–27, where Paul describes the consequences of unbelief and the exchange of God for idols. As a consequence, "God gave them over to shameful lusts. Even their women exchanged natural relations for unnatural ones. In the same way the men also abandoned natural relations with women and were inflamed with lust for one another." The most common interpretation of this passage is that it is a Jewish expression of the lenient historical attitude toward pederasty. Whatever the correct historical meaning may be, these verses have evoked very different interpretations in modern Christianity. Those interpretations have led to restrictions within the Roman Catholic Church regarding who is eligible for the clergy.

In the Qur'an, the story of Lot is mentioned several times (7:81; 27:55; 26:165–66; 29:29; 54:36–38). As with other mentions of biblical stories, the text assumes general knowledge of the tale and the Qur'an only has a moral conclusion about the episode. 54:37 is the most outspoken verse concerning the guests of Lot. "And they even sought to snatch away his guests from him, but We blinded their eyes. (They heard:) 'Now taste ye My Wrath and My Warning.'"

A clearer reference to homosexuality can be found in 7:80–81. "We also (sent) Lot: He said to his people: 'Do ye commit lewdness such as no people in creation (ever) committed before you? For ye practice your lusts on men in preference to women: ye are indeed a people transgressing beyond bounds.'"

The most common word for homosexuality in the Arab world is *Lūṭī* or *Līwāt*, which comes from the same root, *l.w.t*, and so from the same name, as Lot. These views leave little room for scriptural openings regarding homosexuality. Yet, among others, John Nahas, a consultant to the Dutch foundation for the study of Islam and homosexuality found room for reinterpretation. In a book published in 2002, Nahas reinterprets the Lot story as a ban on sex under compulsion of one party, especially between adults and young children, or between humans and animals, and in cases of prostitution. God created people with homosexual inclinations and God cannot hate what He created. Therefore, "sound and sincere homosexuality" is not forbidden by Islam (see Nahas 2002; Rowson 2002, 444–45; Safi 2003).

These liberal interpretations are not always helpful. Sometimes they may even introduce new issues into the debate, such as a rejection of homosexuality as part of the Western world's aggressive rejection of Islam. In a modern Indonesian commentary of the Qur'an, prominent scholar and former Minister of Religion Dr. Quraish Shihab commented upon 4:15. "If any of your women are guilty of lewdness, Take the evidence of four (Reliable) witnesses from amongst you against them; and if they testify, confine them to houses until death do claim them, or Allah ordain for them some (other) way." Although it is not overt in the text, Shihab ponders, along with a long line of modern (not medieval) commentaries that if a lesbian or other homosexual couple is seen in action by four witnesses, should they be punished by flogging, as is commanded by 23:2 in the case of adultery, or should they be punished with lifelong detention? Shihab also continues with some considerations about HIV/AIDS. "For the intimate relations between male people we have already seen its effect in the disease of AIDS and we have now only to wait what sanction will be given to sexual relation between females" (Muh 2000).

Interreligious Communication or Apartheid?

People are different and all human societies institutionalize those differences. The most basic difference is between men and women. Most would agree that ethnicity and age are important differences. Religious classifications have started to become irrelevant for public life in many Western countries, but in other regions, religious identity still plays an important role. To take the Indonesian example again, in official documents people have to declare their religious affiliation to one of the six religions recognized by the Indonesian state. Until 2005, only five religions enjoyed recognition: Hinduism, Buddhism, Islam, Catholicism, and Protestantism (including all non-Roman Catholic denominations like the Adventists, Armenian, Greek or Russian Orthodoxy). In 2006, Confucianism joined the list after being illegal for many years because most consider it a national not global religion. For various reasons, political leaders and civil administrators find it useful to ask for this kind of religious listing. A reason from recent history was the fight against Communism, during which authorities viewed religions as the strongest antidote against an antireligious ideology.

Since the rise of political Hinduism in India in the 1980s, and its institutionalization in the Bharata Janata Party (BJP), a religious identity has again gained importance. What are the motives behind the pressure to emphasize religious identity? Certainly, by laying more stress on differences, on the otherness of foreign religions, it is easier to exploit nationalist sentiments for social, political, and even economic goals. Indonesia, Malaysia, and other countries that exclude ethnic Chinese from land ownership and from public jobs evince this trend.

Religious leaders often join this call to stress the differences between religions and even between denominations. The Vatican declaration of August 6, 2000 *Dominus Iesus. On the unicity and the salvific universality of Jesus Christ and the Church* is an example of such renewed emphasis. It uses exclusivist texts like John 14:6, "I am the way and the truth and the life. No one comes to the Father except through me," and Acts 4:12, "there is no other name under heaven given to men by which we must be saved." The great danger for our time is seen here as *relativismus*. The document argues that "the church's constant missionary proclamation is endangered today by relativistic theories which seek to justify religious pluralism, not only *de facto* but also *de iure* (or in principle). As a consequence, it is held that certain truths have been superseded." Consequently, even the common celebration of the Eucharist between Roman Catholics and Protestants is not possible, with only few exceptions.

This argument from the Catholic Church is similar to that of a fatwa of the Majelis Ulama Indonesia, issued on July 27, 2005 as one in a series of eleven fatwas. The fatwas addressed various issues, but concentrated on a ban of what was labeled as "liberal Islam, acceptability of religious pluralism and secularism." A special fatwa forbade common prayer of Muslims and non-Muslims as a religious innovation, per se a kind of heresy. As previously discussed, the MUI also issued a fatwa against mixed religious marriages. During the interreligious conflicts that occurred between 1995 and 2005, however, groups of Christian and Muslim women protested the abuse of religious differences, mostly at the hands of men. The women came together in many regions and promoted common prayer sessions. As in all cases where official or unofficial religious bodies express strong positions, a strong countermovement developed. In this case, the *Jaringan Islam Liberal*, the "Liberal Muslim Network" led the movement.[6]

Some Conclusions on the Elasticity of Religious Structures: Hermeneutic Possibilities rather than Principles

Religions use various mechanisms in the adaptation of religious texts to old and new conditions. They can declare some older rulings as no longer valid, either because of a separation between the secular and the religious spheres, or because of the temporary validity of the expression of scripture. Religions can also conclude that various sections of sacred scripture contradict each other. The religion can then either opt for the earlier or later version. In this way, the rich internal variety found in various scriptures offers the possibility to skip from one possible interpretation to another. To say it in biblical terms, "every teacher of the law who has been instructed about the kingdom of heaven is like the owner of a house who brings out of his storeroom new treasures as well as old" (Mt. 13:52). Modern hermeneutic language translates this passage into a theory about the text and together with the reader, they create meaning. Finally, religions can also decide that an older text is specifically set within a different culture and must be adapted to modern circumstances.

The above approaches allow the world's religions to have flexibility in the application of classical texts to modern times. However, they may also lead to some conclusions that seem arbitrary to outsiders. The situation becomes even more complicated when we take into consideration the methods of individual or collective decision making, whether for private use or as an authority for a religious community. However, this contribution is not an effort to sketch a complete and balanced overview of hermeneutic principles and practice. Its purpose is to stress the bizarre arbitrariness sometimes found in the varied religious circles, through examples taken from Christianity and Islam. In the process, it also shows the elasticity and flexibility of religious traditions.

Notes

1. See http://www.secularislam.org/articles/wtc.htm.
2. Ascha (1989) states that all religions suppress women ("Toutes les religions répriment la femme") and he also emphasized that Islam is not the only reason although "it constitutes a fundamental reason for the oppression of women for their development at this moment" ("Il en constitute sans aucun doute une cause fondamentale, et demeure un obstacle majeur à l'évolution de cette situation"). In *Marriage, polygamie et repudiation en islam*, Ascha presents a very precise, open, critical, and honest record about the legal position of women in modern countries of the Middle East.
3. See also the first five verses of Surah 79, where the disturbing powers of the last judgment are put forward as the beginning of an admonition not to attach one to earthly goods.
4. *E-Jubilee: E-Newspaper of the 8th Assembly of the World Council of Churches*. No. 8, December 12, 1998. http://www.wcc-coe.org/wcc/assembly/ejubilee/number8.htm.
5. Although these topics have no reference to the technical and scientific developments, for abortion, see 2270–75, and for euthanasia, see the *Catechism of the Catholic Church* 2276–79. http://www.vatican.va/archive/ENG0015/__P7Z.HTM.
6. Since 2001, *Jaringan Islam Liberal* has published their Web site in English as well as in Indonesian. It functions as a powerful medium for debate about modern Islam: see http://islamlib.com/en/ for the English version.

6

Changing Hermeneutics in Reading and Understanding the Bible

The Case of the Gospel of Mark

Geert van Oyen

The present chapter addresses the preliminary hermeneutical work required before reading the Bible, more specifically in the Gospel of Mark.[1] The chapter seeks to illustrate ways to comingle the new hermeneutical insights in biblical criticism with an interpretation of this gospel. To that end, the author is convinced it is helpful and meaningful to approach Mark from the perspective that there is something like a Markan code, the meaning of which will become clear later in the chapter.[2] It is the author's hope to contribute to a better understanding of how the Bible can function as a religious text and as a living text in the contemporary world.

Reading a Biblical Book as a Novel: Plurality of Meanings

Let me start with a personal note. I started my research into the oldest of the gospels in 1985. The most important discovery I made in more than twenty years of study is nothing sensational and is hardly likely to reach the headlines. I did not discover an ancient fragment that shed new light on the figure of Jesus and unmasked the gospels as forgeries. I did not discern some spectacular vision of Jesus that would unleash revolution among believers. There is no secret in the Gospel of Mark to which only a select elite have access while to others it remains hidden. It has also become clear to me that specialists and nonspecialists alike, in spite of the fact that scholarly debate rages over almost every word of the text, can understand the book. In short, I have nothing sensational to offer.

What then are the results of my years of study? Let me try to sum them up in a single sentence: the more you read the Gospel of Mark as a novel, the more the book's potential meanings rise to the surface and touch people. How do you read the gospel as a novel? Are we even permitted to do such a thing? Aren't we being disrespectful? Surely, for many readers the books of the Bible are "sacred scripture" and not mere novels. "They are the word of God," believers will insist. "They are interesting historical documents," religious academics will argue. I will return to those issues later in more detail. Now, though, I will restrict myself to an initial explanation of the notion of "plurality of meanings" that can be derived from the text.

Not everyone appreciates such a possibility. It is much easier to presuppose that there is only one meaning present in the text. In fact, many follow this path and they are rooted in the conviction that it provides many advantages. Some people, for example, insist on an uncritical reading of the gospel, which would appear to provide a solid foundation for believers: everything in the text really happened and we need not and should not doubt it. Those who understand the truth of the gospel in this way may have established a firm foundation for themselves, but they will be unable to enter into dialogue with more critical voices who also consider themselves believers.

Others swear by a particular exegetical method, hoping, for example, that they can recover the evangelist Mark's intention by reconstructing a particular historical situation, which in turn purportedly occasioned the evangelist's writing. The endeavor to read Mark's mind, however, is far from easy. Scholars differ from one another on the identification of the historical background. The explanation for this difficulty is simple: we do not know the identity of the author of Mark, we do not know where he wrote his gospel and we do not even know exactly when he wrote it (Botha 1993). Such an approach, moreover, gives rise to several other problems. How can we explain the enormous influence exercised by Mark if we limit its interpretation to its historical setting? What does it mean for us today if historical reconstruction has become the goal of our interpretation? Last, but not least, his text has undergone the fate of all texts: its meaning falls to the interpretation of its readers despite what Mark may have wanted to say when he wrote it. As I said, these are only a few initial thoughts on the notion of plurality of meaning. Once again, I will return to the question in detail below.

Is There Anything New to Be Said?

Many have asked with the necessary irony, "haven't we said all there is to say about the gospel?" This is a challenging question: do I have anything new to say about Mark's gospel?[3] My answer depends on the reader of the present chapter. As with the Gospel of Mark, my own text has been handed over to an audience. If anything, the purpose of these pages is to initiate dialogue between readers. My audience is a diverse group. It includes readers familiar with Mark from their own faith tradition, but also those who have never read the gospel from beginning to end. It encompasses readers carried along by the spirit of the age, who are open to questions about God or the divine, and who are open to the fundamental options in life. Readers engaged on behalf of others because of their faith, readers in search of spirituality, readers who are critical of the Bible, readers for whom the very idea of reading a book of the Bible is a departure from custom, and readers who are members of non-Christian religious traditions.

I hope the reader will consider these pages in parallel with the Gospel of Mark, in the hope that the gospel itself will take pride of place.[4] My contribution will be effective if readers are led by it to read the gospel and ask questions about the text. It does not matter if every reader finds a different truth in the text. The gospel's narrative is an open one. The present day climate, in which biblical texts function within a variety of ecclesial contexts and generate genuine interest from outside the church, is not one for a standardized reading of the Bible acceptable to everyone. Rather, dialogue about the meanings of the narrative is a more realistic goal for our present circumstances.

The Markan Code

The worldwide best seller in 2004 was Dan Brown's *The Da Vinci Code*. Although critics were not particularly impressed with the literary qualities of the book, the spirit of the age is a better explanation for its success. For those unfamiliar with the novel, it is a detective story that exposes the existence of secret organizations within the Roman Catholic Church. Suppressed documents, cryptic codes, secret conspiracies, the role of men and women in religion, and the influence of elite groups are all part of a story about power and knowledge within the world's most powerful religious institution. *The Da Vinci Code* is also a story about different levels of truth, whereby only the superinitiated have access to the hidden knowledge that forms the foundation of truth. Further, it is about a code that has to be deciphered in order to understand a message that can turn the world and the church upside down. The book is determined to unmask Christianity as a 2000-year-old fraud. The reader instinctively believes in and joins the search for a hidden truth of momentous proportions.

Bearing this in mind, the title of the present section, "The Markan Code," requires some explanation. I presume that the reader is able to distinguish the difference in genre. Dan Brown's book is a fictional novel, while "The Markan Code" refers to a narrative study of a gospel. In the context of this section, the question of whether it is appropriate to speak of a code in the Gospel of Mark remains. At first glance, an affirmative answer is evident. Anyone even vaguely familiar with the study of the Gospel of Mark throughout the twentieth century will be aware of the theme that has dominated Markan exegesis: "the messianic secret." In 1901, the German exegete William Wrede published a book titled *Das Messiasgeheimnis in den Evangelien* (Wrede 1901, 1969; Tuckett 1983; Fendler 1991; Tuckett 2002; Telford 1999). He pointed out that the Gospel of Mark did not present Jesus as the Messiah during his earthly life. The significance of Jesus was not evident during his own lifetime. Rather, the key to identifying Jesus as the Messiah appears only after his resurrection. In dialogue with Wrede, scholars studied this theme throughout the twentieth century. The discussion tended to focus on whether Jesus was the Messiah prior to his resurrection, and, if so, whether he was recognized as such. In line with recent hermeneutics, the following pages will endeavor to explain the mystery surrounding Jesus from a reader's perspective.

There may be some merit to the idea of the presence of a secret in the Gospel of Mark. It is important to bear in mind while reading the gospel that the author incorporated two layers of meaning into his narrative. On the one hand, we have the words he wrote, present for all to read. On the other hand, there is also a hidden, suppressed significance reserved for a "select few." A number of texts in his gospel incline the reader to speak of a code, in much the same way as Dan Brown's book speaks of a code. The parables, for example, seem to be for the edification of all, yet Jesus takes his disciples aside on more than one occasion to explain their precise significance. Even then, sometimes his explanations seem as obscure as the parable itself. Jesus himself speaks of the secrets in the parables and appears to distinguish between a group that understands their deeper significance and a larger group of outsiders for whom the secrets of the gospel remain inaccessible. One of the most puzzling texts in Mark is 4:10–11. "When he was alone, those who were around him along with the twelve asked him about the parables. And he said to them, 'To you has been given the secret of the kingdom of God, but for those outside, everything comes in parables; in order that they may indeed look, but not perceive, and may indeed listen, but not understand; so that they may not turn again and be forgiven.'"

The gospel also suggests a sense of mystery. The text does not explain or clarify every word of the narrative. Take, for example, an expression such as "the kingdom of God." Scholars agree that this expression is central to what Mark wants to say about Jesus, yet the author used it without providing a definition (see Chilton 1996). Instead, the author only provides images. Some specific events likewise remain unexplained. The miracle stories or the depiction of the disciples on the mountain where Jesus appears swathed in a white garment (9:2–9) serve as examples. Moreover, the climax of the gospel is clearly difficult to comprehend at first read. Why did Jesus have to die on the cross? What was the resurrection about? What exactly happened to the disciples after the event? All the text says about the resurrection is that it happened, but none of the characters in the narrative witnessed it personally. A group of women made their way to the tomb but they were too late to see what had happened (16:1–8). Factors such as these might incline the reader to suspect and perhaps even accuse the evangelist of being deliberately obscure. They also reinforce the idea that special knowledge is necessary to understand his gospel. The ingredients of an exciting detective novel seem to be present, inviting the reader to search for a secret code that can help decipher the message of the gospel.

A Public Secret

The mystery surrounding the Gospel of Mark creates a sense of tension for the reader, a clear parallel with many novels. That sense of mystery, though, can potentially create a negative experience for readers. Since only a portion of the readership has access to the real meaning of the book, the majority of readers are left with a sense of dissatisfaction because they are deprived of the book's "final truth." Readers of Mark might be inclined to think that the gospel is not true because it is hiding something. This is exactly what happens with many present day readers. They accuse the church of being an institution that deliberately maintains secrecy in order to avoid losing power and authority.

However, is Mark really a coded book in this sense? I am inclined to respond in the negative. There can be little doubt that the gospel is mysterious and that a key is necessary to understand the narrative. However, anyone hoping to find a story about detectives trying to crack a code will be disappointed. Mark's code and Brown's code are essentially different. The evangelist does not conceal or suppress information. There is no code hidden in Mark's gospel that refers to secrets outside the text itself, intended for a select few, or kept hidden for centuries, only revealed at a particular point in history. The key to the Gospel of Mark resides in the text itself and the reader has access to it at all times.

Why, then, use the expression 'the Markan Code'? There are many reasons: because the content of the gospel is not free of obligation, rather it challenges its readers to make choices and decisions; because the book is incomplete if the reader does not decide to unlock its meaning; because the *reading* process is ultimately a *learning* process. The reader unravels the secret to the extent that he or she is able to respond affirmatively to certain insights from the narrative. Thus, a successful reading of the gospel is the responsibility of the reader. It goes without saying that there would not be a text without the author. From the moment the text appeared, however, the author shared responsibility with the reader; perhaps the author even passed it on to the reader. Depending on their response to the text, readers achieve insight into certain aspects and dimensions of Mark's message. The narrative is an invitation and a challenge. Decoding the gospel is only possible if we realize that the narrative is also about the reader as an individual. We have to search the text for the important questions with respect to which a decision applies.

The reason Mark wrote his book in this manner has to do with the innovative, if not revolutionary, dimension of his subject, Jesus. His description of Jesus as Messiah and son of God is extraordinary for the time. Furthermore, Mark's description also contains a vigorous appeal to the reader to follow Jesus as a model. That appeal runs counter to the customary understanding of the way people organized their lives in those days. The uniqueness of Mark's gospel code is very specific and consists of two inseparable dimensions. First, it leads the reader to see the words and life of Jesus as a revolutionary step in his relationship with people and with God. This dimension of the gospel involves recognition and understanding of the man Jesus. The second dimension of the gospel is that Mark does not distinguish between theory and practice. He wants people to model their behavior on Jesus. The reader is obliged to make decisions about his or her behavior, to act in line with Jesus or not. The present chapter deals with the way in which Mark approached this project in a literary fashion.

The theory that the reader ultimately applies their own subtlety to the meaning of the book is also a potential contribution to the relationships Christians have with those of other faiths. Eventually, interreligious dialogue comes face to face with the value of a particular tradition or faith perspective in the context of a variety of religious and other fundamental life options. Christians themselves frequently employ two models themselves. According to the first model, Christians and their God are better than other religious and fundamental choices. Much missionary engagement that has taken place over the years is rooted in such a vision.

Christians see their faith as the universal religion, the only or best way to obtain salvation. According to the second model, believers understand their own religion as one of many possible ways to happiness, redemption, and salvation. Under that view, Christianity is one of many religions and is equal to the other religions.

Both models have their disadvantages. In the first approach, the uniqueness and value of non-Christian religions is underestimated. The second risks taking the value of one's own tradition too lightly. It is not easy to establish a middle path between the two extremes and there may always be some degree of tension between them. An attractive contemporary insight might argue that no single faith is capable of legitimacy, especially when it claims a universally valid truth. Rather, the truth of faith emerges in dialogue between sources, tradition and the personal acceptance thereof by believers and nothing about it can be compelled. Faith's true significance shows when recognized freely at a certain moment in a person's development. Mark has written his gospel from this very perspective. Ultimately, it calls upon the reader to decide whether he or she considers the narrative meaningful. All the evangelist can do is share his own perspective and persuade the reader to trust him.

My own vision of the gospel is not directly inspired by the problems associated with interreligious dialogue. I am more concerned with people's concrete experience of the Bible as something inaccessible. It is possible, however, to establish a parallel between both interreligious dialogue and the comprehensibility of the Bible. The primary condition for respectful dialogue between religions is the conviction that one's own beliefs are not to be understood as an inescapable obligation but rather as potentially life fulfilling. The primary condition for a successful reading of Mark's gospel is no different. The text only becomes comprehensible for the reader if not presented, not as an obligation, but rather as a possibility or an opportunity. This is the approach taken by Mark himself. He realizes he is writing a book about faith, about a fundamental life option, and that one can never force people to believe. Thus, he uses his skills to tempt the reader into reading his message, in the hope that they will accept his story.

Narrative Approach

Exploring the specific themes of Mark's gospel extends beyond the limits of this chapter. It is appropriate here, therefore, to focus attention on a few more general issues. The Bible has become an unfamiliar book and much is required to introduce the reader to biblical literature and its current understanding. Our point of departure that the gospel is a narrative requires a specific approach that deals with the characteristics of a narrative. I will refer to this approach as the "narrative reading" in the broadest understanding of the expression. Such an approach has the capacity to allow for different points of emphasis including the three supporting elements of communication: author, text, and reader (Utzschneider 1999). The narrative reading can draw attention to the author's rhetorical strategy (rhetorical analysis), or to plot development (narrative reading in the narrow sense; Best 1983, 1988; Rhoads and Michie 1982, 1999; Delorme 1997). It can also highlight reception of the text by the reader (reader response criticism; Vorster 1989; Fowler 1991; van Iersel 1998; Marguerat 1993). I am convinced that these approaches are complementary and should not be considered separately. This combined approach is the narrative method (Powell 1990; Rhoads 1999).[5] However, before employing this method, it is necessary first to remove some obstacles.

Antivirus Protection for the Bible

A Moth-Eaten Book?

Computer people know all about viruses. They disrupt programs and send your hard disk into a spin. The announcement of a new computer virus can cause global panic. If a virus shuts down a bank's computer system for an hour, for example, it can cost millions of dollars. The digital world cannot survive without antivirus protection. The Bible also seems damaged by some kind of virus. The information in the Bible has become difficult to comprehend, and those who claim they understand it are often incapable of communicating their knowledge. No one seems to be interested in the book's message. The use and abuse of certain passages in the Bible throughout the centuries has diluted their original vitality. As a result, many people treat them with suspicion. This confusion and disinterest distance us even further from the Bible. We should also bear in mind that the church, the institution in which the book has been central since time immemorial, is in the midst of a crisis. We must admit that the Bible has become uncharted territory for many, both as a global cultural inheritance and as a foundational book for a global faith.

Positive Signs, but . . .

The picture painted might appear overly pessimistic. It is hard to deny after all, the existence of reading groups, church movements, centers for the study of theology, and university faculties in which the study of this ancient book is thriving. There have even been praiseworthy endeavors to establish a presence on the Internet, although those efforts are not without problems. Unaware of recent developments in biblical studies, many run the risk of surfing in the same waters as fundamentalists and eccentrics. Interested Internet users should make their way to http://ntgateway.com/, for example, in order to view a useful, wide ranging, reliable, and informative Web site on the Bible.

Curiosity and a genuine desire to learn about the Bible often come to the fore in personal conversations. New translations of the Bible can even capture significant media attention and sell in large quantities. For example, hundreds of thousands of copies of the new Dutch translation sold in the first weeks. It was also the first time that the Bible was officially presented not only as a "religious" book, but also as a literary document that had won a prominent place in Western culture. In this way, the Bible not only reached believers within ecclesiastic circles, but also those alienated from Western-Christian tradition.

The question remains, however, whether such initiatives do not simply serve to highlight the fact that the Bible has become a strange and incomprehensible book for many. While opportunities to read the Bible might be numerous, the lack of well-trained interpreters capable of explaining the Bible can turn opportunity into calamity. Until the middle of the last century, there was no need for the public to receive an explanation of the Bible. The environment in which people read the Bible in those days rarely promoted critical questions. Currently, occasional lectures on the Bible tend to attract an overwhelmingly older audience. In spite of the many accessible publications explaining recent developments in biblical studies, that audience is not always able to relate to new insights and often leaves the lecture with more questions than answers. "Why were we kept ignorant?" many ask. While opinions differ on what lies behind such questions, it is probably fair to say that a complex interplay of historical and cultural factors from both the past and the present is to blame. In any event, it would not be an exaggeration to argue that the Bible's status as a holy book and as a cultural inheritance has been tarnished and eroded over the years.

Between the Academy and the Church: Where Do People Read the Bible?

If the Bible is infected with a virus, isn't it time to disinfect it? Shouldn't we rid our collective memory of the ballast that prevents us from seeing how a biblical book can be read in our present day and age? Isn't it time to start with a *tabula rasa* and reestablish the Bible's significance? The present contribution is an endeavor to read the Gospel of Mark in an alternative manner. I take the questions ordinary men and women find important today as my point of departure.[6]

There remain two privileged public places wherein people still read the Bible in dialogue, the academy and the church. Although the academy and the church are often at loggerheads with one another, they remain the two most important places in which those interested in reading the Bible can satisfy their curiosity. For the majority of people, however, neither the academy nor the church are realistically accessible places. At the beginning of this contribution, I spoke of reading the Gospel of Mark as a novel and I hoped to reach those people who search for meaning and faith outside the academy and the church. The majority of people in search of meaning do not identify themselves with either of these traditional institutions. We are evidently witnessing a movement whereby the traditional church is set aside as the privileged location in which meaning and faith are to be found. At the same time, there appears a lack of creativity in both the academy and the church when it comes to spanning the gulf between those who refer to themselves as believers and those in search of meaning in their lives.

While the target audience of the present chapter is broad, it is not composed exclusively of those outside the church and the academy. Narrative analysis, which applies the insights of narrative studies to biblical texts, is now an established aspect of the academic study of the Bible. The presupposition that the Gospel of Mark is a story, therefore, does not mean that the narrative approach is unjustified and unscholarly. At the beginning of this chapter, I suggested that we read Mark as a novel. In so doing, I hope to remain neutral on the historical content of the gospel because I believe that the text best expresses itself when it interacts with the reader as a narrative. At the same time, the choice to write for a broader public is not to contradict the textual approach preferred by the church and the faithful. Indeed, the narrative approach can also be enriching for those who read the gospel in the context of their faith.

In short, the gospel deserves treatment as a story for every interested reader. In order to do so, it has to become a story once again. "The bible is a narrative. Dogmatic formulas, by contrast, are constructed from carefully reasoned concepts, which are rooted moreover in an ancient conceptual world and focused on complex disputed questions from centuries past."[7] Ongoing secularization implies that fewer and fewer people are, or want to be, familiar with such dogmatic formulas. Forgotten formulas, however, need not imply the death of narrative.

Why the Gospel of Mark as a Test Case?

The Gospel of Mark is the oldest of the gospels. Its composition and content bear witness to a writer who does not radiate the self-confidence of a person for whom every question about Jesus has been solved. In their own ways, the other gospels (Matthew, Luke, and John) present a clearer and more definite image of Jesus than found in Mark. Mark, on the other hand, struggles with questions about Jesus and tries to reveal the mystery of Jesus's life and death, a struggle many modern readers may identify with. Thus, the Gospel of Mark can leave its readers with the feeling that the author understands them.

Mark repeatedly draws our attention to an important component in our understanding of Jesus: the identification of Jesus as Son of God by others is not a matter of course. This dimension of the gospel gives expression to the thoughts and sensitivities of many, even today. Mark leaves the reader with the impression that knowledge of Jesus is the fruit of a relational event. The reader does not learn about Jesus in an objective way, rather he or she gets to know him (or deny him) because the author facilitates an encounter with Jesus. Although the readers themselves determine the extent to which they are open to such an encounter, the evangelist provides the opportunity. Mark seems to have written his gospel for "whoever is willing to listen," not a select group. If Mark's gospel is for everyone, then that intention provides the most fundamental reason for explaining the gospel in an open manner.

An additional reason for dealing with the Gospel of Mark is that the core of the book contains a revolutionary message, a message that few are spontaneously inclined to welcome. I will endeavor to encapsulate it in a single verse, precisely because it is Mark's intention that the message unfolds as the reader progresses through the text. Mark's answer to the many questions surrounding the meaning of Jesus can be summarized as "but whoever wishes to become great among you must be your servant, and whoever wishes to be first among you must be slave of all" (Mk. 10:43–44). If this is the evangelist's message, then it is apparent that only an extremely talented author could motivate his readers to accept and follow it.

A New Program: Reading from the Perspective of the Contemporary Reader

We must determine whether it is possible to write about a gospel in an understandable language, which relates to the everyday experience of men and women and does not expect them to be professional exegetes or even active churchgoers. I am aware that biblical scholars tend to employ different criteria for establishing whether an interpretation should be taken seriously. I have consciously opted, however, to use the present as a point of departure, not the past. There are positive reasons for accepting this challenge. In the last twenty-five years, alternative visions about the precise meaning of the term "scholarly" have evolved. The predominant understanding was rooted in the conviction that the gospel was a source of historical or theological information, through which the inquirer approaches the text statically. In recent approaches, the text functions in a dynamic fashion. It is an instrument within a much broader process of communication and the text acquires meaning because people read it. As a result, the text has a variety of interpretations depending on the reader's context. In a certain sense, one can describe the text as "lazy" because dialogue and creativity on the part of the reader are necessary for meaning to evolve. It makes some degree of scholarly sense, therefore, to look at the text from the perspective of contemporary readers rather than that of an unknown author who lived more than nineteen centuries ago.

The approach outlined above has its roots in the shifts that have taken place within the science of hermeneutics in combination with what literary theories teach us about the function of a text. In contemporary understanding, the human person is more and more the provider of meaning, such that the concept of objectivity is no longer easy to maintain. Since a variety of perspectives combine to constitute the meaning of a text, interpretation is necessary. It is impossible to speak about *the* meaning of a text. The problem with biblical texts, however, is that they have functioned for centuries within a single frame of interpretation, namely that which supported the confession of faith within the church. The variety of denominations accounted for interpretive differences.

From the nineteenth century onward, however, scholars set their sights on a different goal: the universal and objective interpretation of the Bible according to the historical method. However, this also turned out to be impossible. Sandra Schneiders correctly pointed out that it is difficult to speak of the "correct" or the "true" interpretation. Instead, it is better to presuppose that there are several *valid* interpretations (Schneiders 1999). For an interpretation to be valid, it has to meet certain criteria within a given method. The point of departure here is that there are several methods of analyzing a text. At the same time, each method has its own rules, which one is obliged to follow in order to acquire a better understanding of the text. A particular method focuses on specific aspects of a text and suppresses others. Awareness of the method one employs is an immediate recognition that there are limits to interpretation.

Many in the church object that they can no longer anchor their faith in a biblical book if it does not have one fixed meaning. Such reactions are often full of tension and confusion because they confront people's own relationships to their faith traditions. In order to clarify that relationship, they ask themselves questions such as how important is my personal understanding of the gospel. Do I only accept the gospel based on an external authority? People frequently leave the church when they realize that the gospel is a human text and that the search for personal meaning in the Bible is their own responsibility. Consequently, such individuals not only turn their back on the church, they simultaneously sever communication with the text.

This kind of reaction is often rooted in misunderstanding. Many people are inclined to believe that there is such a thing as the church's interpretation of a text, but this is not the case. The church does not have its own set of official commentaries. Rather, the faith community maintains a variety of methods for the interpretation of biblical books. Those interested in the most recent statements from the Roman Catholic Church on the methodology used for reading the Bible will find "The Interpretation of the Bible in the Church" helpful (http://www.ewtn.com/library/curia/pbcinter.htm). However, the church still insists that the seeds of dogmatic teaching are always in the Bible. After providing a clear presentation of the narrative method, for example, the above document concludes with a critical note, not to allow this approach to relapse into a tendency to banish every form of doctrine from the biblical texts, which is something many find difficult to reconcile.

The primary goal of my decision to use readers' perceptions as the point of departure in my discussion of Mark is to assist those readers to find their way in the text. People at every stage of life have acquired their own voice. Society increasingly requires the individual to exercise responsibility. At the level of religiosity, people will follow their own path in the future and become less dependent on the institutions that once provided answers without also requiring personal reflection. Given that trend, then, people will likely seek guidance to help them focus. The work of the biblical scholar is to guide readers in ways to approach the Bible, in this case the Gospel of Mark.

The Evangelist's Intention and the Reader's Interpretation

Whether the evangelist's original intentions can be recovered, and whether it is possible to transport his intentions across the boundaries of time and space to the present day are common issues in the debate surrounding the evangelist's original intention. A glimpse at the academic *status quaestionis* concerning the Gospel of Mark, however, reveals that there is little, if any, unanimity on the author's original intention. In other words, anyone who endeavors to recover the evangelist's original intention necessarily invests some of his or her own meaning in the text, making the idea of objectivity impossible. It is no longer feasible to maintain the model of interpretation that understood the Bible as historical, in its purest form. The goal of biblical exegesis is no longer a contest between "the evangelist's intention" and "the reader's interpretation." Rather, today both aspects exist permanently intertwined. By using the reader as a point of departure, I do not deny that Mark had a specific intention when he wrote his gospel. Instead, I recognize that the evangelist and his gospel have undergone the same fate as every writer and every text: once a text is written, it becomes the property of the reader. Each reader brings his or her culture and personal history into the process of interpretation. It makes sense, therefore, to chart those observations and allow potential readers to give voice to their questions.

Some might object to the above approach in the following way: "What if we take the ideal that Mark's initial intention can ultimately be formulated as our point of departure? Surely the role of the reader would then be reduced to an absolute minimum." Perhaps, but what relevance might the intention of an author writing almost 2,000 years ago have for the present? A further objection might be that the endeavor to formulate Mark's initial intention would at least bring us closer to the truth because it would force us to think in line with Mark. However, this is precisely where the complexity of the matter lies. That line of argument assumes that the gospel functions by creating fixed meanings transplantable to different historical periods. What if a time comes (perhaps it is already here) in which the one fixed meaning of the gospel no longer connects with the everyday lives of men and women? For example, the language may be incomprehensible or the historical and cultural circumstances may have changed beyond recognition.

Some people continue to protect the original intention of the author in spite of such arguments. They insist that the gospel has always been a contrary voice and that its power lies precisely in a message that runs counter to the world, a message forbidden, hidden, and incomprehensible to the world. "The times are mistaken, the gospel is right" is an argument employed with relative frequency when Christianity faces a repeat of the early persecutions. In those situations, Christianity adopts the position of a minority and the gospel functions as an antidote to the prevailing culture, which does not understand its message. Once again, this is only a limited vision of the gospel rooted in the conviction that human nature or culture is necessarily at odds with the "good news." In fact, there is no evidence to suggest that the gospels came into existence outside the existing Jewish and Roman-Hellenistic environment of the first century. Rather, this is the original context of early Christianity and all its writings bear the marks thereof.

I am inclined, therefore, to choose a more nuanced reflection on the relationship between gospel and culture. At one moment in history, the gospel runs counter to culture. At another, it is congruous with life and culture. This process occurs without reference to the original message. Interpreters who explain the gospel in the temporal and cultural context of the current reader determine it. The evangelist wrote the gospel to coincide within the prevailing linguistic and cultural context and the mindset of its readers. Sometimes the gospel connected with the culture and its religiosity; sometimes it was a critical voice. It should now be clear why I chose the perspective of the reader as my point of departure. The choice is rooted in the conviction that men and women must be given the opportunity to deal with the questions that preoccupy them; otherwise the gospel cannot survive.

Who Wrote the Gospel and for Whom Was It Written?

The identity of the evangelist and his audience is a subject of considerable importance because it relates to the cultural transformation that has taken place in the way we treat the Bible. A willingness to be open toward a plurality of interpretations implies that we accept the responsibility to seek our own meaning and to respect the visions upheld by others. This does not make the interpretive process easier for the reader. Unlike those who maintain that there is only one possible interpretation, the readers who are open to a plurality of meanings must engage in the process of reflection. This does not mean, however, that a reader-oriented interpretation is free to do whatever it wants with the text. Nor does it imply that every interpretation is a good interpretation. To borrow an expression from David Rhoads, what we need now is an "ethics of reading" (Rhoads 2004).

Rhoads points out that we must treat the text with respect just as we should treat another person with respect. If we wish to enter into dialogue with someone, it makes no sense to set an objective tone to the conversation. On the contrary, we only get to know the other person to the extent we are engaged in the dialogue. The same is true for texts. If a reader wants to understand 2,000-year-old texts, he or she will need empathy for the text. It is important, therefore, to be aware of the factors that make our interpretation subjective, the factors that define our interpretation as *our* interpretation. Readers will be obliged, for example, to distinguish their motivation for reading the gospel. Some may be in search of a political dimension, some for spirituality, others for a point of departure to criticize tradition, and others still for a historical foundation of the Christian faith. This level of awareness is important because it exposes our tendency to read *what we want* to read in the gospel. The ethics of reading requires us to identify our own perspectives in order to have a better understanding of our own interpretation of the text. This is necessary because it allows us to develop our own response to the text. For example, the way we examine the role of women in Mark or interpret the suffering of Jesus depends on the perspectives we developed on those subjects.

Insights of this nature confirm that the result of biblical exegesis cannot be an absolute or objective interpretation. It is better to recognize instead that "relative perspectives" are possible and must be allowed to enter into communication with one another. The ethnic, social, economic, national, and religious groups in which we live determine the ways in which we interpret a text and how we communicate our interpretation with each another. One of the challenges facing biblical studies, therefore, is the need to listen to the enormous diversity offered by such a wealth of contexts. Dialogue with the other is the only way to detect blind spots in our own interpretation. The ethics of reading encourages readers to become aware of the need to refine and adjust their own methods through dialogue with others. Rhoads does not hesitate to insist that the ethics of reading must teach us humility.

Rhoads concludes by offering some advice on our present-day approach to the Gospel of Mark. He invites the reader to be open to change and to the challenge of allowing the text to question the reader. Possible questions the gospel might pose include: Do I have more hope, greater courage and why? Am I more inclined to be of service to others? What do I think of people living on the margins of society? What kind of faith is important? The reader is free to accept or reject such invitations to change. Even if we reject them, however, change is an inevitable result of our confrontation with the text (see also van Oyen 2000). Rhoads warns against the notion that every text in the gospel applies in every circumstance and to every person. In concrete terms, the conditions and identity of the person to whom we say: "All things can be done for the one who believes" (9:23) makes a considerable difference. An ethics of reading further requires us to be particularly careful in the way we transfer old authoritative texts to the present day. Undoubtedly, those texts contain a dimension that is still critical of contemporary wrongs and abuses. It is also possible that those texts contain obsolete elements. Finally, an ethics of reading requires the reader to account for the effects of his or her application of a text. The reader is responsible for the consequences of his or her interpretation, and, as Rhoads concludes, they should bring life and not death.

Dealing with Misconceptions Prior to Reading

The preceding pages focused on the difficulties that flow from the nature of the Bible itself. The following pages will focus on the obstacles that emerge on the side of the reader. The fact that biblical books are currently not popular is not only a result of the gulf between the world in which they emerged and the contemporary world. The critical attitude toward the Bible found in the secularized West also plays an undeniable role. Outside of the Western world, we encounter cultures that contend with the Christian texts and religious traditions in a completely different way. In such cultures, the Bible is a familiar text and is rarely subject to the criticisms characteristic of the West. This observation is not a reproach. The uncritical reading of the Bible in the non-Western world has its own set of problems. An analysis of those cultures, however, is beyond the scope of the present contribution.

In the West, those who consider it important to read the Bible will have to account for the fact that we no longer live in a culture with a biblical orientation. In addition, we must respect today's culture and mentality. The word respect might sound unusual in this context, but I am convinced that whatever one writes or says about the Bible will be counterproductive if one does not account for the reality in which the target audience lives. The first step of effective communication involves the formulation of widely held misconceptions about the Bible.

The negativity surrounding the Bible is the result of centuries-long evolution, which has lead to a series of misunderstandings. Many of those misconceptions have developed into preconceptions that make it impossible to address the Bible honestly. In practice, the Bible has disappeared from the concrete lives of contemporary men and women to such an extent that the majority know little, if anything, about it and consider the Bible a closed book. In the following pages, I will endeavor to inventory the ideas that currently prevent people from opening the Bible or reading about it. Of course, one cannot hope to clarify in a few paragraphs deeply rooted misconceptions that have governed Bible reading for centuries. Indeed, when such misconceptions are rooted in collective experience, many might consider clarification a hopeless task.

The Bible Is Not True

The most significant misconception about the Bible deals with truth. Contemporary language primarily understands "truth" as historical accuracy. This view has deep roots and relates to certain features of Enlightenment thinking. The misconception in the biblical context is the temptation to see every literary writing as an informative source intended to provide accurate historical information. When we combine this with the conviction that only historically accurate information is true, what remains is a highly specific vision of the truth, which unfortunately only applies to a limited number of documents. There is a widespread idea that before the Bible is widely accepted, it must be understood historically. People often refuse to read the Bible when they discover that its contents are not accurate. The idea that not every text tries to provide its readers with historical information, however, challenges that strict approach. For example, is the Bible a historical book, written by and for historians? The evolution of the Bible does not allow us to consider it a historical book.

A multitude of problems exists with respect to the scientific claim that historical authenticity is the ultimate criterion we must use to determine whether something is true. Scientists have long been aware that information is seldom purely historical. While there may be a few exceptions, almost every source, be it textual or archaeological material, contains interpreted information and must undergo further interpretation to become meaningful. In other words, data only acquires meaning when someone understands it. If we bear in mind that interpretation always surrounds information, it becomes necessary to analyze each piece of information in order to determine its historical reliability. The results of such analyses might reveal that the text itself was never intended to communicate exact information. Such cases may leave the reader with the misconception that the text is therefore meaningless. In fact, the opposite is true. Texts have meaning because they contain interpretations. When interpreted, texts acquire new meaning.

As a historical source, the Bible is subject to the same analysis as any other historical source. This is nothing new, of course, but the results of several hundred years of historical criticism are striking to say the least. First, one is obliged to admit that as a whole the Bible is neither historically true nor historically false. It is important to study every statement and every event to determine whether a relationship with history exists. Second, the Bible contains an enormous variety of literary genres. Only a small number of texts in the Bible were written with the intention of providing historical information. Rather, virtually the entire Bible was written to express an interpreted reality, namely a community's experience of God in the world, in the cosmos, in history, and in human beings. Searching for history where it does not exist can only lead to misunderstanding. We cannot expect a myth, for example, to be historically correct. The creation narrative in the book of Genesis is not history. One can historically analyze a parable to determine whether Jesus could have used it, but not to determine whether the parable itself actually took place. Wisdom sayings give expression in words or concrete examples to people's experience, which they desire to pass on to others as good advice. Psalms are prayers. Those who ignore the Bible because of its historical inaccuracy and those who swear by the Bible because it is historically accurate base themselves on the same misconception.

The only response to the misconception that the Bible has to be true is to insist that the Bible *does not have to be* true from a historical perspective. The authors of the biblical books did not set out to provide their readers with information they could verify as historically correct. The Bible's first audience did not believe its narratives because they thought everything happened as described in the text. Why, then, are some contemporary readers so obsessed with the historical dimensions of the Bible? If we can demonstrate certain passages of the Bible are historically accurate, we will have made an interesting discovery, but that discovery does not affect the Bible's credibility. Historical truth can never determine whether the Bible is worth reading. When people speak about biblical truth with respect to their faith, they mean something different. To accept a text as true is the result of a longer process of communication. Such a process might lead us to discover that a text contains something that can serve as a source of inspiration and orientation for the way we lead our lives. Therefore, a text is not judged according to historical criteria, but according to the capacity of its content—the potential for a text to give life, to offer space, to bear fruit. In this sense, the truth of the Bible is itself a metaphor. It is an image to express our conviction that the Bible narrative offers us a meaningful perspective on life.

You Have to Be a Believer to Read the Bible

Many people refuse to read the Bible because they think it is for believers only. They do not want to identify themselves with faith, which they consider has its proper place in the church. Further, the church's current image hardly attracts outsiders in droves. No one can deny that the Bible is an established aspect of the Christian faith. The church is the traditional place where religious believers read the Bible, and the majority of readers are associated in some way with a church. However, there is a difference between that admission and the argument that one must be a believer and church member in order to read the Bible.

The meaning of faith is a key concept that underscores the Bible's availability to church members and nonmembers alike. There is an enormous amount of diversity within a group of believers. Research shows that a large number of people who refer to themselves as Christian do not believe in the resurrection, but believe in reincarnation. This is in spite of the fact that resurrection, in contrast to rebirth, is a core feature of the Christian faith. There are also enormous differences surrounding issues such as the Bible, prayer, politics, images of God, revelation, and interreligious dialogue. Furthermore, one is likely to discover that many people who do not consider themselves believers have respect for the figure of Jesus and are interested in his life. Many nonbelievers also maintain positions on social justice, solidarity, respect for human rights, and respect for the religions of others. Those views are often difficult to distinguish from Christian perspectives on the same issues. Moreover, many people describe themselves as religious but refuse to associate themselves with traditional religious institutions. The boundary between Christian believers and nonbelievers, therefore, no longer coincides with the boundary between church members and nonmembers.

As a result, I support a new dialogue on matters of meaning, religiosity, and spirituality that proceeds beyond the boundaries of institutional religions. The Bible is a tool to stimulate such a dialogue. People in search of meaning are attracted often to wise words passed down through the ages, whatever their source. In order for the dialogue to be successful, though, people within the church will have to suppress their inclination to claim that they alone know how to understand the Bible. At the same time, those outside the church will have to make an effort to read a book that they have always identified with ecclesial tradition. Perhaps the postmodern world in which we live can provide a positive environment for such dialogue.

The Real Truth Is Hidden

We already observed with respect to *The Da Vinci Code* that books that describe religious secrets enjoy enormous popularity these days. This phenomenon is remarkable and paradoxical. Readers who have not followed developments in the study of the Bible for years are suddenly capable of accepting something as true. That truth is usually something sensational, something that runs counter to the traditional faith of the church. Against the background of our earlier observation is an explanation for this: people do not feel at home in the classical framework within which they read the Bible. As a result, they create their own new gospels or use old apocryphal (i.e., hidden) gospels to substantiate their new faith. This process feeds on the claim of long hidden texts as part of a conspiracy among the dominant ecclesial authorities.

Those who are part of this new trend often see no reason to be critical. Yet their uncritical attitude toward the newly discovered ancient texts does not square with their critical attitude toward classical biblical texts. Now, a recurring pattern emerges. A book comes out exposing hitherto concealed truths. Take the Dead Sea Scrolls, for example, which purportedly demonstrate that Jesus was not the founder of a new religion. The Gnostic texts of Nag Hammadi and their revolutionary vision of Christianity are another example. At the time of writing, the newspapers are brimming over with discussion concerning the publication of the Gospel of Judas. Once again, we will be confronted with an image of Jesus that differs from the one proposed by the four gospels found in the Bible. People will accept this image without question. It is strange that people are so inclined to accept hypotheses and reconstructions based on unstable foundations. We remain more ignorant with respect to the history, context, milieu, and origins of the apocryphal texts, for example, than we are with respect to the texts found in the canon of the Bible. Nevertheless, such revolutionary theories gain easy acceptance as an alternative to the biblical tradition.

It is not my intention to explore the theological, sociological, and psychological rationale of this phenomenon in any detail. However, I will focus on one particular element that has to do with the texts themselves. Currently, there is a misconception with respect to the value of hidden texts and their relationship with more familiar texts such as those found in the Bible. A common argument is that texts hidden for centuries are more reliable than familiar classical texts. Many people believe that hidden texts are more authentic. Readers are suspicious about well-known texts, which supposedly contain false truths in which people have mistakenly believed for centuries. The need for a common sense response to this trend is evident.

The discovery, publication, and distribution of apocryphal texts need not imply that we should stop reading the Bible. On the contrary, apocryphal texts and the Bible are better understood when they are read in parallel with each other. Our reading and analysis of noncanonical texts helps us to acquire a better understanding of what we find in the Bible. The New Testament and the apocryphal texts demonstrate the existence of tension in the early church regarding the person of Jesus. Different perspectives on the matter arose side by side. The New Testament itself actually provides evidence of various approaches to Jesus. Apocryphal texts thus become interesting in the sense that they illustrate various points of discussion within the early church. If we want to acquire a more complete understanding of the development of early Christianity, knowledge of such hitherto unknown documents is essential.

The common sense approach described above can temper the emotional reactions that lead to an overvaluation of apocryphal texts. The fact that certain texts have remained hidden for centuries does not make them more authentic or reliable than the texts we find in the biblical canon.

Only by comparing all the texts at our disposal can we develop a clearer understanding of the images of Jesus and of God within early Christianity. This understanding allows the reader to find the tradition he or she prefers. It makes little sense, however, to treat apocryphal and canonical texts in opposition to one another. Rather, both groups stem from the same tradition and share many common features. From a historical perspective, it is clear that after a few centuries, the church reached a consensus about which texts to collect as a canon.

However, there is little advantage in eliminating either apocryphal or canonical texts from consideration. On the contrary, people who wish to explore the depths of Christianity should investigate as many documents as possible in order to make a responsible choice. The commotion surrounding the publication and distribution of unknown texts provides a positive argument in support of rereading known texts. The more apocryphal texts we have at our disposal, the more interesting our discussion of Jesus will be. Each time we discover a new text, we relive events from centuries past. We go back in time to discover new elements that contribute to our understanding of early Christianity.

Conclusion

By way of conclusion, I would like to synthesize a few of the ideas presented in the preceding pages. Individuals, church, and society can benefit from treating the Bible as a book that is open to discussion in the public forum. The atmosphere of contemporary society can enable that open treatment. Currently, many traditional religions are in crisis. However, this does not signify the end of religion. The elements that caused religious expression to deteriorate can also contribute to the possibility that religion can resume its place in our personal and social agenda. Ever-increasing secularization spawned suspicion of the church's power among members and nonmembers alike. The perception of the church as an intimidating institution diminished. We would be missing an important opportunity, therefore, if we overlooked the role the Bible can play in bringing people back to religion. At the personal level, people now have liberty to explore the Bible and see where it inspires new perspectives. This exploration will involve a wider variety of interpretive approaches than has hitherto been the norm. If the Bible regains an important position in individual lives and society, then it can contribute to social debates concerning multiculturalism or specific ethical dilemmas. In order for biblical texts to be used in a respectful way, however, it is necessary to treat the Bible as an open book. It cannot be exploited by a select few, but must be available for everyone to read.

Notes

1. References to the gospel are abbreviated with "Mk" whereas "Mark" is used when referring to the author. For readers of this volume unfamiliar with biblical literature, see introductions of recent commentaries on Mark: J. R. Donahue and D. J. Harrington, *The Gospel of Mark*, Sacra Pagina 2 (Collegeville: Liturgical Press, 2002); R. T. France, *The Gospel of Mark*, The New International Greek Testament Commentary (Grand Rapids: Wm. B. Eerdmans, 2002).
2. Application of the hermeneutics to the gospel itself can be found in (in Dutch): G. van Oyen *De Marcus Code* (Averbode: Kampen-Kok, 2006) [*The Markan Code*]. This chapter is a revised translation of the first part of the book.
3. For an overview of the publications on Mk, 1950 until 1990, see F. Neirynck, et al. *The Gospel of Mark. A Cumulative Bibliography 1950–1990* (BETL) (Leuven: University Press and Peeters, 1992). More recently, D. Dormeyer, *Das Markusevangelium* (Darmstadt: Wissenschaftliche Buchgesellschaft, 2005).
4. A translation of the Greek text of Mark can be found on the Internet.
5. On the rise of new methods in Markan exegesis, see J. C. Anderson and S. D. Moore (eds.) *Mark and Method: New Approaches in Biblical Studies* (Minneapolis: Augsburg Fortress, 1992).
6. See the application of this view in F. Segovia and M. A. Tolbert (eds.) *Reading from this Place. Vol. 2. Social Location and Biblical Interpretation in the Global Perspective* (Minneapolis: Fortress Press, 1995).
7. More than twenty years ago, Han Renckens published a book in Dutch: H. Renckens, *Je eigen Schrift schrijven: Meegroeien met de bijbel* [*A Scripture of Your Own: Growing with the Bible*] (Baarn: Ambo, 1983).

Part II

Hermeneutics, Religious Freedom, and Exclusion

7

The Qur'an and Religious Freedom

The Issue of Apostasy

Ali Mirmoosavi

The Universal Declaration of Human Rights recognizes religious freedom as a fundamental right. Other conventions and declarations also deal with its different dimensions and limitations. Nevertheless, in Islamic societies, the violation of this right was justified according to Shar'ia (Islamic law). Considering the diverse interpretations of Islamic scriptures, however, it is difficult to determine the exact view of Islam on the issue of religious freedom. Some Qur'anic verses reject compulsion in religion, while others denounce apostasy, which is turning back from religion. According to Shar'ia, apostasy is punishable by death or several civil sanctions. Does this view reflect and show the whole view of Islam? Or, can the Qur'anic texts be interpreted in a way that is not incompatible with religious freedom? How can we rethink Shar'ia to bring about a compromise between Islam and religious freedom?

These questions lead us to hermeneutics and the possibility of new interpretations. In light of dominant and current interpretations, religious freedom is not consistent with Islam. If we understand the holy text in relation to context, however, we can argue that the above view is open to challenge. To critique the view that Islam and religious freedom are incompatible, it is first necessary to establish a theoretical framework from which to explore the interaction between text and context. Second, it is important to establish foundations of religious freedom based on the Qur'an. Accordingly, it is necessary to reconsider the punishment for apostasy and its incompatibility with religious freedom.

Hermeneutics and Interpretation

The science of interpretation known as hermeneutics has developed since the eighteenth century and includes several approaches divisible into the following categories: author-oriented (traditional), text-oriented (modern) and interpreter-oriented (postmodern). However, some new approaches concentrate on the interaction between text and context. According to those approaches, the text is essentially a collection of signs formed within a special context. As a result, there is a dialectical relation between text and context. To understand the meaning, then, it is imperative to consider the political, social, and cultural context surrounding the text.

To interpret the Qur'an based on these approaches requires adopting the following assumptions. The first assumption is to regard scripture as a text like other texts. This may not be an easy assumption to adopt because the Qur'an is a divine revelation and thus considered different from other kinds of texts created by man. Because of its sacredness, some people reject comparison of the Qur'an with other texts. This tendency doubts the text's historical roots and denies the textual relation to the context. On the other hand, if we can consider the scripture to be a text, then one can investigate the interaction between scripture and context.

A second assumption to adopt is that a text is a systematic combination of linguistic signs that bears a message and a meaning. The type of message within the text is the only thing distinguishing sacred texts from nonsacred. Linguistic signs represent the facts and the content of the mind. Having developed in a social context, they have a communicative function. Since linguistic signs form socially, the surrounding social facts also influence the text. As a result, to understand the message it is necessary to understand the context.

The third assumption to adopt is that the text and context have a reciprocal relationship. They each have a bearing on the other. When a community accepts a particular text as a religious or cultural work, it affects that community. Scriptures are no exception and they influence social and political events.

A fourth, and final, assumption is that interpretation of the Qur'an, in light of its context, involves at least three levels. Those contextual levels include external, internal, and interpreter. External context includes the social, political, and cultural situation dominant in the age of revelation. One important attribute of the Qur'an's external context is that the tribal community experienced a decentralized political system in three major cities based on racial relations. Internal context, on the other hand, includes the process of the genesis, evolution, and transformation of the text. In relation to the Qur'an, gradual revelation, abrogated verses, different readings, and the history of collecting and unifying the copies represent its internal context. Finally, the interpreter's context involves the circumstance that surrounds the interpreter and that directly or indirectly, consciously or unconsciously influence the process of interpretation. This level of context includes both the theoretical and sociological conditions that surround the interpreter. For example, global values of human rights are so widespread that no one can deny them.

Keeping in mind the four assumptions stated above, the way is clear to evaluate the unfamiliar interpretation that Islam is compatible with religious freedom. In order to develop this interpretation completely, the following section sets forth a definition and description of the theoretical foundations that support the interpretation that Islam can support religious freedom.

Conceptual Dimensions of Religious Freedoms

According to the preamble of the Declaration on the Elimination of All Forms of Intolerance and of Discrimination Based on Religion or Belief (hereinafter referred to as the "1981 Declaration"), a religion or belief, for anyone who professes either, is one of the fundamental elements in the conception of life and should be fully respected and guaranteed. What does that statement really mean? What is the theoretical basis of religious freedom? Why is freedom of religion valuable and why is discrimination on the basis of religion and beliefs specifically prohibited?

Freedom of religion and belief is a broad concept that is subject to varying interpretations. Those interpretations vary between different states, cultures, religions, and individuals. Even if a group of states agrees to the general principle of freedom of religion or belief in an international treaty, for example, it is quite possible that they do not share an understanding of the values at stake when making such an agreement (Evans 2001, 32). In its ordinary sense, freedom of religion means to have the right to choose, profess, manifest, and propagate one's own religion. A definition of the term "freedom of religion," then, centers on an expression of those dimensions.

To profess means to make an open or public declaration of one's faith in or allegiance to, a particular religion, belief, or opinion (Webster's, 1436–37). With regard to religion, profession is the right of a person to declare freely that he believes or does not believe in any religion. The right to profess essentially means the right to choose, which also includes the right to convert.

Freedom of manifestation allows anyone to reveal his religion through worship, observance, practice, and teaching. The ability to practice rituals and tenets is an essential part of religion and includes the norms or customs of religion as well. Freedom of religion means that anyone, individually or in community with others, in private or in public, can practice his own religious rituals and worship. Article 6 of the 1981 Declaration expresses those aspects of religious freedom. Freedom of propagation is a third dimension of religious freedom. Propagation includes the rights to teach, train, call, preach, reproduce, and cause to grow in number or amount and spread from place to place.

Freedom of religion also deals with tolerance, nondiscrimination and religious equality. The term "tolerance" connotes that what one is tolerating is to some extent undesirable, improper, misguided, or wrong. Nevertheless, reasons for permitting the objectionable behavior to continue exist (Evans 2001, 22; Raz 1986, 401–2). The principle of religious equality involves a simultaneous recognition of unity and diversity. Different religions do not have to be the same in order to be united.

Religious freedom is incomplete and ineffective without the freedom of religious association, assembly, and speech. The right to association is an important aspect of religious freedom because an individual cannot establish or promote an idea or a religion unless he joins another or others join him. Freedom of assembly means to gather for a special purpose or practice, such as worship. It also enables individuals to meet each other, to discuss their religious ideas, and perform their practices. Finally, freedom of speech includes the vocalization of words in order to communicate with others.

The terms discussed above are important aspects of religious freedom, but different justifications for religious freedom will lead to different interpretations regarding the scope and importance of each aspect. Thus, to elaborate the concept, the next section discusses the different foundations of religious freedom.

Foundations of Religious Freedom

The theoretical premises that form the foundation of freedom of religion relate to the view of religious truth and faith. This chapter discusses the idea that these premises are necessary for freedom of religion to find effective acceptance.

Almost every religion claims to be the best and most complete religion in the world. The claim that a monotheistic religion is the most complete derives from the notion that all other beliefs are erroneous. This exclusive attitude toward religion denies the right of everyone to be different. Additionally, claims to a monopoly of religious truth historically served as a basis for intolerance and countless "holy, divine, or just wars" and "crusades" waged against so-called "heretics" or "infidels" (Tahzib 1996, 31).

In opposition to the exclusive attitude toward religion, a pluralistic view recognizes that common core teachings underlie many religions. For example, many religions share the "Golden Rule," which means to treat others as we would wish to be treated. In the words of a 1960 UN study: "Truly great religions and beliefs are based upon ethical tenets such as the duty to widen the bound of good-neighborliness and the obligation to meet human need in the broadest sense. The precept that one should love one's neighbor as oneself was part of Christianity even before it had been organized as a Church. The same idea permeates Judaism and Islam, as well as various branches of Buddhism, Confucianism and Hinduism, and it may also be found in the teaching of many non religious beliefs" (Krishnaswami 1960, 44).

Considering other religions to be various readings of truth and different ways of life leads to tolerance and prevents religious discrimination, a pluralistic perception of religion, therefore, is a necessary assumption that underlies acceptance of religious freedom.

A liberal conception of faith is another precondition for religious freedom. Faith is an internal and intentional matter and must develop freely, not by compulsion. Since religion and faith are inseparable, a liberal conception of faith leads to religious freedom. On the other hand, the belief that faith is a matter of fate determined by God's will, or that it only involves believing religious teachings, is comparable to compulsion and hence not easily compatible with religious freedom.

These above premises underlie religious freedom. If religious truth is pluralistic and religious faith develops freely, then there will not be obstacles to overcome in order to realize religious freedom. Without these, however, freedom of religion can still exist. The next section discusses that religions may also pragmatically accept freedom of religion.

Justifications for Religious Freedom

Many arguments justify the existence of religious freedom. These arguments tend to answer the questions of why freedom of religion is valuable and why it is imperative to prohibit discrimination based on religion or belief. Since these arguments influence the conceptions of religious freedom, they are worthy of notice. These arguments divide easily into four main types: instrumental or pragmatic, historical, religious, and philosophical.

Pragmatic or Instrumental Approach

Instrumental arguments emphasize tolerance as a means of achieving another important end. Although some people perceive that the best society is one where all people accept the same true religion, they might also understand that religious diversity is a reality. Further, they might recognize that intolerance causes many social problems without bringing about religious cohesion. Thus, religious freedom can be justified as a means to other desirable ends.

This type of pragmatic argument commonly arises in international discussions on religious freedom. The preamble of the 1981 Declaration refers to the fact that "the disregard and infringement of human rights and fundamental freedoms, in particular of the right to freedom of thought, conscience, religion or whatever belief, have brought directly or indirectly, wars and great suffering to mankind." Religious freedom can contribute to achieving the goals "world peace, social justice and friendship among people."

Although pragmatic approaches play a significant role in developing liberty of religion throughout the world, they are of limited value. According to instrumental or pragmatic arguments, freedom of religion is valuable only insofar as it helps to achieve other ends. Thus, in a predominantly religiously homogenous society, for example, it may be very easy to violate religious freedom rights.

Historical Approach

Historical justifications of religious freedom emphasize the use of religion to justify persecution and repression. Religious freedom, therefore, is necessary in order to prevent undesirable outcomes of intolerance, such as torture, imprisonment, and all the other horrors once visited on religious dissenters.

Religious Approach

Religious arguments are another form of justification for religious freedom. Those whose own religion is a minority adopt one line of religious arguments. Those believers often see the importance of promoting religious freedom in order to support themselves. Thus, that line of religious reasoning is a pragmatic argument. Another line of religious argument is the belief that it is easier to convince people to believe in one true religion from an environment of religious freedom. Both Locke and Mill, for example, argue that some degree of religious freedom would benefit true religion. A third line of religious argument attempts to extract from scriptures a core commitment to religious freedom. In the holy Qur'an, for example, are many verses that contain some teaching useful for this purpose. This religious justification is an effective reason for believers who adhere to the superiority of their religious truth to all other human thinking and knowledge. Such justifications are valuable, however, only to the extent that the teachings of the religion can accommodate them.

Philosophical Approach

The pluralistic philosophical approach argues that freedom of religion or belief is an essential component of treating human beings as autonomous persons who deserve dignity and respect. As Raz notes, "The ruling idea behind the ideal of personal autonomy is that people should make their own lives. Coercion in matters of fundamental importance, such as belief in the existence of God, or of an afterlife, or in a religiously based set of morals or obligations towards others, would deny people the ability to be authors of their own lives" (Evans 2001, 29–30).

Based on this approach, other authors discuss the issue of religious freedom as a fundamental aspect of human life and self-definition. In his *Theory of Justice*, Rawls comments that "it seems that equal liberty of conscience is the only principle that the persons in the original position can acknowledge. They cannot take chances with their liberty by permitting the dominant religious or moral doctrine to persecute or to suppress others if it wishes" (Rawls 1972, 17–22).

Unlike some religious arguments, autonomy arguments do not claim that freedom of religion is an absolute value. Some religious arguments claim that religious teaching is the highest truth. As a result, the state cannot legitimately limit the practice of religious adherents. Autonomy arguments, on the other hand, are more limited. They do not accept that one religion has a monopoly on truth or that all religious practices are permissible. From the viewpoint of those arguments, religious freedom is only one aspect of autonomy and may conflict with other aspects. The conflict between one person's religious duty to punish apostasy with death, and the apostate's right to life is one clear example that supports placing limitations on religious freedom.

In light of the above arguments, it is reasonable to categorize the discussion about the Qur'an and religious freedom as a religious argument. The introductory discussion above describes the text and context of human rights as a basis for religious freedom. To elaborate on the context, this chapter discusses the Islamic view of religious freedom with regard to the Qur'an and Shi'a tradition. The next section will first focus on Qur'anic teachings that support religious freedom. Then the chapter argues for reinterpretation of the teachings incompatible with religious freedom in light of the human rights context.

Religious Context of Revelation

To study the Qur'anic attitude toward freedom of religion, it is first necessary to consider the religious context of a pre-Islamic community. In addition to lineage and property, religion was a basic dimension of tribal structure. Individuals were identified by tribal membership and by belief in the tribal religion. The role of religion in social and political life, however, was not as important as lineage. Lineage more often than religion distinguished tribes.

In the pre-Islamic age, called the Ignorance period, the four major religions were polytheism, Judaism, Christianity, and a monotheistic religion called *hanifi'iah*. Polytheists believed in Allah, but they also accepted that other gods and goddesses fulfilled God's will. The town-state of Mecca was the center of polytheism. Monotheists were a minority in Mecca. Jews and Christians lived in *Yathreb*, renamed Medina in the Islamic period and was another important town-state of Arabia. According to some narratives, the main religion of Arabia was a version of monotheism later distorted to polytheism (Ali 1978, 6). Monotheists were a minority within that society, however, and could not manifest their religion.

As historical documents witness, the Prophet endured many troubles after he began proclaiming Islam because most people followed their family religion and religious freedom was not recognized. Since Islamic revelation occurred in the tribal context, the Qur'anic teachings about religion interacted with the tribal community. After making a few changes, Islam recognized the tribal society and used its structure to expand and propagate religious teachings. In response, the tribe also imposed its own conditions on Islam. As mentioned above, the concept of lineage played a more important role in pre-Islamic society than the concepts of religion and property. After the establishment of Islam, however, religious belief became more important than lineage. Islamic society became a religious tribe, called *Ommah*, in which people joined based on their faith, not their lineage. The Qur'an 49:13 says, "O mankind! We created you from a single (pair) of a male and a female, and made you into nations and, that ye may know each other (not that ye may despise each other). Verily the most honoured of you in the sight of Allah is (he who is) the most righteous of you. And Allah has full knowledge and is well acquainted (with all things)."

Qur'anic Concept of Religion

The Qur'anic term for religion is *din*, which is used in at least four different ways: (1) judgment and dispensation (1:3); (2) obedience, servitude, slavery, devotional service to Allah (82:9, 3:82, 39:2); 3) the way, method, custom, and rule of obedience and submission (3:19, 42:13, 109:6); and (4) legislation or governance (12:76). The second and fourth uses of the word *din* have opposing meanings. Thus, *din* has a dual meaning and its meaning depends on the context (Izotso 1982).

To some extent, the word *din* and *Islam* have the same meaning. In other words, Islam is the only true religion acceptable to God. For example, Allah says, "the Religion before Allah is Islam (submission to His Will)" (3:19). Allah also said, "If anyone desires a religion other than Islam, never will it be accepted of him; and in the Hereafter he will be in the ranks of those who have lost" (3:85). The word *Islam* also has a more general meaning that encompasses submission and surrendering one's will before the will of God. Divine religions, like Judaism, Christianity, and Islam, share this meaning (Tabatabaiee 1973, 3:121).

The Qur'an positions Islam as the true religion that is supposed to overcome other religions, even though the polytheists or unbelievers may be averse to Islam. According to their attitude toward the Islamic faith, people fall into three main groups: believer, unbeliever, and hypocrite. Believers are on the right course and salvation (2:5) and deserve civil rights. Unbelievers have set a seal upon their hearts and upon their hearing, there is a covering over their eyes, and there is a great punishment for them (2:7). Hypocrites have illness in their hearts, so Allah increases their illness and they shall have a painful chastisement because they lied (2:10).

The general meaning of "unbelief" includes all types of disbelief of Islam. According to some verses, however, its exact meaning is to unjustly and proudly deny the Lord's clear communications or signs even though the soul is convinced by those signs (27:14, 29:47, 49). Therefore, those verses denounce unbelief when the soul has been convinced. In light of these verses, the Qur'an does not denounce believers in other religions, such as Christianity and Judaism. Like Islam, those religions also invite their followers to believe what convinces their souls and to fulfill what their Book says.

Through an emphasis on commonality, the Qur'an recognizes other divine religions and invites their believers to agree on common teachings. Allah instructed the Prophet to agree on beliefs shared by Muslim and non-Muslim. "Say: 'O People of the Book! Come to common terms as between us and you: that we worship none but Allah; that we associate no partners with Him; that we erect not, from among ourselves, Lords and patrons other than Allah.' If then they turn back, say yes, 'Bear witness that we (at least) are Muslims (bowing to Allah's Will)'" (3:64). On the other hand, the Qur'an denounces polytheism and negatively describes it as grievous iniquity (31:13). Those guilty of adhering to polytheistic beliefs will not be forgiven. Idolaters are unclean and must leave the Islamic community. In the *Tobeh* surah, Allah announces, "Away with polytheists who had agreement with Muslims and commands Muslims to fight and kill them anywhere. But those who had agreement and have not violated their agreement and have not been harmful for Muslims must be accepted" (9:1–6).

In summary, the Qur'an recognizes Islam as a high and complete religious truth that includes the undistorted teaching of previous divine religions in addition to new teachings. The Qur'anic attitude toward other monotheistic religions is positive and invites their followers to agree on the common points. On the other hand, the Qur'anic view toward polytheists and unbelievers is negative and intolerant. Thus, the Qur'an invites people to break their relation with polytheists and unbelievers. These views lead to the conclusion that the Qur'an recognizes religious boundaries and a division of communities along religious lines. Islamic believers, as members of the community called *Ommah*, deserve civil rights. Does it also mean that freedom of religion is incompatible with Qur'anic teaching? The next section will discuss Qur'anic views about that subject and attempt to answer the question.

Qur'anic Principle for Religious Freedom

The main Qur'anic principle about religion is that "Let there be no compulsion in religion" because "Truth stands out clear from Error" (2:256). As Tabatabaiee, the famous contemporary Shi'a interpreter says, refusing the compulsion can be interpreted either predicatively or prescriptively. A predicate interpretation refers to the fact that religion cannot be imposed on anyone. Religious faith essentially is an internal action differentiated from external action. While external action may happen under pressure, internal action needs intention and cannot occur under coercion. Religious faith, which is an internal action, is impossible to coerce. A prescriptive interpretation forbids any compulsory action that seeks to impose religion. This prohibition relies upon the fact that belief and faith cannot be an object for compulsion. Everyone must choose his own religion through free will (Tabatabaiee 1973 2,342–43). The prescriptive interpretation introduces a principle to establish religious freedom in the Qur'an.

The Qur'anic vision of faith also leads to a pluralistic view of religion. According to the Qur'an, salvation depends on faith and doing well. It makes no difference who is the believer and in what religion he believes. The Qur'an says, "Those who believe (in the Qur'an), and those who follow the Jewish (scriptures), and the Christians and the Sabians,—any who believe in Allah and the Last Day, and work righteousness, shall have their reward with their Lord; on them shall be no fear, nor shall they grieve" (2:62). Other verses also invite the followers of religions to believe what their soul accepts and to do what their religions say. Joy and happiness in the hereafter depends only on believing in God and the Last Day and doing well. To some extent, this attitude is a pluralistic view and recognizes religious freedom.

Qur'anic teachings that concern the appropriate attitude and behavior toward non-Muslims are another potential source for a religious freedom principle. Allah ordered the Prophet to "Call to the way of your Lord with wisdom and goodly exhortation, and have disputations with them in the best manner; surely your Lord best knows those who go astray from His path, and He knows best those who follow the right way"(16:25). When he disputed with unbelievers, the Prophet did not insist on his position. Rather, he said "certain it is that either we or ye are on right guidance or in manifest error" (34:24). These teachings reject pressuring someone to believe in Islam and suggest that believers should tolerate followers of other religions or unbelievers. As a result, those teachings are useful to justify a pluralistic view and attitude toward religion. However, the teachings that limit the role of man in adopting his own religion undermine such a conclusion. Noticeably, the issue of apostasy is one of the most important examples of a violation of religious freedom, and the next section discusses it.

Issue of Apostasy

The right to change religions is one of the most important elements of religious freedom. Many scriptures of Islam reject this right and denounce apostasy as a crime punishable by death or other civil sanctions. Those texts, found both in the Qur'an and in tradition, clearly contradict human rights and present an obstacle to the recognition of religious freedom.

Muslim scholars take two approaches to the issue of religious freedom in light of the texts that denounce apostasy. Classical and traditionalist Muslim scholars do not support a Muslim's conversion to another religion. Some contemporary Muslim jurists or intellectuals disagree with the established law and opinion. They argue that the Qur'an is silent on any worldly punishment on apostasy, so one must interpret any other texts according to the Qur'an and cannot frustrate God's purposes. Thus, whatever *Sunnah* may claim for apostasy is no longer applicable in accordance with evolutionary principles (An-Na'im 1990, 109). This chapter will now discuss the issue of apostasy from two viewpoints. First, the concept and its decrees in view of the Qur'an and Shar'ia undergo examination and then the issue in light of present circumstances.

The Qur'anic term for apostasy is *Al Irtedad*. The ordinary meaning of the term is to turn back or leave one's religious faith or belief. In the Qur'an, however, apostasy does not merely mean turning back from religion. It means to change one's belief after clear guidance and confidently understanding true religion. The Qur'an says, "Those who turn back as apostates after Guidance was clearly shown to them,—the Evil One has instigated them and busied them up with false hopes" (47:25). If someone does not truly believe in the religion and changes his religion because of that disbelief, then he is not an apostate.

Traditionalist Viewpoint

Qur'anic verses related to apostasy fall into six divisions. The first encompasses those verses that denounce apostasy and declare that it deserves punishment on the Last Day. Verse 217 of Al Baqareh falls under this category.

> They ask thee concerning fighting in the Prohibited Month. Say:
> Fighting therein is a grave (offence); but graver is it in the sight of Allah to prevent access to the path of Allah, to deny Him, to prevent access to the Sacred Mosque, and drive out its members. Tumult and oppression are worse than slaughter. Nor will they cease fighting you until they turn you back from your religion if they can. And if any of you Turn back from their faith and die in unbelief, their works will bear no fruit in this life and in the Hereafter; they will be companions of the Fire and will abide therein. (2: 217)

Implicitly, "then he dies while an unbeliever" implies that if the apostate turns back to Islam before his death, then his acts will not be spoiled. This phrase supports the claim that the repentance of an apostate is acceptable and can cancel the punishment he would have received. Some interpreters claim that is a worldly punishment for an apostate. However, "spoiling" means to cancel or nullify. It does not indicate worldly punishments. The phrase "and they will not cease fighting with you" points to some of the causes of apostasy and reveals the moral attitude of the Qur'an toward apostasy.

Verse 25 of Surah Mohammad also falls under the first category:

> Surely (as for) those who return on their backs after that guidance has become manifest to them, the Satan has made it a light matter to them; and He gives them respite. That is because they say to those who hate what Allah has revealed: We will obey you in some of the affairs; and Allah knows their

secrets. But how will it be when the angels cause them to die smiting their backs. That is because they follow what is displeasing to Allah and are averse to His pleasure, therefore He has made null their deeds.

This verse points out that apostates can only receive blame in certain situations, such as when guidance has become manifest to them. The term apostasy does not include those who believe in Islam, but then change their religion after experiencing doubt. Other verses, like 85, 88, 91 and 106 of Al Emran (3); 71 of an' am; 109 of Nahl; and 65 of Zomar, also blame apostasy and set a punishment for the last day.

The second category of verses that address apostasy promise that repentance by the apostate is acceptable. Verses 86 through 89 of Al Emran fall within this category: "How shall Allah Guide those who reject faith after they accepted it and bore witness that the Messenger was true and that Clear Signs had come unto them? But Allah guides not a people unjust. Of such the reward is that on them (rests) the curse of Allah, of his Angels and of all mankind;—In that will they dwell; nor will their penalty be lightened, nor respite be (their lot);—Except for those that repent (Even) after that, and make amends; for verily Allah is Oft-Forgiving, Most Merciful."

These verses clearly indicate that repentance of the apostate is acceptable even for those who disbelieve after they had confidently believed in Islam.

Verses 106 through 110 of Nahl also indicate a similar meaning:

> Anyone who, after accepting faith in Allah, utters Unbelief,—except under compulsion, his heart remaining firm in faith—but such as open their breast to Unbelief, on them is wrath from Allah, and theirs will be a dreadful Penalty. This because they love the life of this world better than the Hereafter: and Allah will not guide those who reject Faith. Those are they whose hearts, ears, and eyes Allah has sealed up, and they take no heed. Without doubt, in the Hereafter they will perish. But verily thy Lord,—to those who leave their homes after trials and persecutions,—and who thereafter strive and fight for the faith and patiently persevere,—Thy Lord, after all this is oft-forgiving, Most Merciful.

This verse demonstrates that apostasy resulted from persecution, and that the way is still open for the persecuted to struggle and come back to Islam. In addition to forgiving apostasy and its last day punishment, these verses also indicate the possibility of cancelling worldly punishments like the death penalty.

The third type of verses that address apostasy includes those that reject acceptance of the apostate's repentance if the apostate repeated the apostasy or increased disbelief. Verse 90 of Al Emran states that, "but those who reject Faith after they accepted it, and then go on adding to their defiance of Faith,—never will their repentance be accepted; for they are those who have (of set purpose) gone astray." Similarly, verse 137 of Al Nessa states, "Those who believe, then reject faith, then believe (again) and (again) reject faith, and go on increasing in unbelief,—Allah will not forgive them nor guide them on the way." These verses pose a challenge to those who emphasize that God absolutely accepts repentance. Tabatabaiee solved that problem by interpreting the last verse in light of its context. He suggests that the verse refers to hypocrites who change their ideas many times and do not seek repentance. If they choose to seek repentance, though, they will be accepted (Tabatabaiee 1973, 5:114).

The fourth category of verses includes those that indicate apostasy depends on free will. Under that view, a change of beliefs that occurs under pressure or coercion is not apostasy. Verse 106 of Nahl declares: "Anyone who, after accepting faith in Allah, utters Unbelief,—except under compulsion, his heart remaining firm in Faith—but such as open their breast to Unbelief, on them is Wrath from Allah, and theirs will be a dreadful penalty."

The fifth division encompasses verses that explain the causes of apostasy. These causes include loving life, friendship, obeying of disbeliever, and the cheating of Satan. The verses in this category are 107 and 108 of Nahl, 100 of Al Emran, 89 of Nessa, 51 of Meade, and 25 and 26 of Mohammad. The sixth, and final, verse divisions to address apostasy are those that explain that apostasy is not harmful to God because He is able to replace the apostate with a believer. Verse 54 of Maedeh, for example, says: "O ye who believe! If any from among you turn back from his Faith, soon will Allah produce a people whom He will love as they will love Him,—lowly with the believers, mighty against the rejecters, fighting in the way of Allah, and never afraid of the reproaches of such as find fault. That is the grace of Allah, which He will bestow on whom He pleaseth. And Allah encompasseth all, and He knoweth all things."

The above discussion of verses reveals several points about the Qur'anic viewpoint toward apostasy. First, apostasy does not simply mean to change religion or disbelief. More specifically, it means to change one's religion after guidance has become manifest and a person believes in the religion freely and confidently. Changing one's belief because of doubt about the truth of the religion is not apostasy.

A second point is of interpreting the Qur'anic attitude toward apostasy morally. The moral interpretation concentrates on the causes and conditions that make believers change their ideas. According to this approach, the Qur'anic teachings about apostasy provide moral guidance for believers to resist and be firm. Conversion usually occurs when people believe an idea, then face problems because of their beliefs. God denounces that kind of behavior and orders believers to be firm. The Qur'an says: "O you who believe! whoever from among you turns back from his religion, then Allah will bring a people, He shall love them and they shall love Him, lowly before the believers, mighty against the unbelievers, they shall strive hard in Allah's way and shall not fear the censure of any censurer" (5:54).

The main purpose of denouncing the apostasy is not to limit freedom, but to reject mental uncertainty under undesirable conditions.

A third point regarding the Qur'anic viewpoint toward apostasy is that the Qur'an does not directly condemn apostasy with worldly punishment or sanctions. Juristic interpretation, which considers apostasy a civil crime that deserves punishment, raises the issue of punishment. Since the Qur'an is silent about worldly punishment of apostasy, the jurists interpret the Qur'an in light of the *Sunnah* narratives. The *Sunnah* considered apostasy in terms of *reddah* and conferred upon it a worldly punishment. As the prophet (saw) commands, "whoever change his religion kill him." The prophetic decree on this matter is very clear, explicit, and unambiguous. This decree was executed several times during his lifetime and by all four caliphs after him. In addition to the punishment of death, apostasy alternatively led to severe civil sanctions. Those sanctions include annulment of the marital relationship, deprivation of inheritance, and deprivation of property. Both Sunni and Shi'a Muslim jurists more or less accepted these sanctions (Sarrami 1997, 313–32; Mahbubul Islam 2002, 211–14).

The *Sunnah* also sets forth four broad measures that constitute apostasy. These include faith, action, abandonment, and statement, and all have in common disbelief and denial of the teachings of Islam. According to Shar'ia, a declaration of apostasy depends on essential conditions. Submission to Islam, maturity, soundness of mind, and free will are those four essential conditions (Sarrami 1997, 334–40; Mahbubul Islam 2002, 228–31). The person punished as an apostate must be Muslim. It does not matter whether he originally believed in Islam or converted to Islam. Shi'a jurists, however, do differentiate between those who converted to Islam and those who originally believed Islam when deciding to accept their repentance. Submission to Islam also means that one must believe confidently and without doubt. Whoever doubtfully chooses Islam may not receive punishment as an apostate.

Maturity (*Bulugh*), the second condition required before declaring someone an apostate means that the person must be mature in age. The third condition, soundness of mind (*Aql al Salim*), is applicable to all litigation in Islamic law. Free will, the last condition, means that one must act from an internal, personal desire. If forced to act, then the fixed punishment cannot be imposed.

In light of the jurists' views toward apostasy, it is possible to conclude that they unanimously consider apostasy a civil crime punishable by death and the civil sanctions mentioned. As a result, there is a clear difference between the Qur'an and Shar'ia when it comes to punishments for apostates. This difference can be reconciled in one of two ways. The first is to rely on the *Sunnah* to interpret the Qur'an. The second is to rely on the Qur'an, then interpret Shar'ia.

Modernist Viewpoint

Most modern Muslim thinkers follow the second way. They argue that the Qur'an never suggests any punishment, let alone death, for a Muslim who renounces Islam (Hasan 1982, 61). Some also claim that the death penalty and other punishments in *Sunnah* are for apostates whose disbelief equates to high treason. Following this argument An-Na'im writes: "Sunnah can be understood to support the death penalty for apostasy only if disbelief equated with high treason on the assumption that citizenship is based on belief in Islam. That assumption, in turn, is valid only under a view of the responsibilities of belief as pre-requisite of membership of the community whose members enjoy those rights. Moreover, this reasoning is premised on a conception of freedom of belief as a conditional right of citizens and not as a human right to which all human beings are entitled" (Brems 2001, 212).

As An-Na'im mentioned, and in view of the context, citizenship is based on belief in Islam. On the contrary, lineage formed the basis for most pre-Islamic tribal structures. Islam subsequently replaced lineage with belief. Citizenship, therefore, is now a conditional right, which depends on responsibility of belief. A comparison of Islam with Judaism makes this clear. Judaism, like Islam, established a religious community and considered apostasy a serious crime punishable by death. The localized, traditional existence of past Islamic societies made this conception relevant. Islamic Shar'ia and jurisprudences reflect this existence in the decrees and punishments of apostasy. Those decrees and punishments are not original to Islam and depend on time and space.

Today, societies differ from past Islamic communities in many aspects. In contemporary multireligious nation states fully incorporated into a globalized world of political, economic, and security interconnections, religious belief does not play a role in citizenship. This new reality supports the claim that everyone is entitled to religious freedom. This is a human right rather than a conditional right of membership within a religious community. Accordingly, the decrees of apostasy link to the context of the revelation and to the conditions that existed for historical Islamic communities. The Qur'anic verses that confer worldly punishment to apostates relate to the society in which religious belief was a criterion to distinguish citizens from foreigners.

Conclusion

Human rights developed historically and in correlation with social and theoretical transformations. Freedom of religion gained recognition of an important human right in response to historical religious wars and challenges. Religious freedom also affects modern multireligion states where different religions and beliefs coexist. Several arguments developed since the sixteenth century can justify the theoretical foundation of that right. According to the UDHR and the 1981 Declaration, religious freedom is multidimensional. It includes the right to choose, profess, manifest, and propagate one's own religion. Religious freedom also addresses tolerance, nondiscrimination, and religious equality, and remains incomplete and ineffective without the freedom of religious association, assembly, and speech.

The Qur'an manifested in a tribal context states that a man receives his identity through his relationship to his tribe and his position within that community. The notion of inherent human dignity, and consequently the idea of human rights, was unfamiliar and unthinkable in the tribal context. The Qur'anic text and its context had a reciprocal relationship. The main influence brought by the Qur'an was to replace lineage with religious belief. Thus, the Qur'an emphasizes religious responsibility and recognizes human rights as conditional on that responsibility. In some verses, though, the Qur'an recognizes some universal and unconditional rights through an emphasis on human dignity.

The Qur'anic scriptures establish a general principle described as the Qur'anic principle of religious freedom. The main rule is that "there is no compulsion in religion," which rejects any pressure on belief. Yet, in connection with other verses that put some limitation on belief, this principle cannot justify religious freedom in its broad dimensions.

The issue of apostasy is the most controversial issue, which increases the gap between Islam and religious freedom. According to the Qur'an, apostasy does not mean just simple changing of religion or disbelief. It implies to change religion after confidently believing and because of an unjustified motivation, usually concerning treason. However, the Qur'an does not directly impose any worldly punishment for apostasy. This deduction discloses a possibility for reconciliation between the Qur'an and religious freedom.

Freedom of religion was not compatible with past Islamic society where the basis of citizenship was religious belief. The jurist decrees and punishment of apostasy, which conflict with freedom of religion, derive from past society and reflect those conditions. The current transformation of society and state leads to different jurisprudence, which should be compatible with new conditions. Modern Islamic society experiences a completely different life in the globalized world of political, economic, and security interdependence. Freedom of religion in this world is not only the legitimate right based on several arguments, but also a necessary condition for a peaceful and stable life. Even though traditional interpretations can justify themselves as the best ones, pragmatic necessities cancel and frustrate these interpretations. These pragmatic necessities lead Muslim jurists to appeal to some facilities that can reconcile their jurisprudence with freedom of religion.

8

Dignitatis Humanae

A Hermeneutic Perspective on Religious Freedom as Interpreted by the Roman Catholic Church

Kurt Martens

International declarations, covenants, and treaties guaranteeing the right to religious freedom, not only for individuals, but also for groups, marked the second half of the twentieth century. The right usually includes a number of elements, such as the right to have a religion, the right to adopt a religion, the right to change one's religion, the right to religious education, the right to worship and practice, the right to preach, and others. Civil authorities guarantee these rights. But what about the various religions? How do religious institutes themselves see religious liberty and the role of the state? An appositional illustration of the dialectics of religion in the sense of binding people to absolute and eternal truth is the opinion of Theodore Beza, Calvin's successor, whereupon tolerating other religions was a diabolical idea "because it means everyone should be left to go to hell in his own way" (Robertson 2005, 39). This chapter shall examine particularly the view of the Roman Catholic Church on the right to religious liberty or religious freedom, as expressed in various documents and especially in the Declaration *Dignitatis humanae* of Vatican II.

People often hold the Roman Catholic Church accountable for its involvement in a number of proselytizing activities that sometimes included even the use of force or violence. The Inquisition and the Crusades are two examples frequently mentioned in this context, but also the prosecution of witches fits this list. The concern for the one true faith leads to both the protection of that faith and the salvation of those who abandoned the faith, such as heretics, or those who did not find the faith yet. While the church always rejected the use of violence and force, it is not always easy to determine the involvement of individuals, if any, and of certain church authorities in such acts. In his apostolic letter *Tertio Millennio Adveniente* for the preparation of the Jubilee of the year 2000, Pope John Paul II brought to mind that intolerance and violence have been used in the service of truth.

> Another painful chapter of history to which the sons and daughters of the Church must return with a spirit of repentance is that of the acquiescence given, especially in certain centuries, to *intolerance and even the use of violence* in the service of truth. It is true that an accurate historical judgment cannot rescind from careful study of the cultural conditioning of the times, as a result of which many people may have held in good faith that an authentic witness to the truth could include suppressing the opinions of others or at least paying no attention to them. Many factors frequently converged to create assumptions which justified intolerance and fostered an emotional climate from which only great spirits, truly free and filled with God, were in some way able to break free. Yet the consideration of mitigating factors does not exonerate the Church from the obligation to express profound regret for the weaknesses of so many of her sons and daughters who sullied her face, preventing her from fully mirroring the image of her crucified Lord, the supreme witness of patient love and of humble meekness. From these painful moments of the past a lesson can be drawn for the future, leading all Christians to adhere fully to the sublime principle stated by the Council: "The truth cannot impose itself except by virtue of its own truth, as it wins over the mind with both gentleness and power." (*Dignitatis humanae* 1) (Pope John Paul II 1995)[1]

While Pope John Paul II did not mention the Inquisition, clearly this paragraph is a reference to it. Bishop Piero Marini, then Master of Papal Liturgical Celebrations, suggested as much during the press conference for the presentation of the Day of Pardon. As examples of sins committed, he mentioned in the service of truth sins of intolerance and violence against dissidents, wars of religion, acts of violence, and oppression during the Crusades and methods of coercion employed in the Inquisition.[2] On Sunday, March 12, 2000, Pope John Paul II presided over the Holy Mass for the Day of Pardon: the prayer of the faithful included the confession of sins and a request for forgiveness from God.[3] In a specific way, it included a confession of sins committed in the service of truth. A representative of the Roman Curia introduced the prayer: "Let us pray that each one of us, looking to the Lord Jesus, meek and humble of heart, will recognize that even men of the Church, in the name of faith and morals, have sometimes used methods not in keeping with the Gospel in the solemn duty of defending the truth."

Pope John Paul II continued with the following prayer:

> Lord, God of all men and women, in certain periods of history Christians have at times given in to intolerance and have not been faithful to the great commandment of love, sullying in this way the face of the Church, your Spouse.
> Have mercy on your sinful children and accept our resolve to seek and promote truth in the gentleness of charity, in the firm knowledge that truth can prevail only in virtue of truth itself. We ask this through Christ our Lord.

Almost two years earlier, at the request of Pope John Paul II, historians and theologians studied the Inquisition. They presented the results at an international conference and in an impressive published volume (Borromeo 2003). One of the conclusions of the scholars involved in the project was that from the thirteenth century onward, special commissions (inquisitors) were delegated by the Apostolic See to fight heresy in certain regions. Gradually, this institution became permanent and developed. Ecclesiastical and civil tribunals held about 100,000 trials according to procedures set by the Inquisition. In less than 100 cases, ecclesiastical tribunals condemned the accused to death by fire. The work demystified certain myths and legends surrounding the Inquisition that arose in an atmosphere of anti-Catholicism. The same goes for the processes against witches: often the church was not even involved in such affairs, but civil authorities were very active (Monballyu 1994, 1996). Indeed, processes against witches not only took place in Catholic areas, but also in Protestant areas.

No matter the actual involvement of the Roman Catholic Church in extreme acts of religious intolerance, it is definitely important to take a hermeneutic look at its own teachings on religious liberty and the search for and protection of the truth. The teaching of the Second Vatican Council is the central point of attention in this chapter in connection with the teachings of the popes leading to Vatican II.

With the announcement of an ecumenical council on January 25, 1959, Pope John XXIII envisioned an *aggiornamento* of the Catholic Church. At the same time, he also announced two other events: (1) a synod for the diocese of Rome and (2) the revision of the 1917 Code of Canon Law.[4] For about twenty-five years, this revision of the Code of Canon Law would dominate, in one way or another, the discussions among canon lawyers and even theologians. The promulgation of the 1983 Code of Canon Law[5] would mark the end of this revision process and the beginning of a new era: the application of the revised law of the church. The teachings of Vatican II are important documents for the life of the Roman Catholic Church, and the conciliar debates can enlighten us in the interpretation of these documents.[6]

The Second Vatican Council produced a number of documents, namely sixteen, organized in three categories: four constitutions, three declarations, and nine decrees. Among the four constitutions rank the dogmatic constitution on Divine Revelation *Dei verbum* (Vatican II 1966a), the dogmatic constitution on the church *Lumen gentium* (Vatican II 1965a), the constitution on the sacred liturgy *Sacrosanctum Concilium* (Vatican II 1964a), and the pastoral constitution on the church in the modern world *Gaudium et spes* (Vatican II 1966b). The nine decrees are the decree *Ad gentes* on the mission activity of the church (Vatican II 1966c), the decree on the ministry and life of priests *Presbyterorum Ordinis* (Vatican II 1966d), the decree on the apostolate of the laity *Apostolicam actuositatem* (Vatican II 1966e), the decree on priestly training *Optatam totius* (Vatican II 1966f), the decree on the adaptation and renewal of religious life *Perfectae caritatis* (Vatican II 1966g), the decree concerning the pastoral office of bishops in the church *Christus Dominus* (Vatican II 1966h), the decree on ecumenism *Unitatis redintegratio* (Vatican II 1965b), the decree on the catholic churches of the eastern rite *Orientalium Ecclesiarum* (Vatican II 1965c), and finally the decree on the media of social communications *Inter mirifica* (Vatican II 1964b). The three declarations are the declaration on Christian education *Gravissimum educationis* (Vatican II 1966i), the declaration on the relation of the church to non-Christian religions *Nostra aetate* (Vatican II 1966j), and the declaration on religious freedom *Dignitatis humanae* (Vatican II 1966k).

This chapter will examine the traditional teachings of the Roman Catholic Church on religious freedom. In part two, the renewed understanding of that religious freedom since the Second Vatican Council will be covered. Is this a renewed understanding, or a new interpretation of the same teaching? Or is the teaching of Vatican II on religious freedom a rupture with the past?

The Roman Catholic Church and Religious Tolerance or Religious Freedom

The traditional teaching of the Roman Catholic Church on religious freedom can be found in the classical handbooks. One of those handbooks, the *Institutiones iuris publici ecclesiastici*, was published by Alfredo Ottaviani (Ottaviani 1958–1960; Hendriks 1987, 1993), cardinal and at the time secretary of the Holy Office (now the Congregation for the Doctrine of the Faith). The key notion for a good understanding of the traditional teaching of the church on religious freedom is the concept of the *societas perfecta* (Granfield 1979, 1982). Once it is clear what this concept means, the consequences are also clear: freedom for one, tolerance at most for the rest. The teaching of the Roman Catholic Church on religious freedom is also closely connected with its view on the relationship between church and state.

The Idea of a Societas Perfecta

Since the concept of *societas perfecta* is essential for a good understanding of the traditional vision of the Roman Catholic Church on religious freedom, it is necessary first to know what it means. A *societas perfecta* or perfect society is a society that in itself possesses all necessary means and tools to achieve its goal.[7] Joseph Kleutgen offers a helpful definition of the *societas perfecta*. As a side note, Kleutgen was a Jesuit who contributed to the drafting of the documents of Vatican I. In his view, "a *societas perfecta* is a society, distinct from every other assembly of men, which moves towards its proper end and by its own ways and reasons, which is absolute, complete and sufficient in itself to attain those things which pertain to it and which is neither subject to, joined as a part, or mixed and confused with any society."[8]

Pope Benedict XV used the term *societas perfecta* in his apostolic constitution *Providentissima Mater Ecclesia* promulgating the 1917 Code of Canon Law.[9] In the code, however, the term *societas perfecta* is not used, but it is clear that it is the underlying idea of the code.

According to the traditional teaching of the church, there are only two such perfect societies: the state and the church. While the state is the highest instance in the temporal, worldly sphere, the church is the highest authority in spiritual matters. Huysmans points out that comparison with the political state power emphasizes that the ecclesiastical jurisdiction is directed to the eternal or supernatural salvation of all the baptized, as distinct from their earthly well-being. The latter is the responsibility of the state. Based on its orientation toward salvation, the holder of ecclesiastical jurisdiction has the required competence to guide the faithful to this salvation. Such an approach leads to the consequence that ecclesiastical laws do not bind this holder of ecclesiastical jurisdiction, should that be necessary or useful for the church. In other words, if the ecclesiastical authority believes something is necessary or useful for the church, and more in particular for the salvation of souls, he can act even against ecclesiastical laws (Huysmans 1996, 10; Ottaviani 1958–1960, 178, 112).

Although both are the highest authorities in their respective spheres, one has certain precedence over the other: the church must have precedence over the state, since spiritual matters are more important than temporal matters.

In both societies—the church and the state—authority comes from God. Therefore, people exercising civil authority must do so in accordance with God's law and its demands. Indeed, those in charge of civil society, the civil rulers, have a personal moral obligation to be good and just rulers and to fulfill diligently their mission given by God. Consequently, the ruler has a personal liability and the state, represented by this ruler, has moral obligations to proclaim the truth and thus to protect the true religion. The state must honor God and listen to the magisterium of the church. From this perspective, the Catholic state is the ideal (Hendriks 1993, 127).

Such a vision resides in the encyclical *Quanta cura* and the *Syllabus errorum* (Noether 1968). Both documents comprise the teaching of the church on the ideal organization of the state. On December 8, 1864, Pius IX published his encyclical *Quanta cura* (Denzinger and Hünermann 1991). Here, Pope Pius IX calls it an "insanity" to claim that "liberty of conscience and worship is each man's personal right, which ought to be legally proclaimed and asserted in every rightly constituted society; and that a right resides in the citizens to an absolute liberty, which should be restrained by no authority whether ecclesiastical or civil, whereby they may be able openly and publicly to manifest and declare any of their ideas whatever, either by word of mouth, by the press, or in any other way."[10]

Pope Pius IX also seems to condemn certain forms of democracy, when he writes "some . . . dare to proclaim that 'the people's will, manifested by what is called public opinion or in some other way, constitutes a supreme law, free from all divine and human control; and that in the political order accomplished facts, from the very circumstance that they are accomplished, have the force of right.'"

On the same day, the *Syllabus errorum* was promulgated (Denzinger and Hünermann 1991, 2901–80). While the encyclical *Quanta cura* focuses on issues such as the relations between church and state and the freedom of speech and of religion, the *Syllabus errorum* is a list of concrete errors in a number of areas. These errors are contrary to the teaching of the church and must be avoided. The document contains no new elements, but is a collection of previous papal statements on modern issues, hence the reference at the end of each statement to the specific document upon which the statement is based. In the context of the present contribution, the following errors are relevant:

> The Church is not a true and perfect society, entirely free—nor is she endowed with proper and perpetual rights of her own, conferred upon her by her Divine Founder; but it appertains to the civil power to define what are the rights of the Church, and the limits within which she may exercise those rights.[11]

The ecclesiastical power ought not to exercise its authority without the permission and assent of the civil government.[12]
The Church has not the power of defining dogmatically that the religion of the Catholic Church is the only true religion.[13]

In the vision of *Quanta cura* and the *Syllabus errorum*, a state organized on democratic principles constitutes a tricky endeavor as that could endanger the protection and promotion of the true faith by the state.

Religious Freedom or Religious Tolerance?

According to the traditional teaching of the church, at most only religious tolerance is possible. The traditional doctrine is the doctrine of the thesis and hypothesis. Félix Dupanloup, Bishop of Orleans (1849–1878) formulated the doctrine that was originally an interpretation of the *Syllabus errorum*. According to the thesis, the state has the duty to protect exclusively the true religion, represented by the Roman Catholic church. The hypothesis, however, took into consideration that circumstances could give the state the possibility to tolerate the freedom of those who did not share the Catholic faith (Troisfontaines 2007). That does not come as a surprise, since the only true religion is the religion wanted and founded by Christ. Therefore, it is incorrect to state that everyone has the freedom to choose his own religion. Civil authorities might have sufficient arguments to tolerate other religions than the Roman Catholic religion, but tolerance is not a right, or, in other words, while the state might tolerate other religions, there is no such right as religious freedom. Moreover, the state has the duty and obligation to protect and promote the Roman Catholic religion, as far as possible in any given situation. The aforementioned *Syllabus errorum* clearly expresses this idea. Pope Pius IX condemned religious freedom and labeled the following proposition as erroneous: Every man is free to embrace and profess that religion which, guided by the light of reason, he shall consider true.[14] Furthermore, as erroneous is also condemned the permission to grant the public exercise of non-Catholic worship in a Catholic country, as formulated in the following proposition: Hence it has been wisely decided by law, in some Catholic countries, that persons coming to reside therein shall enjoy the public exercise of their own peculiar worship.[15]

Evolution in the Thinking of the Church?

There is, of course, a close link between the form of government and religious liberty. In the liberal democracy, citizens have rights, including the right to religious liberty. Such is problematic from the traditional perspective. Indeed, the state has to protect and to promote the one true religion. What, then, is the attitude of the Roman Catholic Church vis-à-vis certain forms of government? While the encyclical *Quanta cura* and the *Syllabus errorum* did not directly condemn democratic forms of government, Pope Leo XIII approached the matter from a positive side, first with his encyclical *Diuturnum illud* (June 29, 1881; Pope Leo XIII 1881) and later in his encyclical *Immortale Dei* (November 1, 1885; Pope Leo XIII 1885). He declared that the democratic form of government is not against the teaching of the Catholic Church and that it is acceptable that people share in the government of their country. The church does not reject any form of government that is suitable for taking care of the welfare of the people. However, it is important to note that this concerns only the designation of those who will exercise power in the state; in no way does it affect the content of that power. The basis of a community and power is not just a contract between humans. In both encyclicals, Pope Leo XIII emphasizes that according to St. Paul's letter to the Romans (13:1) all power comes from God (Fawkes 1918; Rommen 1950; Sigmund 1987). Pope Pius XI states in the encyclical *Divini Redemptoris* (March 19, 1937) that "society is for man and not vice versa."[16]

Pope Pius XII (1939–1958) laid down some of the fundamentals of the church's current teaching on religious freedom, more particularly in his Christmas addresses of 1942 and 1944. He accepted the self-understanding of democratic regimes about the nature and scope of their authority, namely that they are, as governments, legally limited by constitutions and morally obliged by a commitment to human rights (Pope Pius XII 1943, 1944; Hittinger 2008). In his encyclical *Pacem in terris* (April 11, 1963; Pope John XXIII 1963), Pope John XXIII (1958–1963) declared that authority or power coming from God should not be seen as an obstacle for the people in the election of their leaders and to set the methods and the limits for the exercise of power. In the pastoral constitution *Gaudium et spes*, the democratic form of government and an active participation of citizens in the government of their country is recommended.[17]

Pope Paul VI (1963–1978), in his apostolic letter *Octogesima adveniens* (May 14, 1971; Pope Paul VI 1971) to Cardinal Maurice Roy, President of the Council of the Laity and of the Pontifical Commission for Justice and Peace, on the occasion of the eightieth anniversary of the encyclical *Rerum Novarum*, goes even further and writes that preference should be given to a democratic form of government in which the people can participate as much as possible. "In order to counterbalance increasing technocracy, modern forms of democracy must be devised, not only making it possible for each man to become informed and to express himself, but also by involving him in a shared responsibility."[18]

Obviously, this new understanding of the role of the state was to lead to a different approach of religious freedom. A state that can judge religious affairs and accept the truth of the Catholic faith, and that has the task to protect the truth and the true church, cannot grant religious freedom. At most, it may tolerate other religions because of specific circumstances and because of the freedom inherent in the act of faith. If, however, civil authorities become merely service-oriented, responsible for the temporal general well being, then the state has no supporting function for the church (Hendriks 1993, 130). The texts of the Second Vatican Council, and more in particular *Gaudium et spes*, together with the declaration *Dignitatis humanae* and the declaration *Nostra aetate*, are witnesses of an evolution in the mind of the church. Finally, the church came to terms with the principles of the French Revolution of 1789 and the ideas of a liberal democracy. While the *Syllabus errorum* was a firm attack against modernism and in the historical context of 1864 understandable, the documents of Vatican II have a positive tone and attitude toward modern society and constitute in a way, as then Cardinal Ratzinger, now Pope Benedict XVI, called it, a "countersyllabus."[19]

Declaration on Religious Freedom *Dignitatis Humanae*

On December 7, 1965, Pope Paul VI promulgated the declaration on Religious Freedom, called *Dignitatis humanae* (Carter 1976; Hittinger 2008; Salvini 2008). A not very well-known document of the Second Vatican Council, based on its title and description, some presume a content without having read the document and assume that the Roman Catholic Church promotes religious liberty as proclaimed in constitutions and international treaties. That is not true. However, the declaration is exceptionally important. Roughly, twenty years after the declaration on religious freedom by the World Council of Churches, the Roman Catholic Church produced its own declaration on religious freedom.

The Declaration on Religious Freedom in a Broader Context

Reading and understanding the Declaration on Religious Freedom, *Dignitatis humanae*, requires a broader context. This context is first that of the church. While preparing for the Second Vatican Council and commenting on draft texts, attention was paid to the position of the Roman Catholic Church toward religious freedom. Cardinal Alfrink, archbishop of Utrecht, stated in an intervention on December 1, 1962, that the world was looking forward to what the Roman Catholic Church would have to say about religious freedom, rather than listening again to a statement on the rights of the church (van Schaik 1997, 333).

There is also the secular context within which the declaration finds its own place. In the aftermath of World War II, and most likely because of the atrocities committed during this frightful confrontation, the idea of reaffirming, guaranteeing, and protecting human rights through international declarations and treaties gained importance and was brought into practice. The affirmation of religious freedom is a habitual part of such declarations and treaties. One of the first international documents in the postwar context is of course the Universal Declaration of Human Rights. This General Assembly of the United Nations adopted the declaration on December 10, 1948 (Lauterpacht 1948; Hannum 1995–96). The assembly called upon all member countries to publicize the text of the declaration and "to cause it to be disseminated, displayed, read and expounded principally in schools and other educational institutions, without distinction based on the political status of countries or territories" (G.A. Res. 217). The freedom of thought, conscience and religion, without any limitation, is in article 18. Although the declaration as such is not formally binding, it was certainly "a breakthrough and a revolution in international relations and has remained a continuing source of inspiration since 1948" (Stamatopoulou 1998, 1998–99). Other international instruments were deemed necessary for the adequate implementation and protection of human rights. One of these is the International Covenant on Civil and Political Rights. Adopted and opened for signature by United Nations General Assembly Resolution 2200A (XXI) on December 16, 1966, the covenant entered into force on 23 March 1976 (Starr 1967). The right to religious freedom is included in article 18 of this text.

In a European context, the European Convention for the Protection of Human Rights, signed in Rome on November 4, 1950, by twelve member states of the Council of Europe, goes further in the same direction (Robertson 1950; Schaffer 1991; Black-Branch 1996–97; Evans 1997; Ovey and White 2006). The authors of the convention had the 1948 UN Universal Declaration of Human Rights in mind, but added a system for the collective enforcement of certain rights set out in the Universal Declaration. The convention provided a mechanism for the enforcement of the obligations entered into by the contracting states: the European Commission of Human Rights, the European Court of Human Rights (the two are now replaced by one full-time Court), and the Committee of Ministers of the Council of Europe.[20] As such, this is a unique system for a more effective protection of human rights, as guaranteed by the convention. The convention also proclaimed as a principle, the freedom of religion in article 9, while allowing strict exceptions:

1. Everyone has the right to freedom of thought, conscience, and religion; this right includes freedom to change his religion or belief and freedom, either alone or in community with others and in public or private, to manifest his religion or belief, in worship, teaching, practice, and observance.
2. Freedom to manifest one's religion or beliefs shall be subject only to such limitations as are prescribed by law and are necessary in a democratic society in the interests of public safety, for the protection of public order, health or morals, or for the protection of the rights and freedoms of others.

As these international documents had already emerged in a different postwar context, they were there at the time of Vatican II. Moreover, at its first assembly in Amsterdam in August 1948, the World Council of Churches (WCC) adopted a Declaration on Religious Freedom (Martin and Stahke 1998; Neophitos 1974). The Declaration of the WCC contains four parts, or rather, four aspects of religious freedom. In this document, these are called "rights of religious freedom," which means that there is, at least in the spirit of this declaration, more than one right.

Thus, from the contextual perspective, the Declaration *Dignitatis humanae* did not come as a surprise.

Declaration Nostra Aetate

Before we deal with the Declaration *Dignitatis humanae*, let's briefly turn to the Declaration *Nostra aetate*. It is the shortest document of the Second Vatican Council. Pope John XXIII asked the Secretariat for the Unity of the Christians to prepare a declaration on the Jewish people.[21] Later, in 1962–63, it was decided that the document would also deal with the non-Christian religions in general, perhaps to counter protests from Arab countries (Hendriks 1993, 120). While the Declaration *Dignitatis humanae* deals with religious freedom, the Declaration *Nostra aetate* focuses on relations with non-Christian religions.

The document contains five parts or sections. In the opening paragraph, the globalized world is the point of reference because there is more mobility and because people of various nations encounter each other on a daily basis, the church wants to pay attention to its relationship to non-Christian religions. "In our age, when the human race is being daily brought closer together and contacts between the various nations are becoming more frequent, the church is giving closer attention to its relation to non-Christian religions."[22]

The first two paragraphs are general in nature. The Catholic Church praises, recognizes, and respects the ways of acting and living and the precepts and teachings of each religion. At the same time, however, the church confirms that she continues to preach Christ, in whom people find the fullness of religious life and in whom God has reconciled all things. In other words, the Roman Catholic Church looks with respect to other religious traditions, but in no way is the Declaration *Nostra aetate* a sign of indifference or indication that all religions are equal and equally lead to salvation; such relativism cannot be read in any of the conciliar texts.[23]

The third and fourth paragraphs focus on the Muslims and Jews respectively. In spite of the considerable dissensions and enmities between Christians and Muslims over the course of centuries, the council urges all parties to educate themselves toward sincere mutual understanding. The fourth paragraph, the paragraph on the Jews, is rather lengthy. It mentions and confirms the many ties between the Jews and the Roman Catholic Church as well as confirming the Jewish roots of Christianity. Because of the common spiritual heritage of Christians and Jews, the paragraph draws three conclusions: (1) biblical and theological studies and dialogues through which Christians and Jews get to better know each other are recommended; (2) the Jews should not be presented as rejected by God and accursed, and such misrepresentation should be removed from all religious instruction and preaching; and (3) the church deplores feelings of hatred, persecutions, and demonstrations of anti-Semitism against the Jews at whatever time and by whomever.

In the fifth and concluding paragraph, the church condemns as foreign to the mind of Christ any kind of discrimination whatsoever between people, or harassment of them, done because of race or color, class, or religion.

Declaration Dignitatis Humanae

Originally, the Declaration *Dignitatis humanae* was not a separate document. While it was understood that the Second Vatican Council would address the issue of religious freedom in the civil sphere, the earlier drafts of such a statement in relationship between church and state were at first included in the *schema* on the church. Later on, the subject moved to the *schema* on ecumenism. Finally, the *schema* on religious freedom had become an independent document. The Secretariat for the Unity of the Christians would play an important role in the drafting process of a document on religious liberty (Declerck and Troisfontaines n.d.; Hittinger 1993, 359; Pavan 1967; Scatena 2003; Tagle 2003; Troisfontaines 2007). The American Jesuit John Courtney Murray and the American view on religious liberty also influence the document. The state must guarantee the free exercise of religion and should not favor any religion at all. While before the council the writings of Murray were under investigation by the Holy Office, one cannot ignore his contribution to the Declaration *Dignitatis humanae* (Connell 1948; Fenton 1952; Gonnet 1994; Kennedy 1995; Komonchak 1996, 1999). Pope Paul VI was to visit New York and the UN on October 4, 1965. A general vote was organized: the Fathers of the council were asked whether they would approve such a document, knowing that it needed correction. On September 21, 1965, this vote was organized. With 2,222 Fathers present, only 224 voted against (*non placet*). The pope could visit the UN. On November 19, 1965, the Fathers voted on the amended text with 1,954 voting in favor (*placet*), 249 against (*non placet*), and 13 votes were invalid. The final vote took place on December 7, 1965: 2,308 voted in favor of the document (*placet*), while 70 voted against (*non placet*; Troisfontaines 2007, 773–76; Salvini 2008, 338). The Declaration *Dignitatis humanae* on religious freedom would, together with the liturgical reforms of the Second Vatican Council, constitute the major cause for the schism with Archbishop Marcel Lefebvre and his followers (Congrégation pour les Évêques 1988, 789; Pope John Paul II 1988: 1495–98; Perrin 1989).

The right to religious freedom, understood in the sense that one cannot be forced to be baptized, is part of the tradition of the church. The church has always taught that nobody may be forced to receive baptism. This principle is also expressed in the current Code of Canon Law (1983), in which we find the rule that an adult in danger of death cannot be baptized unless he has manifested in one way or another the intention to receive baptism: "C. 865 §2. An adult in danger of death can be baptized if, having some knowledge of the principal truths of the faith, the person has manifested in any way at all the intention to receive baptism and promises to observe the commandments of the Christian religion."[24]

The Declaration *Dignitatis humanae* contains three parts: after an introduction, the first part sets out the general principles of religious freedom, while the second part deals with religious freedom in light of revelation.

The Declaration *Dignitatis humanae* starts in a positive way with the dignity of each human person. Indeed, human dignity is so important that the name of the document reflects it, *Dignitatis humanae*. The first paragraph sketches the evolution of civil society. As the dignity of the human person increasingly gains recognition, people should enjoy the use of their own responsible judgment and freedom and decide on their actions based on duty and conscience, without external pressure or coercion. In this light, there is a demand that the law set boundaries of the government, in order to assure this freedom of the people is unlimited. In the same first paragraph, the council proclaims that God has himself made known to the human race and that the one and only true religion subsists in the catholic and apostolic church. All people are bound to seek the truth, especially about God and his church, and, once found, bound to embrace and keep this truth. This obligation touches human conscience. The demand of people for religious freedom in carrying out their duty to worship God concerns the freedom from compulsion in civil society. While in the introduction to the declaration, the Fathers of the council affirm that the traditional Catholic teaching on the moral obligation of individuals and societies toward the true religion and the one Church of Christ remains intact. In respect of religious freedom, the council sets out to develop the teaching of recent popes on the inviolable rights of the human person and on regulating society by law.

The second paragraph proclaims the right to religious freedom for everyone. Religious freedom is defined here as the immunity from coercion by individuals, groups or any human power. Nobody should be forced to act against her or his conscience in religious matters and, vice versa, nobody should be prevented from acting according to that conscience, whether in private or in public, whether alone or in association with others. The declaration recognizes that there are due limits. Freedom of religion is based on the dignity of the human person and hence should be recognized in the law of a civil society in such a way that it becomes a civil right. Yet, human dignity has another side: it entails the obligation to seek the truth.

In paragraph three of the declaration, attention goes to the search for the truth. While this is an internal act, voluntary and free, as is the practice of religion, the social nature of human beings requires that they can express their religious acts externally: free and communal practice of religion within the limits set by due public order must be possible. It is the task and duty of the state to guarantee that.

Freedom from coercion in religion must also be allowed when people act together. The fourth paragraph deals with the collective aspect of religious freedom. Religious communities have the right to train their own ministers, to communicate with religious authorities, to construct buildings for religious purposes and to acquire and use appropriate property. Furthermore, these communities also have the right to teach and give witness to their faith.

In the fifth paragraph, the religious life of the family—seen as a little society on its own—is the subject matter. Every family has the right to organize its own religious life at home under the supervision of the parents. In this context, the state has the duty to recognize the right of parents to have a truly free choice of schools or other means of education.

The protection of the right to religious freedom is the subject of paragraph six. Every civil authority must safeguard and promote the inviolable human rights. Therefore, the state is obliged to protect the religious freedom of all citizens effectively by just laws and other suitable means, and must ensure favorable conditions for fostering religious life.

The right to religious freedom is not limitless, as explained in paragraph seven. In the use of their rights, the moral law to respect the rights of others restricts individuals and social groups. Moreover, society has the right to protect itself against abuses that can occur under the guise of religious freedom. The state must provide the necessary guarantees.

Finally, paragraph eight deals with the duty to educate people so that they can make their own judgments and decisions in light of truth.

The second part of the declaration focuses on religious freedom in the light of revelation. Here again, there is confirmation that no one must be forced to embrace the faith against his or her will: the act of faith is by its very nature voluntary. The apostles followed Christ's word and example and strove to convert people, not by coercion, but by the power of God's message. In human society and in the presence of any civil power, the church claims for herself spiritual authority. The faithful likewise have the civil right not to be prevented from living their lives as conscience directs. The council puts responsibility in the hands of the civil powers to protect and promote religious freedom and to make sure that this freedom receives not merely solemn recognition in a constitution or an international text, but real, practical application and makes life for individual believers and for religious communities possible.

In sum, the Declaration *Dignitatis humanae* is an elaboration of the teaching of the recent popes in matters of religious freedom. The subject matter links with the vision on the tasks of the state or civil authorities closely. In no way does the declaration promote the freedom to choose any religion whatsoever. The document contains the teachings of the church on the duty of civil powers. Where in the past, civil powers were to protect and promote the one true faith, namely the Roman Catholic Church, now the civil powers must grant the freedom to seek the truth. The state cannot limit the right to search for the truth, namely that which is found fully only in the Roman Catholic Church. In other words, the message is still the same, but the method has changed.

Conclusion

Did the Declaration *Dignitatis humanae* change the teaching of the Roman Catholic Church on religious freedom? Alternatively, is it merely a fine elaboration of earlier teachings of the church in this matter? That is not an easy question to answer. Some will say that, given the opposition against the declaration, the changes are considerable and not merely a change of tone. Others will say that the negative approach from the past—no liberty, tolerance at most—has been replaced by a positive attitude.

It seems fair to state that the teaching of the Roman Catholic Church has not considerably changed, but a renewed interpretation of the role of the state, related to changes in society and the rise of the multicultural society, has led to this fine-tuning. In the past, the church required the state to protect and promote the one true faith. With this declaration on religious freedom, the church claims the freedom for everyone to seek the truth. The state must guarantee this freedom. In other words, there can be no coercion on the part of the state. However, while other religions and denominations are valuable, the truth is found fully only in the Roman Catholic Church.

The declaration does not lead to relativism, but on the contrary emphasizes the duty of each human being to search for the truth. The dignity of the human person is key to the whole approach. Each human person is free, but has a moral duty to find the truth. Only Christ leads to salvation through the Roman Catholic Church. The state has a specific task: it must take care of the temporal well-being of its citizens. In this context, the state has the duty to protect the right to religious freedom, too, both for individuals and for religious communities.

In other words, the declaration does not recognize the freedom to believe whatsoever. It is thus somewhat misleading to call the document a declaration on religious freedom: that would give the impression that the church does not care about the truth. What it does proclaim is the freedom to search for the truth, a truth found only fully in the Roman Catholic Church. The ultimate goal is that all human beings may once find the way to Christ through the Roman Catholic Church. However, according to the declaration, that is not achievable with force and fear exercised by the state in an attempt to protect and promote the true faith, but only by guaranteeing the freedom for each human being to search that truth. This is, perhaps, the ultimate synthesis to which the dialectics of absolute truth and religious freedom for individual human beings could be lifted.

Notes

1. The text is available in English translation on the Web site of the Holy See: http://www.vatican.va.
2. For the text of the press conference, see http://212.77.1.245/news_services/bulletin/news/6618.php?index=6618&po_date=07.03.2000&lang=en.

3. The entire text of the universal prayer of the faithful of this celebration can be found on http://www.vatican.va/news_services/liturgy/documents/ns_lit_doc_20000312_prayer-day-pardon_en.html.
5. "Pronunciamo innanzi a voi, certo tremando un poco di commozione, ma insieme con umile risolutezza di proposito, il nome e la proposta della duplice celebrazione: di un Sinodo Diocesano per l'Urbe, e di un Concilio Ecumenico per la Chiesa Universale... Esse condurranno felicemente all'auspicato e atteso aggiornamento del Codice di Diritto Canonico" (Pope John XXIII 1959, 68).
6. Code of Canon Law (1998): All subsequent English translations of canons from this code will be taken from this source unless otherwise indicated.
7. For a comprehensive overview of the history of Vatican II, see Alberigo and Komonchak (1995-2006) and Alberigo (n.d.).
8. "Societas iuridice perfecta ea est quae bonum in suo ordine completum tamquam finem habens, ac media omnia ad illud consequendum iure possidens, est in suo ordine sibi sufficiens et independens, id est plena autonoma" (Ottaviani 1958–1960, 46, 23).
9. "Qua de causa ecclesia etiam iure merito societas perfecta dicta est: quippe quae ad finem proprium propriis viis et rationibus tendens, a quovis alio hominum coetu distincta, atque ita in se absoluta et completa est, ut sibi ad finem consequendum sufficiens, in iis, quae eo pertinent, nulli alii societati sive subiecta sive tanquam pars innexa sive permixta et confusa est" (Mansi 1961, 315).
10. All subsequent English translations of canons from this code will be taken from this source unless otherwise indicated. The beginning of the apostolic constitution reads as follows, "Providentissima Mater Ecclesia, ita a Conditore Christo constituta, ut omnibus instructa esset notis quae cuilibet perfectae societati congruunt, inde a suis primordiis, cum, Dominico obsequens mandato, docere ac regere omnes gentes incepit, aggressa est iam tum sacri ordinis virorum christianaeque plebis disciplinam datis legibus moderari ac tueri." In English: "That most provident Mother, the Church, endowed by her Divine Founder with all the requisites of a perfect society, when, in obedience to the Lord's mandate, she commenced in the very beginning of her existence to teach and govern all nations, undertook by promulgating laws the task of guiding and safeguarding the discipline of the clergy and the faithful" (Peters 2001).
11. Pope Pius IX refers in fact to the encyclical *Mirari vos* (August 15, 1832) of his predecessor Gregory XVI.
12. "Ecclesia non est vera perfectaque societas plane libera, nec pollet suis propriis et constantibus juribus sibi a divino suo fundatore collatis, sed civilis potestatis est definire quæ sint Ecclesiæ jura ac limites, intra quos eadem jura exercere queat" (Denzinger and Hünermann 1991, 2919, statement 19). Reference is made to Pope Pius IX, Allocution *Singulari quadam* (December 9, 1854).
13. "Ecclesiastica potestas suam auctoritatem exercere non debet absque civilis gubernii venia et assensu" (Denzinger and Hünermann 1991, 2920, statement 20). Here, reference is made to Pope Pius IX, Allocution *Meminit unusquisque* (September 30, 1861).

14. "Ecclesia non habet potestatem dogmatice definiendi, religionem Catholicæ Ecclesiæ esse unice veram religionem" (Denzinger and Hünermann 1991, 2921, statement 21). Reference made to the Damnatio *Multiplices inter* (June 10, 1851).
15. "Liberum cuique homini est eam amplecti ac profiteri religionem, quam rationis lumine quis ductus veram putaverit" (Denzinger and Hünermann 1991, 2915, statement 15). Reference is made to Pius IX, Allocution *Maxima quidem* (June 9, 1862), and to the Damnatio *Multiplices inter* (June 10, 1851).
16. "Hinc laudabiliter in quibusdam catholici nominis regionibus lege cautum est, ut hominibus illuc immigrantibus liceat publicum proprii cuiusque cultus exercitium habere" (Denzinger and Hünermann 1991, 2978, statement 78). Reference made to Pope Pius IX, Allocution *Acerbissimum* (September 27, 1852).
17. "Civitas homini, non homo" (Pope Pius XI 1937, 79).
18. GS 31 and 75.
19. "Ut vero gliscenti technicorum potestati obsistatur, novae popularis imperii formae inveniendae sunt, hodiernae vitae consentaneae, ita ut non modo cuique homini tribuatur facultas res cognoscendi suamque de iis opinionem exprimendi, verum etiam is communi munerum et officiorum susceptione obstringatur" (Pope Paul VI 1971, 436).
20. "If it is desirable to offer a diagnosis of the text as a whole, we might say that (in conjunction with the texts on religious liberty and world religions) it is a revision of the *Syllabus* of Pius IX, a kind of counter syllabus. Harnack, as we know, interpreted the *Syllabus* of Pius IX as nothing less than a declaration of war against his generation. This is correct insofar as the *Syllabus* established a line of demarcation against the determining forces of the nineteenth century: against the scientific and political world view of liberalism. In the struggle against modernism this twofold delimitation was ratified and strengthened. Since then many things have changed. The new ecclesiastical policy of Pius XI produced a certain type of openness toward a liberal understanding of the state. In a quiet but persistent struggle, exegesis and Church history adopted more and more the postulates of liberal science, and liberalism, too, was obliged to undergo many significant changes in the great political upheavals of the twentieth century. As a result, the one-sidedness of the position adopted by the Church under Pius IX and Pius X in response to the situation created by the new phase of history inaugurated by the French Revolution was, to a large extent, corrected *via facti*, especially in Central Europe, but there was still no basic statement of the relationship that should exist between the Church and the world that had come into existence after 1789 ... Let us be content to say here that the text serves as a counter syllabus and, as such, represents, on the part of the Church, an attempt at an official reconciliation with the new era inaugurated in 1789. Only from this perspective can we understand, on the one hand, its ghetto-mentality, of which we have spoken above; only from this perspective can we understand, on the other hand, the meaning of this remarkable meeting of Church and world. Basically, the word 'world' means the spirit of the modern era, in contrast to which the Church's group-consciousness saw

itself as a separate subject that now, after a war that had been in turn both hot and cold, was intent on dialogue and cooperation" (Ratzinger 1987, 381–82).
21. The Committee of Ministers of the Council of Europe is composed of the Ministers of Foreign Affairs of the Member States or their representatives.
22. The Secretariat for the Unity of the Christians was established in 1960 by Pope John XXIII, aside from the eleven antepreparatory commissions for the Second Vatican Ecumenical Council (1962–1965). The Secretariat had two tasks: establish and maintain contacts with the separated Christians, so that they would be able to follow the work of the Council, and study possibilities for reestablishing the union. In 1962, the Secretariat was given the rank of conciliar commission and was responsible for the preparation of a schema on ecumenism, which would later become the decree *Unitatis redintegratio*. The Secretariat would also collaborate intensively in the preparation of other important documents such as the decree *Orientalium Ecclesiarum*, the declaration *Nostra aetate* and the declaration *Dignitatis humanae*. After the Council, the Secretariat became the curial department responsible for the ecumenical dialogue, and since the last curial reform in 1988, through the apostolic constitution *Pastor Bonus* (June 28, 1988), the Secretariat became the Pontifical Council for Promoting Christian Unity (del Re 1998).
23. NA, 1: "Nostra aetate, in qua genus humanum in dies arctius unitur et necessitudines inter varios populos augentur, ecclesia attentius considerat quae sit sua habitudo ad religiones non-christianas." English translation from Tanner (1990). All subsequent English translations of documents of ecumenical councils are taken from this source, unless otherwise indicated. The original Latin text of the document is also taken from this source.
24. Such is confirmed in recent teachings. See Congregation for the Doctrine of the Faith (2000).
25. C. 865 § 2. Adultus, qui in periculo mortis versatur, baptizari potest si, aliquam de praecipuis fidei veritatibus cognitionem habens, quovis modo intentionem suam baptismum recipiendi manifestaverit et promittat se christianae religionis mandata esse servaturum. In the 1917 Code of Canon Law, this was formulated as follows: C. 752. § 2. In mortis autem periculo, si nequeat in praecipuis fidei mysteriis diligentius instrui, satis est, ad baptismum conferendum, ut aliquo modo ostendat se eisdem assentire serioque promittat se christianae religionis mandata servaturum.

9

Strangers and Residents

The Hermeneutic Challenge of Non-Jewish Minorities in Israel

Deborah Weissman

This chapter addresses the complicated question of majority and minority rights in Israel, from the point of view of the interpretation of classical Jewish texts. While not wishing to minimize the importance of political and security issues, this chapter will concentrate on the texts and their interpretations, with only secondary mention of their concrete political ramifications. The reason is that this book addresses "text and context, religion, and human rights," and Israel is a sovereign secular state whose actions are not necessarily motivated by the interpretation of religious texts. Generally speaking, *realpolitik* is the basis, rightly or wrongly understood (depending on one's personal, political point of view) of its decisions. However, many of the actors involved, especially the religious settlers and their opponents, are indeed motivated by religious texts and have various ways of interpreting them. Thus, the classical sources do bear some relevance on the complexities of the contemporary situation.

Another dimension of the complex contemporary situation is visible through the example of ancient texts that deal with the rights of non-Jews in the Land of Israel. First, most of those texts date from the pre-Islamic period, and some date even from the pre-Christian period. The non-Jews referenced in those texts were idol worshippers. That fact raises the question of whether the rules might be different with regard to adherents of monotheistic faiths. Second, the texts appeared before the rise of the modern nation-state. At that time, the notion of citizenship did not exist in the modern sense of the term. Thus, the texts, and those who read them, would not have recognized the important distinction between Palestinian Arabs who are citizens of the state of Israel and those who live in the occupied territories. Based on the above considerations, there are several questions to discuss. In general, how does the tradition look at non-Jews? In particular, how does it look at non-Jews living in the Land of Israel? Does the tradition offer a way to combine traditional religious commitments with modern democratic values?

Before delving into the texts themselves and the historical understanding involved, I would like to add one more point regarding contemporary reality. For almost thirty-five years, small but noteworthy groups within Israeli society have used the religious texts as a basis for opposition to the settlements and to other policies of the Israeli government. One of the best-known groups is Rabbis for Human Rights.[1] This organization unites rabbis from the various movements within Judaism. Another transdenominational group is the Inter-religious Coordinating Council in Israel.[2] A reform rabbi, Dr. Ron Kronish, founded the ICCI and it promotes interfaith dialogue in the service of peace. One of its most important projects is the *Kedem* Dialogue, which fosters dialogue and cooperation among Orthodox rabbis, imams, and priests.[3]

On the Orthodox side of the spectrum, a number of groups have remained as extraparliamentary movements, such as *Oz V'Shalom, Netivot Shalom*,[4] the now-defunct Religious Women for the Sanctity of Life, and *Meimad*.[5] Meimad became a political party and gained a seat in the Knesset (Israeli parliament), and usually runs as a faction on the Labor Party ticket. The leader of Meimad, Danish-born Rabbi Michael Melchior, has served in the Israeli cabinet for several terms and has brought a dovish approach based on his understanding of traditional Jewish religious values. On at least two occasions, Meimad has had two seats in the Knesset. Despite its position as a minority within the Orthodox community, its position finds expression.

I would argue that the existence of these groups, as well as the activities of dedicated religious Jews working in secular frameworks, such as Peace Now, attest to the possibility of a hermeneutic different from that of the hardcore, right-wing settler movement. Some of the groups might even be comfortable with the label "religious humanists." "Religious humanism" may seem oxymoronic because religion is theocentric, while humanism is anthropocentric. However, if religion supports the view that human beings are created in the image of God, then in both religion and humanism the Divine Image occupies the center.

Let us begin our journey with a story, related by Israel's Nobel Prize laureate for literature, S. Y. Agnon:[6]

Dr. Meir Weiss told me that when Hermann Cohen[7] was in Poland, he worshipped on Yom Kippur eve in a Chassidic house of prayer. When they reached the verses of *Sh'ma Kolenu*, there was a fervent awakening within the congregation. And when they arrived at, "For My house shall be called a house of prayer for all the nations", the *Ba'al Tefilla* wept. Hermann Cohen thought to himself, "How profoundly this Polish Jew must feel that great prophetic vision, when all nations will recognize that they are one, and all will worship in one house of prayer."

After the service, Cohen approached the *Ba'al Tefilla*, blessed him and asked, "Why did you weep so at that verse, 'For My house shall be called a house of prayer for all the nations?'" And the *Ba'al Tefilla* answered, "How shall I not weep, when the house of our holiness and glory shall be filled with *Goyim*?"[8]

A Traditional Dialectic

The Agnon story juxtaposes the liberal consciousness of Western European Jewry (as exemplified by Cohen) with the more traditional approach of the Eastern European Chassidim (represented by the *Ba'al Tefilla*). The dilemma, or, if you prefer, dialectic, between the universal and particular dimensions in a traditional approach can also be found in many passages from earlier rabbinic literature. In *Pirkei Avot* 3:14, for example, in the name of Rabbi Akiva, we read, "beloved is man (*adam*) for he was created in the image of God." In the tractate *Yevamot* of the Babylonian Talmud, however, the following appears in the name of R. Shimon bar Yocha, "you are called '*adam*,' and foreigners [the Hebrew reads *nochrim* or *goyim*, some translations give "idolaters" for *nochrim*] are not called '*adam*.'"[9] Is the lofty, apparently humanistic statement of Rabbi Akiva intended to apply only to his fellow Jews? Some would argue that this is indeed the case. That view seems highly unlikely, however, since Rabbi Akiva's dictum continues, "beloved are Israel for they were called the children of God." If *adam* and Israel were synonymous, the text would be redundant. Akiva's formulation certainly accords a special status to Israel, but doesn't necessarily detract from the uniqueness and worth of the entire human race.

Two different approaches, the universal and the particular, the concern for all of humankind and the special concern for our fellow Jews, have their foundations in traditional Jewish culture. Both themes are present in the High Holiday liturgy. On the one hand, "now, therefore, O Lord our God, impose Your awe upon all Your works, and Your fear upon all that You have created . . . that they may all form a single band to do Your will with a perfect heart." On the other hand, "give then glory, O Lord, unto Your people . . . joy to Your land, gladness to Your city." Are the universal and the particular to be understood as contradictory, complementary, or integrated in some more complex way?

Leon Roth, an important twentieth century Jewish philosopher, writes about this problem in an article titled "Moralization and Demoralization in Jewish Ethics" (1973). Roth makes reference to the famous *Mishnah* in *Sanhedrin* 4:5, "if any man saves a single soul from Israel, Scripture imputes it to him as though he had saved a whole world." Roth points out that in earlier manuscripts, the words "from Israel" were omitted. Indeed, in terms of the context—namely, the Creation of Adam—the words do seem to distort the simple meaning of the text. Roth refers to the process by which a more universal text becomes particularized as the demoralization of the text. He writes: "the addition of the word *me-Yisrael* (from Israel) produces a sudden, and ludicrous, deflation."

Moshe Greenberg, the great Bible scholar and teacher at the Hebrew University, pointed out the tremendous educational challenge we have today, particularly in Israel, to deal with questions of the universal and particular in our study of traditional Jewish culture. Greenberg is also a member of an interfaith dialogue group in Jerusalem known as the Rainbow.[10] Several years ago, the theme for the group's discussions was "Embarrassing Texts in our Respective Religious Traditions." Greenberg opened with a presentation on embarrassing texts in the Jewish tradition that negatively relate to non-Jews. His views appear in a Hebrew book published in 1984, *Al HaMikra v'Al HaYahadut*, and an English article published in 1996, "A Problematic Heritage: The Attitude towards the Gentile in the Jewish Tradition—An Israel Perspective." In the latter, Greenberg indicates that in Israel he became aware "that the main stream of Jewish thought is permeated by notions of the genetic spiritual superiority of Jews over gentiles" (1996, 23). To this, he responds: "I am more than ever convinced that the hold that Judaism will have on this and future generations will be gravely impaired unless these notions are neutralized by an internal reordering of traditional values—a reordering by which the cherished value of the universality and oneness of God is matched by an equally cherished value of the universality and oneness of humanity" (Greenberg 1996).

The problematic tendencies that Greenberg finds within the Jewish heritage originate in the Torah's notions of the separation and election of the people of Israel. Many texts express that view, from "you shall be My own treasure from among all peoples"[11] to "it is a people that shall dwell alone and not be reckoned among the nations."[12] These notions are articulated in a more balanced way in the prophets, especially Isaiah, in whose prophecy we find, "blessed be Egypt, My people, and Assyria, the work of My hands, and Israel, Mine Inheritance."[13] This passage implies that the election of Israel does not place it in a completely separate category from other nations (as in the famous *Midrash* on the word *ivri*).[14] Rather, Isaiah also develops the concept of Israel's role in the world as a "light unto the nations,"[15] in order that salvation may come to all. Moreover, in the prophet Micah's vision of the End of Days, there exists a universal harmonious order, "many nations shall go and say, 'Come ye, and let us go up to the mountain of the Lord ... and He will teach us of His ways, and we will walk in His paths'... For let all the peoples walk each one in the name of its god."[16] The last phrase would seem to imply that redemption would bring a balance of the universal and the particular.

These kinds of universalistic formulations found in the prophets are much less evident in rabbinic literature and later medieval texts. The work of Yehudah HaLevi is one example. According to Greenberg, the Kabbalah played the largest role in the development of the chauvinistic trend in Jewish thought. For example, Greenberg presents the work of Shmuel de Uzeida, a disciple of R. Isaac Luria in the sixteenth century, who denied that Gentiles were created in the image of God. These tendencies reached a peak, Greenberg maintains, in the writings of the *Maharal* of Prague, *Ba'al HaTanya*, the founder of the Chabad movement, and even HaRav Kook and some of his disciples. For the record, one can also find articulations of a much more universalistic approach in the writings of HaRav Kook, the elder. Some of those writers were mystics, not systematic philosophers. As a result, perhaps they can be forgiven certain inconsistencies in their belief systems. The accusation of racism in medieval writings may indeed be anachronistic. Yet, those writers have followers in contemporary Israeli religious society and their views have led to unfortunate acts of violence, culminating in the 1994 atrocity in the Cave of the Machpela, in which twenty-nine Muslim worshippers were killed as they bowed in prayer.

Concept of "Chosenness"

In dealing with the dialectic described above, our first challenge is to confront the implications of the concept of Jewish "chosenness." Clearly, an exhaustive study of the different approaches to this concept is beyond the scope of a short chapter. There have been many different approaches to this issue (*Commentary Magazine* 1996; Eisen 1983), ranging from a belief in the inherent superiority of Jews over other human beings to a rejection of the concept as chauvinistic, irrational, and inappropriate for a modern Jew (perhaps most notably in the work of Mordecai Kaplan, founder of the Reconstructionist movement; *Commentary Magazine* 1996, 121). The "Chosen People" have also been called "the Choosing People." These types of interpretations treated the concept of election as a component of the Abrahamic

Covenant, as the meaning of the Mosaic Revelation, or as an embarrassment and affront to our moral sensibilities. Eliezer Berkovits wrote, "God did not choose the Jews, but the people that God chose became the Jewish people as a result of their taking upon themselves the task and responsibility for the realization of Judaism" (*Commentary Magazine* 1996, 26).

Jacob Agus, in a critique of such attempts to reinterpret the concept of "chosenness," wrote: "It is not enough to resort to the usual homiletical devices—the Jews were chosen for service, not for lordship; they were given greater responsibilities; they were to consider themselves aristocrats of the spirit, endowed with the ardor of *noblesse oblige;* they were in the actual unfolding of their historic destiny the 'Suffering Servant' of humanity" (*Commentary Magazine* 1996, 12).

Agus perceived those attempts as apologetic. In their stead, he suggested the following: "As a component of faith, the feeling of being 'covenanted' should be generalized; every person should find a vocation and dedicate himself to it. So, too, the pride of belonging to a historic people should be universalized. All men [sic] should take pride in the noble achievements of their respective peoples, scrutinize their national feelings, and guard against their collective weaknesses, even as we Jews are bidden to do" (*Commentary Magazine* 1996, 13).

His suggestion seems to draw from the idea, first found in the works of Samson Raphael Hirsch[17] that every nation was chosen for some purpose. Nevertheless, it is difficult to deny certain unique features of Jewish history and culture. For example, few other peoples share the historical and geographical breadth of Jewish existence. The complex amalgam of religion and nationhood, the diaspora experience, the history of suffering and persecution, the modern renaissance—all of these taken together seem to point to a special heritage. Still, following Agus, we can offer the possibility that other nations might learn from the very dialectic of universalism and particularism with which we are concerned in this chapter. As Agus summarized, "we ought to be a chosen people, as example, not as exception" (*Commentary Magazine* 1996, 13).

The Golden Rule

Leviticus 19:18 is the biblical text that the Christian tradition refers to as "the Golden Rule." That passage reads, "you shall not take vengeance, nor bear any grudge against the children of your people, but you shall *love your neighbor as yourself*: I am the Lord" (emphasis added). Most readers of this text probably assume that it is of universal import, equally applicable, for example, to both Jews and non-Jews. Even Sara Schenirer, a leading

Orthodox figure in the early twentieth century and founder of Beis Ya'akov, the pioneering movement for girls' Torah education, says the following in *Em B'Yisroel* 2:75–78 (translation from *The Jewish Political Tradition* 1): "When we state that it is a mitzvah to love people, this means that it makes no difference who the person is, whether Jew or alien . . . Thus Abraham our father, through love and devotion, extended his hospitality to guests, dressing them and feeding them. He endangered his life for the sake of the King of Sodom and begged G-d's[18] mercy for Sodom and Gomorrah. Moses our master, too, was quick to come to the aid of alien shepherds and defended them from attackers."[19]

Another commentary, this time from northern Italy in the nineteenth century, states,

> *And love your neighbor as yourself* - Not that one should love every person as he actually loves himself, for that is impossible, and Rabbi Akiva already taught that "Your life takes precedent over your friend's life". Rather *as yourself* in the sense of *[your neighbor] who is like you* - as in [the verse] *for you are like unto Pharaoh*. So here too as well *Love your neighbor who is as yourself*; he is equal to you and similar to you in that he was also created in the image of God, he is a human being just as you are, and that includes all human beings, for they were all created in the divine image. The Torah concluded [in the passage] everything with this commandment, just as it began with *each man shall fear his mother and father*, because one who honors the human image and considers it excellences, treats himself and all other people well (R. Yitzhak Shemuel Reggio on Leviticus 19:18).[20]

These humanistic interpretations are not the only ones. Let us see how another very traditional approach might interpret Leviticus 19:18.

The Hebrew of the Torah is not easily translatable. The customary translation of *veahavta l'reyacha kamocha*—"you shall love your neighbor as yourself" (Leviticus 19:18)—seems to imply that all "neighbors", regardless of creed, are to be loved equally. This implication, based upon the inadequate translation of *reyacha*, is not accurate.

First let us observe the context in which the above phrase appears in the Torah: "You shall not hate *your brother* in your heart. You shall not take revenge or feel resentment against *the children of your people*, you shall love *your companion [reyacha]* as yourself." From this it is clear that "your companion" refers to the same category as "your brother" and "the children of your people", all explicitly referring to one's fellow Jew.

Thus we see that in the Torah, the Hebrew word *reyacha* explicitly means "your fellow Jew". It does not refer to anyone outside the Jewish faith. "Neighbor" is not an accurate translation for the word *reyacha*. The Hebrew

> word for "neighbor"' is *shachen*. The Hebrew word *reyah* means "a very close companion". Sometimes it is used to mean "spouse". Just as a Jewish soul is commanded to unite in marriage only with another Jewish soul, so there is also an explicit commandment in the Torah that a very close friendship and companionship with another should be established only with someone referred to as *reyah*. A Jew is not allowed to develop a very close relationship with a non-Jew for the simple reason that the non-Jew's faulty faith system might have negative influence on the Jew.
>
> The Jew is commanded to respect all human beings. The Torah prohibits any negative behavior toward a non-Jew, so long as he is not an enemy. He is instructed, however, not to become too close a companion to him. Thus the above verse, *veahavta l'reyacha kamocha*, "You shall love your neighbor as yourself", does not imply a universal neighbor. To be honest with the text, the parenthetical "a fellow Jew" must appear.

This quotation comes from the Web site called "The Inner Dimension: Authentic Jewish Mysticism."[21] It is based on the work of Rabbi Yitzchak Ginsburgh, a contemporary Israeli rabbi. It might be possible to marginalize Rabbi Ginsburgh, simply as a kind of fringe phenomenon. After all, he wrote a booklet praising Baruch Goldstein, the murderer who perpetrated the Hebron atrocity. Two points should be noted however: (1) Rabbi Ginsburgh's students, and those whom he influences, extend beyond the marginal fringe of those who supported the massacre and (2) the views he espouses have been part of mainstream Jewish legal thought for centuries. Must we then abandon the notion of a universal Golden Rule, at least in Jewish hermeneutics?

Rabbi Akiva, one of the most important second century rabbis, said the major principle of Torah is "love your neighbor as yourself." Another sage, Ben Azzai, argued that Genesis 5:1 is an even greater principle, "this is the book of the generations of Adam [the Hebrew could also mean 'man' or 'human being']."[22] Azzai's argument may revolve around whether it is preferable to base an ethical system on a subjective standard (i.e., "as you love yourself") or on the more objective statement of our common human origins. Some commentators have suggested Rabbi Akiva's formulation actually presents two commands—to love your neighbor, but also to love yourself. Thus, Ben Azzai's principle apparently solves two problems that might arise if we make Rabbi Akiva's principle the more authoritative: (1) what are we to do with people who do not love themselves, or, who love themselves in masochistic ways? (2) Ben Azzai has shown us that "Love thy neighbor as thyself" may be dangerous in that it can imply "'the neighbor *who is as thyself*.' All children of Adam—and the Hebrew phrase for that would be *b'nei Adam*, which means 'human beings'—are 'as ourselves,' not just the children of Abraham, Isaac and Jacob."

In Leviticus 19: 33–34, the *Torah* teaches, "and if a stranger should sojourn with you in your land, you shall not do him wrong. The stranger that sojourns with you shall be unto you as the home born among you, and you shall love him as yourself; for you were strangers in the Land of Egypt: I am the Lord your God."

These verses, I submit, teach us two things. First, in Leviticus 19:18, the "neighbor" referred to is, indeed, a "neighbor like yourself." Second, Ginsburgh and other commentators performed a serious disservice, at least educationally, by ignoring these later verses. The *Torah* does contain a message of love that is universal. That message is echoed in Genesis 5:1 and, indeed, in the first eleven chapters of Genesis, as a more universal introduction to the *Torah*. The universal themes of the *Torah* then appear in many of the later prophetic books. Thus, with regard to Leviticus 19:18, we can say that although the Bible contains universal messages, the above verse does not set forth a universal Golden Rule. Other verses, however, can function as such.

Theological Rationale

In a number of sources, Jews are commanded to "walk in the paths of the Lord."[23] This command is interpreted as *imitatio dei* that is, imitating the attributes and deeds of the Almighty. That process of imitation has been understood to include being compassionate and merciful, clothing the naked, visiting the sick, burying the dead, and comforting the mourners. The law, as codified by Maimonides and others, also mandates such behavior toward non-Jews by using the rabbinic phrase, *mipnei darkei shalom*. The phrase means "in the interests of peace," often interpreted as a social precaution. The Jewish community should be charitable toward the Gentiles for its own good, so that there will be no negative consequences, such as violent reprisals that result from their overly parochial behavior.

However, many commentators suggested a more literal interpretation of the phrase. The literal meaning is "because of the ways of Peace." If peace, as noted earlier, is one of the names of the Almighty, then Jews who are compassionate toward all human beings are indeed walking in the paths of God.[24] As an amateur theologian, I would like to add one additional consideration. Racism and xenophobia are widespread—indeed, almost universal—phenomena in human societies. As a student of anthropology, I learned that in many tribes, the words for "human being" are the same as the name of the tribe. Divine revelation, therefore, did not make us narrow and chauvinistic. Rather, divine revelation provided us with the revolutionary insight that all human beings are created in the Divine Image.

Thus, it would appear that the universal hermeneutic is more authentic than the particular. For those of us who see the Torah as having a transcendent source, a humanistic message may be the more religiously authentic of the two approaches.

Our Common Humanity

Given the above considerations, let us now examine how a Jewish religious-humanist hermeneutic might proceed. The Hebrew Bible (known to Christians as the "Old Testament") begins with eleven chapters about the creation of the world and the origins of humankind before it even comes to the first Hebrew, Abraham. Before the covenant made with Abraham's descendants (Genesis 17), we read about the Rainbow Covenant made with the children of Noah (Genesis 8:21–9:17). Rabbi Adin Steinsaltz, a contemporary scholar in Israel, comments on the discussion of the rainbow symbol in the *Talmud*, "the very form of the rainbow, not like a bow of war aimed at the earth, is in itself an indication that the rainbow is not a sign of war, but, on the contrary, a symbol of peace."[25]

Anyone conversant with the strictures of traditional Judaism knows Jewish law sets the Jewish people apart and demands of them various behaviors not demanded of other people. Strict dietary laws are one example. Even within this separation, we can find an intimation of unity, as in the following rabbinic homily:

> Twice in the Torah—once in Leviticus 11 and once in Deuteronomy 14—we find a list of nonkosher birds. Among those listed is the *chassida*, the stork. It would appear that the name of this bird is derived from the word *chessed*, "loving-kindness". Our great medieval biblical commentator Rashi, following the *Midrash*, asks, "Why is the bird called *chassida*? Because it performs acts of *chessed* by sharing its food with other storks." It took hundreds of years for the next logical question to be addressed; namely, then why isn't it Kosher? This question was asked in the 19th century by the Gerer Rebbe known as *Chiddushei HaRim*. The answer he gave: "Because it performs acts of *chessed* by sharing its food with other storks. Only with other storks."[26]

This short parable presents the strength and the weakness of religious communities: the dilemma of particularism and universalism. Strong particularistic communities do *chessed* toward members of their own group. The true question, however, is how do the religious communities relate to outsiders? A rabbinic statement teaches, "Who is a hero? The one who turns his enemy into his friend."[27] Even our (hopefully, temporary) enemy is a human being with the potential of becoming our friend.

A Vision and a System

The prophets gave us visions of a better world in the future, both on the macro level ("nation shall not live up sword against nation"[28]) and on the micro level ("but they shall sit everyone under his vine and under his figtree, and none shall make them afraid"[29]). In this is a vision of redemption: "For let all the peoples walk each one in the name of its god"[30] and the world will be full of righteousness, equity, and harmony. Often, in Jewish thought, the term for this vision is "the Messianic era." Human action with the aid of divine intervention can initiate it. The belief that it can come though human action is a shield against despair; the belief in the need for divine intervention is a shield against hubris.

How does such a lofty vision translate into a human program for living? Jewish culture, like Islam and some of the Eastern traditions, but unlike Christianity, emphasizes a legal system for the regulation of everyday life. That system, called *Halakha* (from the root "to walk") is like a *tao*, a path, which Jews are summoned to walk on a daily basis. The laws govern everything from eating to marital relations to business or medical ethics. The ideals embodied in the prophetic visions are concretized through incremental steps on a day-to-day basis. The educational philosophy underlying the *Halakha* emphasizes habituation, but not blindly. The biblical source for this approach is Exodus 24:7 when the people tell Moses, "All that the Lord has spoken, we will do and we will hearken." Sometimes, as an educational strategy, especially with children, one has to encourage and develop in them patterns or habits of good behavior, even before they understand all the reasons for the behavior. As they grow and mature, their understanding develops, along with their behavioral practices.

An ethical human being cannot be a blind, unquestioning conformist because new situations will arise in which he or she will have to exercise reasoned judgment to make ethical decisions. The actual definition of what is right and good in newly arising situations is a matter of discussion and debate, since the Holy Books did not describe every situation. The issue of whether one should be obedient to authority or exercise autonomous judgment is a classic question in Jewish thought (Safrai and Sagi 1997). Except for some ultra-Orthodox sects that might require someone to consult a rabbi before making any decision, most Jews believe the ideal mindset consists of faithfulness to the law through understanding, intentionality, and commitment to critical thought.

Lessons from Jewish History

Jewish history has been characterized as lachrymose or as "the history of literature and of suffering." Persecution has been a major part of the history of the Jewish people. Some Jews have drawn from this history very anti-Gentile lessons; others have learned the opposite. The story of the French Huguenot town of Le Chambon-sur-Lyon provides an example for this discussion. During World War II, 5,000 Christians saved approximately the same number of Jews. Pierre Sauvage, an American Jewish filmmaker hidden in the town as an infant, went back in the early 1980s to research the motivation for this impressive rescue operation. In his outstanding documentary *Weapons of the Spirit*, he reached the conclusion that several factors were responsible, including the inspired leadership of the local pastor, Father André Trocmé. The townspeople—a fierce, mountainous lot—had a long tradition of resisting the central authority in Paris. Ultimately, though, Sauvage maintained that the main reason for their resistance was the collective historical memory of having been persecuted as a religious minority in the seventeenth century. This, to be sure, was an echo of the biblical injunction, "And you must understand the soul of a stranger, for you were strangers in the land of Egypt."[31]

In his testimony before the English-American investigative commission in 1946, Rabbi Yitzchak HaLevi Herzog, chief rabbi of the Land of Israel said,

> False claims have been heard that a Jewish majority would act cruelly to a non-Jewish minority living amongst it. It has also been claimed that the non-Jewish religions would be hurt by the change of the present status of the Land of Israel and its becoming a Jewish community. Claims like these can be sounded only by those who forget that more than 3000 years ago, G-d could think of no better rationale for His commandment to the Jews to love the stranger than the memory of the injustice that was done to them in Egypt out of hate for the stranger. True, our exile has taught us to hate—to hate hatred.[32]

Given all that we have written above, a logical question arises: Why are there relatively few religious Jews in the "Peace Camp"?

Some would find the very formulation of the above question problematic. It assumes that people who disagree with the way the peace process in the Middle East is being conducted are opposed to peace. To quote a colleague,[33]

> They would presumably reply that they want peace no less than you but that . . . the more left-wing position will in fact not lead to peace but to more terror . . . The phrasing of the question presumes that the camp

favoring accommodation with the Palestinians should be called "the peace camp", implying that those who read the situation differently are not in favor of peace, and that is simply not correct. With the exception of extremists on both sides, most of the rest of us disagree not on peace as a goal but on what is likely to be attainable with the neighbors we happen to have, especially in light of what's actually happened on the ground since the beginning of the Oslo "peace process",[34] and even more, since the failure of Camp David.[35]

Still, many of the rabbis and other right-wing Orthodox Jews who talk about peace are referring to some ideal, messianic peace as described in the prophetic visions of the end of days, when "the lion will lie down with the lamb" (Isaiah 11:6). It is difficult to reconcile these prophecies with the fragmented reality represented in the actual world. Rabbi Michael Melchior, mentioned earlier, suggested that we should be striving for a "piece of peace."[36]

In line with the adage that "the perfect is the enemy of the good," the very prophetic messages that inspire us to work for peace in the long run, can sometimes get in the way of actually achieving some modicum of peace in the short run. Having said that, it would appear that there are a number of other reasons why the Orthodox in Israel remain alienated from the so called "peace camp."

1. The doves in Israel, largely secular in orientation, are often alienated from traditional Jewish symbols and rhetoric. Instead, their slogans are typically based on Western sources. A good example is Shalom Achshav, a Hebrew translation of "Peace Now," which is the largest and longest-lasting group in the Israeli peace camp. For some Orthodox Jews, the use of foreign terms and symbols is an example of cultural assimilation and should be rejected. Unfortunately, for some of the Orthodox Jews, one of the foreign values that must be rejected is democracy. That value is particularly suspect coming, as it does, out of Greek culture.[37]

2. There is an increasing awareness that, for Israel, achieving peace with the Palestinians involves giving up land that is part of the biblical *Eretz Yisrael*, or Land of Israel. For some Orthodox Jews, this is a religious transgression. Still, respected Orthodox authorities as disparate as Rabbi Ovadiah Yosef of the Sephardi Shas party, or the late Rabbi Joseph B. Soloveitchik of Yeshiva University permitted returning parts of the land in return for a viable peace settlement. I will not develop this point further, as it is concerned with ending the conflict between Israel and the Palestinians of the occupied territories. Our

present concern is the status of Arabs in Israel, no matter what the borders of the state may be.

3. For many religious Zionists, the state of Israel is "the beginning of the flowering of redemption."[38] In such a pre-Messianic situation, there is a reluctance to give away land, as well as a mystical fervor that clouds issues of *realpolitik*. A good example is the disengagement from Gaza, which many settlers refused to believe would happen at all, until it was over.
4. A religious ideology of "chosenness," as well as a history of persecution, led many Jews to distrust deeply the religious and ethnic "other." Again, this issue seems to hold greater weight for Orthodox Jews who may in general be more insular (this point would certainly be truer of ultra-Orthodox than of modern Orthodox Jews.) There is sometimes a reluctance to hold dialogue sessions between Israeli Orthodox schools and their Arab counterparts for fear that the mixing might lead to interdating or even intermarriage. This is true even when the Arabs are Israeli citizens, not Palestinians from the territories (perceived as "The Enemy").
5. Proportionally, the recent intifada (2000–2004) killed and injured more Orthodox than non-Orthodox Jews. One reason for this is singling out of Orthodox settlements in the Gaza Strip and the West Bank for attack. Several of the major attacks in Jerusalem were in specifically religious neighborhoods or bus lines to those neighborhoods. Finally, the Orthodox and traditional populations are, overall, less affluent than the secular population. As a result, when buses, bus stations, and open-air markets are attacked, a high percentage of the people who patronize them are religious Jews. Moreover, I would maintain that the events within both Israel and Palestine are happening within deeply wounded, posttraumatic societies.

Now that we have entered a realm of incredible complexity, it is time to return to the hermeneutical task. We now face the most difficult question of all: can traditional Jewish sources be reconciled with an acceptance of both the individual and group rights of non-Jews in the Land of Israel? Thus far, this chapter has proceeded in a descriptive-analytical mode. It is now time to interpret classical religious texts within a modern political context.

Status of *Gerim*

I would like to present a philosophical/*Halachic* controversy from my own perspective as an educator. Many contemporary rabbis and scholars noted that traditional Jewish sources characterize non-Jews in the Land of Israel by three different terms and different status. Idol worshippers are not permitted to reside in the Land of Israel. The biblical passages that speak most vehemently about conquest of the land and driving out its inhabitants refer to idolaters. Exodus 23:23–33 or Deuteronomy 7 are examples of such passages. According to most Jewish authorities in medieval and modern times, Muslims are not in this category.[39] Islam is generally recognized as a radically monotheistic faith. Some authorities would similarly exempt Christians (Greenberg 2004; HaLevi 2001), although the monotheistic status of Christianity is less clear-cut, especially because of the Trinitarian beliefs. The whole question of the contemporary relevance of the category idolater is a fascinating one, but it goes beyond the bounds of the present discussion (Halbertal and Margalit 1998). Having mentioned Muslims and Christians, however, it is important to quote from the thirteenth century Jewish scholar in Provence, R. Menachem HaMeiri. He distinguished "the nations who are constrained by the ways of religion and worship the Deity," (including Christians and Muslims) from others "who have not any religion and are unconcerned with the responsibilities of human society." Jews, he taught, have different legal obligations toward the two groups (Linzer 2004).

The two other terms used in the biblical derive from the root word *ger*, or stranger. First, there is the *ger tzedeq*, "the righteous stranger," who is a convert to Judaism and accepts all of the biblical and rabbinic legislation as binding. Second, there is the *ger toshav*, a "resident alien" or "stranger-sojourner." The term itself is interesting, even before we actually define it. It derives from two words that represent "dwelling" in Hebrew: *lagur* and *lashevet*. *Lagur* means a kind of temporary residency; *lashevet* means to strike roots (for example, see Genesis 47:4). What complicates matters, though, is that English translations of the Hebrew Bible often use the term "to sojourn" for both Hebrew words. The term *ger toshav* is, in one respect, an oxymoron. The Jewish legal system defines *ger toshav* as a non-idol-worshipping Gentile who accepts as binding the Seven Noachide Laws (Lichtenstein 1981). The laws are rabbinic extrapolation of the Rainbow Covenant with Noah in Genesis 9 and include (1) justice (an imperative to pursue social justice and a prohibition of any miscarriage of justice); (2) blasphemy; (3) idolatry; (4) illicit intercourse; (5) homicide; (6) theft; and (7) limb of a living creature (prohibits the eating of animal parts severed from a living animal).[40] Except for the seventh law, the others are basic moral and ethical laws found in most civilized societies. The seventh law may reflect the idea that eating flesh was forbidden to human beings until the Rainbow Covenant made after the Flood. In addition, biblical dietary laws teach a reverence for life. Thus, a *ger toshav* is a civilized, law-abiding worshipper of the One God, who is not part of the Covenant of Israel. Such a Gentile may remain in the Land of Israel.

To be fair, we must indicate that there are some extreme approaches regarding the *gerim toshavim*. For example, even Maimonides does not permit them in the Holy City of Jerusalem, but only in other parts of the Land. Other Halakhic authorities require them to recognize the revelation given to Israel, although they are not a part of it. Some even require them to recognize the Jewish claim over the entire Land of Israel (Steiner n.d.). To complicate the issue further, some authorities say that we are not permitted to receive *gerim toshavim* without a Sanhedrin. For lack of a better alternative, the liberal approach taken toward non-Jewish minorities today generally relies on this legal category of the *ger toshav*.

Amid this whole discussion, there is a particular challenge when we examine the text in its context. How can Palestinian Arabs be "strangers" or "aliens" in their own land? Can the category of *ger* apply to them, or must we coin a new phrase such as "b'nei HaAretz," which would literally translate as "children of the Land"? It is offensive to hear the term strangers applied to Palestinian Arabs. The term is also misleading and counterproductive to those who use it. Even if we can ultimately use *ger* to promote understanding and love, doesn't it still connote condescension? The biblical admonitions not to oppress the stranger might be helpful. Their message can encourage a more humane policy vis-à-vis the so-called "foreign workers." With regard to Palestinian Arabs, however, those admonitions may harm the situation more than they help. Is there, then, another approach to follow with regard to the Arab citizens of Israel?

Different Suggestion

Each week, in Jewish synagogues throughout the world, a particular portion of the Torah is read. In a fortuitous coincidence, the portion read on the Shabbat of our conference, May 20, 2006, is the last part of the Book of Leviticus, chapters 25–27. In 25:23, God says to the children of Israel, "and the land shall not be sold in perpetuity, for the land is Mine; for ye are strangers and residents with me [the Hebrew uses both *gerim* and *toshavim*]." This passage echoes an earlier biblical passage, Genesis 23:4, in which Abraham purchases a burial plot for Sarah from the children of Heth, saying, "I am a stranger and a resident among you." Here, we unexpectedly see Israel referred to as the stranger! A Chassidic commentary on this sentence is worth bringing in at this point:

> Between Me and you, says the Holy One, there is always a relationship of strangers and residents (sojourners.) If you see yourselves as strangers in the world, remembering that your entire existence here is only temporary, as in a hallway leading to the next world, then I will reside among you and My Presence will always be within you. But if you see yourselves as permanent residents in the world—then I will be as a stranger in your midst. In any case, here we are—you and I—strangers and residents. Either you are strangers and I am a resident, or else you are residents and I am a stranger.[41]

The recognition that we are temporary residents in the world might lead to a different ecological consciousness that includes humility and a sense of responsibility or stewardship for the integrity of God's creation.

Suppose that we begin to view ourselves and the Palestinians as strangers and residents in the same land. The land belongs to God; we must not sell it in perpetuity for it is His. If we sincerely believe this, might we adopt a more humble approach, with more openness to the other? A number of Israelis suggested that both the Jewish and Palestinian sides of the conflict share a common experience of exile and of having been refugees. Those Israelis would maintain based on such common experiences that the two sides might develop a sense of empathy for one another. Post-Zionist academic Amnon Raz-Karkotzkin wrote an important essay titled "Exile Within Sovereignty: Towards a Critique of 'Negation of the Diaspora' within Israeli Culture," in which he suggested a new approach vis-à-vis Palestinians as well as Diaspora Jews, based on an awareness of the exilic experience (Raz-Karkotzkin 1993–94). Religious Zionist Professor Tzvi Mazeh also coined a phrase while speaking at the Kehilat Yedidya[42] Israel Independence Day service in Jerusalem in 1999, "and you understand the soul of a refugee, for you yourselves were refugees." On May 1, 2006, the Common Ground News Service sent out over the Internet a piece that appeared originally in the daily "HaAretz" on April 26. Bradley Burston wrote,

> It was the experience of exile that forged the Jews and the Palestinians both . . . We are who we are, in no small part, because of the hardships, longings and insecurities conferred by displacement from home . . . For the Jews, the insecurity manifests itself as fear, fear of being annihilated, fear of being cast out by force. For the Palestinians, the insecurity finds expression in humiliation and profound loss of honour, that stretches over the decades that the State of Israel has existed . . . We are, all of us, Jew and Palestinian, victims of our refugee mentality, the one we cannot shake, that makes us into villain and victim both.

Mutual recognition of each other's exile narratives would be an important beginning step toward solving the conflict. This suggestion poses two basic difficulties, though. For Palestinians, it would be difficult to accept the idea that the Jewish people had been exiled from the Land of Israel since the Palestinian narrative officially denies any historical (i.e., prior to the late nineteenth and twentieth centuries) ties between the Jewish people and the land. Acceptance, or recognition, of the Jewish narrative would render the land "Israel" as well as "Falestin." For Jews, recognition of the Palestinian narrative of *nakba* (the Arabic word for the national catastrophe of 1948, as the Palestinian people see it) would also involve some assumption of responsibility for the Palestinian refugee problem.[43] Despite these challenges, it is difficult to see how to solve the conundrum of Israeli-Palestinian relations in the near future without mutual recognition.

I mentioned earlier that this chapter would not confront the Israeli-Palestinian conflict. Instead, I am concerned here with the status of non-Jewish minorities within the state of Israel. Thus, we must concern ourselves with local Arabs, who are natives of the land, and with Jews, both natives and, like me, immigrants. Israeli Arabs are citizens of the state. They vote and are, as of this writing, represented by ten members of the Knesset. However, their status in Israeli society is unequal to that of Jewish citizens. Serious inequalities in budgets, housing, employment, and education exist. Some people feel that it must be this way since Israel defines itself as a Jewish state.[44] Others feel that it cannot be this way since Israel defines itself as a democratic state. Can the Jewish textual heritage and its subsequent interpretations be of any help in resolving this dilemma?

I believe we have seen the hermeneutic possibilities contained within the phrase *ger toshav*. Now, in several important biblical passages, *ger* is juxtaposed with *ezrach*. For example, Leviticus 24:23 reads, "you shall have one law, for the ger as well as for the ezrach." In biblical Hebrew *ezrach* is usually translated as "home-born," and rabbinic interpretation limits its meaning to males. In Modern Hebrew, however, the term means "citizen." Clearly, citizenship is a modern concept that stems from the democratic nation-state. The term in the twentieth century is founded on equality of men and women, as well as Jews and non-Jews. Perhaps a biblical statement such as "the stranger that sojourns with you shall be unto you as the home-born among you, and you shall love him as yourself, for you were strangers in the land of Egypt: I am the Lord your God" (Leviticus 19:34) can be a key toward equalizing the status of Israeli Arabs and Jews. Both are *gerim-toshavim* and both can be *ezrachim*.

On June 28, 2006, I met a settler rabbi, Shlomo Kimchi, with whom I was engaged in a debate. He quoted the Or Chayim, a classic Torah commentary written by the Moroccan-born rabbi Chayim ben Attar. In this commentary, the following Hebrew homily appears. The Hebrew word *ezrach* is made up of four letters. The outer two letters (*Alef* and *Chet*) spell *ach*, "brother." The inner two letters (*zayin* and *raish*) spell *zar*, "stranger." Thus, the deeper meaning of *ezrach* is a stranger who becomes a brother.

Tentative Conclusions

I hope that the reader now has a sense of the complexity involved in the interpretation of Jewish religious texts within the highly charged political context of the state of Israel. I tentatively suggest that traditional commentaries can inform a modern worldview if we build on the notion that all of us are *gerim toshavim* (resident strangers), certainly with respect to the Divine Presence. Mutual recognition of alienation-exile-refugee status will go a long way in helping to solve the Israeli-Palestinian conflict. I believe the Palestinian Arabs who are citizens of Israel, my main concern in this chapter, will be able to achieve the status of first-class citizens when the Jewish-democratic state clarifies their status and, in so doing broadens the biblical notion of *ezrach*. To some extent, a new understanding of *ezrach* developed when women achieved suffrage (Weissman 2004). This expansion should continue to include the non-Jewish minorities living within the state. Although they are full-fledged citizens from a legal point of view, they will not truly be first-class citizens unless we can develop a new understanding of their status in the Jewish state. I hope that my chapter can serve as a contribution to the advancement of this important process.

One final point: interpretation takes place within communities, communities that share a common sense of meaning. I know there are many Jews who will not accept my hermeneutic approach or who may even deny the legitimacy of my effort. I offer this contribution instead to those Jews (and non-Jews) who are committed to the double character of Israel as both a Jewish and democratic state, and are looking for creative solutions to the challenge of integrating the two.[45] I attempted to use traditional texts and language to suggest that liberal views of equal citizenship for non-Jewish minorities in Israel may be grounded in, or at least connected with, biblical language. The concepts themselves, though, may have undergone significant development in the millennia that elapsed since those texts were first written. It may be that our motivation for a new hermeneutic comes "from the outside" that is, from modern liberal-democratic values. Still, I believe that to the extent with which a new hermeneutic resonates with our ancient texts; it will have more depth, meaning, and opportunity for success in influencing public policy.

Notes

1. Rabbais for Human Rights, http://www.rhr.israel.net (accessed June 2007).
2. http://www.icci.co.il.
3. *Kedem* is a Hebrew acronym for Voices of Religious Conciliation. One of the projects spawned by Kedem is a joint Jewish-Muslim institute for the reinterpretation of texts.
4. http://www.netivot-shalom.org.il.
5. http://www.meimad.org.il.
6. This is my translation of a story that appeared in S. Agnon (1985) *A Shroud of Stories*. My attention was first drawn to this story by Dr. Steve Copeland of Boston's Hebrew College.
7. An important liberal German Jewish philosopher of the late nineteenth and early twentieth centuries.
8. Although in the Bible, *goyim* means simply nations—the nation of Israel is considered a *goy*—in later Jewish usage, the term has taken on a pejorative connotation.
9. *Yevamot* 61a.
10. I am privileged to be a member of this group.
11. Exodus 19:5.
12. Numbers 23:9.
13. Isaiah 19:24.
14. "The whole world on one side and Abraham on the other" (*Breishit Rabba*: 42).
15. Isaiah 49:6.
16. Micah 4:2, 5.
17. Nineteenth century German rabbi, founder of neo-Orthodoxy
18. Writing the name of the Deity this way is an Orthodox convention, intended to prevent a transgression of the commandment not to take the Lord's name in vain.
19. I am indebted to the modern Orthodox organization Edah for this passage. See: www.edah.org
20. Appeared in *Shabbat Shalom* (445), May 2006.
21. http://www.inner.org.
22. The controversy is recorded in several places in rabbinic literature, including Jerusalem *Talmud Nedarim* 30B and *Midrash Sifra* 7:4.
23. For example, Deut. 13:5, as developed in Babylonian Talmud *Sotah* 14a.
24. For this insight, I am indebted to Professor Moshe Halbertal of the Hebrew University in Jerusalem.
25. Steinsaltz commentary on Babylonian Talmud *Rosh Hashana* 23b-24a.
26. As cited in A. Z. Friedman, *Ma'ayana shel Torah* 3: 61.
27. *Avot d' Rabbi Natan* 23
28. Isaiah 2:4; Micah 4:3
29. Micah 4:4
30. Micah 4:5

31. Exodus 23:9
32. From Simone, Uriel. "The Land of Israel and the State of Israel," can be found on the Netivot Shalom Web site.
33. Excerpt from a private communication with a religious Israeli academic.
34. September 13, 1993
35. Summer of 2000
36. Rabbi Melchior, a native of Denmark and very much a European social democrat in his outlook, has been the leader of the Meimad party, an Orthodox but dovish party that has, on several occasions, run in the elections together with the Israeli Labor Party.
37. Note should be taken of the important work done by Shlomo Fischer and his colleagues at the Jerusalem-based Yesodot Center for the Study of Torah and Democracy, which works within the Orthodox schools (see Gross 2005).
38. This phrase is best-known from the "Prayer for the State of Israel," attributed to Nobel Laureate S. Y. Agnon, and recited in modern Orthodox synagogues throughout the world every Sabbath and festival. In recent years, some modern Orthodox Jews have questioned the validity of continuing to recite this prayer, given their opposition to the Israeli peace process.
39. Although several rabbis suggested that radical Islamisists who call for the killing of innocent people through suicide bombings may remain in the category of idolaters.
40. Babylonian Talmud *Sanhedrin* 56a, as cited in Lichtenstein (1981, 12).
41. As cited in Friedman (op. cit.) p. 147.
42. A modern Orthodox congregation of which I am a founding member.
43. It should be noted that unofficial discussions of this topic have begun on the Israeli side, among academics and other public intellectuals.
44. For example, Rabbi Avraham Giesser of the settlement of Ofra, speaking at a symposium at Yedidya on May 8, 2006.
45. See the collection of essays on Judaism and democratic values put out in Hebrew by the Jerusalem-based Yesodot Center for the Study of Torah and Democracy (2001). I would also like to mention an unpublished paper by Fuchs (2005).

10

Religious Texts as Models for Exclusion

Scriptural Interpretation and Ethnic Politics in Northern Nigeria[1]

Niels Kastfelt

In the autumn of 1999, a major national crisis erupted in Nigeria. The governor of Zamfara State, one of the predominantly Islamic states of northern Nigeria, declared that from January 2000 Shar'ia law would form the legal basis of the state. This led to serious political confrontations between Christians and Muslims. Muslims argued that the Nigerian constitution secured them freedom of religion and that being a practicing Muslim implied the right to live in society based on Islamic law. Christians argued that since Nigeria was a secular country, neither the Qur'an nor the Bible could form the basis for the organization of the state. In their view, religion and politics were two separate spheres, and any religious influence on the foundation of the state would violate its secular nature (Imo 2008).

The Nigerian case is but one of many recent attempts at organizing society and the state based on canonical religious texts. The Nigerian debate parallels other African countries, not the least is the Sudan. Yet, it is also part of a wider international development, growing in force since the late 1970s, where explicitly political forms of Islam, Christianity, Judaism, Hinduism, and other religions forced scholars and the public to rethink the political role of religion, as well as the alleged secular nature of many modern states, and the political implications of particular hermeneutic principles applied to religious texts.[2] This development was supplemented by the interpretive turn in the social and human sciences and its interest in the connection between textual interpretation and political power. Both developments contributed to growing interest in the political aspects of interpreting religious texts, or on scriptural politics (Ricoeur 1981; Foucault 1999, 1969).

The function of religious texts as political models conforms to two sets of defined characteristics. First, they can be used as a general or a partial model. A general political model is all-encompassing, containing precepts, which outline in detail how society should be organized and providing specific rules for the establishment of political institutions, offices, laws, and taxation to name a few, all of them unified in a coherent and total system. A partial political model provides precepts applicable only to parts of society or to specific spheres of human behavior without constituting a coherent and comprehensive order. Second, religious texts can be used as institutional or symbolic models. As an institutional model, the religious texts are used to establish and legitimate political institutions, offices, and laws. When they are used as symbolic models, they serve as sources of inspiration for political ideas, symbols, metaphors, narratives, language, and imagery. Whether the Qur'an and the Bible should be seen as general versus partial models or as institutional versus symbolic models depends on particular historical configurations of three elements: the words of the texts, the interpretation of these words, and the practical application of these terms.

It is a widely held view that the Qur'an contains a general political model and that it's both an institutional and a symbolic model. The general view of the Bible, in contrast, is as a partial model, which today is mainly a symbolic model. This view needs to be qualified. Although generally true that the Bible does not contain the same kind of comprehensive political model as the Qur'an, it is important not to exaggerate the difference between the two texts in this respect. Just as a particular interpretation or application may weaken the model in the Qur'an, a particular interpretation may see explicit and comprehensive models in the Bible. Today, the use of the Bible as a general political model is limited but this was not always the case, and in contemporary Africa, the Bible is widely used as a partial political model.

Throughout most of its history, the Bible has been interpreted as a political model providing the fundamental laws for society. Until the American and French revolutions, many Christians implemented a theocratic image of the Bible according to which "God has laid down the way in which society ought to be governed and its affairs conducted. The essential constitution for human society has been written by God. These are not human regulations worked out by people . . . these are explicit divine regulations" (Barr 1980, 94).

All through the history of Christendom, this scriptural principle was used to legitimate a monarchical political order, which was seen as a divine creation. Although the theocratic political model was gradually questioned from the late medieval period, it was strengthened during the Reformation in Protestant Europe, where the Bible, and especially the Old Testament, was used as a *ius divinum* (divine law), not the least in criminal law. Although the Bible might not contain regulations for specific political institutions, it has nevertheless been widely used as a collection of divine laws governing society.

In a discussion of the Bible as a political document in Africa, Paul Gifford introduced the concept of "Biblical paradigms" (2003). He defines biblical paradigms as "overarching paradigms," which reflect different fundamental ways of interpreting the Bible and then relates these paradigms to their political implications. Biblical paradigms, then, are links between scriptural interpretation and political thought and Gifford identifies seven different paradigms of which three are particularly relevant here—a theocratic, a dualistic, and a prophetic paradigm—each with their specific political implications. Gifford then distinguishes biblical paradigms from "Biblical motifs," which are more specific ideas or lines of thought that are supposed to be derived from the Bible and then interpreted into a political context.

In contrast to the Bible, most Muslims view the Qur'an as containing a general political model. Different hermeneutical and epistemological principles shape contemporary Muslim debates about Qur'anic interpretation. However, a process of rapid social change is also reshaping the social conditions for Qur'anic interpretation. To mention a few examples, one can point to the interpretative and political consequences of mass higher education and mass communication in the Arab world, whereupon individual Muslims now examine and debate fundamental aspects of the Qur'an to an unprecedented degree, creating a new kind of religious activism, which threatens to marginalize the interpretative authority of traditional religious leaders (Eickelman 1998). In most African countries, however, this situation is different. Mass education and mass communication may have the same hermeneutical consequences for African as for Arab Muslims and contribute to the erosion of traditional textual authority, but the political implications of this development will probably be different in sub-Saharan Africa. Power relations may change in local Muslim communities but this is unlikely to have national political consequences for the state as most African states have a secular basis. Moreover, most African countries have a longer experience with mass education and with a public political and religious space than most Arab countries do (Brenner 1993).

A different tradition of Qur'anic hermeneutics that has become more influential in Islamic reform movements goes back to such thinkers as Abu-al-A'la al-Mawdudi, Hasan al Banna and Sayyid Qutb (Moussalli 2003). The starting point for this group of thinkers is the poverty of human reason as opposed to the richness and completeness of divine revelation. True knowledge is only attainable through the Qur'an and therefore, Islamic political models have their credibility through their Qur'anic origin. True knowledge entails action, and action is able to satisfy the material, spiritual, and intellectual needs of human beings. Qutb stresses that the Qur'an also aims at developing a nation through a creed because the Qur'anic not only provides a belief system but also a revolutionary political model, which is opposed to and surpasses all human models. To these Islamic thinkers, all human beings and all human activity can be defined through an opposition between the God-given and the man-made. The God-given is derived from divine scripture, and those people and institutions that organize their activities accordingly, are *hizb Allah*, the party of God. Man-made activities, on the other hand, are based on human systems and their followers constitute the *hizb al-Shaytan*, the party of Satan. In this understanding, religion is a method of belief that includes metaphysics, politics, society, and morality.

Sayyid Qutb's hermeneutical procedure is interesting in a comparative perspective (Simonsen 2003). His Qur'anic exegesis is personal and individual and has only few references to the century long tradition of Qur'anic commentary or to the *hadith*. Qutb insisted, for instance, that *sunna* should not be understood as the *sunna* of the Prophet Muhammad but should be explicitly linked to God. Qutb thereby disentangled himself from the principle of *taqlid* (imitation) and stressed that following the path of previous generations would be a serious threat to Islam and to its expansion. Qutb's hermeneutical position, then, has one striking similarity to contemporary liberal trends in Islam, which insist upon the right of individual Muslims to bypass previous generations of Qur'anic commentators and to make a personal and individual interpretation of the Qur'an. Their serious differences apart, Qutb and liberal Muslims join hands in undermining established textual authority.

Trends in contemporary biblical interpretation in Africa have interesting parallels to developments in the Islamic world. One of the most significant developments in modern African Christianity is the dramatic rise of Pentecostalism throughout the continent (Maxwell 2006). Rijk van Dijk has pointed at a historical transformation in African Christianity, which is interesting when compared to the Islamic world (2003). Van Dijk's point of departure is the religious transformation from prophetism to Pentecostalism visible in many parts of Africa. The African Christian prophets who emerged from the early twentieth century developed combinations of traditional and modern culture and generally rejected Western religious leadership in the churches. In contrast, these Pentecostal churches, especially the so-called second Pentecostal wave from the 1970s onward, were based on direct personal inspiration and were strongly opposed to traditional culture. Prophetic and Pentecostal movements represent two different models of religious power and two ways of using the Bible as a model for practice because their kinds of Christianity derive from different views of the relationship between the believers and God.

In the prophetic churches, there is a mediated access to God and to religious knowledge, and the mediation takes place through a prophet. Pentecostalism, on the other hand, is based on unmediated access to God, as any believer can be inspired and filled with the Holy Spirit, thus involving a more "democratic" scriptural practice. It is significant that Pentecostalism is based on a principle of scriptural interpretation, which stresses personal and individual access to God through the Holy Spirit, independently of theological authorities. This does not mean that Pentecostal churches do not have leaders of great power and authority, but there abides a generally accepted principle that any believer may have direct access to God. In this way, African Pentecostalism shares a fundamental hermeneutical procedure with liberal Muslims and reformers like Qutb by insisting upon the legitimacy of personal and individual scriptural interpretation independent of traditional textual authorities.

Scriptural Interpretation and Cultural Politics in a Northern Nigerian Community

Since the 1980s, Nigeria experienced a dramatic intrusion of religious matters into local and national politics. Antagonism between the Christian and Muslim communities created a long series of political conflicts that have at times threatened the survival of the Nigerian state. The radicalization of religious politics has been experienced in many contexts, most of them reflecting fundamental aspects of state and society in Nigeria. At the national level, the political controversies between Christians and Muslims involved fundamental debates about the role of religion in the state, about the nature of secularism, about the role of religion in foreign policy, and about religion's place in the country's legal system. Likewise, political competition between the major regions has often been defined as opposition between the predominantly Muslim north and the predominantly Christian south (Falola 1998).

During the 1980s and 90s, Nigeria experienced a dramatic intrusion of religious matters into national and local politics. At the local level, the convergence of ethnic and religious loyalties does not determine the political importance of religion. During the 1980s and 90s, numerous communal conflicts occurred in the central and northern parts of the country, most of them between communities that defined themselves in ethnic and religious terms. In the north, Hausa and Fulbe groups defined themselves as Muslim, and many smaller ethnic groups saw Christianity as a defining element of their ethnic identity. Religion and politics became closely entangled and overlapping (Falola 1998, 137–62, 193–225). This situation is the result of a historical development that facilitated the blending of politics, ethnicity and religion. The rapid spread of Christianity and Islam as well as the European colonization in the nineteenth and twentieth centuries created a situation where political competition within the colonial state and later, within the postcolonial state, organized increasingly along ethnic and religious lines. Citizens in the Nigerian state came to define their public identity through affiliation with a religious or an ethnic community, and these communities became the actors in national political competition (Coleman 1958; Osaghae 1998).

In this chapter, I discuss one particular aspect of this development, the role of the Bible and of Christianity as religious and political models in the making of new ethnic identities and new political communities. The empirical focus is on the Bachama, a community of some 300,000 people living in Adamawa State in northeastern Nigeria.[3] Today, most Bachama are Christians, the largest and politically most significant denomination being the Lutheran Church of Christ in Nigeria (LCCN), which grew out of the work initiated in 1913 by missionaries from the Danish branch of the Sudan United Mission (Nissen 1968; Kastfelt 1994). The following discussion of the role of the Bible and Christianity in the making of new ethnic identities and new political communities takes off from two analytical traditions. The first has to do with the history of African ethnicity, the other with the vernacularization of African Christianity.

The general trend in studies of African ethnicity, as of ethnicity in general, has long been to stress the historicity of ethnicity, to emphasize that ethnic identities and boundaries are constantly being created, debated and negotiated, and that ethnic groups are being reconstructed according to changing political and cultural circumstances (Vail 1989).[4] Ethnicity should not, however, be seen in exclusively constructivist and contextual terms. It seems more useful to follow John Lonsdale's distinction between a "moral ethnicity" and a "political tribalism," which opens for a more complex historical understanding of ethnicity. Lonsdale defines moral ethnicity as "the common human instinct to create out of the daily habits of social intercourse and material labour a system of moral meaning and ethical reputation within a more or less imagined community." He defines political tribalism as "the use of ethnic identity in political competition with other groups" and adds that, "Ethnicity is always with us; it makes us moral—and thus social—beings. Tribalism is contingent upon political intention and context" (Lonsdale 1994, 132).

The second thematic context of this analysis is that of the vernacution of African Christianity. There is a long tradition of studies on the interplay between Christianity and local African cosmologies. The thematic emphasis has varied. Some studies focused on the development of African Christianity as part of a general process of African religious change;[5] others have seen the history of African Christianity as a translation process (Sanneh 1999), while many theologians approached the problems through the concept of contextual theology (Parratt 1995).

Research on the history of African Christianity and on African ethnicity converges in studies emphasizing how religious vernacularization and ethnic reconstruction go hand-in-hand. They share a common focus on the crucial role of language, arguing that the translation of the Bible into the vernacular produced written languages and literature. Access to the Bible in the vernacular enabled Africans to apply biblical stories and images to their own history, and combining this with a newly shared written language enabled them to strengthen existing ethnic identities or to create new ones (Peel 2000; Lonsdale 2002; Hastings 1997).

At this point, let's consider a case of the converging trajectories of African Christianity, ethnicity, and politics. The case shows how the reconstruction of ethnic identity accompanied new interpretations of history and traditional religion and by attempts at creating a vernacular theology. Moreover, how this accompanied the rise of political tribalism, all of it by drawing upon the Bible as a key model and inspiration. The case is a political and cultural movement that emerged among the Bachama in the 1950s and which continued into the 1990s. It was a movement of political mobilization and ethnic reconstruction, and at its center were the new Christian Bachama elite that grew out of the Lutheran churches in the Adamawa area. The present focus is on four aspects of the movement: how the new Christian political class among the Bachama developed new and modern political organizations, how Bachama intellectuals and others redefined Bachama ethnicity, how this redefined ethnicity formed the basis of a new political community, and finally, how the Bible provided the new political community with its own political language.

To the Bachama political elite in Adamawa, as well as to other Christians in the Nigerian Middle Belt in the 1950s, the Bible served as a political model in different ways. The Bible provided them with a mirror in which they could see and understand their own history in a new way and make sense of their place in history, as well as by explaining their relations with other communities in the region. The Bible provided Bachama intellectuals with a new language and a set of images, allegories, metaphors, and symbols that made the politics of their time meaningful and at the same time helped them to create a platform for political action.

Religion, Ethnicity, and Politics in the Nigerian Middle Belt

The Bachama are one of the many ethnic groups in the Nigerian Middle Belt. From the early colonial period in the first decades of the twentieth century, the status of the Middle Belt in the colonial state largely carried a negative definition, as being neither in the Muslim north nor in the Christian south. The Middle Belt was the "pagan" zone in the middle. Especially since World War II, however, people in the Middle Belt have worked to create a positive definition of the area as a region in its own right and with its own distinct history, culture, and identity.[6] In political terms, it makes good sense to see the Middle Belt as a separate region because over the last 150 years, a special structure of political conflict, based on ethnicity and religion characterized the region. Political conflicts raged between the so-called ethnic minority groups. The Fulbe and Hausa, and Bachama political history is a good example of this. A series of confrontations began in the mid-nineteenth century when Fulbe groups in the Middle Belt tried to extend the Fulbe-led *jihad*, proclaimed by Usman dan Fodio in 1804. This led to the Islamization of major parts of northern Nigeria, resulting in the establishment of a large number of emirates under the umbrella of the Sokoto Caliphate (Last 1967; Abubakar 1977). Parallel to this, the Hausa settled throughout the Middle Belt, often as trading communities (Adamu 1978).

During the twentieth century, Christianity expanded rapidly in the Middle Belt and many communities became predominantly Christian. A new religious component joined in regional politics, as mainly Christian ethnic groups and Muslim Fulbe and Hausa were competing for power. The material basis of political conflict remained unchanged: competition over land, grazing, and fishing rights, and access to bureaucratic state power, but the political communities increasingly defined themselves in ethnic and religious terms.

This was part of a general development in much of colonial Africa where competition in the emerging colonial labor market and in the new colonial state increasingly became a competition between ethnic groups, resulting in a strongly politicized ethnicity: "Ethnic groups became political tribes" (Lonsdale 1994, 137). In the Adamawa region this phenomenon took a local shape. The British largely based their colonial administration on what they saw as traditional Fulbe domination over other ethnic groups, and the colonial state consequently had a strong ethnic and religious component. Precolonial conflicts merged into the colonial state, and the British favoring of one ethnic group intensified the political role of ethnicity. As colonial politics became increasingly ethnic, it became politically expedient for other ethnic groups as well to define themselves in unambiguous ethnic terms. This development became even more prevalent in the period of decolonization in the 1940s and 1950s where the impending national independence led to a dramatic increase in ethnic and religious politics. Both the rise of political tribalism and the linking of ethnicity, religion, and political opportunity implied that ethnic and religious boundaries became more sharply defined than before (Kastfelt 1994, 11–29; Logams 2004).

The political importance of Christianity in the Middle Belt was organizational as well as intellectual. Organizationally, the churches formed regional networks originally intended to promote contact between Christians throughout the region, but which soon came to function as political networks as well, as they were the only regional, interethnic networks that were not Muslim and at the same time, allowed by the British colonial administration. Intellectually, the Bible became the key political text for the Middle Belt Christians. The Bible provided them with a narrative, a language, and an imagery that they applied to their political competition with the Muslims and that they used to develop strong new Christian identities (Crampton 1976; Kastfelt 1994).

Making of a New Bachama Political Community

Decolonization changed the political landscape in Nigeria in the 1940s and 50s. Regional parliaments and political parties were established, and national and regional elections were organized for the first time (Dudley 1968; Whitaker, Jr. 1970). Like other communities, the Bachama were drawn into this new world of modern politics where ethnic groups competed for access to national power in the coming independent Nigeria. To the new emerging political class among the Bachama, the main concern was how to avoid Muslim domination, whereas the issue of national independence in itself was relatively unimportant (Kastfelt 1994, 65–12). In their universe, local and regional interests always overshadowed national politics.

Throughout the Middle Belt, new political organizations arose to deal with the challenges of the new political situation, and a large number of associations and political parties formed. Middle Belt Christians had to take part in the project of creating new political communities that could operate efficiently in a situation of highly politicized ethnicity and religion. Among the Bachama, this project began in the late 1940s and continued through to the 1990s. Individual contributors to the project changed with time, but the central ideas remained the same and formed a continuous historical concern: to use the Bible and Christianity to promote the interests of the Bachama community.

Western-style party politics was the domain of the new Bachama political class that emerged after World War II. It was a group of mission trained young men, mainly in their twenties, students in mission schools, teachers and ex-soldiers from World War II, most of whom were associated with the Lutheran church. Once party politics came in to it, they set out to promote Bachama interests, and in this political project, the Bible and Christianity became important sources (Kastfelt 1994, 127–31).[7] The first step in their attempt at developing a new political community was to establish an ethnic association, the "Peneda Bwaré" ("the coming together of the heads of the people") around 1954, aimed primarily at bringing more schools to the Bachama area.[8] The next step was to take an active part in the establishment of new political parties, first the Middle Zone League in 1951 and later the United Middle Belt Congress in 1955. These were Christian political parties with most of their members from the Middle Belt churches, particularly from small ethnic groups like the Bachama. Their main political objective was to promote the interests of their communities against the Muslims and their party, the Northern People's Congress. Christianity was crucial in this development. The new parties were from church networks throughout the Middle Belt, and church services functioned as political rallies. At the local level, church and party networks overlapped to such an extent that in effect the parties functioned as the political branch of the churches and the churches as the religious branch of the parties (Kastfelt 1994, 69–75, 103–24; Dudley 1968).

Having established new political organizations, the young intellectuals of the Bachama political class began a major "cultural work" intended at creating the intellectual and moral basis for a new political community.[9] It was a political community, equally embedded in biblical ideas and in traditional Bachama culture, drawing on both as reservoirs of ideas, symbols, and moral values. If we see their work in the context of West African politics of the 1950s, the case of Kwame Nkrumah is useful for comparison. In his famous rephrasing of Jesus's words in the Sermon on the Mount, "But seek ye first the kingdom of God, and his righteousness; and all these things shall be added unto you" (Matthew 6:33), Nkrumah said "Seek ye first the political kingdom," assuring his followers, in David Birmingham's words, "that all else would then be added unto them" (Birmingham 1999, 32). The Bachama politicians followed Nkrumah part of the way, like him insisting on the need to take part in secular politics, but unlike Nkrumah, they remained on firm biblical ground. They sought not only the political kingdom, but the kingdom of God as well, and the core of their cultural work was to unite the two into a Christian political kingdom, or a Christian political community. If Nkrumah secularized the Sermon on the Mount, the Bachama politicians sanctified Nkrumah.

The Bachama use of the Bible as a political model derived from a typological interpretation of the Bible. Bachama politicians identified particular types of biblical situations with their own and thus found the model for contemporary action. As in many other parts of colonial Africa, the most fundamental model narrative from the Bible was the Exodus story. Exodus became a master narrative in postwar Bachama politics, to such an extent that one can almost talk about a Bachama "Exodus politics" (Walzer 1985, 131 ff). In Michael Walzer's words *Exodus politics* is, "A characteristic way of thinking about political change, a pattern that we commonly impose on events, a story that we repeat to one another. The story has roughly this form: oppression, liberation, social contract, political struggle, new society" (Walzer 1985, 133).

The Exodus story and the figure of Moses were widely used by Bachama politicians in the 1950s and early 60s to conceptualize and make sense of their political struggle. The Exodus interpretation of Bachama politics implied that the Christian Bachama—like God's chosen people—were oppressed by the Muslim Fulbe, and the task of the Christian political class was to lead the people out of political captivity through a contract—a covenant—with God which would eventually lead them to a just society. Likewise, Moses became one of the most popular biblical figures, a political model for how to lead the people out, to free them from oppression and persecution.[10]

The popularity of the Old Testament story of Exodus and Moses was determined by the postwar political context. In the Middle Belt, the Old Testament as an ethnic text, telling the story of a people in the making, Christians perceived as particularly relevant to their political situation. In the period of decolonization with its promotion of political tribalism, the political relevance of the Old Testament was obvious. The creation of the new Christian political community among the Bachama came, therefore, from a particular reading of the Bible, which resulted in an ethnic covenant theology. In the religious and political spheres, respectively, covenant theology and political tribalism facilitated each other.

Moses was not only important as part of the Exodus story. He was also important as a biblical model, justifying that Christian Bachama politicians were involved in politics at all. In the 1950s and '60s, there was a lively discussion going on among Bachama Christians about the moral status of political power. One of the two main views was roughly that Christians should stay out of politics because politics and worldly power were morally corrupting. This view was held by Bachama Christians as well as by Danish missionaries in Adamawa and was based on such well-known biblical references as Matthew 22:21: "Render therefore unto Caesar the things which are Caesar's; and onto God the things that are God's."[11]

In the face of such a biblically founded critique, Bachama politicians pointed to Moses as a man of action whose political activism led his people out of captivity into freedom, because God intervened in history through es.[12] They also defended their own political activities by reference to Matthew 3:13, "Ye are the salt of the earth." In Mark 11:15–17, where Jesus drove out those who bought and sold in the temple, it was taken to show that Jesus involved himself in worldly affairs, or by referring to King David, seen both as a man of the world and a man of God.[13]

The interesting thing about these new political ideas is not only the biblical foundations, but also the reflection of a more general system of symbolic dualism. The theological dualism between the people of God and his opponents corresponded with an ethnic dualism between the Bachama and the Fulani and Hausa, as well as with a political dualism between the Christian Middle Belt parties and the Northern People's Congress. The more the Bachama political community saw itself as a Christian community, the more were local and regional communal conflicts interpreted as religious conflicts. Politics were increasingly perceived in religious terms, and religion increasingly provided the language and symbolism of political thought.

Ethnic and Religious Reconstructions in the Bachama Political Kingdom

The cultural work of the Bachama intellectuals continued from the 1960s to the 1980s. During this time, a series of events took place that marked a temporary culmination of the process of ethnic and religious reconstruction. Three main developments took place and the Bible was a key model in all three. First, a reconstruction of Bachama ethnicity, which led to an increase in the population of the Bachama political community. Second, a Christianization of Bachama traditional religion and history, which, in turn, strengthened the Christian character of the Bachama political community. Third, Christianization of Bachama kingship, which helped to Christianize the leadership of the Bachama political community.

Ethnic Reconstruction

From the mid-1970s, a Bachama movement of ethnic reconstruction gathered momentum, its main concern to launch the new ethnic category of "Bwatiye." Originally, Bwatiye was the vernacular name of the Bata, the neighboring people of the Bachama. Up to the mid-twentieth century, the Bachama and Bata understood themselves as two separate but closely connected communities. They based this on a common tradition of origin, which related how a pair of twins originally travelled together, and came to Adamawa where they quarreled and eventually split. One of them settled in the village of Lamurde and founded what became the Bachama kingdom;

the other settled in Demsa and founded the Bata kingdom (Carnochan 1967; Dalli 1976; Stevens 1973; Magaji 1982).[14]

In the early 1950s, these ethnic labels and the tradition of origin underwent reinterpretation as part of a Bachama political and cultural mobilization. Before the 1950s, the tradition of origin had been used to stress that the Bachama and the Bata were two different peoples after their split. Now an interpretation emerged that emphasized that the two peoples had originally been one people before the split. The tradition was used as evidence of ethnic unity instead of ethnic difference, and from there the new understanding of the term Bwatiye began. Bwatiye came to stand as a common category for both the Bachama and the Bata, and the two communities began to be seen as one (Kastfelt 1994, 142–43). The political advantage of this move was obvious, creating an ethnic unit that was larger and potentially more influential in the ethnic politics of postwar Nigeria.

The intellectual foundation of this ethnic reconstruction was laid in the 1950s, but its organized political implementation was not seen until the 1970s. Bachama and Bata intellectuals now came together and launched a movement whose aim was to promote the idea of Bwatiye and of unity between Bachama and Bata. On June 3, 1976, they published an advertisement in *The New Nigerian* newspaper, reporting that members of the Bachama and Bata communities had met in December 1974 and passed a resolution stating that they had agreed to call themselves by the name Bwatiye, "the original name of the Bachama/Batta people."[15]

This was followed by the launching of new ethnic associations in the 1980s and early 1990s, the Bwatiye Development Association Fund and the Gwaha Foundation, set up to promote social development in the Bachama community.[16] The launching of the Gwaha Foundation in the town of Demsa in 1993 was accompanied by a speech that demonstrated how strongly the Bible had by now permeated public political oratory, and how closely intertwined biblical models and ethnic politics had become. Dr. Samuel Aleyideino, a retired professor of education at Ahmadu Bello University in Zaria and a prominent member of the Bachama intellectual elite, as well as third generation of an influential Christian Bachama family gave the speech (Aleyideino 1993).

Aleyideino took as his starting point the words of Nehemiah, "come, and let us build up the wall of Jerusalem" (2:17). He narrated the story of the prophet Nehemiah who during his exile in Babylon was allowed by the king to return to Jerusalem to rebuild the walls of the city and restore it to its former glory. Nehemiah returns to Jerusalem and tells its citizens, "come, let us build up the wall of Jerusalem." This is the story of a prophet who is chosen by God to perform great things—to rebuild the city of God's chosen people and to reconstruct the greatness and glory of the people.

Aleyideino then went on to compare Nehemiah's situation with that of the founders of the Gwaha Foundation: as Nehemiah was chosen to rebuild Jerusalem, so the Gwaha founders were chosen to rebuild the Bwatiye community. Now the Bwatiye must rally around the Gwaha Foundation and rebuild their educational, medical, and cultural institutions, which are on the decline. And what needs to be rebuilt is seen from the following. "Again, this area, represented by our chiefdoms, was among the first places in Adamawa State to embrace modernisation and development, which, in our case arrived hand-in-hand with the liberating light of the Gospel" (Aleyideino 1993, 6).

In this way, Aleyideino linked the work of the Gwaha Foundation with the key Old Testament idea of a covenant between God and his chosen people. The special religious status of the Bwatiye gained emphasis, as they were among the first peoples in Adamawa to hear the Christian Gospel, and with Christianity came modernization, development, and liberation. This was what was now threatened and needed rebuilding. The biblical story then became a model for ethnic reconstruction, social modernization, and political mobilization.

Christianizing Bachama religion and history was a movement of historical reconstruction and theological vernacularization accompanied the movement of ethnic reconstruction. The main idea, promoted by a growing number of Bachama intellectuals and others, was to reinterpret Bachama history and traditional religion by Christianizing it. The ideas behind this date back to the 1910s, when Bachama Christians began to reflect on how to interpret Christian ideas in the light of traditional Bachama religion and to develop a Christian vocabulary in the vernacular. Some of these ideas shall be briefly sketched here.[17]

A starting point was to forward a particular interpretation of Bachama migrations that placed Bachama origin in Egypt and the Arab world, from where they migrated to their present location in Nigeria. This interpretation—strongly inspired by the work of the British government anthropologist C. K. Meek and the Danish missionary Niels H. Bronnum in the 1920s—provided the clue through which to Christianize Bachama traditional religion (Meek 1931, 42ff; Kastfelt n.d.).[18] The supposed origin of the Bachama in the Arab world was used to explain what was seen as striking similarities of character between the main Bachama spirit Nzeanzo and Jesus Christ. According to this interpretation, the Bachama encountered Christian ideas when they migrated from the Arab world to West Africa, and the similarities between Nzeanzo and Jesus are a product of this assumed historical connection. Through this parallel, Nzeanzo becomes a local manifestation of Jesus Christ and the qualitative difference between traditional Bachama religion and Christianity is narrowed. In this perspective, the Bachama are a Christian people who encountered Christianity centuries before the arrival of Christian missionaries from Europe in the twentieth century and, consequently, the Bachama political community is part of the long history of Christendom.[19]

Christianising Bachama Kingship

The third major event in the 1970s, which helped to promote a Christian political community among the Bachama, was the election of a new Bachama king in 1975. The new king (*hama*), Rev. Wilberforce Myahwhegi, was an ordained pastor in the Lutheran church and the first Bachama king to be a dedicated Christian. One of his predecessors, King Mbi, who ruled from 1921 to 1941 supported the Christian church actively but never received baptism. However, he did initiate a secularization of Bachama kingship by refusing to perform some of the rituals traditionally presided over by the king.[20] The election of King Wilberforce was therefore a major new development. He was not just a baptized Christian, but also a pastor in the Lutheran church, and his appointment implied the clear public symbolic statement that a Christian king now ruled the Bachama, and this further stressed the point that the Bachama were a Christian people and their kingdom a Christian community. A man who took the Bible as his main guidance in the handling of the affairs of the kingdom and who was convinced that God had placed him in his office now led them. Unlike previous kings, he insisted upon having only one wife, and he maintained a subtle and difficult balance between the duties of a traditional ruler and his personal convictions as a Christian. Until his death in 1994, he preached regularly in the Lutheran church, and he saw God as the ultimate source of his power and himself as a ruler through whom God channeled his blessings to the Bachama. The metaphysical nature of Bachama kingship changed, as the king now perceived royal power as having a biblical foundation channeled through a prophet-like king (Agijah 1985).

The election of King Wilberforce completed that project of cultural reconstruction that Bachama intellectuals had worked on since the 1950s. King Wilberforce was himself part of the same generation and a member, although not always very active, of the new political class that emerged after World War II and what his contemporaries achieved in the field of "modern" politics, he achieved in the field of "traditional" politics. Together, they helped to create the modern Christian political kingdom of the Bachama.

A Snake in the Grass: The Bible and Bachama Politics in the 1990s

The project of creating a Christian political community gradually progressed through Bachama political history from the 1950s to the 1990s. Different political, religious, and intellectual trends moved in the same direction and in the end resulted in a relatively homogenous body of political ideas and organizations. All of them served the purpose of defending the political interest of the Bachama community. Bachama intellectuals carried out the most public part of this development, but the project enjoyed wide popular support in the community in general. Support was not unanimous, however. It was initially a Christian elite project, and many non-Christian Bachamas had mixed feelings about the blessings of Christianity and its erosion of traditional Bachama culture. Irrespective of religious preferences, however, there was widespread support of those Christian Bachama leaders who fought for Bachama interests on the regional and national political levels. It was at these levels, in relation to other ethnic and religious groups in northern Nigeria, and less in the sphere of domestic politics within the Bachama community, that the project of the Christian intellectuals was important.

By the 1990s, Bachama political culture had become so permeated by biblical ideas and language that it makes sense to talk about a biblical political culture in the same way as Christopher Hill described Tudor England as having a "biblical culture" (Hill 1993). In Hill's words, "The vernacular Bible became an institution in Tudor England—the foundation of monarchical authority, of England's protestant independence, the textbook of morality and social subordination ... Society was in turmoil, and the Bible was expected to supply solutions for pressing problems. Translation of the Bible into English had made it available to new and far wider social groups than hitherto, including artisans and women, and they read their own problems and solutions into the sacred text" (Hill 1993, 4).

Much the same was the case with Bachama society in the 1990s. The Bible had become a fundamental political text, a model for politics and personal morality, as well as a model for royal power and for Bachama independence in relation to other ethnic groups.

In the 1990s, then, Bachama politics—especially in its regional and national context—continued along the same lines as in the preceding decades, and the main opponent was still defined in religious and ethnic terms. The 1980s and 90s, however, also saw the first serious threat to the unity of the Christian political community among the Bachama, and it is in itself a sign of the great role of Christianity in Bachama politics that this threat grew out of a church conflict.

The conflict arose from a dispute over the number of dioceses in the Lutheran Church of Christ in Nigeria (the LCCN), the largest Protestant church in the area. In the late 1980s and early 1990s, church membership had grown so much that the leadership of the LCCN decided to increase the number of dioceses in the church from one to five, and there to be five bishops led by a presiding bishop.

This decision met with widespread dissent by the Bachama members of the LCCN. Until then, the only Nigerian bishop of the LCCN had been a Bachama who retired in 1987 and succeeded by a bishop from the Longuda people. This was bad enough in Bachama eyes and challenged the widespread Bachama feeling of having a special position in the church, being the first people in the LCCN area that heard the Christian Gospel. Increasing the number of dioceses made matters worse and eroded Bachama influence in the church further. Many Bachama Protestants now came together in an "antidiocese" group claiming the true leadership of the church as opposed to the "prodiocese" group. This caused a split in the Bachama community between followers of the two groups, and the split had devastating effects, causing broken social relations, violent confrontations, and court cases.[21] The conflict is ongoing and no matter its outcome and long-term political effects, its very existence is proof of the crucial political role of Christianity in the Bachama community.

Conclusion

The general theme of this chapter is the use of the Bible as a model in ethnic politics, based on the Bible's place in modern Bachama political and intellectual history.

The political use of the Bible by Bachama intellectuals was founded on a biblical interpretation, which identified biblical situations with similar contemporary situations among the Bachama. With this principle of interpretation, Bachama intellectuals derived three general ideas from the Bible as relevant to their political situation. The first was the Old Testament idea of an ethnic religion and a chosen people that had made a pact with God. The second idea related to prophecy, of a person or a people through whom God carries out his plans. This also involved the idea of prophetic leaders through whom God channels his blessings to his people. This applied to the Bachama church and to Christian Bachama political leaders who fought for the interests of the Christians. The third idea concerned notions of political power and activism. Bachama politicians needed a moral justification of their political activism, and they obtained this by identifying their situation with biblical situations of the same kind.

To which political ends, then, did Bachama intellectuals and politicians apply these biblical ideas? First, they used the Bible to reconstruct and strengthen their ethnic identity, important as this was in a context of ethnic pluralism with a close link between ethnic boundaries and political opportunities. Ethnic reconstruction involved a reinterpretation of Bachama history and traditional religion based on the Bible, and it implied a Christianization of both. In this way ethnic reconstruction, new historical interpretations and the making of a vernacular theology went hand in hand. Second, Bachama intellectuals used the Bible to create a new political community with new political organizations and, third, they used the Bible to provide this new political community with its own distinct political language and imagery.

The frequent use of the Bible did not mean, however, that Bachama politics had a particularly religious basis. Political relations between the Bachama and other ethnic groups had a material substance which was more or less unchanged throughout the nineteenth and twentieth centuries and which was concerned with the control of farmland and water, access to grazing areas for cattle, competition for office and bureaucratic power, the acquisition of social resources for the community, and so on. Neither the political substance nor the principal political agents, then, changed much. In regional politics, the main agents were still ethnic communities, although the boundaries of these communities changed and became more rigid. What changed most significantly was the cultural definition of political communities as well as the language and imagery of politics, and the Bible shaped them both.

In more general terms, the Bachama case shows how religious and ethnic identities have become almost completely overlapping, not only among the Bachama but also in many parts of the Nigerian Middle Belt. It also shows that the Bachama use the Bible as a model for modernization, through which the Bachama political community has simultaneously made itself part of a global Christian community and remained in an indigenous tradition, modernized by biblical interpretation.

The Bachama case also reflects a general trend in national politics and religion in Nigeria. The growing overlapping of ethnic and religious identities contributed to the transformation of ethnic conflicts into conflicts between Christianity and Islam. Local communal conflicts are increasingly perceived as part of a national religious conflict and this perception, in turn, contributes to the further religious polarization in Nigeria.

Notes

1. This chapter, based on revised and renewed synthesis of Kastfelt (2003a, 2003b) and Kastfelt (2005a), is the result of a parallel and related work on religion and war in sub-Saharan Africa.
2. Published by The Fundamentalism Project in five volumes beginning with Marty and Appleby (1991) and concluding with Marty and Appleby (1995).
3. Today most Bachama, together with the neighboring Bata, refer to themselves as Bwatiye. This contemporary use of the term Bwatiye reflects part of the historical development analyzed in this chapter. For most of the period covered by the analysis, the term Bwatiye would be anachronistic.
4. For analysis of the historiography of "tribe," see Lonsdale (1994).
5. An early example is Ranger and Weller (1975).
6. For the political and cultural history of the Middle Belt, see Logams (2004).
7. Based on interviews with Dr. Nicholas Pweddon (July 15, 1985); Mr. Esly Tanyishi (January 31, 1987); Senator Gayus Gilama (May 29, 1985) and Mr. Shadrach Jarah (June 18, 1985).
8. Interviews with Mr. Ezekiel Nabo (August 21, 1982); Dr. Nicholas Pweddon (August 20, 1982); Mr. Jonah Assadugu (May 27, 1985) and Mr. Shadrach Jarah (June 5, 1985).
9. For the notion of cultural work, see Peel (1989).
10. Interviews with Dr. Nicholas Pweddon (June 23 and July 15, 1985); Mr. Gilbert Ananze (July 14, 1985) and Mr. Jonah Assadugu (July 19, 1985). See Biliyong (1964).
11. 'Årsmødet 2' (November 1954) *Sudan*, 1646–5. Interviews with Dr. Nicholas Pweddon (June 23, July15 and July 16, 1985) and with Mr. Gilbert Ananze (July 14, 1985).
12. Interviews with Dr. Nicholas Pweddon (23 June and 15 July 1985); Mr. Gilbert Ananze (14 July 1985) and Mr. Jonah Assadugu (19 July 1985).
13. Interviews with Dr. Nicholas Pweddon (July 16, 1985 and February 21, 1987) and with Mr. Esly Tanyishi (January 31, 1987).
14. Recorded versions of this tradition of origin can be found in "Bachama History as written down by Mbi, D. H. Bachama," The District Head, Numan, to the Resident, Yola, December 13, 1926, no. 112/1926/14, Nigerian National Archives, Kaduna, Yola Prof., 101/3126, ACC7.
15. "Change of Name from Bachama/Batta to Bwatiye," *New Nigerian*, June 3, 1976; see G.G.S.L.N., no. 40 of 1987, The Re-designation of the Bachama and Bata Communities/Tribes as the Bwatiye Order, 1987, Gongola State of Nigeria Gazette no. 51, vol. 12, December 17, 1987, supplement part B.
16. Speech by the promoter of Bwatiye Association Development Fund, Mr. E. B. Mamiso, during the 3rd Launching on December 19 and 20, 1980, at Yola: The Bwatiye Development Association Constitution 1989, Yola, The Government Printer, 1989.
17. This development is treated in N. Kastfelt (forthcoming) *The New Way of the Bachama*.

18. Modern Bachama interpretation is Magaji (1982). The idea of the origin of the Bachama in the Arab world is part of a cluster of migration stories in West Africa. Many of them are related to the Hamitic hypothesis, see Sanders (1969).
19. An early influential missionary view of Nzeanzo and Jesus Christ can be found in Brønnum (1926: 33–46). For modern Bachama views along similar lines is Asodati (n.d.).
20. See N. H. Brønnum, "En stor Begivenhed i Bachamaland," enclosed letter to "Venner i Sudanmissionen," The National Archives, Copenhagen, Archives of the Sudan United Mission, correspondence from N. H. Brønnum 1910–21, file 3.
21. For a useful account of the conflict up to 1998, see Filibus (1998). For more recent developments see Kastfelt (2005b, 2007).

11

In the Name of Allah

Jihad from a Shi'a Hermeneutic Perspective

Seyed Sadegh Haghighat

Ask the Holy Qur'an, since it does not speak on its own.

—Imam Ali (Nahjolbalaqeh, sermon 158)

From time to time, especially regarding the aftermath of September 11, scholars come together at conferences to discuss the relationship between Islamic schools of thought, human rights, extremism, and terrorism.[1] Among them, some are in favor of the compatibility of Islam and human rights, while others are against it. They all assume unequivocally that Islam has different, and sometimes contradictory, readings. Some people believe that the logic of religious commitment in Islam reveals that the motivations for the often-violent actions taken by Islamic extremists are rooted in the original tenets of Islam.[2] However, the text cannot speak by itself. Rather, it needs the context—the political, geographical, social, and cultural conditions—to have meaning. Accordingly, dialectical interaction between text and context shows the real meaning of jihad, as well as the misconceptions of both Islamic extremists and some non-Muslims.

This chapter will first identify and explain the types of jihad followed by a description of the fundamentalist, traditionalist, and modernist Shi'a approaches to jihad. This will be followed by a comparison between Shi'a and Sunni readings of jihad and conclude with a new reading of jihad by using Quentin Skinner's hermeneutical approach.

Jihad: Definition and Typology

The word jihad means "struggle, strive." The Arabic root of the word is *jahada* "to strive for." The Arabic word for war, on the other hand, is *harb*.[3] The semantic meaning of its Arabic terminology, therefore, does not relate to holy war or even war in general (Firestone 1999, 16). In much of the English-speaking world, however, jihad is associated with the phrase "holy war." The concept of jihad encompasses more than just warfare, though, and a more accurate translation is "holy struggle," "righteous struggle," or "holy endeavor."

In *Muqaddimaat*, Averus (Ibn-Rushd) divides jihad into four types: "jihad by heart; jihad by tongue; jihad by hand and jihad by sword." He defines jihad by tongue as the duty "to commend good conduct and forbid the wrong, like the type of jihad Allah ordered us to fulfill against the hypocrites in His Words, 'O Prophet! Strive hard against the unbelievers and the hypocrites.'"[4] The Prophet struggled against the unbelievers by sword and against the hypocrites by tongue.

Al-Mawardi, an eleventh-century Shafi'i jurist, developed a different distinction according to which the infidels of *Dar al-Harb* (i.e., the arena of battle) encompass two groups. The first group is composed of those to whom the call of Islam has reached, but who refused it and took up arms. The second group includes those to whom the invitation to Islam has not reached. Such people are now few since Allah has made the call of His Messenger clear. An attack on infidels cannot begin before making an invitation to Islam. This invitation must inform the infidels of the miracles of the Prophet and make clear the proofs to encourage acceptance on their part. If they still refuse to accept this invitation, war may then be waged against them and they are treated as those to whom the call has reached. Ibn Taymiyya, a fourteenth century Hanbali jurist, explained that lawful warfare is essentially jihad. Since it aims to advance God's word, those who stand against that aim must be fought. Those who cannot fight, such as women, children, monks, the elderly, the blind, and the disabled, shall not be killed unless they actually fight with words (i.e., by propaganda) and acts (i.e., by spying or assisting in the warfare). A war may only be waged against an oppressive regime, not innocent people.

Jihad against infidels can be offensive, where the enemy is attacked in his own territory, or defensive, which means to expel the invaders from Islamic lands. Defensive jihad is a compulsory duty upon all. Ibn Taymiyya remarked, "if the enemy enters a Muslim land, there is no doubt that it is obligatory for the closest and then the next closest to repel him, because the Muslim lands are considered to be one territory. It is obligatory to march to the territory even without the permission of parents or creditor, and narrations reported by the Prophet (pbuh) are clear on this."

Combat against infidels, whether offensive or defensive, is the outer, or lesser jihad. The inner, or greater jihad, is the struggle against inner evils. In other words, the lesser type of jihad is the struggle against religious or political oppression. The greater type is the soul's struggle with evil. Thus, ranking of jihad is as follows: (1) the inner jihad, (2) the defensive jihad against invaders, (3) the defensive jihad against those who forbid Islamic propagation, (4) the offensive jihad against unbelievers. The first type relates to morality. The second and the third types are less controversial because everyone justifies fighting against aggressors. This chapter, then, will concentrate on the fourth type of jihad, which is the type that most directly relates to human rights, radicalism, extremism, and fundamentalism.

At this point, it is illustrative to examine a definition that disregards the relationship between text and context. The United States Department of Justice developed its own definitions of jihad in indictments of individuals involved in terrorist activities. Those definitions are as follows: "As used in this First Superseding Indictment, 'jihad' is the Arabic word meaning 'holy war.' In this context, jihad refers to the use of violence, including paramilitary action against people, property or governments deemed to be enemies of a fundamentalist version of Islam. As used in this Superseding Indictment, 'violent jihad' or 'jihad' includes planning, preparing for, and engaging in, acts of physical violence, including murder, maiming, kidnapping, and hostage-taking."[5]

These kinds of misconceptions, which ignore the relationship between text and context, attempt to apply contemporary understandings to ideas that originated several centuries ago in order to condemn those ideas. Methodologically speaking, however, each text should be examined in its context. In terms of that specific focus, jihad cannot be defined as extremist and nondemocratic.

Contradictory Shi'a Readings of Jihad: Fundamentalist, Traditionalist, and Modernist Approaches

Shi'a intellectuals, who study the Holy Qur'an and narrations of the prophet and Imams, like every interpreter of holy texts, can be categorized as fundamentalist, traditionalist, or modernist. Fundamentalist scholars primarily rely on the text. The core meaning and modern implications are secondary. Traditionalist scholars, on the other hand, concentrate on the core of the message more than the text itself. Modernist scholars apply modern ideas to the text. If traditional and modern ideas contradict each other, modernist scholars interpret the text in light of modern conditions. Borrowing from Max Weber, however, the ideal type of interpretation involves a combination of all three categories. According to Weber, there is no homogenous legitimacy as any political regime has a combination of charismatic, traditional, and legal legitimacy. In practice, every interpretation of texts involves a combination of fundamentalism, traditionalism, and modernism.

Fundamentalist Approach

When fundamentalists interpret the meaning of jihad, they focus on the shell of religion rather than its core meaning. For example, they refer to the following Qur'anic verses about jihad. "Fight those who believe not in Allah, nor the Last Day, nor hold that forbidden which hath been forbidden by Allah and His Messenger, nor acknowledge the religion of Truth [Islam], (even if they are) of the People of the Book [Jews, Christians, and Zoroastrians], until they pay the Jizya with willing submission, and feel themselves subdued."[6] Some argue that this verse means that Muslims should support jihad as a continual war upon non-Muslims until they repent and accept Islam, or until they pay *jizya* (referred to as poll tax).

In response to Qur'anic verses, radical fundamentalists may argue that (1) fighting infidels is compulsory; (2) infidels include Zoroastrians, Jews, and Christians; and (3) Qur'anic and *Fiqhi* (jurisprudential) precepts are divine, timeless, and therefore beyond the faculty of human ability. Fundamentalists seek to Islamize society fully, through the application of Islamic rules. Sayyid Qutb, for example, justifies jihad in order to establish Allah's authority on earth, to arrange human affairs according to the true guidance, to abolish the satanic forces, and to end the lordship of some men over others (Koylu 2003, 43, 156). According to fundamentalists, offensive jihad as a violent action against other people, including innocents, is compulsory at this time. Radical Islamic fundamentalists assume that a jihad is a war without constraints. This chapter argues that radical fundamentalists do not consider the context of the text. As a result, the above statements are controversial.

Traditionalist Approach

Unlike fundamentalists, traditionalists place more importance on the greater (inner) jihad rather than the lesser (outer) one. According to Hossein Nasr, the inner jihad essentially refers to all the struggles that a Muslim could go through while adhering to his or her religion. In addition, inner jihad also includes a dimension of the greater jihad, since it encompasses overcoming selfish motives, desires, emotions, and the tendency to grant primacy to earthly pleasures and rewards. This traditionalist approach, which identifies interior jihad (i.e., nonmilitary) as the greater jihad, was profoundly influenced by Sufism (Islamic mysticism), which is an ancient and diverse mystical movement within Islam (Nasr n.d.).

To understand the spiritual significance of jihad and its wide application to nearly every aspect of human life, it is necessary to remember that Islam bases itself upon the idea of establishing equilibrium within the human being, as well as within society where he functions to fulfill the goals of his earthly life. To fulfill the entelechy of the human state, which is the realization of unity (*al-tawhid*) or total integration, Nasr argues that Muslims, as both individuals and members of Islamic society, must carry out jihad. They must exert themselves at all moments of life to fight both inwardly and outwardly against those forces that, if not combated, will destroy the equilibrium that is necessary to maintain the spiritual life of the person and the functioning of human society.

Nasr's argument is especially true under the view of society as a collective. Man is a spiritual and corporeal being, a microcosm complete unto himself. Yet he is also the member of a society within which he develops and fulfills certain needs. The external forms of jihad would remain incomplete, and in fact would contribute to an excessive externalization of the human being, if not complemented by the greater or inner jihad. According to traditionalism, all the pillars of Islam relate to jihad. Through the utterance of the principal testimonies, "there is no divinity but Allah" and "Muhammad is the Messenger of Allah," a person becomes a Muslim. These are not only statements about the Truth as seen from the Islamic perspective, but also weapons in the practice of inner jihad. They are forms of spiritual warfare. The daily prayers (*salat*) that constitute the heart of the Islamic rites are a constant jihad that harmonizes human existence with the rhythm of the cosmos.

For the spiritual man, every breath is a reminder that he should continue the inner jihad until he awakes from all dreaming, and until the very rhythm of his heart echoes that primordial sacred Name through which all things were made and through which all things return to their origin. The Prophet said, "Man is asleep and when he dies he awakens." Through inner jihad, the spiritual man dies in this life in order to cease all dreaming. In order to awaken to that reality, which is the origin of all realities, in order to behold that beauty of which all earthly beauty is but a pale reflection, and in order to attain that peace which all men seek but which can only be found through the inner jihad (Nasr n.d.).

Although traditionalists acceptably emphasize the inner jihad, they cannot explain offensive jihad, even in the Prophet's era. Rather, they magnify some parts of the holy texts, and diminish other sections. Since no one can ignore offensive jihad in Islam, its relationship with the inner jihad requires clarification.

Modernist Approach

Modernist interpreters believe that while jihad might refer to an active war against an oppressive regime, such a war may be waged only against that regime, not innocent people or regimes who do not want to engage in war. Modernists consider jihad the most misunderstood aspect of their religion by non-Muslims. Islamic modernism seeks to make Islam relevant and responsive in the context of modern society. They try to establish positive links between Islam and modern thought by interpreting modern institutions from the moral-social orientation of the Qur'an and Sunnah. In furtherance of those views, modernists do not believe in the offensive kind of jihad, especially in contemporary society (Koylu 2003, 25–27). Modernist theology, a study of modern Islamic political theory, rejects the radical reading of jihad, since that reading is not compatible with modernity and human rights.

Although considered an Islamic modernist, Abulkarim Soroush neither accepts nor rejects modern civilization in its entirety. He does not see an inherent relationship between its various components, such as humanism and modern sciences or liberalism and industry (Soroush 1994; Jalaei Pour 1997). He does not accept modernity as a whole, because, as mentioned earlier, a combination of modernism, traditionalism, and fundamentalism is the ideal approach.

Each of the three approaches has weaknesses. According to traditionalist criticism, we must turn to the premodern consciousness in order to determine the essence of jihad. Only then can we interpret its significance within modern Islamic political thought. In addition, the modernist approach cannot illustrate how and why modern thought comes before the holy texts (i.e., the holy Qur'an and narrations). In the following section, Skinner's hermeneutics is used to establish a new reading of jihad based on the relationships between the text and the context. That new reading will serve as a critique of the fundamentalist, traditionalist, and modernist readings of jihad.

Skinner's Hermeneutics

Five important approaches can be traced in the field of hermeneutics: (1) Schleiermacher and the romantic hermeneutics, (2) Dilthey, who proposed hermeneutics as the methodology of humanities in contrast to the natural sciences, (3) Heidegger and Gadamer, who represent ontological hermeneutics, (4) Ricoeur, who synthesized analytical and continental philosophy (i.e., hermeneutics), and (5) Skinner, who advanced the idea of reading text through context. I personally believe in the dialectic between text and context as an approach that falls between the two extremes of textualism and contextualism. I also stress the relationship among the author, the text and the interpreter. Of the various approaches to hermeneutics, then, Skinner's approach is the most appropriate for this discussion of jihad.

Skinner's procedural analysis involves five steps that are best seen as a way to answer the following five questions: (1) How does the author's text relate to other available texts that make up the ideological context? (2) How does the author's text relate to contemporaneous political action that makes up the practical context? (3) How should ideologies be identified, and how should their formation, criticism, and evolution be examined and explained? (4) What is the relationship between political ideology and political action that best explains the diffusion of certain ideologies, and what effect does this have on political behavior? and (5) What forms of political thought and action disseminate and conventionalize ideological change (Tully 1988)?

Skinner is not solely concerned with history and method. For example, he applied his method to Machiavelli and Hobbes (Skinner 2002). Almost since its inception, his work has revolved around a tripartite axis that includes interpretation of historical texts, survey of ideological formation and change, and analysis of the relation of ideology to the political action it represents. The following section will explain the five major components of Skinner's approach by applying his work to the case of jihad.

Toward a New Reading of Jihad

Jihad is one of the most misunderstood concepts of Islam, which is a religion based on unity, love, and rational action. When the Prophet (pbuh) returned from a battle he said, "We are now returning from the lesser jihad to the greater one, the jihad against the self." The Prophet also reportedly said during the Farewell Pilgrimage that "the fighter in the way of Allah is he who makes jihad against himself for the sake of obeying Allah." Critics of Islam insist, however, that Islam and Muslims are openly hostile and intolerant toward communities other than their own. In support of that position, critics refer to Qur'anic verses that exhort believers to fight infidels and they point to the battles of early Islam and the eventual confrontation between the Muslims and the Crusaders. In contemporary times, the stereotype of the Muslim as "terrorist" also supports the critics' position.

When one applies Skinner's hermeneutical approach to the concept of jihad, it is clear that we cannot interpret Qur'anic or Prophetic texts without adequate knowledge of the human situation and cultural milieu of their revelation and first application. We must also determine which verses take precedence over others based on order of revelation or the possibility of abrogation. In other words, the context of Qur'anic revelation and traditions (*Hadith*) are crucial in coming to terms with jihad. It is an error to judge Islam and Muslims based on the jihad that has fallen victim to ideological tendencies. Rather, it is vital to understand the Qur'anic meaning of jihad within the context of Arab wars that occurred at the time of first introduction. At that time, tribal members felt no responsibility to those outside their kinship group. To a certain extent, the system of mutual revenge served to prevent wanton killing across tribal boundaries.[7] If seen from the viewpoint of that practice, Islamic jihad was more progressive than its contemporaneous traditions.

Jihad by Tongue

God states in the Qur'an, "Invite (all) to the Way of thy Lord with wisdom and beautiful preaching; and argue with them in ways that are best and most gracious: for thy Lord knoweth best, who have strayed from His Path, and who receive guidance."[8] This is the first type of jihad in Islam and involves calling people to Islam and making them acquainted with tenets of the religion through dialogue and peaceful persuasion. This definition of jihad contrasts the imagined belief that jihad is always combative. By returning to the first and second questions of Skinner's hermeneutics, which concern the ideological and practical context of the text, we see that faith is not compulsory and the inner jihad is more important than the outer one.

When Allah says, "Therefore listen not to the Unbelievers, but strive against them with the utmost strenuousness, with the (Qur'an)," support that proposition.[9] According to M. H. Tabatabaiee, the word strive (*jaahidu* in the above passage means "struggle by means of the tongue"). In other words, "to strive" means to preach, exhort, and persevere despite the obstinate resistance of some unbelievers to the ideals of Islam (Tabatabaiee 1973, 228). Tabatabaiee is famous for interpreting the Qur'an via parts of the Qur'an and by other means other than tradition. As mentioned earlier, every text should be interpreted by other parts of itself and by its context. This approach is an alternative to textualism and metatextualism.

Since the foundation of jihad is Islamic propagation (*da'wah*) many people ask whether Islam condones and teaches the forced and armed conversion of non-Muslims. The Qur'an clearly states, "Let there be no compulsion in religion: Truth stands out clear from error."[10] In this verse, the word *rushd*, or "path of guidance," refers to the entire domain of human life, not just to the rites and theology of Islam. No reliable evidence exists that Muslims ever intended or attempted to impose the specific rites and beliefs of Islam. The histories of Spain, India, and the Balkans offer concrete proof of that view.

There is no debating that pre-Islamic Arabia was a misguided society dominated by tribalism and blind obedience to custom. In contrast, the clarity of Islam and its emphasis on reason and rational proofs made it unnecessary to impose religion by force. The verse cited in the above paragraph is a clear indication that the Qur'an is strictly opposed to the use of compulsion in religious faith. According to the fourth step of Skinner's hermeneutics, which examines the relationship between political ideology and political action, each action originates from a theory and the theory and action survive in a dialectical relationship. It is not possible then, to understand Muslim jihad correctly and completely without understanding its relationship with its theoretical foundations.

Offensive Jihad

The ruler, the Imam, is completely answerable to the people and their legal apparatus, the most important representatives of which are the scholars. The position of the law is that offensive jihad is allowed only when it can be reasonably proven that (1) there are aggressive designs against Islam, (2) there are concerted efforts to eject Muslims from their legally acquired property, and (3) that military campaigns are being launched to eradicate Muslims. At such time, the ruler can declare and execute the provisions of jihad. A leader of the Muslims, an Imam, must be the one to declare combative jihad. Allah said, "Enter into Islam whole-heartedly; and follow not the footsteps of the evil one."[11] The Prophet said, after establishing the Islamic state in Medina, that the way of the Muslims is one. No single group can autonomously declare war or fight, nor can any one group make peace by itself. The nation's leader can make a peace treaty and all subjects of the nation are bound by that decision, regardless of whether the leader was appointed or elected.

In the case of offensive jihad, the whole community has an obligation to fight. This is based on the Prophet's statement that "He who is killed in defense of his belongings, or in self-defense, or for his religion, is a martyr." It is evident from the Qur'an and other sources that the armed struggle against the polytheists was authorized in the context of specific circumstances that developed after the Prophet had migrated from Mecca to Medina. In Medina, he secured a pact with the Jewish and Arab tribes of the city, who accepted him as the leader of their community. In the setting of this newly founded base of operations, and under the governance of divine legislation and the leadership of the Prophet, Islam attained the status of a nation with territory. As a result, it developed the need to protect its self-interests.

After several circumstances developed, the divine command permitting jihad appeared. The persistent refusal of the Mecca leadership (the Prophet being in Medina at the time) to allow the peaceful propagation of Islam in Mecca was one such circumstance. In fact, this is the basic reason for armed jihad. Another development was the unabated persecution of Muslims who remained at Mecca after the Prophet's emigration to Medina triggered an armed insurrection against Qurayshite interests in the Hijaz. A third circumstance that led to the authorization of offensive jihad developed when the Meccans began military campaigns against the Muslims at Medina with the sole objective of eradicating Islam. Finally, a number of tribes allied to the Prophet unilaterally abrogated key security pledges and forced him into a vulnerable position.

The above conditions clearly met the requirements for combative jihad specified in the Qur'an: "Fight in the cause of Allah those who fight you, but do not transgress limits; for Allah loveth not transgressors"[12] and "Will ye not fight people who violated their oaths, plotted to expel the Messenger, and took the aggressive by being the first (to assault) you?"[13] In later times, Muslims engaged in warfare to establish the Islamic Order. "But when the forbidden months are past, then fight and slay the Pagans wherever ye find them, and seize them, beleaguer them, and lie in wait for them in every stratagem (of war); but, if they repent, and establish regular prayers and practice regular charity, then open the way for them: for Allah is Oft-forgiving, Most Merciful."[14] The following verse also supports that purpose for warfare: "If one amongst the Pagans asks thee for asylum, grant it to him, so that he may hear the Word of Allah, and then escort him to where he can be secure. That is because they are men without knowledge."[15]

The picture that emerges from the above verses is that the command to fight was in response to specific conditions. Thus, the declaration of war is not an arbitrary act. Beyond the conditions described above there exists no valid reason for hostility because the Qur'an states, "Allah forbids you not, with regard to those who fight you not for (your) Faith nor drive you out of your homes, from dealing kindly and justly with them: for Allah loveth those who are just"[16] This verse refers to non-Muslims in general. Therefore, in the Prophet's time outer jihad, the combative type was strictly defensive. In a narration, Auf bin Malik said, "O Prophet of Allah, do you recommend that we fight them? He said, 'No, don't fight them as long as they do not prevent you from your prayers. And if you see from them something that you dislike, dislike their acts, do not dislike them. And do not take your hand out from obedience to them.'"[17] As M. Mutahhari argues, the unconditional Qur'anic verses of jihad, those that do not require conditions to fight, should be interpreted by the conditional verses, that is, those that limit the practice of jihad, those that limit it to a form of retaliation (Mutahhari 1981, 69–70).

Applications to Modern Jihad

In order to complete this discussion of jihad, it is necessary to present some crucial points. Most importantly, jihad, even the combative type, was not considered an unusual phenomenon at that time. According to Skinner's hermeneutics that point is important because it is necessary to consider other ideologies that existed at the writer's time. Within the context of the tribe-state or town-state of Medina, non-Muslims also resorted to jihad. Since infidels at that time launched wars against Muslims to eradicate Islam, it was the Prophet's right to use the sword against them in return.

Second, the relationship between tribes in the Prophet (pbuh) era is different from the relationships seen in modern times. The dichotomy of Muslim versus infidel evolved into a three-fold demarcation of Muslim versus secular versus infidel. The third element, however, is continually fading. Since most countries at this time are secular, the relationship between Islamic and secular states is not the same as in the Prophet's era. Hence, modern Islamic states cannot begin an offensive fight against secular countries, especially if those countries signed a peace convention with them. We live in a time of modern nation-states, neither in the Prophet's era nor in the Middle Ages. Thus, Mutahhari's argument on offensive jihad, which permits it in modern times because of its defensive nature and its relationship to human rights and religious values (Mutahhari 1981, 49, 75), is not convincing because the practice of offensive jihad in modern times inhibits a peaceful relationship between Islamic states and other nations. This reasoning is something more than *social analysis* that situates hermeneutics of religious scriptures within a given social-historical context. Rather, it seems that it is one of the *interpretative explications*, which go beyond formal scriptural hermeneutics in order to justify action.

Finally, in modern times no state can survive without international bilateral and multilateral conventions. Although modern Islamic states might have transnational responsibilities outside of their borders, they are confined by both international conventions and conditional limitations. Islam does not allow Muslims to violate conventions, even though they are against the benefits of Muslims. Based on Islamic precepts, every state must act according to the treaties that have been accepted or signed (Haghighat 1997). Accordingly, modern Islamic states can establish a reasonable and peaceful relationship with other states and groups in the international milieu.

Conclusion

In conclusion, Shiites and Sunnites have different, and sometimes contradictory, readings of jihad. Among those readings the fundamentalist, traditionalist, and modernist views are considered in terms of an "ideal type." The weaknesses of each approach, however, lead to a dialectical reading of jihad, between text and context. That dialectical approach supports the argument that no form of jihad, including the offensive (preemptive) one, contradicts freedom of religion. Further, the nature of combative jihad is defensive. As a result, unconditional Qur'anic verses require interpretation in light of conditional verses. Methodologically speaking, premodern phenomena cannot be interpreted in light of modern circumstances. As a result, the Prophet's jihad cannot be labeled a "terrorist" action that violated "human rights." No text can be interpreted without its specific context. Jihad, of all kinds, must be read in the context of tribe-state conditions. The offensive kind of jihad—allowed in the time of the holy Prophet and the innocent Imams (according to the majority of Shi'a jurisprudences)—addresses anti-Muslim countries, not secular ones. International conventions confine transnational responsibilities of Islamic states.

Notes

1. For example see *Changing Patterns of Security in the Middle East and Central Asia*, 2005, a workshop cohosted by the Department of National Security Affairs at the Naval Postgraduate School and the Center for Strategic Studies at the CNA Corporation. On May 19, 2005, the Naval Postgraduate School and the Center for Naval Analyses held a workshop on Islamic extremism and terrorism in the Gulf and Central Asia. This conference was third in a series of Center for Naval Analyses-Navy Postgraduate School cohosted events.
2. *Changing Patterns of Security in the Middle East and Central Asia*, 2005, "Qualitative vs. Quantitative Schools of Thought on Trends in Radical Islam."
3. Islamic Dictionary: http://muttaqun.com/dictionary3.html.
4. Qur'an: 9:73. All passages from the Quran are taken from Ali, Abdullah Yusuf *The Meaning of The Holy Qur'an* [English translation], http://www.wrighthouse.com/religions/islam/Quran.html.
5. http://www.answers.com.
6. Qur'an: 9:29.
7. Reuven, p. 35
8. Qur'an: 16:125.
9. Qur'an: 25:52.
10. Qur'an: 2:256.
11. Qur'an: 2:208.
12. Qur'an: 2:190.

13. Qur'an: 9:13.
14. Qur'an: 9:5.
15. Qur'an: 9:6.
16. Qur'an: 60:8.
17. Other narrations with similar purpose are: 1) "There will be upon you leaders who you will recognize and disapprove of; whoever rejects them is free, whoever hates them is safe as opposed to those who are pleased and obey them," they said, "should we not fight them." He said, "No, as long as they pray." 2) "The best of your leaders are those you love and they love you, you pray for them and they pray for you. The worst of your leaders are those who anger you and you anger them and you curse them and they curse you." He said, we replied: "O Messenger of Allah should we not remove them at that"? "No, as long as they establish the prayer amongst you."

12

Views on Women in Early Christianity

Incarnational Hermeneutics in Tertullian and Augustine

Willemien Otten

The issue of women in the early church received much attention in the latter half of the twentieth century and this interest continues today. This is a topic of immediate interest to contemporary ecclesial concerns. The Roman Catholic Church, through its claim of direct continuity of apostolic succession, still denies women's ordination. For many of its members the continuation of that practice is disappointing after Vatican II raised the hope for change. In response, it is clear that some studies will advocate the opposite point of view and state that the early church did not share the conservative contemporary viewpoint. Such is the case in Karen Jo Torjesen's book *When Women Were Priests: Women's Leadership in the Early Church and the Scandal of Their Subordination in the Rise of Christianity* (1993). Although the book's thesis as stated in its title has not won the general acceptance that the author may have intended, a steady stream of anthologies and other source collections in recent decades has given us better access to, and insight in, the variegated nature of women's roles in this period (see Daniélou 1961; Gryson 1972; Wilson-Kastner 1981; Brooten and Greinacher 1982; Laporte 1982; Clark 1983). Meanwhile, the range of interest reflected in them is shifting from the institutional to the sexual, as contemporary critical theory is applied to the issue of sex and gender in antiquity (Boswell 1980, 1994; Brooten 1996; Burrus 2000, 2004, 2007). An example of the latter is Bernadette Brooten's *Love Between Women; Early Christian Responses to Female Homoeroticism* (1996), which seems underpinned by disappointment that Christianity reflected, rather than reversed, the *mores* of late ancient culture by condemning homoerotic relationships between women.

In addition, recent studies try to open our eyes to the ideological manipulation involved in the shaping of orthodox doctrine and practice. The denial of a leading role for women went hand in hand with the establishment of an increasingly ascetic mentality in the church that displayed misogynist overtones while simultaneously empowering women. That trend continued into the Middle Ages (Clark 1986a, 1986b; Elliott 1993, 16–50). Careful analysis of misogynist tendencies in the church fathers (Power 1995; Clark 1999; Stark 2007), however subtle, coupled with attention to the heroic efforts of women ascetics (Elm 1994), led to a deeper awareness of the fraught gender relations in this period. In the most recent turn of events, this awareness resulted in a more critical theological approach to Christianity's central tenets, since the anti-Arian doctrine of the consubstantiality of Christ the Son with God the Father can be seen as both employing and imposing a constructive notion of masculinity (see Burrus 2000).[1]

These preliminary reflections are relevant insofar as they heighten the reader's awareness of the hermeneutical difficulties involved when tackling as difficult and charged a topic as women in the early church. Let me add two reflections of a more personal nature, which relate to the religious and the academic sphere respectively, as these hopefully, clarify my scholarly perspective.

The first has to do with my Dutch Reformed background. Reformed churches may be deprived of apostolic succession, but they often compensate for this perceived lack by seeing their theological position uniquely informed by the wisdom of the early church, to which they show a persistent attachment. Nevertheless, it has taken me a long time, and some insightful prodding from Catholic colleagues, to realize that reformed and patristic positions are not necessarily the same. Reformed circles are often plagued by an unreflectively usurping historigraphical outlook toward the early church ("we" *know* what the early church was really like), which prevents them from employing more critical distance by stating that this is what "we" *think* that the early church looked like. Adopting an approach to the period that is ecumenically open, insofar as it combines religious familiarity with an appreciation of its historical alterity, will exclude triumphalism and mitigate undisguised outrage by studying such themes as women's ordination, asceticism, or Gnosticism in less propagandistic ways. In the end, this may enable future generations, including non-Christians, to develop a broader perspective on early Christianity by seeing its foundational nature as separate from concrete ecclesial manifestations. The point about reformation attitudes toward early Christianity can also be made vis-à-vis Eastern Orthodoxy. Indeed its relevance extends to the entire span of Christian churches. There are no monopolies on Christianity's past and no institutional patents on the theological tradition.

The second reflection pertains to methodology. This chapter will follow what one may call a textual theological approach, as this reflects both my own interest and my theological training. While I am greatly indebted to recent contextual studies by Peter Brown and others, historians and social scientists alike, I am not ready to concede that their studies diminished the need for a textual theological approach. The aim of this introduction is precisely to point out how opportune such analyses are, as decades of historical scholarship on late antiquity prepared us well for a renewed reading of familiar texts. In an interesting departure from her previous work, Elizabeth Clark's recent book *History, Theory, Text* argues that patristic studies may benefit greatly from such a new reading. She recommends that the discipline reconfigure itself as a form of the new intellectual history.[2] Taking Clark's lead, and keeping the above introductory reflections in mind, let us now move closer to the position of early Christian women.

Approaching Women in Early Christianity: Dueling Dualisms

When approaching the role of women in early Christianity through a study of early Christian texts, one faces various dualistic typologies that both help and hinder the development of a stable view. For this reason, it's best to give them separate attention here. The most pervasive is obviously the dualism between man and woman. While originally based on sexual differences, this dualism embedded increasingly in a structure of interlocking sets of oppression due to its pervasive nature. Elisabeth Schüssler Fiorenza termed that structure "kyriarchy," rather than patriarchy.[3] Anchored in the mythical division of Adam and Eve, the mildly hierarchical, archetypal relationship between men and women according to which humanity was originally created quickly turned into an unbridgeable and divinely ordained gender gap. This theological development both reflects and explains the muddled view of hierarchy and spiritual companionship found in the second-fourth centuries.

The issue of gender difference becomes even more complex and theologically charged when accounting for the different textual genres in which early Christian authors wrote. Here I want to highlight the division between descriptive and prescriptive texts. Early Christian prescriptive texts generally aim at imposing a certain kind of behavior on the members of Christian communities. In so doing they tend to highlight women's servility and inferiority throughout the indicated period.[4] The focus on the lowliness and humility of women arises out of a triple dynamic. First, women symbolically represent the purity of the new Christian community. As such, they become the object of special scrutiny and their dress and external conduct merit detailed attention. Second, rhetorical contrast with the impurity of non-Christians intensifies the need for their purity. The impact of this contrast on the social status of Christians is not to be underestimated. Third, the more we see male Christian authors conform their moral attitude to the standards of society, the more they tend to "make women the object of their invasive gaze" and the subject of especially restrictive injunctions.

Around the fourth century, during which religion achieved social acceptance and began moving toward cultural dominance and suppression, Christianity began to make use of and cultivate the so-called rhetoric of empire, to use Averil Cameron's apt term for the triumphant nature of their views and the self-glorifying tone with which they were expressed (Cameron 1991). It is no surprise that in this rhetorical hotbed the theological role and conduct of women became especially charged. There is little reason to suspect that this rhetoric was born overnight when Constantine made Christianity a public religion in 313. Therefore, it is valuable to follow the evolution of this rhetoric-theological tradition. More importantly, by approaching early Christian texts on women from the perspective of the rhetoric of "earthly" triumph,[5] we can use female identity or womanhood as a theological prism. Through that prism, we can read the texts at hand in an attempt to gain a better grip on the dynamic cauldron that was the shifting culture of the early church.

A final dualism affecting the position of women in early Christian texts involves the difference between a constructivist and an essentialist position on gender. This difference extends beyond the literary genre and has become an important tool of cultural deconstruction in the hands of contemporary feminist scholars. Given the importance of early Christianity for contemporary ecclesial power structures, the most interesting question is whether early Christian authors themselves held an essentialist view of gender. According to an essentialist view, women's proclaimed inferiority is forever sealed and ordained in creation. If early Christian authors ascribed to a constructivist view, however, they would have allowed for theological development. If that is the case, then there may be light at the end of the tunnel for those women who hope that the Vatican will one day lift the ban on women's ordination. The precise anchoring of women's lowly state in creation is a charged topic and receives ample attention in this chapter.[6]

Armed with an awareness of the above-mentioned dueling dualisms that form a matrix in which many of the difficulties involved in "reading early Christian women" are situated, I will proceed by presenting my own reflections on the position of women in the early church by focusing on two western theologians of North African descent, namely Tertullian (160–225 CE) and Augustine (354–410 CE). Both have been the target of feminist criticism.

Tension between Creation and Incarnation: Tertullian on Eve and Mary

Given the dualisms mentioned above, it may seem as if there are few redeeming qualities in early Christian texts on women. Yet, there is a way in which we can see the various slights and prohibitions as part of the wider rhetoric-theological tradition of Christianity. Although that Christian tradition was unable to prevent the movement from becoming grounded in the ordinariness of late antique society whose norms and values it increasingly adopted once its eschatological outlook was on the wane, it still struggled to retain a concrete sense of "otherness" in culture as much as in language.

Intrigued by this struggle, my own take on early Christian texts has especially focused on their suspended and malleable rhetoric-theological character. Leaving their indulgence in prescriptive texts aside, the church fathers evoke, rather than define, the early Christian movement as one that desires to meet the challenges of a society in which it felt increasingly at home while still maintaining its eschatological identity. Theologically, the resulting tension between earthly belonging and heavenly citizenship reflects the distance between creation and incarnation. In what follows, I will focus on how this tension yields various paradoxes. While these paradoxes especially affect the position of women, in my view, they need not automatically be seen as affirming "kyriarchy." This view will ultimately bring me to regard Augustine's view of marriage more positively than do Brooten and Clark (Brooten 2003, 181–93; Clark 1986, 139–62). Before I embark on a discussion of Augustine, I will comment on some biblical passages and on the theology of Tertullian.

It seems clear that in Christianity's initial stages the imitation of Jesus Christ was aimed at lifting boundaries between the sexes rather than erecting them. The key text in support of this notion is in Paul's Letter to the Galatians 3:23–29 (NRSV), where Paul states,

> Now before faith came, we were imprisoned and guarded under the law until faith would be revealed. Therefore the law was our disciplinarian until Christ came, so that we might be justified by faith. But now that faith has come, we are no longer subject to a disciplinarian, for in Christ Jesus you are all children of God through faith. As many of you as were baptized into Christ have clothed yourselves with Christ. There is no longer Jew or Greek, there is no longer slave or free, there is no longer male and female; for all of you

are one in Christ Jesus. And if you belong to Christ, then you are Abraham's offspring, heirs according to the promise. (Osiek 2003, 191–92)[7]

This suspended difference between male and female was hard to prolong, however, given the threat of anarchy implied by the undermining of social institutions like marriage, we obtain a first taste of Paul's own tendency to compromise in 1 Cor. 7:9, where he states that "it is better to marry than to be aflame with passion." Peter Brown takes this Pauline comment as indicative of the apostle's hesitation toward the consequences of the new social vista that his proclamation of radical freedom made possible (Brown 1988, 44–57). From this Pauline reservation it is but a small step to the more conventional atmosphere of the Pastoral Letters, where women's subordination is affirmed and rooted in a theology of creation in 1 Timothy 2, 8–15 (NRSV).

> I desire, then, that in every place the men should pray, lifting up holy hands without anger or argument; also that the women should dress themselves modestly and decently in suitable clothing, not with their hair braided, or with gold, pearls, or expensive clothes, but with good works, as is proper for women who profess reverence for God. Let a woman learn in silence with full submission. I permit no woman to teach or to have authority over a man; she is to keep silent. For Adam was formed first, then Eve; and Adam was not deceived, but the woman was deceived and became a transgressor. Yet she will be saved through childbearing, provided they continue in faith and love and holiness, with modesty.

We can see the latter development not just as a shift from incarnation to creation but also as a simultaneous transition from a constructivist to an essentialist and moralizing view of women. The cited text from 1 Timothy hearkens back to the opening chapters of Genesis where God made Adam "a helper as his partner" (NRSV Gen. 2:18) and Eve was seduced by the serpent only to draw Adam with her in her fall (Gen. 3).

The prescriptive tenor of 1 Timothy resonates with Tertullian, who magnified its impact by reading it as a moral condemnation not only of Eve but of all women. In the opening passage of his *On the Apparel of Women*, Timothy addresses his female audience as direct descendants of the accursed Eve:

> If there dwelt upon earth a faith as great as is the reward of faith which is expected in the heavens, no one of you at all, best beloved sisters, from the time that she had first known the Lord and learned the truth about her own condition, would have desired too gladsome, not to say too ostentatious a style of dress; so as not rather to go about in humble garb, and rather to affect meanness of appearance, walking about as Eve mourning

and repentant, in order that by every garb of penitence she might the more fully expiate that which she derives from Eve the ignominy, I mean, of the first sin, and the odium of human perdition. "In pains and in anxieties dost thou bear, woman; and toward thine husband is thy inclination, and he shall be your master" (Gen. 3:16). Do you not know that you are each an Eve? The sentence of God on this sex of yours lives in this age: the guilt must of necessity live too. You are the devil's gateway: you are the unsealer of that tree: you are the first deserter of the divine law. You are she who persuaded him whom the devil was not valiant enough to attack. You destroyed so easily God's image, man. On account of your desert—that is death—even the Son of God had to die. And do you think about adorning yourself over and above your tunics of skins? Come, now; if from the beginning of the world the Milesians sheared sheep, and the Serians [i.e., Chinese] spun trees, and the Tyrians dyed, and the Phrygians embroidered with the needle, and the Babylonians with the loom, and pearls gleamed, and onyx-stones flashed; if gold itself also had already issued, with the cupidity (which accompanies it), from the ground; if the mirror, too, already had license to lie so largely, Eve, expelled from paradise, already dead, would also have coveted these things, I imagine! Accordingly these things are all the baggage of woman in her condemned and dead state, instituted as if to swell the pomp of her funeral. (Roberts and Donaldson 1994,14)[8]

In this passage, Tertullian does not simply sketch an essentialist position toward women. His position is hyper-essentialist, mythological, and miserable. Through Eve, death entered the world and there is little women can do to make amends other than to bear their grief patiently and assume an attitude of humble subordination. As he often does, Tertullian revels in paradox to the point of shamelessly condemning all women. He specifically portrays a woman's glamorous jewels as pomp for her funeral instead of any other festive occasion.

It is understandable why Tertullian's treatise is often compared to other Stoicizing early Christian texts.[9] Bishop Cyprian of Carthage in the West and Bishop John Chrysostom of Constantinople in the East echo similar sentiments about women's dress. Their "cosmetic theology" represents what Elizabeth Clark called a "rhetoric of shame." That style places the full spotlight on women as a way of forcing them to behave in accordance with male-enforced social standards (Clark 1991). In reading and rereading these texts, my reaction has not so much been one of outrage, but one of persistent amazement: why would these authors bother to write them in the first place? This question has especially haunted me about Tertullian. In other works, he was remarkably sensitive, as when he exhorts his wife not to remarry in *To His Wife*, and nuanced, as in the treatises *On Monogamy* or the *Exhortation to Chastity*.[10]

In my own search for answers, I am not content with relegating these patristic diatribes to the prescriptive domain of ethics and morality. As a quick comparison with Cyprian and Chrysostom reveals, Tertullian was never a bishop, which puts the behavior of his audience outside the scope of his formal authority, and makes the exercise of behavioral control as the possible aim of his treatises unlikely. I generally wondered whether the tendency in various patristic handbooks to differentiate between dogmatic and moral works[11] while facilitating thematic comparisons among early Christian authors, does not undervalue the serious theological interest expressed in the latter. In the case of Tertullian, this is all the more relevant, as his rhetoric seems closer to the tenor of early New Testament texts like Paul's proclamatory statements in Galatians than to various Episcopal attempts to organize their flock. At times, the powerful, prophetic force of his literary style puts Tertullian on par with the apostle. Tertullian not only sees himself fighting the same cause but may even feel at liberty to disagree.[12] He does not primarily aim to influence social or ethical behavior, but to project the truth of the gospel and will further his goal by using whatever discourse carries the most rhetorical weight (Otten 1997, 251–55).[13]

Just as I counsel against separating Tertullian's moral comments from his theological ones, I likewise counsel against tabulating his rhetoric according to the conventions of antiquity (Otten 1997, 247–51; Dunn 2005, 6–9; 2007, 471–72, 475, 480–81). Classifying the instances where he departs from convention as aberrations may make us lose sight of the deliberate theological choices they represent. His idiosyncratic view of Christ's birth from a virgin, expressed in *De carne Christi*, is a striking example. That work is a theological treatise in which he defends the reality of Christ's flesh against Gnostic detractors of the incarnation, chiefly Marcion and Apelles. Tertullian tries to be true to Isaiah's prophecy that effectively announces the incarnation: "the virgin will conceive and she will bear a son." Tertullian feels forced to defend this passage against Gnostic opponents like Apelles, whose perception of a logical contradiction makes him dismiss not just the prophecy, but also, more damagingly, its fulfillment in Christ's incarnation. After all, it seems impossible for a virgin to deliver a child, since she has a closed womb.

In an interesting chapter toward the end of his treatise, Tertullian posits a rather unusual solution to this problem by identifying Mary as the door to salvation. Mary's identity is in opposition to Eve's role as the "devil's gateway." Thus in Ch. 23, Tertullian argues that while Mary conceived as a virgin, she gave birth as a wife, thus solving the problem of how a virgin can give birth. Mary gave birth as all wives and mothers do: by adhering to nature's "law of the opened body." In Mary's case, though, the womb opened in an unusual fashion. Rather than being opened by a human spouse through regular intercourse, Christ himself opened her womb through his human birth as God's (and her) son:

> She (scil. Mary) bore who really did bear: and if as a virgin she conceived, in her child-bearing she became a wife. For she became a wife by that same law of the opened body, wherein it was quite immaterial whether the violence was of the male let in or let out: it was the same sex that unsealed her womb. This in fact is the womb by virtue of which it is written also concerning other wombs: Everything male that openeth the womb shall be called holy to the Lord. Who is truly holy, except that holy Son of God? Who in a strict sense has opened a womb, except him who opened this that was closed? For all other women marriage opens it. Consequently, hers was the more truly opened in that it was the more closed. Indeed she is rather to be called not-virgin than virgin, having become a mother by a sort of leap, before she was a bride. Why need we discuss this any further? In stating, on these considerations, not that the Son of God was born of a virgin, but of a woman (Gal. 4:4), the apostle acknowledges the nuptial experience of the opened womb. (Evans 1956, 77)

Assuring himself again of apostolic authority, Tertullian affirms Paul's "nuptial experience of the opened womb" and salvages Mary's decency even if he sacrifices her virginity in the process.[14] He does not hesitate to be idiosyncratic and even controversial by explaining that the unique event of Christ's birth opened Mary's womb rather than the conventional occasion of a wedding night. More important in terms of early Christian feminist hermeneutics, however, is the fact that by stressing Mary's "nuptial experience of the opened womb" he gives the strongest possible answer to his own vocal accusation of Eve. Just as Eve was the devil's gateway, so Mary's womb becomes quite literally the door to redemption. Further, one could argue that just as Tertullian signals out the bedecked women in the Christian community as visible signposts that mark Eve's fall, he also implicitly acknowledges that the chain of ordinary child-bearing women are visible testimonies to Mary's delivery of Christ, which is the preface to Christ's deliverance of humanity. Although Tertullian frequently uses the rhetoric of shame, he also embraces the most shameful moment of human life in the eyes of his Gnostic opponents, physical birth. By doing so, he powerfully proclaims the primacy of human life and resurrection over death and sin. Tertullian offsets creation's fall through Eve with the event of the incarnation and makes Mary the prime passageway to redemption and resurrection.[15]

Changing Times: Augustine on the Good of Marriage

If my analysis of Tertullian is correct, then his condemnation of Eve in *On the Apparel of Women* may not be all he has to say to her daughters. Mary is held up as a positive and praiseworthy example of the good woman,[16] virgin as well as wife. As such, she is a counterexample of equally paradigmatic impact to Eve in providing the human race with the passageway to redemption and resurrection. It is important to keep in mind that for Tertullian and his contemporaries, the end of time, and hence the era of resurrection and redemption was unmistakably near. In *On the Apparel of Women* (Schaff n.d., 23), Tertullian embeds the ethical portions of this treatise into a larger theological vision. "We have been predestined by God, before the world was, to arise in the extreme end of times. And so we are trained by God for the purpose of chastising and so to say castrating the world. We are the circumcision—spiritual and carnal—of all things; for both in the spirit and in the flesh we circumcise worldly principles."

According to the view I expressed above, his ascetic views represent a call to universal sanctity more than a moral injunction.[17] In that regard, they apply to men as well as to women, even if the latter are singled out specifically. Yet as Tertullian's reflection on the incarnation, itself a paradoxical sign (*signum contradicibile*), makes clear, eschatological time is neither marked by an about-face of created reality, nor by the suspension of its laws. Rather it must inexorably lead to its affirmation (Otten 1997, 257). This is due to the purifying effect "the circumcision of worldly principles" has on reality. Tertullian probably expected the time prior to the general resurrection to be short and intense, and could therefore tolerate no distractions in the interim. All Christian believers are called to focus their energy and rally around this chastisement as the preamble to Christ's fulfillment, which is their ultimate and universal goal. Treatises like *On the Apparel of Women* or *On the Veiling of Virgins* are hence suffused with urgency.[18]

In moving from Tertullian to Augustine, there is no denying that times have changed. Or rather, not just the times have changed, but temporality itself is a factor in Augustine's views of creation and incarnation. For Augustine, Christ is above all the mediator, who reconnects heaven and earth and who binds time and eternity. His transcendence represents the fullness of divine grace and embeds, rather than isolates, the incisive force of eschatological time. Yet it can only manifest itself to us in horizontal terms, as time becomes stretched out, alienating the soul from God through *distentio animi*, and separating humans from themselves through the effects of sin.[19] The problem is not that the introduction of temporality creates a kind of linear distance between God's promise and its fulfillment, that is between the moment of Christ's incarnation and his *parousia*. As a matter of principle, Augustine is quite adamant in opposing any apocalyptic reading of the end of time (Fredriksen 1992). The problem of temporality is rather a problem of humanity's failure to grasp and hold on to the incarnation's presence as a firm present-ness.[20] Because of sin, time is fleeting to us as the present of the present, in the same way we can only know the present of the past or the present of the future.[21] Just as there is no guarantee that the incarnation will be a lasting presence, we do not possess a memory that can be durably anchored outside the human self, which is always struggling to orient itself, collapsing and even confusing the earlier and the later, the old and the new.[22] As a result, we notice in Augustine that the eschatological urgency that dominated Tertullian's agenda has clearly subsided. When Augustine approaches the topic of marriage in *On the Good of Marriage*, he does so in a historical-exegetical context:

> Nor is it now necessary that we enquire, and put forth a definite opinion on that question, whence could exist the progeny of the first men, whom God had blessed, saying: Increase and be ye multiplied, and fill the earth; (Gen. 1:28), if they had not sinned, whereas their bodies by sinning deserved the condition of death, and there can be no sexual intercourse save of mortal bodies. For there have existed several and different opinions on this matter; and if we must examine, which of them be rather agreeable to the truth of Divine Scriptures, there is matter for a lengthened discussion.[23]

While Tertullian made clear that earthly and temporal institutions such as marriage had no place in Christ's Kingdom, he proved pragmatic about affirming them for as long as they needed to stay in place after the incarnation's circumcision of the world. For Augustine, however, the question had become a completely different one. He could have chosen to follow the direction of his ascetic contemporaries, who held that with the indefinite deferral of the *eschaton*, eternity should dictate the unfolding of time. Concretely, this implied that marriage was to be phased out and virginity accepted as the Christian norm. Since the ascetic movement made a great impression in the time between Tertullian and Augustine, the question was why Augustine would not simply accept Jerome's position and state that "marriage is evil and virginity is good."[24]

Finding himself at this important juncture after examining the effects of the incarnation, Augustine's resistance to sacrificing the value of marriage is remarkable. Since his acceptance of marriage included his acceptance of its patriarchal and "kyriarchical" accretions, his attitude met with harsh accusations from contemporary feminist scholars. Elizabeth Clark argues that he is unable to maintain a nonreproductive view of marriage, of which *On the Good of Marriage* gives some examples with its attention for friendship between the partners. Bernadette Brooten is another critic who argues that Augustine caves in to ancient natural law. The expectations placed on this church father by contemporary women scholars are unusually high, and their evaluations of his position accordingly negative. Among the passages most severely criticized is his *De Genesi ad litteram* (IX.5.9) where Augustine states that if God had wanted to create a friend for Adam he would have created a second man. This passage rejects the view of marriage as friendship and summarizes the purpose of Eve's creation exclusively in terms of biological motherhood (Reynolds 1994).

Although Augustine may at times be relaxed in discussing exegetical possibilities, he eventually embraces a new urgency that he wishes to impose on Christian society. This urgency is deliberately universal, firmly anchored in scripture, and seemingly marked by an increasing preoccupation with the meaning of creation rather than incarnation. It's as if the first chapters of Genesis are his theological workshop, through which he focuses on the pilgrimage of humanity and of the church. Augustine's church, meanwhile, is no longer Tertullian's community of the chosen few, which foreshadows eschatological fulfillment. Rather, it represents a mixed society that attempts to live out of the past of its frozen incarnational memories. Given Augustine's universal perspective, the reading of Genesis no longer provides a mere foil for imposing a strict female morality in the church. Instead, it piques a much more fundamental interest, as it can help him to uncover humanity's common origin as willed by God.

Augustine goes about his task in a manner that combines Stoic views of sociopolitical concordance with a fresh reading of the biblical text of Genesis. This brings him to a creative view of human kinship as stated in chapter 1:

> Forasmuch as each man is a part of the human race, and human nature is something social, and had for a great and natural good, the power also of friendship; on this account God willed to create all men out of one, in order that they might be held in their society not only by likeness of kind, but also by bond of kindred. Therefore the first natural bond of human society is man and wife. Even those God did not create separately and join him as if strangers, but He made the one from the other, indicating also the power of union in the side where she was drawn and formed. A consequence is the union of society in the children who are the only worthy fruit, not of the joining of male and female, but of sexual intercourse. For there could have been in both sexes, even without such intercourse, a kind of friendly and genuine union of the one ruling and the other obeying. (Schaff, vol. 3 n.d., 399)

With this last comment, about the friendly union of partners even without sexual intercourse, Augustine no doubt harkens back to his Manichean days, when he preferred to read Genesis allegorically rather than historically. Still, even this spiritualizing view of marriage was not devoid of patriarchal bonds. As he develops his arguments in the course of *On the Good of Marriage*, he no longer privileges friendship as he did early in this treatise. Rather, Augustine comes to endorse the traditional goods of marriage, sacrament, loyalty of its partners (*fides*) and offspring (*proles*), which were to have a long afterlife in Roman Catholic theology. Viewed from this perspective, his blunt comments in *De Genesi ad litteram*, written more than a decade later, merely crown a development already under way. Not only is the reason for Eve's creation seen in biological terms here, unlike in apologists like Irenaeus and Tertullian, there is no Mary in sight to elevate the figure of the woman to a more spiritual level.

Yet Augustine's view of Adam and Eve that underlies his defense of institutional marriage seems colored more by his attempt to create a presentness for their past than by the ancient natural law-approach. Increasingly aware of the weight that the correct view of their creation carried for maintaining the universal effect of Christ's incarnation, Augustine takes great care to formulate a balanced and responsible judgment on humanity's progenitors. Unlike Tertullian, he does not blame only Eve for human sinfulness. He sees Adam and Eve as committed social partners, even in crime. As he states in *City of God* 14.11,

> For as Aaron was not induced to agree with the people when they blindly wished him to make an idol, and yet yielded to constraint; and as it is not credible that Solomon was so blind as to suppose that idols should be worshipped, but was drawn over to such sacrilege by the blandishments of women; so we cannot believe that Adam was deceived, and supposed the devil's word to be truth, and therefore transgressed God's law, but that he by the drawings of kindred yielded to the woman, the husband to the wife, the one human being to the only other human being. For not without significance did the apostle say, "And Adam was not deceived, but the woman being deceived was in the transgression" (1 Tim. 2:14), but he speaks thus, because the woman accepted as true what the serpent told her, but the man could not bear to be severed from his only companion, even though this involved a partnership in sin. He was not on this account less culpable, but sinned with his eyes open.

Augustine defends this position by saying that the apostle (cf. 1 Tim. 2:14) does not say that Adam did not sin, only that he was not deceived, for only Eve was deceived. By admitting that Adam also sinned, Augustine changes Tertullian's harsh verdict about Eve as the devil's doorway into a critical evaluation of Adam as humanity's collective passageway to sin. He emphasizes his view of the fall, which hinges on the sociohistorical priority of Adam as the first human being, by his imaginative (although exegetically flawed) reading of Romans 5:12 that "by one man sin entered into the world." This allows him to shore up the connection between Adam and Christ as the axial bond linking creation and incarnation (Bonner 1983).[25]

We can best explain Augustine's desire to safeguard humanity's eschatological future by taking a balanced approach to its origin, by seeing it as stemming from a deep desire to hold on to the present-ness of the incarnation. Creating a representative "present" of humanity's collective "past" was the only responsible way for Augustine to anchor his ecclesial concerns in a universal fashion. In the same way, he expressed his views of the creation and the fall of Adam and Eve, he espoused their marriage. In so doing, he anchored the institution and retained its integrity even in the case of the polygamous Old Testament patriarchs (Schaff, vol. 3 n.d., 408, 410–13). While Brooten accuses him of merely upholding ancient standards of nature (Brooten 2003, 189–90), I argue that in the final analysis it is the preservation of incarnational time that is of importance here.

Conclusion: Early Christian Women as Theological Prism

The unfolding of time and the need to hold on to the present-ness of the incarnation by appropriating the past in responsible fashion is ultimately what separates Augustine from Tertullian's eschatological and pragmatic approach to marriage. Although Augustine solidified the institutional aspects of marriage,[26] we risk shortchanging the complexity of this process when we describe it exclusively in terms of natural law. What makes Augustine's position distinctive is that he tries to maintain humanity's incarnational focus by appropriating a responsible social-historical past that while allowing for collective guilt is open toward redemption. In the end, his view is directed toward the same eschatological goal as Tertullian's proclamations that are more forthright. This occasionally comes to the surface, as when Augustine states the difference between the era and *mores* of the patriarchs and his own time and manners in *On the Good of Marriage*. Here again, we find him judging what happened in the past on the sole basis of what it contributes to the future of the church and humanity. "As therefore the Sacrament of marriage with several of that time signified the multitude that should be hereafter made subject unto God in all nations of the earth, so the Sacrament of marriage with one of our times signifies the unity of us all made subject to God, which shall be hereafter in one Heavenly City" (Schaff, vol. 3 n.d., 408).

I would modify Brooten's position and argue that it is Augustine's conception of time rather than nature that defines his view of marriage.

Inherent in this incarnational view of time, furthermore, is the idea that it allows for change, hope, and redemption.

I wholeheartedly agree with Brooten, however, on the need to develop a fuller historical picture as a basis for contemporary Christian sexual ethics (Brooten 2003, 193). One can extend that to the need for a fuller contemporary theological anthropology. As I have tried to demonstrate, isolating what the church fathers have to say about women can lead to a misrepresentation of the complexity of their texts. In my opinion, this complexity is caused in part by the position of women as a theological prism that allowed early Christian authors to highlight issues of particular importance to them. This makes the study of early Christian hermeneutics a particularly useful, but also delicate matter. It forces us to read and interpret early Christian theological texts in a way that includes women without isolating them, but instead by magnifying their position. In terms of feminist hermeneutics, female and male theologians may develop fruitfully and jointly a keen eye for the incarnational focus of the church fathers.

Notes

1. Other authors who problematized masculine notions of the Trinity from a systematic rather than a historical perspective are Catherine LaCugna, Elizabeth Johnson, and Sarah Coakley. For a brief assessment with mention of their respective positions, see Soskice and Martin (2002) and Slee (2002).
2. Clark (2004) pays increasing attention to the rhetorical complexity of early Christian texts, suggesting that the field of patristics move beyond the social science approach and reconfigure itself as a kind of new intellectual history.
3. Schüssler Fiorenza (2001) develops such analytical tools as kyriocentrism, kyriarchy, and wo/men. For a brief definition of the term "kyriarchy," see Brooten (2003, 182).
4. For an analysis of the tension between diversity and conformity, as the eschatological horizon of early Christianity receded, see Sawyer (1996).
5. For reflection of a more general theological nature on Christianity's "earthly" triumph see Otten (2001).
6. Pagels (1988) links the theological oppression of women to the imperial changes set in motion by Constantine with Augustine as the main theoretician.
7. Osiek points out that the male-female pair is found only here, while the pairs of Jew-Greek and slave-free occur in similar statements in 1 Corinthians 12:13 and Colossians 3:11. Osiek also comments that this pair is connected by a coordinating conjunction (male and female), whereas the other pairs are connected by correlative conjunctions (slave or free, Jew or Greek). She gives five possible interpretations: (1) Emancipation proclamation ahead of its time; (2) a formula used in the baptism of new Christians; (3) reference to the order of creation but not to the order of the Fall; (4) the time of salvation anticipated in

the present; and (5) a glimpse of the still distant future. My own preference is a modification of four along incarnational lines. I rule out three because of the inextricable links between creation and fall in Western Fathers like Tertullian and Augustine, who generally abstain from cosmological speculation along Platonic lines.

8. Although the translation is old, it has the advantage that it can be consulted online at http://www.ccel.org/fathers.html as part of the Library of Christian Classics.
9. Colish (1990) actually sees Tertullian's cosmetic theology as turning Stoic ethics inside out by rejecting the moral equality of men and women and the assessment of moral acts based on the agent's intentionality. See also her comments on p. 34 on Cyprian's *De habitu virginum*, which she sees as more Stoic than Tertullian's work even while it is more narrowly Christian in focus, as he addresses only consecrated virgins. For insight in the different dynamics of Chrysostom's *On Virginity* which is set against the ascetic movement in the East, see Brown (1988, 305–22).
10. For more information, see *Ante-Nicene Fathers* vol. 4, edited by Roberts and Donaldson (1994).
11. For more information, see *Ante-Nicene Fathers* vol. 3; Schaff's edition follows standard patristic practice here and lists Tertullian's dogmatic and anti-Marcionite treatises in separate categories.
12. See chs. 3 and 4 of his *Exhortation to Chastity*, *Ante-Nicene Fathers* vol. 4, p. 52 where Tertullian distinguishes Paul's personal suggestions from his speaking of divine precept as a way to bring up his own reading of Paul's words.
13. Another way of putting this is to say that Tertullian is not only defending orthodox tradition against Gnosticism but that his performative rhetoric polemically establishes tradition by accusing opponents like Marcion of undermining it.
14. It is a lacuna in Dunn's analysis that he does not explicitly deal with Christ's opening of Mary's womb through His birth, especially when Dunn is concerned with anchoring ch. 23 more firmly within a rhetorical division of Tertullian's treatise. Dunn's concern is more with preserving Mary's virginity, while I see Tertullian as concerned with Mary's decency as a wife and the regularity of Christ's birth as fully human.
15. In light of the wider symmetry between Eve and Mary to which my argument draws attention, I fail to understand Dunn's comment that Tertullian's typology of Eve in *De carne Christi* is imperfect. See Dunn (2007, 478).
16. Turcan (1990) exonerates Tertullian of many of the feminist charges by underscoring his great reverence for Mary. She does not mention the passage discussed here from *De carne Christi*.
17. I use the term "universal" here in the way it is used in Badiou (2003).
18. Here I disagree with Brown (1988, 76–82) in that I deem Tertullian's interest in prophecy to express a deeper, more fundamental sense of urgency, which I label eschatological.

19. Augustine calls our current state the so-called *regio dissimilitudinis*, cf. *Confessions* VII.10.
20. Colish (1983) focused on another consequence of the incarnation in Augustine, namely the empowerment of human speech through the redemption of the divine Word. This is not unlike what I argued above about Tertullian. My focus in Augustine, however, is on the issue of temporality.
21. Augustine's reflections on time are found in *Confessions* XI.20: "From what we have said it is abundantly clear that neither the future nor the past exist, and therefore it is not strictly correct to say that there are three times, past, present, and future. It might be correct to say that there are three times, a present of past things, a present of present things, and a present of future things."
22. Cf. *Confessions* X.27: "I have learnt to love you late, Beauty at once so ancient and so new! I have learnt to love you late! You were within me, and I was in the world outside myself and, disfigured as I was, I fell upon the lovely things of your creation. You were with me, but I was not with you."
23. Although Schaff's translation like Tertullian's is old, it also can be easily checked online at http://www.ccel.org/fathers.html as part of the Library of Christian Classics.
24. This in itself is a reaction to Jovinian who thought asceticism did not make one a better Christian, since only baptism marks the true believer. See Otten (1998, 393–97).
25. Prior to Augustine, Ambrosiaster engaged in a similar reading of Rom. 5:12.
26. Brooten (2003, 189–90) criticizes Augustine's use of gender subordination as a value, when he accepts the polygamy of the patriarchs but makes no allowance for polyandry. Yet this also may be more a matter of time and history than of natural law, as there is no biblical counterexample of polyandry.

13

Women's Rights and the Interpretation of Islamic Texts

The Practice of Female Genital Mutilation

Isatou Touray

Feminist critique of religious texts stems from a desire to find meaning for women's lives in the context of their religion. Accordingly, feminist scholars noticed patriarchal control over Muslim religious texts. "Through the centuries of Muslim history, these sources have been interpreted only by Muslim men who have arrogated to themselves the task of defining the ontological, theological, sociological and eschatological status of Muslim women" (Sharma and Young 1999, 248).

Indeed, interpretations of the Qur'an tended to incorporate the prevailing practices in Arabia, transmitting patriarchal values. This system still governs religious interpretations and social expectations. Its effects are discernable in all Muslim communities where patriarchal norms and expectations prevail, and where the vantage point of men, or even male superiority over women, underlies interpretation of the religious text.

Correspondingly, culture is an area of contestation regarding women's sexuality and autonomy over their bodies. Culture has many faces and does not exist in isolation from other discourses that shape its various contexts. The term "culture" refers to the various practices and ways that societies choose to pattern themselves. Symbols and rituals, tradition, language, dress, food, behavior, and ethics mediate these practices. Other factors such as gender, class, religion, wealth, position, and laws also influence them. The laws can be written, unwritten, or based on consensus of the people. Depending on all the factors that shape it, culture as a social construct can be acceptable or unacceptable. As we know, cultural practices can be either positive or negative as seen from distinct perspectives.

Some aspects of African cultures are beautiful and hence Africans have good reason to be proud to show them everywhere. However, it is also necessary to look at one's own culture with a critical eye in order to locate the axis of gender inequalities and subordination, and to examine how religion is used to shape women's sexual rights and autonomy. The practices of female genital mutilation, early or forced marriage, and gender-based violence both at a community level and at a household level are features of many cultures. These practices are gender-specific and if women do not bring them to the public domain, little or no attention will be given to them. Even feminist activists sometimes try to gloss over these negative issues. Indeed, patriarchal resistance can be so strong that some, eventually, give up the fight or take on compromising views, to allow the perpetuation of these practices. These are the areas of female subordination, however, and I am of the view that the conditions of African women can be improved only if there is a general acknowledgement that cultural practices can, indeed, contribute to gender inequality and oppression. Many women and children suffer in silence, not because they accept what is happening to them, but because their culture sanctions it. Many times there is no cultural space available for these victims of cultural oppression to express their objections. It is particularly in the practice of female genital mutilation that the culture of silence prevails.

This chapter looks at that practice. Female genital mutilation is gender-specific and affects the bodily integrity and dignity of women and girls in the name of honor for men. I shall look particularly at religious arguments, based on text interpretation, which are used to reinforce the practice. A discussion of female genital mutilation also involves a discussion of sexuality. Sexuality not only includes the realm of sexual carnal experience, but all concepts that relate to the social and sexual construction of women in our society. Religion is not divorced from the concept of sexuality. Rather, the nexus of religion, culture, and tradition informs us how women are viewed.

I take a feminist approach to Islam here that challenges traditional interpretations of religious texts. The chapter will attempt to look at how female sexuality is shaped in Muslim religious discourses and will provide some examples of women's personal status law. My empirical focus is particularly gender-based violence against women. Furthermore, I will examine how religious texts are used to justify female genital mutilation, which is a practice that affects the health and well-being of more than 30 million women and children in Africa and elsewhere. Throughout the chapter, I attempt to show the contextual situation by drawing on various sources that discuss cultural practices in an Islamic context.

Feminist Approach to Islam

The practice of female genital mutilation is associated with culture and reinforced by religious misinterpretations. Traditional practices in African communities are justified by religious scholars and they resist stopping the practice in the name of Islam. Their arguments are drawn from religious, cultural, and traditional points of view. Shar'ia law and a weak and unauthenticated Hadith are also used to justify these practices. These multi-layered perspectives, therefore, legitimize certain practices in the name of culture and religion.

General observations confirm that cultures are fluid and interactive rather than distinct from each other. They exist on a continuum. Internal and external forces influence cultural adaptations and reformations. Those forces usually operate from a patriarchal point of view. In light of those developments, feminist scholars are challenged to delineate the gender specific issues, while emphasizing the agency of women. This agency will influence an understanding of culture and religion from the perspective of women who can read the subtexts that influence contemporary practices. Personally, as a woman who wishes to remain true to the Islamic values that are grounded in the search for social justice and gender equality (*musawah*), I engage in critical thinking that is consistent with the Islamic notion of *Ijtihad*, or reasoning, which is a domain where both men and women are required to participate and engage in the advancement of knowledge.

The message of Islam is universal and addressed to the entire people (*Umma*). Islam recognizes and respects all revealed religions, prophets, and messengers. It is based on moderation, peaceful coexistence, constant common values (the five pillars), cooperation and mutual understanding between civilizations. It further emphasizes religious and moral education. Islam also seeks constructive dialogue among religions and cultures, and thereby forms part of human civilization. What genuine scholars are entitled to is to dig into the various sources and come up with analyses and outcomes that respect the dignity of the person. However, some Muslim scholars or preachers ignore or misunderstand this fact or process, particularly on aspects relating to women's strategic concerns and interests. I observed that most of the issues affecting women's personal status are misinterpreted or partially applied resulting from the misapplication of justice for women. It is essential that Islamic and universal principles of justice, equality, and dignity be reflected in the social relationships between men and women.

Naturally, women's rights must not be seen from a homogenous perspective but in light of the diversity and individuality of women. Recognition of diversity is necessary to understand women's rights from the context of our lived realities better. In addition, it is important to interrogate the sources scholars use since most, if not all, tend to have gender-biased perspectives. There is a need to understand the context—the classification and authenticity—of the referenced *Ahadith*, as well as the nature of the issues.

For example, Ayesha Imam, in her paper titled "Recovering Women's Reproductive Rights: Classical Muslim Scholars Versus Contemporary Fundamentalist Alliances," outlined how Muslim laws are constructed on the basis of five central principles. The first principle is to rely on the Qur'an (Imam 2005). If there are no explicit provisions in the Qur'an, then the *sunnah* plays a role in construction. Muslim laws are further developed through *qiyas* (analogy), through *ijtihad* (interpretive reasoning), and finally through *ijma* (consensus about what the law is). Amina Wadud further noted that although the words of the Qur'an are unquestioned, what they mean, how they should be understood in contemporary times, which verses take priority, and how they should be construed in *Fiqh* (Islamic Jurisprudence) and thence into *Shar'ia* (Muslim laws), is and has always been subject to discussions or even controversy (Wadud 1999). Notably, these levels in Islam always created controversy between progressives and conservatives regarding women's rights. Contradictions between text and the interpretations of various schools of thought exist when it comes to issues regarding female sexuality and sexual rights. Female genital mutilation is a case in point. There are also disputes over what constitutes the *Sunnah* as well as issues about the validity and authenticity of the *Ahadith*.

The *Hadith* that many scholars use as justification for the practice of female genital mutilation is drawn from the narrations of Abu Dawud, who himself acknowledges that his sources are weak and unauthenticated. Some scholars do not even refer to the *Ahadith* because of the disputes it generates. Others, however, use it to control women. Most of the sources do not recognize the role played by the wives of the prophet in transmitting the *Ahadith*. Ayesha, for example, notably provided most of the authentic *Ahadith*. As stated by the Prophet, "take half your religion from that woman."

While not putting in any doubt that the Qur'anic text was revealed to the Prophet of Islam, it remains clear that the whole text was subjected to different understandings in various social contexts. Indeed, the text of the Qur'an was the subject of interpretations by scholars contributing to different understandings of the text. Thus, a plurality of views regarding textual understanding provides wide discretion for interpretation. Normally, male scholars consider this area their preserve. In light of the current circumstances and situations women face, however, feminist scholars question the validity of some of these interpretations.

Women's rights activists and Muslim women in particular stimulated current debates in Islamic eschatology and discourses. Among these are Sisters In Islam (SIS), Women Living Under Muslim Laws (WLUML) and other feminist sororities throughout the world. The interpretation, and especially the distortion, of religious texts create a divide among women even within the same faith. This divide centers on sexuality, politics of control, and dominance. For example, women who do not wear the *hijab* are sometimes considered "good women" as long as they appear covered. Circumcised women are also considered good Muslims. Some cultures teach that an uncircumcised woman will not cross *Serat* (the bridge of salvation) and therefore the possibility of their going to heaven is remote. These myths about the sexuality of women, however, affect the extent to which they are able to self-actualize.

Grassroots activism has noticeably revealed that progress in the realization of women's rights in the name of Islam remains frozen. Women in both rural and urban communities seem to accept the conservative interpretations of their personal status law, despite the fact that they consider it unfair. The critical areas of contention involve issues of personal status law for women. Various interpretations of those issues originate from traditionalists who base their views on political economy and the self-perpetuation of men as superior. Women's sexuality, in particular that of Muslim women, has been used by various civilizations as a political tool influenced by capitalism and unequal power relations. The policies of the Taliban, who used women's dress codes as a negotiation tool during the war, constitute just one testimony of double standards.

The recent "Rabat Declaration" on children's rights by the Organization of Islamic Conference (OIC), and the Islamic Educational, Scientific and Cultural Organization (ISESCO) regarding female genital mutilation, are steps in the right direction. The stance taken by these religious bodies opened up an opportunity for feminist theologians and activists to find vindication. To some extent, those groups directly addressed women's sexual rights, bodily integrity, and violence against women. They also extricated the blurred Islamic perspectives of female genital mutilation and other harmful traditional practices, such as early marriage and wife inheritance.

In Gambia, like in many sub-Saharan countries, the practice of female genital mutilation is, indeed, associated with the religion of Islam. Recently, women challenged religious views posited by some Islamic scholars. These challenges created a universal debate where interpretations of religious texts occupy center stage. Such debates open up the wide horizon of *ijtihad*, in which different scholars, including feminist academics, engage in a discussion of women's rights in Islam. These debates also lead to a convergence of religious practices (Sunni and Shi'a) in defining women's sexuality. In addition, differences occur on matters of personal status. For example, regarding marriage, the Maliki School recognizes a father's right to give away his never married daughter without her consent. On the other hand, the Hanafi School allows or accepts women and men to choose their own marriage partners without a guardian. These nuances provide the existing lacunae in Islamic jurisprudence for feminist interpretations of the text. Already more than a century ago, Amin observed,

> The scholars for whom these schools of law were named did not see themselves as setting down a God-given legal code to be obeyed by all Muslims for all times. On the contrary they were quite categorical that Muslims were not obliged to follow them if they did not believe that their reasoning from the Qu'ran and the sunnah were right. Imam Malik cautioned: "I am but a human being. I may be wrong and I may be right. So first examine what I say. If it complies with the Book and sunnah, then you may accept it. But if it does not comply with them, then you should reject it."[1]

Human subjectivities can affect peoples' interpretations and result in injustices. Thus, gender politics is quite apparent in the debate on women's rights across all religions. The commonality among all faiths is that women are lesser beings and the dictates of the religion is to control them. The following section looks at discourses that shape women's sexuality in the context of Islam.

Discourses on Female Sexuality from the Islamic Perspective

I shall now provide a brief overview of issues related to sex and sexuality in Muslim societies, starting with a summary of traditional and contemporary discourses. From there I shall draw from various schools of thought and practices that structure female sexuality, trying to develop the nuances found throughout those various interpretations. However, this chapter is not an attempt to provide answers. Rather, its aim is to raise various critical questions concerning the validity of theological interpretations and to examine the viewpoint of those who propagate these interpretations. This section sets out to provide examples of the practices and the prescriptions regarding aspects of personal status law of women.

Definition and Purpose of Sex

Sex refers to an individual's biology. This may be male, female, or both in the case of intersexed individuals. Sex also refers to activity associated with being sexual, though it often only applies to the act of sexual intercourse in most cultures. Sexuality, on the other hand, refers to social behaviors associated with or arising out of an individual's biological sex. Different sexualities emerge out of various interpretations of biological sex and take form in various socially acceptable (at times less acceptable) means for realizing and expressing the needs associated with biological sex. For example, female genital mutilation is associated with controlling female sexual urges and sexual pleasure. Some Muslim scholars interpreted the practice as a sign of honor and respect for men.

Sexuality as a function of gender creates many interpretations, with particular sexual behaviors associated with specific notions of gender (Dunne 1998, 9). The Qur'anic notion of sexuality recognizes the active nature of both male and female sexuality. Indeed, Qur'anic notions of sexuality promote physical and emotional love since the Qur'an affirms that God has ordained "love and mercy" between mates. Celibacy plays a lesser role in Islam. The Qur'an places a high value on marriage and reproduction, but they are not necessarily obligatory. The erotic dimensions of sexuality are well founded in Islamic literature of medieval times. The poems and song lyrics all support the eroticism of sexuality in Islam:

> And of his signs is this that He created for you from yourselves mates that you may find tranquility in them; and He placed between you affection and mercy. Indeed, these are signs for people who give thought (S30:21).[2]
> O mankind! Lo! We have created you from a male and a female and have made you nations and tribes that you may know one another. Indeed, the most noble of you in the sight of Allah is the most righteous. (S49:13)[3]

The Qur'an affirms sex differences as a means of differentiating humanity in a manner that promotes awareness about the equal existence of both sexes. Men and women are different from each other, so that they may come to know each other. Since people may know each other in numerous ways, these include a possibility of knowing those of different sexes and learning about their particularities. However, verses that speak of sexual differences are often read to mean that men have strength and are the protectors and maintainers of women. Some interpretations have shown that men will be above women if they fulfill the conditions laid down by Allah regarding the responsibility of men to protect women. Given the current political economy and the emerging trend of female-headed households in Africa, the idea that men are protectors of women is no longer tenable. The rise in domestic violence resulting in divorce increasingly makes women assume more responsibility for their children and for themselves, thus causing the question of inheritance and the portions ordained for men to be revisited.

The Qur'an also views the physical differences between the sexes as a means of explaining different social phenomena. In the following verses, the Qur'an explains that where men are stronger than women, and where men support women, there they play the role of protectors and maintainers of women:

> Men are in charge of women[4] by (right of) what Allah has given over the other and what they spend (maintenance) from their wealth. So righteous women are devoutly obedient, guarding in (the husband's) absence what Allah would have them guard.[5]
>
> Men are the protectors and maintainers of women, because Allah has given the one more (strength) than the other, and because they support them from their means. (S4:V34)

While the above verses purportedly derive from the same divine source, they raise a fundamental question as to whether the Qur'an is being rewritten. The issue of interpretation in terms of engagement with the text has gender implications. Marriage is the expected norm in most Muslim communities. Marriage laws legitimize the control and subjugation of women. In the area of divorce, the next verse of the Qur'an shows that when men have a greater right to revoke a divorce than women, then men inevitably have a degree of advantage over women: "Divorced women shall wait concerning themselves for three monthly periods. Nor is it lawful for them to hide what Allah hath created in their wombs, if they have faith in Allah and the Last Day. And their husbands have the better right to take them back in that period, if they wish for reconciliation. And women shall have rights similar to the rights against them, according to what is equitable; but men have a degree (of advantage) over them. And Allah is exalted in Power, Wise" (S2:V228).

Assumptions from Different Scholars Regarding Female Sexuality in the Context of Religion

While sexuality entails a complex set of sexual feelings and practices, reproductive health and rights of men and women in the context of their existence, behavior, and personality, the gendered nature of Islamic interpretation presents a basis for differentiation and discrimination between the sexes. Muslim scholarship over time created myths and beliefs to support these differentiations. Menstruation and pregnancy have been associated with weakness emanating from biological sex, and historical texts list a host of associated "deficiencies" that include monthly physical weakness, inability to pray, and excessive emotions. Women are also seen as *fitra/fitna*[6] to mask male weakness for not controlling their sexual feelings or urges. Notions of women as lesser beings, of defective female intelligence, and of women's propensity for evil[7] are later developments in Muslim thought and reflect in large part the cultural heritage that Islam incorporated in the areas of its expansion.

Locating Women's Sexuality and Sexual Rights in the Context of Cultural Practices: The Case of Female Genital Mutilation

Naturally, sexual rights are about sexuality, and discourses around them vary. In Islam, there are different schools of thought that attempt to construct women's sexual rights with reference to their personal status. The personal status law of the Muslim woman relates to issues of inheritance, marriage, custody, divorce, widowhood, sex, and sexual autonomy. Traditionally anything related to sex and sexuality in Islam takes place within the framework of marriage. Fulfillment of sexual desire and pleasure abide solely within a heterosexual relationship. Classical and medieval Islamic scholarship, on the other hand, has shown a markedly different perspective of sex and sexuality. For example, the works of Al Ghazali and of the Sufis have shown the erotic dimensions of sexuality in Islam. The departure from that medieval view took place when modern Muslim society was becoming more politicized and restricted. Similarly, Western notions of sexuality changed in response to Victorian cultural ideals of sex and sexuality within the framework of the church. However, postmodern discourses of sexuality are crossing boundaries and reclaiming some of the practices of the past. Within the context of Islam, such trends become evident when Muslim feminists are involved in *ijtihad* and analyze sexuality, particularly women's sexuality. They reveal that the organization of sexuality in Islam is influenced by the notion of what an ideal woman should be (Ilkaracan 2005; GAMCOTRAP 2003).

A particular contextual setting is, indeed, female genital mutilation in the context of Gambia. More than 80–90 percent of Gambian women are circumcised and all the major ethnic groups, such as the Mandinka, Fulla, Serahuli, Jahanka, and Jola, practice female genital mutilation. Most women suffer either clitoridectomy or excision. Data revealed that only a few Gambian women undergo infibulations. Some of the women who marry men from the practicing culture are forced to undergo the practice in order to be accepted, due to social pressure from other women within the community. In Gambia, the practice is associated with culture, tradition and religion. From a cultural perspective, female genital mutilation is a form of cultural identity and cohesion that bonds the group together. It is also a symbol of being an ideal woman in the culture. From a traditional point of view, the practice has been passed on from one generation to another. Indeed, it has been a long-standing practice among women, supported by men. The third explanation associated with female genital mutilation in Gambia is the Islamic religion. Some Muslim scholars wrongly associated the practice with Islam and misinterpreted an unauthenticated *hadith* to justify it.

Imam Abdoulie Fatty of the State House mosque in Banjul narrates that female genital mutilation is a religious injunction and hence he urges women to continue the practice. His arguments are based on the *hadith* of Umm Attia, a woman known to have practiced it in Medina during the time of the prophet Mohamed. In their religious sermons (*hudba*), those scholars associate female genital mutilation with cleanliness for women. According to them, uncircumcised is unclean and her prayers will not be answered. Another interpretation of scholars referring to Islamic texts regarding the practice relates to the story of Sarata who was the first wife of the Prophet Abraham. It is narrated that Sarata subjected Hajara, the second wife of the Prophet Abraham, to female circumcision because she was jealous due to the attention given to her cowife. The first wife Sarata was demonized and accused of inflicting pain on her cowife Hajara. Almost all serious Muslim scholars, however, concluded that the *hadith* of Umm Attia is unauthenticated and have shown the fallacy of that interpretation of female genital mutilation from the Islamic perspective. Undoubtedly, female genital mutilation has nothing to do with the religion. The call for circumcision was directed at Abraham and his sons. It was also associated with improving sexual hygiene for men. As a result, many Muslims embraced the practice for their sons, but even this was not an obligation. Female genital mutilation, on the other hand, negatively affects women's sexual rights and reproductive health, as well as their bodily integrity.

The recent debates in Africa regarding women's rights underwent various challenges by Islamic scholars who interpret issues of sexuality and sexual rights in a way that prevents women from attaining sexual autonomy. Looking at the current trends, the areas affecting female sexuality and women's sexual rights are the ones addressed in the *African Protocol on Human Rights and the Rights of Women in Africa*. Article 5 is meant to eliminate traditional harmful practices such as female genital mutilation[8]; article 6 attempts to ensure equal rights in marriage[9]; article 7 regulates equality in divorce[10]; article 14 deals with health and reproductive rights[11]; and article 26 aims to ensure monitoring and implementation.[12]

Initially, many African countries rejected the articles because they are not in line with people's religion. The same trend of resistance also occurred in Beijing in 1995. Consequently, feminist scholars and activists engaged in *ijtihad* in order to reinterpret the religious texts in accord with the *African Protocol on Human Rights and the Rights of Women in Africa*.

They asserted those rights as against the state and/or religious scholars. However, the level of resistance in Beijing was formidable, which led to further negotiations in subsequent conferences. It is, indeed, important to note that progress in the struggle for women's rights has come but there remains much to accomplish.

It is the manner of women's socialization that they believe only male scholars read and interpret the Qu'ran. Ignorance of the religious text resulted in dependence of too many women on male scholars whose opinions shape the way they appear, think, and act. One has to acknowledge though that ignorance of their rights in Islam is a contributing factor. Recently in Gambia, some women adopted the use of *hijab*, a practice alien to Gambian religious culture. This may be a manifestation of Muslim fundamentalism and a gradual process of control over women's bodies, minds, and spaces. Throughout history, women have been patriarchal gatekeepers, by responding and defending discriminatory practices that affect women's rights in the name of Islam. Similarly, gender discrimination is apparent in the way that Shar'ia applies on matters of adultery. One example is the case of Amina Lawal, a Nigerian woman accused of adultery. She was convicted and sentenced to death by stoning in March 2002, but the decision was overturned through the efforts of NGO movements in Nigeria as well as from international networks of women's rights and human rights activists. The creative use of Shar'ia, statutory, customary, and international human rights instruments has shown how to interpret these texts to assert and protect women's rights. The laws against female genital mutilation passed by some countries constitute another example of alternative interpretations of Islam that influence the implementation of policies to promote women and children's rights. However, alternative interpretations of the text are not encouraged in our communities. Female scholars who attempt to contribute to an alternative interpretation of the text are hardly encouraged to do so. Therefore, efforts to protect women's rights are still urgently needed.

Suggestions for Improving the Interpretations

With regard to religious texts, the foregoing discussions revealed the limitation of human interpretations and demonstrated the necessity that both men and women be recognized as authorities. Customary laws, statutory laws, and Islamic jurisprudence (*fiqh*) should not be regarded as static. Rather, they are dynamic and exist on a continuum to allow for changes as the need arises. Furthermore, it is necessary to develop progressive interpretations of those texts in order to promote the human rights of women and children. Since the family code of many countries discriminates against women and children, the judiciary, *Qadi* court personnel, lawyers, and the police need to undergo gender awareness training.

The protection of women's rights can improve by creating solidarity and networks of communication among the various organizations that work on women's sexual rights. Those organizations can learn from each other's experiences and share landmark cases where progressive interpretation restored women's rights and equality before the law. The case of Amina Lawal is just one example. Based on the lessons of those cases, NGOs can use strategic impact litigation to advance other cases. Finally, NGOs can work at a grassroots level to raise the consciousness of women and men and create awareness for gender equality.

Conclusion

This chapter set out to contribute to the debate on women's sexual rights and reproductive health, especially from the context of Islamic religion. It raised the issue of female genital mutilation in the context of Islam and explained how misinterpretations of religious texts contributed to the circumcision of more than 30 million women and children in Africa and beyond. It examined the various discourses on female sexuality in the context of the prevailing religion and how those views are used and abused to violate women's sexual and reproductive health and rights. The chapter also provided examples on how women's rights organizations and feminist activists advocate for those rights by using the sacred text and the human rights conventions, while it argued that feminist interpretations are a new way of understanding the text, without changing the text itself. Finally, this chapter suggested various strategies to improve the debate on women's rights from the religious perspective regarding the debates on female genital mutilation.

Notes

1. Qasim Amin, quoted by Imam, *op. cit.*
2. Qur'anic quotations in this chapter follow the edition by Saheeh International.
3. Literally, "he who has the most taqwa" or consciousness and fear of Allah, piety, and righteousness and the "he" is generic applying to both male and female.
4. This applies primarily to the husband-wife relationship
5. Their husband's property and their own chastity
6. The term fitna/fitra is rich in connotation and has a wide semantic field. Its root meaning is affliction or temptation from the straight path. In social or

religious terms, it connotes civil strife within the umma (religious collectivity). It also has a clear field of sexuality where women are seen as the bearers of fitna (chaos and disorder) because they distract men and tempt them to sin.
7. Narrated Abu Said Al-Khudri: Once Allah's Apostle went out to the Musalla (to offer the prayer) o 'Id-al-Adha or Al-Fitr prayer. Then he passed by the women and said, "O women! Give alms, as I have seen that the majority of the dwellers of Hell-fire were you (women)." They asked, "Why is it so, O Allah's Apostle?" He replied, "You curse frequently and are ungrateful to your husbands. I have not seen anyone more deficient in intelligence and religion than you. A cautious sensible man could be led astray by some of you." The women asked, "O Allah's Apostle! What is deficient in our intelligence and religion?" He said, "Is not the evidence of two women equal to the witness of one man?" They replied in the affirmative. He said, "This is the deficiency in her intelligence. Isn't it true that a woman can neither pray nor fast during her menses?" The women replied in the affirmative. He said, "This is the deficiency in her religion" [Buhkari: Volume 1, Book 6, Number 301].
8. Article 5: Elimination of Harmful Traditional Practices: *State parties shall prohibit and condemn all forms of harmful traditional practices which negatively affect the human rights of women and which are contrary to recognised international standards. States shall take all necessary legislative and other measures to eliminate such practices, including*:
    a) creation of public awareness in all sectors of society regarding harmful practices through information, formal and informal education and outreach programs;
    b) prohibition through legislative measures backed by sanctions, of all forms of female genital mutilation, scarification, medicalization and para-medicalization of female genital mutilation and all other practices in order to eradicate them;
    c) provision of necessary support to victims of harmful practices through basic services such as health services, legal and judicial support, emotional and psychological counselling as well as vocational training to make them self supporting; and
    d) protection of women who are at risk of being subjected to harmful practices or all other forms of violence, abuse and intolerance.
9. Article 6: Marriage: *State parties shall ensure that women and men enjoy equal rights and are regarded as equal partners in marriage. They shall enact appropriate national legislative measures to guarantee that*:
    a) no marriage shall take place without the free and full consent of both partners;
    b) the minimum age of marriage for women shall be 18 years;
    c) monogamy is encouraged as the preferred form of marriage and that the rights of women in marriage and family, including in polygamous marital relationships are promoted and protected;
    d) every marriage shall be recorded in writing and registered in accordance with national laws, in order to be legally recognised;

e) the husband and wife shall by mutual agreement, choose their matrimonial regime and place of residence;
f) a married woman shall have the right to retain her maiden name, to use it as she pleases, jointly or separately with her husband's surname;
g) a woman shall have the right to retain her nationality or to acquire the nationality of the husband
h) a woman and a man shall have equal rights, with respect to the nationality of their children except where this is contrary to a provision in national legislation or is contrary to national security interests;
i) a woman and a man shall jointly contribute to safeguarding the interest of the family, protecting and educating their children; and
j) during her marriage, a woman shall have the right to acquire her own property and to administer and manage it freely.

10. Article 7: Separation, Divorce and Annulment of Marriage: *State parties shall enact appropriate legislation to ensure that women and men endure the same rights in case of separation, divorce or annulment of marriage. In this regard, they shall ensure that*:
    a) separation, divorce or annulment of a marriage shall be effected by judicial order;
    b) women and men shall have the same rights to seek separation, divorce or annulment of a marriage;
    c) in case of separation, divorce or annulment of marriage, women and men shall have reciprocal rights and responsibilities towards their children. In any case, the interest of the children shall be given paramount importance; and
    d) in case of separation, divorce or annulment of marriage, women and men shall have the right to an equitable sharing of the joint property deriving from the marriage.

11. Article 14: Health and Reproductive Rights: *State parties shall ensure that the right to health of women, including sexual and reproductive health is respected and promoted. This includes*:
    a) the right to control their fertility,
    b) the right to decide whether to have children, the number of children and the spacing of the children;
    c) the right to choose any method of contraception;
    d) the right to self protection and to be protected against sexually transmitted infections, including HIV/AIDS;
    e) the right to be informed on one's health status and on the health status of one's partner, particularly if affected with sexually transmitted infections, including HIV/AIDS, in accordance with internationally recognised standards and best practices; and
    f) right to have family planning education.

State parties shall take all appropriate measures to:
  a) provide adequate, affordable and accessible health services, including information, education and communication programs to women and especially those in rural areas;
  b) establish and strengthen existing pre-natal, delivery and post-natal health and nutritional services for women during pregnancy and while they are breast feeding; and
  c) protect the reproductive rights of women by authorizing medical abortion in cases of sexual assault, rape, incest, and where the continued pregnancy endangers the mental and physical health of the mother or the life of the mother or the fetus.
12. Article 26. Implementation and Monitoring: *State parties shall ensure the implementation of this protocol at national level, and in their periodic reports submitted in accordance with Article 62 of the African Charter, indicate the legislative and other measures undertaken for the full realization of the rights herein recognized.*

References

Abeyesekera, S. 1995. *Women's Human Rights: Questions of Equality and Difference.* The Hague: Institute of Social Studies, Working Paper No. 186.
Abubakar, S. 1977. *The Lamibe of Fombina. A Political History of Adamawa 1809–1901.* Zaria, Nigeria: Ahmadu Bello University Press.
Adamu, M. 1978. *The Hausa Factor in Westr African History,* 91–111. Zaria: Ahmadu Bello University Press.
Agijah, J. 1985. "The Christian Traditional Title Holder: An Exclusive Interview with His Royal Highness, Rev. Wilberforce Mayhwhegi [sic]: The King of Bachama." *Today's Challenge,* March/April, 16–19.
Alberigo, G. n.d. *A Brief History of Vatican II*; G. Caprile (1965–1969) *Il Concilio Vaticano II: cronache del Concilio Vaticano II edite de La Civilta Cattolica,* 6 vols. Rome: Civiltà cattolica.
Alberigo, G., and J. A. Komonchak (eds.) (1995–2006) *History of Vatican II,* 5 vols. Leuven, Belgium: Peeters.
Aleyideino, S. 1993. "Address Delivered by the Guest Speaker Professor Samuel Aleyideino at the Launching of the Gwaha Foundation at Demsa." *Linto* 1(1): 6.
Ali, Abdullah Yusuf. n.d. *The Meaning of The Holy Qur'an* [English translation]. http://house.com/religions/islam/Qu'ran.html (accessed August 2008).
Ali, J. 1978. *Detailed in pre-Islamic History of Arab.* Beirut: Darol Eilm Lel Malaein.
Amar, Akhil Reed. 2005. *America's Constitution: A Biography.* New York: Random House.
Anderson, John. 2003. *Religious Liberty in Transitional Societies: The Politics of Religion.* Cambridge: Cambridge University Press.
An-Na'im, A. A. 1990. *Towards an Islamic Reformation: Civil Liberties, Human Rights and International Law.* New York: Syracuse University Press.
———. 1995. *Human Rights in Cross-Cultural Perspectives: A Quest for Consensus.* Philadelphia: University of Pennsylvania Press.
Asad, M. 1993. *The Message of the Qur'an.* Gibraltar: Dar al-Andalus.
Ascha, G. 1989. *Du statut inférieur de la femme en Islam.* Paris: Harmattan.
———. 1996. "Moslimvrouwen: tussen sjarie'a en moderne tijd." In *Islam in een ontzuilde samenleving,* ed. R. Lavrijsen, 27–56. Amsterdam: Koninklijk Instituut voor de Tropen.
———. 1998. *Marriage, polygamie et repudiation en islam.* Paris: Harmattan.
Asodati, D. B. n.d. *The Mysteries of Nzeanzo and the Vunon Festival of Fare.* Wukari, Nigeria: Amune Press.

Augustine. *On Free Choice of the Will* (*De libero arbitrio*), Bk I, Chapter II. Trans. Anna S. Benjamin and L. H. Hackstaff (1964) seventh reprint, with an introduction by L. H. Hackstaff. Indianapolis: Bobbs-Merrill Publishing, 1984.

Badiou, A. 2003. *Saint Paul: The Foundation of Universalism*. Stanford: Stanford University Press, pp. 98–10 6.

Barr, J. 1980 "The Bible as a Political Document." In *Explorations in Theology, Vol. 7: The Scope and Authority of the Bible*, ed. J. Barr. London: SCM.

Beitz, Charles R. 2003. "What Human Rights Mean." *Daedalus* 132(1): 36.

Bell, Lynda S., Andrew J. Nathan, and Ilan Peleg. 2001. *Negotiating Culture and Human Rights*. New York: Columbia University Press.

Bell, R. 1969. *The Origin of Islam in its Christian Environment*. London, Cass & Co. (Orig. pub. 1926).

Belton, R. K. 2005. *Competing Definitions of Rule of Law: Implications for Practitioners*. Washington, DC: Carnegie Endowment for International Peace, Working Paper no. 55, p. 5.

Berting, Jan, Peter R. Baehr, J. Herman Burgers, Cees Flinterman, Barbara de Klerk, Rob Kroes, Cornelis A. van Minnen, and Koo VanderWal. 1990. *Human Rights in a Pluralist World: Individuals and Collectivities*. Westport, CT: Meckler.

Best, E. 1983 *Mark. The Gospel as Story* Studies of the New Testament and Its World. Edinburgh: T. & T. Clark.

Bewley, A. A. 1989. *Al-Muwatta of Imam Malik ibn Anas. The First Formulation of Islamic Law*. London: Kegan Paul.

Biliyong, D. B. 1964. "Afrikanske overvejelser om kristendom og politik." In *Under Afrikas Sol*, ed. Agnes Brandt, 33–36. Stockholm: Författares bokmaskin.

Birmingham, D. 1999. *Kwame Nkrumah*. London: Cardinal.

Black-Branch, J. L. 1996–97. "Observing and Enforcing Human Rights Under the Council of Europe: The Creation of a Permanent European Court of Human Rights." *Buffalo Journal of International Law* 3:1–32.

Boff, Leonardo. 1988. *When Theology Listens to the Poor*. Trans. Robert R. Barr. San Francisco: Harper & Row, pp. 24–25.

Bonner, G. 1983. *St. Augustine of Hippo. Life and Controversies*. Norwich, Britain: Canterbury Press, pp. 370–93.

Borromeo, A., ed. 2003. *L'Inquisizione. Atti del Simposio internazionale* (Città del Vaticano, 29–31 ottobre 1998). Città del Vaticano: Biblioteca apostolica vaticana.

Boswell, J. 1980. *Christianity, Social Tolerance, and Homosexuality: Gay People in Western Europe from the Beginning of the Christian Era to the Fourteenth Century*. Chicago: University of Chicago Press.

———. 1994. *Same-Sex Unions in Premodern Europe*. New York: Villard Books.

Botha, P. J. J. 1993. "The Historical Setting of Mark's Gospel: Problems and Possibilities." *Journal of the Study of New Testament* (*JSNT*) 51: 27–55.

Boyle, Kevin, and Juliet Sheen, eds. 1997. *Freedom of Religion and Belief: A World Report*. London: Routledge.

Brems, E. 2001. *Human Rights: Universality and Diversity*. The Hague: Martinus Nijhoff Publishers.

Brock, Peggy, ed. 2005. *Indigenous Peoples and Religious Change.* Leiden and Boston: Brill.

Brønnum, N. H. 1926. *Under Dæmoners Aag. Bachamafolkets Religion og Overtro.* Copenhagen: O. Lohse, pp. 33–46.

Brooten, B. 1996. *Love Between Women: Early Christian Responses to Female Homoeroticism.* Chicago: University of Chicago Press.

———. 2003. "Nature, Law, and Custom in Augustine's *On the Good of Marriage*." In *Walk in the Ways of Wisdom*, eds. S. Matthews, C. B. Kittredge, and M. Johnson-Debaufre. New York: Trinity Press International.

Brooten, B., and N. Greinacher. 1982. *Frauen in der Männerkirche?* Mainz, Germany: Grünewald; Munich: Kaiser.

Brown, D. 2004. *The Da Vinci Code.* New York. Doubleday.

Brown, P. 1988. *Body and Society. Men, Women, and Sexual Renunciation in Early Christianity.* New York: Columbia University Press, pp. 44–57.

Burrus, V. 2000. *Begotten Not Made: Conceiving Manhood in Late Antiquity.* Stanford: Stanford University Press.

———. 2004. *The Sex Lives of Saints: An Erotics of Ancient Hagiography.* Philadelphia: University of Pennsylvania Press.

———. 2007. *Saving Shame: Martyrs, Saints, and Other Abject Subjects.* Philadelphia: University of Pennsylvania Press.

Cameron, A. 1991. *Christianity and the Rhetoric of Empire: The Development of Christian Discourse.* Berkeley: University of California Press.

Canadian International Development Agency (CIDA). 2006. "Governance—Overview." http://www.acdi-cida.gc.ca/CIDAWEB/acdicida.nsf/En/JUD-121132928-PPH (accessed June 2007).

Canon Law Society of America. 1982. *The Art of Interpretation.* Washington: CLSA, pp. 28–34.

Carnochan, J. 1967. "The Coming of the Fulani: A Bachama Oral Tradition." *Bulletin of the School of Oriental and African Studies* XXX(3): 632–33.

Carter, M. 1976. "Dignitatis Humanae Declaration on Religious Freedom." *The Jurist* 36:338–52.

Chakrabarti, A. P. 1993. *Muslim Identity and Community Consciousness: Bengal Legislative Politics.* Calcutta, India: Minerva Associates.

Chakravorty, Pinaki. 1995. "The Rushdie Incident as Law-and-Literature Parable." *Yale Law Journal* 104. http://www.encyclopedia.com/doc/1G1-17150046.html (accessed October 2007).

Changing Patterns of Security in the Middle East and Central Asia, 2005. 2005. Workshop cohosted by the Department of National Security Affairs at the Naval Postgraduate School and the Center for Strategic Studies at the CNA Corporation, May 19.

Chilton, B. 1996. *Pure Kingdom. Jesus' Vision of God*, Studying the Historical Jesus. Grand Rapids: Wm. B. Eerdmans.

Clark, E. A. 1986a. "Adam's Only Companion: Augustine and the Early Christian Debate on Marriage." *Recherches Augustiniennes* 21:139–62.

———. 1986b. *Ascetic Piety and Women's Faith: Essays on Late Ancient Christianity.* Lewiston, NY: Edwin Mellen Press.

———. 1991. "Sex, Shame and Rhetoric: Engendering Early-Christian Ethics." *Journal of the American Academy of Religion* 49:221–47.

———. 1999. *Reading Renunciation. Asceticism and Scripture in Early Christianity.* Princeton: Princeton University Press.

———.2004. *History, Theory, Text: Historians and the Linguistic Turn.* Cambridge: Harvard University Press, pp. 158–61.

———, ed. 1983. *Women in the Early Church.* Collegeville: Liturgical Press.

Codex Iuris Canonici auctoritate Ioannis Pauli PP. II promulgatus. 1998. Vatican City: Libreria Editrice Vaticana, 1983. English translation from *Code of Canon Law, Latin-English Edition: New English Translation.* Washington, DC: CLSA.

Codex Iuris Canonici Pii X Pontificis Maximi iussu digestus Benedicti Papae XV auctoritate promulgatus. 1917. Rome: Typis Polyglottis Vaticanis.

Coleman, J. S. 1958. *Nigeria: Background to Nationalism.* Berkeley: University of California Press.

Colish, Marcia L. 1983. *The Mirror of Language: A Study in the Medieval Theory of Knowledge*, rev. ed. Lincoln: University of Nebraska Press.

———. 1990. *The Stoic Tradition from Antiquity to the Middle Ages. Vol. 2. Stoicism in Christian Latin Thought through the Sixth Century.* Leiden, The Netherlands: Brill, p. 27–29.

Congregation for the Doctrine of the Faith. 2000. Declaration *Dominus Iesus* August 6, 2000 *AAS* 92: 742–65.

Congrégation pour les Évêques. 1988 Décret d'excommunicationJuly 1, 1988, *La documentation catholique*, 70: 789.

Connell, F. J. 1948. "Christ the King of Civil Rulers." *The American Ecclesiastical Review* 119:244–53.

Coriden, J. 1982. "Rules for Interpreters." *The Art of Interpretation.* Cannon Law Society of America CLSA., pp. 1–27. http://www.google.nl/search?sourceid=navclient&ie=UTF-8&rlz=1T4SMSN_enNL340NL340&q=Coriden%2c+J.+1982.+%e2%80%9cRules+for+Interpreters.%e2%80%9d+The+Art+of+Interpretation.++Washington%3a+CLSA.+1982 (accessed August 2008).

Crampton, E. P. T. 1976. *Christianity in Northern Nigeria.* Zaria: Gaskiya Corporation, p. 48–100.

Dalactoura, Katerina. 1998. *Islam, Liberalism and Human Rights.* London: I. B. Tauris.

Dalli, A. 1976. *Double Descent: With Special Reference to the Bachama of Adamawa, North-East Nigeria* (MA thesis, University of London), p. 46–49.

Daniélou, S. J. 1961. *The Ministry of Women in the Early Church.* London: Faith Press.

Davey, N. 2004. "On the Polity of Experience: Towards a Hermeneutics of Attentiveness." *Renascence: Essays on Values in Literature* 56 (1).

Declerck, L., and C. Troisfontaines. n.d. "Paul VI et la liberté religieuse." Paper of the Brescia conference of the Istituto Paolo VI, 2007.

del Re, N. 1998. *La Curia Romana. Lineamenti storico-giuridici.* Città del Vaticano: Libreria Editrice Vatican, p. 249–52.

Fawkes, A. 1918. "The Papacy and the Modern State." *The Harvard Theological Review* 11:376–94.

Fendler, F. 1991. *Studien zum Markusevangelium. Zur Gattung, Chronologie, Messiasgeheimnistheorie und Überlieferung des zweiten Evangeliums.* Göttinger Theologische Arbeiten, 49. Göttingen, Germany: Vandenhoeck & Ruprecht.

Fenton, J. C. 1952. "Principles Underlying Traditional Church-State Doctrine." *The American Ecclesiastical Review* 126:452–62.

Filibus, M. P. 1998. *An Exploratory Study of the History, Nature and Management Model of Conflict Within a Local Congregation with Theological Implications for Pastoral Ministry: LCCN No. 1/Cathedral Numan, Adamawa State, Nigeria, as a Case Study.* Ph.D. thesis, Luther Seminary, St. Paul, Minnesota, p. 187–215.

Firestone, R. 1999. *Jihad: The Origins of Holy War in Islam.* New York: Oxford University Press.

Foucault, M. 1999/1969. *L'archéologie du Savoir.* Paris: Gallimard.

Fowler, R. M. 1991. *Let the Reader Understand: Reader-Response Criticism and the Gospel of Mark.* Minneapolis: Fortress Press.

Fredriksen, P. 1992. "Tyconius and Augustine on the Apocalypse." In *The Apocalypse in the Middle Ages*, ed. R. K. Emmerson and B. McGinn, 20–37. Ithaca, NY: Cornell University Press.

Frishman, J., W. Otten, and G. Rouwhorst, eds. 2004. *Religious Identity and the Problem of Historical Foundation: The Foundational Character of Authoritative Sources in the History of Christianity and Judaism.* Leiden, The Netherlands: Brill.

Fuchs, S. 2005. "The Attitude towards 'the Other' in the Bible, in the Light of Jewish Commentaries Throughout the Generations." December.

G. A. Res. 217 (III) D, U.N. Doc. A/RES/217 (III) D (10 December 1948).

Gadamer, Hans-Georg. 1975. *Truth and Method.* London: Sheed and Ward.

GAMCOTRAP. 2003. Gambia Women, Law and Customary Practices. Banjul, Gambia: GAMCOTRAP. http://www.gamcotrap.gm/index.html.

Garaudy, R. 1993. *Avons-nous besoin de Dieu?* Paris: Desclée de Brouwer, p. 201.

Geertz, C. 1968. *Islam Observed. Religious Developments in Morocco and Indonesia.* New Haven & London: Yale University Press.

Gifford, P. 2003. "The Bible as a Political Document in Africa." In *Scriptural Politics. The Bible and the Koran as Political Models in the Middle East and Africa*, ed. N. Kastfelt, 16–28. London: Hurst & Company.

Gonnet, D. 1994. *La liberté religieuse* à Vatican II. La contribution de John Courtney Murray s.j. (Paris: Cerf).

Granfield, P. 1979. "The Church as *Societas Perfecta* in the Schemata of Vatican I." *Church History* 48:431–66.

———. 1982. "The Rise and Fall of the Societas Perfecta." *Concilium*, 18(7): 3–9.

Greenberg, I. 2004. *For the Sake of Heaven and Earth: The New Encounter between Judaism and Christianity.* Philadelphia: Jewish Publication Society.

Greenberg, M. 1984. Al HaMikra v'Al HaYahadut. In *Communla Life: An International Perspective*, ed. Avraham Shapira. Tel Aviv: Am Oved.

Greenberg, M. 1996. *Conservative Judaism* XLVIII(2): 23–35.

Delorme, J. 1997. "Évangile et récit. La narration évangélique en Marc." *New Testament Studies* 43:367–84.

Dicey, A. V. 1982. *Introduction to the Study of the Law of the Constitution*. Indianapolis: Liberty Fund.

Dilthy, W., and R. Frithjof. 1996. *Rudolf A. Makkreel. Hermeneutics and the Study of History*. Princeton, NJ: Princeton University Press.

Dudley, B. J. 1968. *Parties and Politics in Northern Nigeria*. London: Frank Cass & Co.

Dunn, G. D. 2005. "Rhetoric and Tertullian's *De virginibus velandis*." *Vigiliae Christianae* 59:1–30.

———. 2007. "Mary's Virginity *in partu* and Tertullian's Anti-Docetism in *De carne Christi* Reconsidered." *Journal of Theological Studies* 58:467–84.

Dunne, B. 1998. "Power and Sexuality in the Middle East." *Middle East Report* No. 206, Power and Sexuality in the Middle East, 9.

Durkheim, Émile. 1915. *The Elementary Forms of the Religious Life*. Trans. Joseph Ward Swain. London: George Allen & Unwin Ltd.

Duyverman, J. H. 2005. *Tien jaar in de Minaassa, 1909–1919*. Lichtenvoorde: Terra Incognita.

Dworkin, R. 1978. "Political Judges and the Rule of Law." *Proceedings of the British Academy* 64(259): 262.

———. 2006. "The Strange Case of Judge Alito." *New York Review of Books* LIII(3): 14–16.

Eickelman, D. 1998. "Inside the Islamic Reformation." *The Wilson Quarterly* XXII(1): 80–89.

Eisen, A. 1983. *The Chosen People in America: A Study in Jewish Religious Ideology*. Bloomington: Indiana University Press.

El Fadl, K. A. 2003 "Islam and the Challenge of Democratic Commitment." *Fordham International Law Journal* 27(4): 8.

Elliott, D. 1993. *Spiritual Abstinence in Medieval Wedlock*. Princeton: Princeton University Press, esp. p. 16–50.

Elm, S. 1994. *Virgins for God: The Making of Asceticism in Late Antiquity*. Oxford: Clarendon Press.

Ernstein, R. J. 1983. *Beyond Objectivism and Relativism: Science, Hermeneutics, and Praxis*. Philadelphia: University of Pennsylvania Press.

Evans, C. 2001. *Freedom of Religion under European Convention on Human Rights*. Oxford: Oxford University Press.

Evans, E. 1956. *Tertullian's Treatise on the Incarnation*. London: Speck Press.

Evans, M. D. 1997. *Religious Liberty and International Law in Europe*. Cambridge: Cambridge University Press.

Falola, T. 1998. *Violence in Nigeria: The Crisis of Religious Politics and Secular Ideologies*. Rochester: University of Rochester Press.

Fatemi, S. M. Ghari Seyed. 2007. "Shi'a Fiqh and Universal Human Rights."In *Theoretical Foundations of Human Rights: Collected Papers of the Second International Conference on Human Rights May 2003*, ed. K. Wellman and M. Habibi Modjandeh. Qom: Mofid University Publications.

———. 1986b. *Ascetic Piety and Women's Faith: Essays on Late Ancient Christianity.* Lewiston, NY: Edwin Mellen Press.

———. 1991. "Sex, Shame and Rhetoric: Engendering Early-Christian Ethics." *Journal of the American Academy of Religion* 49:221–47.

———. 1999. *Reading Renunciation. Asceticism and Scripture in Early Christianity.* Princeton: Princeton University Press.

———.2004. *History, Theory, Text: Historians and the Linguistic Turn.* Cambridge: Harvard University Press, pp. 158–61.

———, ed. 1983. *Women in the Early Church.* Collegeville: Liturgical Press.

Codex Iuris Canonici auctoritate Ioannis Pauli PP. II promulgatus. 1998. Vatican City: Libreria Editrice Vaticana, 1983. English translation from *Code of Canon Law, Latin English Edition: New English Translation.* Washington, DC: CLSA.

Codex Iuris Canonici Pii X Pontificis Maximi iussu digestus Benedicti Papae XV auctoritate promulgatus. 1917. Rome: Typis Polyglottis Vaticanis.

Coleman, J. S. 1958. *Nigeria: Background to Nationalism.* Berkeley: University of California Press.

Colish, Marcia L. 1983. *The Mirror of Language: A Study in the Medieval Theory of Knowledge,* rev. ed. Lincoln: University of Nebraska Press.

———. 1990. *The Stoic Tradition from Antiquity to the Middle Ages. Vol. 2. Stoicism in Christian Latin Thought through the Sixth Century.* Leiden, The Netherlands: Brill, p. 27–29.

Congregation for the Doctrine of the Faith. 2000. Declaration *Dominus Iesus* August 6, 2000 *AAS* 92: 742–65.

Congrégation pour les Évêques. 1988 Décret d'excommunicationJuly 1, 1988, *La documentation catholique,* 70: 789.

Connell, F. J. 1948. "Christ the King of Civil Rulers." *The American Ecclesiastical Review* 119:244–53.

Coriden, J. 1982. "Rules for Interpreters." *The Art of Interpretation.* Cannon Law Society of America CLSA., pp. 1–27. http://www.google.nl/search?sourceid =navclient&ie=UTF-8&rlz=1T4SMSN_enNL340NL340&q=Coriden%2c+J.+1982 .+%e2%80%9cRules+for+Interpreters.%e2%80%9d+The+Art+of+Interpretation .++Washington%3a+CLSA.+1982 (accessed August 2008).

Crampton, E. P. T. 1976. *Christianity in Northern Nigeria.* Zaria: Gaskiya Corporation, p. 48–100.

Dalactoura, Katerina. 1998. *Islam, Liberalism and Human Rights.* London: I. B. Tauris.

Dalli, A. 1976. *Double Descent: With Special Reference to the Bachama of Adamawa, North-East Nigeria* (MA thesis, University of London), p. 46–49.

Daniélou, S. J. 1961. *The Ministry of Women in the Early Church.* London: Faith Press.

Davey, N. 2004. "On the Polity of Experience: Towards a Hermeneutics of Attentiveness." *Renascence: Essays on Values in Literature* 56 (1).

Declerck, L., and C. Troisfontaines. n.d. "Paul VI et la liberté religieuse." Paper of the Brescia conference of the Istituto Paolo VI, 2007.

del Re, N. 1998. *La Curia Romana. Lineamenti storico-giuridici.* Città del Vaticano: Libreria Editrice Vatican, p. 249–52.

Brock, Peggy, ed. 2005. *Indigenous Peoples and Religious Change*. Leiden and Boston: Brill.
Brønnum, N. H. 1926. *Under Dæmoners Aag. Bachamafolkets Religion og Overtro*. Copenhagen: O. Lohse, pp. 33–46.
Brooten, B. 1996. *Love Between Women: Early Christian Responses to Female Homoeroticism*. Chicago: University of Chicago Press.
———. 2003. "Nature, Law, and Custom in Augustine's *On the Good of Marriage*." In *Walk in the Ways of Wisdom*, eds. S. Matthews, C. B. Kittredge, and M. Johnson-Debaufre. New York: Trinity Press International.
Brooten, B., and N. Greinacher. 1982. *Frauen in der Männerkirche?* Mainz, Germany: Grünewald; Munich: Kaiser.
Brown, D. 2004. *The Da Vinci Code*. New York: Doubleday.
Brown, P. 1988. *Body and Society. Men, Women, and Sexual Renunciation in Early Christianity*. New York: Columbia University Press, pp. 44–57.
Burrus, V. 2000. *Begotten Not Made: Conceiving Manhood in Late Antiquity*. Stanford: Stanford University Press.
———. 2004. *The Sex Lives of Saints: An Erotics of Ancient Hagiography*. Philadelphia: University of Pennsylvania Press.
———. 2007. *Saving Shame: Martyrs, Saints, and Other Abject Subjects*. Philadelphia: University of Pennsylvania Press.
Cameron, A. 1991. *Christianity and the Rhetoric of Empire: The Development of Christian Discourse*. Berkeley: University of California Press.
Canadian International Development Agency (CIDA). 2006. "Governance—Overview." http://www.acdi-cida.gc.ca/CIDAWEB/acdicida.nsf/En/JUD-121132928-PPH (accessed June 2007).
Canon Law Society of America. 1982. *The Art of Interpretation*. Washington: CLSA, pp. 28–34.
Carnochan, J. 1967. "The Coming of the Fulani: A Bachama Oral Tradition." *Bulletin of the School of Oriental and African Studies* XXX(3): 632–33.
Carter, M. 1976. "Dignitatis Humanae Declaration on Religious Freedom." *The Jurist* 36:338–52.
Chakrabarti, A. P. 1993. *Muslim Identity and Community Consciousness: Bengal Legislative Politics*. Calcutta, India: Minerva Associates.
Chakravorty, Pinaki. 1995. "The Rushdie Incident as Law-and-Literature Parable." *Yale Law Journal* 104. http://www.encyclopedia.com/doc/1G1–17150046.html (accessed October 2007).
Changing Patterns of Security in the Middle East and Central Asia, 2005. 2005. Workshop cohosted by the Department of National Security Affairs at the Naval Postgraduate School and the Center for Strategic Studies at the CNA Corporation, May 19.
Chilton, B. 1996. *Pure Kingdom. Jesus' Vision of God*, Studying the Historical Jesus. Grand Rapids: Wm. B. Eerdmans.
Clark, E. A. 1986a. "Adam's Only Companion: Augustine and the Early Christian Debate on Marriage." *Recherches Augustiniennes* 21:139–62.

Gross, N. C. 2005. "Religious Zionism's Identity Crisis." *The Jerusalem Report*, September 5, 17–20.

Gryson, R. 1972. *Le ministère des femmes dans l'Église ancienne*. Gembloux: Duculot. Trans by J. Laporte and M. L. Hall. 1976. *The Ministry of Women in the Early Church*. Collegeville, MN: Liturgical Press.

Gurr, T. 1986. "The Political Origins of State Violence and Terror: A Theoretical Analysis." In *Government Violence and Repression: An Agenda for Research*, ed. M. Stohl and G. Lopez, 231–72. New York: Greenwood.

Gustafson, Carrie, and Peter Juviler, eds. 1999. *Religion and Human Rights: Competing Claims?* Armonk, NY: M. E. Sharpe.

Gutmann, A., ed. 1994. *Multiculturalism: Examining the Politics of Recognition*. Princeton: Princeton University Press.

Haghighat, S. S. 1997. *Transnational Responsibilities in the Foreign Policy of the Islamic State*. Tehran: Center for Strategic Researches.

Halbertal, M., and A. Margalit. 1998 *Idolatry*. Trans. by Naomi Goldbloom. Cambridge: Harvard U. Press.

HaLevi, H. K. 2001. *At the Entrance to the Garden of Eden: A Jew's Search for God with Christians and Muslims in the Holy Land*. New York: William Morrow.

Hannum, H. 1995–96. "The Status of the Universal Declaration of Human Rights in National and International Law." *Georgia Journal of International and Comparative Law* 25:287–398.

Hasan, R. 1982. "On Human Rights and the Qur'anic Perspective." *Journal of Ecumenical Studies* 25(1): 1–21.

Hastings, A. 1997. *The Construction of Nationhood: Ethnicity, Religion and Nationalism*. Cambridge: Cambridge University Press, p. 148–66.

Hayek, F. A. 1978. *The Constitution of Liberty*. Chicago: University of Chicago Press.

Hefner, R. W., ed. 1993. *Conversion to Christianity. Historical and Anthropological Perspectives on a Great Transformation*. Berkeley: University of California Press.

Hendriks, J. 1987. "De libertate religiosa in concilio Vaticano II disceptata." *Periodica* 76:83–98.

Hill, C. 1993. *The English Bible and the Seventeenth-Century Revolution*. London: Allen Lane, The Penguin Press, p. 3–44.

Hittinger, F. R. 2008. "The Declaration on Religious Liberty, *Dignitatis Humanae*." In *Vatican II. Renewal within Tradition*, ed. M. L. Lamb and M. Levering, 361–62. Oxford: Oxford University Press.

Huysmans, R. G. W. 1996. *De administratieve macht in de r.k. Kerk, brug tussen de wetten en de noden van het godsvolk. Rede uitgesproken op 22 november 1996 door prof. dr. R.G.W. Huysmans bij gelegenheid van zijn afscheid als hoogleraar Canoniek Recht*. Utrecht, The Netherlands: Katholieke Theologische Universiteit.

IDEM. 1991. "A Short Note on Some Developments with Regard to Mixed Marriages in Indonesia." *Bijdragen tot de taal-, land-, en volkenkunde* 147:261–72.

Ignatieff, M. 2001. "Dignity and Agency." In *Human Rights as Politics and Idolatry*, ed. M. Ignatieff, 3–52. Princeton and Oxford: Princeton University Press.

Ilkaracan, P. 2002. "Women, Sexuality and Social Change." *Social Research*, 69 (3): 753–79.

Imam, Ayesha M. 2005. *Recovering Women's Reproductive Rights*. Public Lecture at the University of California, Santa Cruz, 10 November.

Imo, C. 2008. "Evangelicals, Muslims, and Democracy: With Particular Reference to the Declaration of Sharia in Northern Nigeria." In *Evangelical Christianity and Democracy in Africa*, ed. T. O. Ranger, 37–66. Oxford: Oxford University Press.

Izotso, T. 1982. *God and Human in Qur'an*. Translated in Persian by Ahmad Aram. Tehran: Cooperative Publishing.

Jalaei Pour, H. R. 1997. "The Iranian Islamic Revolution: Mass Mobilization and Its Continuity during 1976–96." PhD diss., Royal Holloway, University of London.

Jeanrond, Werner G. 1991. *Theological Hermeneutics: Development and Significance*. New York: Herder and Herder.

Kalscheur, Gregory A. 2007. "Toward A Theory of Human Rights: Religion, Law, Courts." *Theological Studies* 68: 1–56.

Kastfelt, N. 1994. *Religion and Politics in Nigeria. A Study in Middle Belt Christianity*. London: Vhps Distribution.

———. 2003a. "Introduction." In *Scriptural Politcs. The Bible and the Koran as Political Models in the Middle East and Africa*, edited by N. Kastfelt, London: Hurst & Company, p. 1–15.

———. 2003b. "Seek Ye First the Christian Political Kingdom: The Bible as a Political Model in the Nigerian Middle Belt." In *Scriptural Politcs. The Bible and the Koran as Political Models in the Middle East and Africa*, ed. N. Kastfelt, 203–20. London: Hurst & Company.

———, ed. 2005a. *Religion and African Civil Wars*. London: Hurst & Company.

———. 2005b. "History, Religion and Political Culture in Northern Nigeria: The Contexts of a Recent Bachama-Muslim Conflict." In *The "Traditional" and the "Modern" in West African (Ghanaian) History. Case Studies on Co-existence and Interaction*, ed. P. Hernæs, 35–57. Trondheim: Department of History, Norwegian University of Science and Technology.

———. 2007. *The Politics of History in Northern Nigeria*. Copenhagen: Centre of African Studies, University of Copenhagen.

Kastfelt, N. Forthcoming."Historical Thought and Social Aspirations in Northern Nigeria. Christianity and the Making of a New Bachama Ethnic Identity." In *Africans at Home and Abroad. Personal Lives and Social Aspirations*, ed. T. C. McCaskie and K. Shears. Madison: University of Wisconsin Press.

Kennedy, R. T. 1995. "The Declaration on Religious Liberty Thirty Years Later: Challenges to the Church-State Relationship in the United States." *The Jurist* 55:479–503.

Kliever, Lonnie D. 1987. *The Terrible Meek: Religion and Revolution in Cross-Cultural Perspective*. Paragon Press: New York.

Kneal, E. 1982. "Interpreting the Revised Code." *The Art of Interpretation*, 28–34. Washington: Canon Law Society of America (CLSA).

Koby, M. 1999. "The Supreme Court's Declining Reliance on Legislative History: The Impact of Justice Scalia's Critique." *Harvard Journal. on Legislation*. 36: 369–95.

Komonchak, J. A. 1996. "The Silencing of John Courtney Murray." In *Cristianesimo nella Storia: Saggi in onore di Giuseppe Alberigo*, ed. A. Melloni, 657–702. Bologna, Italy: Il Mulino, 122–35.

———. 1999. "The Crisis in Church-State Relationships in the U.S.A. A Recently Discovered Text by John Courtney Murray." *The Review of Politics* 61:675–714.

Kowal, W. 2000. *Understanding Canon 17 of the 1983 Code of Canon Law in Light of Contemporary Hermeneutics*. Lewiston: The Edwin Mellen Press.

Koylu, M. 2003. *Islam and its Quest for Peace: Jihad, Justice and Education*. Washington, DC: The Council for Research in Values and Philosophy.

Krishnaswami, A. 1960. "The Status of Religion in Relation to the State." *Journal of Church & State* 2:44.

Laclua, E. 1994. *The Making of Political Identities*. London: Verso.

Laporte, J. 1982. *Women in Early Christianity*. New York: Edwin Mellen Press.

Last, M. 1967. *The Sokoto Caliphate*. London: Longman.

Lauterpacht, H. 1948. "The Universal Declaration of Human Rights." *British Year Book of International Law* 25:354–81.

Levi, Werner. 1989. *From Alms to Liberation: The Catholic Church, the Theologians, Poverty, and Politics*. Praeger Publishers: New York.

Levine, Samuel J. 1998. "Unenumerated Constitutional Rights and Unenumerated Biblical Obligations: A Preliminary Study in Comparative Hermeneutics." *Constitutional Commentary* 15(3): 511–12.

Lichtenstein, A. 1981. *The Seven Laws of Noah*. New York: Berman Books.

Linzer, D. 2004. "Status of Non-Jews in Halakha." Yeshivat Chovevei Torah Rabbinical School unpublished paper.

Logams, P. C. 2004. *The Middle Belt Movement in Nigerian Political Development: A Study in Political Identity 1949–1967*. Abuja, Nigeria: Centre for Middle Belt Studies.

Lombardi, C. B., and N. J. Brown. 2006. "Do Constitutions Requiring Adherence to Shar'ia Threaten Human Rights? How Egypt's Constitutional Court Reconciles Islamic Law with the Liberal Rule of Law." *American University International Law Review* 21(379): 379–435.

Lonergan, B. 1972. *Method in Theology*. New York: The Seabury Press.

———. 1978, second ed. *Insight*. New York, Harper & Row.

———. 1997. "Imago Dei." *Verbum: Word and Idea in Aquinas*, vol. 2 of *Collected Works of Bernard Lonergan*. Toronto: University of Toronto Press, 38–45.

Lonsdale, J. 1994. "Moral Ethnicity and Political Tribalism." In *Inventions and Boundaries: Historical and Anthropological Approaches to the Study of Ethnicity and Nationalism*, ed. P. Kaarsholm and J. Hultin, 132–42. Roskilde, Denmark: International Development Studies.

Lonsdale, J. 2002. "Kikuyu Christianities: A History of Intimate Diversity." In *Christianity and the African Imagination. Essays in Honour of Adrian Hastings*, ed. D. Maxwell with Ingrid Lawrie, 157–97. Leiden, The Netherlands: Brill.

Lynch, Edward A. 1991. *Religion and Politics in Latin America: Liberation Theology and Christian Democracy*. New York: Praeger.

Magaji, A. 1982. *Myths and Legends of Bachama*. Wukari, Nigeria: Amune Press.

Mahbubul Islam, A. 2002. *Freedom of Religion in Shari'ah: A Comparative Analysis*. Kuala Lumpur, Malaysia: A. S. Noordeen.

Mansi, G. D. 1961. *Sacrorum conciliorum nova et amplissima collection*, vol. 53. Graz, Austria: Akademische Druck- und Verlagsanstalt.

Maodood, Tariq. 2006. "The Danish Cartoon Affair: Free Speech, Racism, Islamism, and Integration." *International Migration* 44 (5): 17–22.

Marguerat, D. 1993. "La construction du lecteur par le texte (Marc et Matthieu)." In *The Synoptic Gospel: Source Criticism and the New Literary Criticism*, ed. C. Focant, 239–62. Leuven, Belgium: Leuven University Press.

Marshall, William P. 2000. "The Culture of Belief and the Politics of Religion." *Law and Contemporary Problems* 63(1–2):2.

Martin, J. P., and T. Stahke, eds. 1998. *Religion and Human Rights: Basic Documents*. New York: Columbia University, p. 207–8.

Martin, J. R. 1994. "Methodological Essentialism, False Difference, and Other Dangerous Traps." *Signs* 19:630–57.

Marty, M. E., and R. Scott Appleby, eds. 1991. *Fundamentalisms Observed*. Chicago: The University and Chicago Press.

———, eds. 1995. *Fundamentalisms Comprehended* Chicago: The University of Chicago Press.

Maxwell, D. 2006. *African Gifts of the Spirit. Pentecostalism and the Rise of a Zimbabwean Transnational Religious Movement*. Oxford: James Currey.

McGovern, Arthur F. 1990. *Liberation Theology and Its Critics*. Maryknoll, NY: Orbis.

McKechnie, Jean Lyttleton, ed. 1983. *Webster's New Twentieth Century Dictionary, Second Edition*. New York: Simon & Schuster.

Meek, C. K. 1931. *Tribal Studies in Northern Nigeria*, vol. 1. London: Kegan Paul, Trench, Trubner and Co., p. 42ff.

Mir, M. 1986. *Coherence in the Qurān. A Study of Islahi's Concept of Nazm in Tadabbur-i Qur'ān*. Washington, American Trust Publications.

———. 1993. "The *Sura* as a Unity: A Twentieth Century Development in Qur'ān exegesis." In *Approaches to the Qur'ān*, ed. G. R. Hawting and Abdul-Kader A. Shareef, 211–24. London/New York: Routledge.

Monballyu, J. 1994. "Was Tanneken Sconyncx een heks? Een analyse van haar proces in 1602–1603." *De Roede van Tielt* 25:94–140.

———. 1996. *Van hekserij beschuldigd. Heksenprocessen in Vlaanderen tijdens de 16de en 17de eeuw*. Kortrijk: UGA.

Moneta, P. 1970 "Errore sulle qualità individuanti ed interpretazione evolutiva." *Diritto Ecclesiastico* 81(2): 31–55.

Moussalli, A. S. 2003. "The Qur'an as a Political Model." In *Scriptural Politics. The Bible and the Koran as Political Models in the Middle East and Africa*, ed. N. Kastfelt, 29–41. London: Hurst & Company.

Mudzhar, M. A. 1993. *Fatwa-fatwa Majelis Ulama Indonesia*. Jakarta: Inis.

Muh, Q. S. 2000. *Tafsir al-Mishbah*. Jakarta: Lentera Hati. 2:356.

Mutahhari, M. 1981. *Jihad*. Trans. by M. S. Towheedi, B'ethat Foundation.

Nahas, O. 2002. *Islam en Sexualiteit*. Amsterdam, The Netherlands: Bulaaq.

Nasr, S. H. n.d. "The Spiritual Significance of Jihad." *Al-Serat*, IX(1), http://www.islamataglance.org/media/Articles/General/Jihad.pdf (accessed June 2008).

Neophitos, A. M. 1974. *The Legal Limitation of Religious Liberty: an Historical Study of the Documents of the World Council of Churches and the Second Vatican Council*. Roma: Pontificia Universitas Lateranensis.

Neuwirth, A. 1993. "Images and Metaphors in the Introductory Sections of the Makkan *suras*." In *Approaches to the Qur'ān*, ed. G. R. Hawting and Abdul-Kader A. Shareef, 3–36. London/New York: Routledge.

Nissen, M. 1968. *An African Church is Born: The Story of the Adamawa and Central Sardauna Provinces of Nigeria*. Viby, Jotland, Denmark: Purups Grafiske Hus.

Noether, E. P. 1968. "Vatican Council I: Its Political and Religious Setting." *The Journal of Modern History* 40:218–33.

Nowak, Manfred. 2003. *Introduction to the International Human Rights Regime*. Leiden, The Netherlands: Martinus Nijhoff.

Orentlicher, D. F., ed. 2003. "Relativism and Religion." In *Human Rights as Politics and Idolatry*, ed. M. Ignatieff, 141–60. Princeton: Princeton University Press.

Ormiston, Gayle L., and Alan D. Schrift, eds. 1990. *The Hermeneutic Tradition. From Ast to Ricoeur*. Albany: State University of New York Press.

Örsy, L. 1979. "Lonergan's Cognitional Theory and Foundational Issues in Canon Law." *Studia Canonica* 13(225): 177–243.

Örsy, L. 1980. "The Interpreter and His Art." *The Jurist* 40:27–56.

Örsy, L. 1992. *Theology and Canon Law*. Collegeville, MN: Liturgical Press.

Osaghae, E. E. 1998. *Crippled Giant: Nigeria Since Independence*. London: Hurst & Company.

Osiek, C. 2003. "Galatians." In *Feminism and Theology*, ed. J. M. Soskice and D. Lipton, 188–96. Oxford: Oxford University Press.

Ottaviani, A. 1958–1960. *Institutiones iuris publici ecclesiastici*, 2 vols. Città del Vaticano: Typis Polyglottis Vaticanis.

Otten, W. 1997. "Christ's Birth of a Virgin Who Became a Wife: Flesh and Speech in Tertullian's *De carne Christi*." *Vigiliae Christianae* 51:247–60.

———. 1998. "Augustine on Marriage, Monasticism, and the Community of the Church." *Theological Studies* 59:385–405.

———. 2001. "Early Christianity Between Divine Promise and Earthly Politics." In *Religious Identity and the Invention of Tradition*, ed. J. W. van Henten and A. Houtepen, 60–83. Assen, The Netherlands: Van Gorcum.

Otten, Willemien, and Theo Salemink. 2004. "Prologue: Religious Identity and the Problem of Historical Foundational Character of Authoritative Texts and Traditions in the History of Christianity." In *Religious Identity and the Problem of Historical Foundation: The Foundational Character of Authoritative Sources in the History of Christianity and Judaism*, ed. Judith Frishman, Willemien Otten, and Gerard Rouwhorst, 3–27. Leiden and Boston: Brill.

Ovey, C., and R. White. 2006. *Jacobs and White, The European Convention on Human Rights* Oxford: Oxford University Press.

Pagels, E. 1988. *Adam, Eve and the Serpent*. New York: Random House.

Parratt, J. 1995. *Reinventing Christianity. African Theology Today*. Grand Rapids: William B. Eerdmans Publishing Company.

Patrick, John J., and Gerald P. Long. 1999. *Constitutional Debates on Freedom of Religion: A Documentary and History*. Westport, CT: Greenwood Press.

Pavan, P. 1967. *Einleitung*, in L.Th.K. *Das Zweite Vatikanische Konzil*, II. Freiburg-Basel-Wien: Herder, p. 704–11.

Peel, J. D. Y. 1989. "The Cultural Work of Yoruba Ethnogenesis." In *History and Ethnicity*, ed. E. Tonkin, M. McDonald, and M. Chapman, 198–215. London: Routledge.

———. 2000. *Religious Encounter and the Making of the Yoruba*. Bloomington: Indiana University Press.

Peerenboom, R. 2004. *Varieties of Rule of Law: An Introduction and Provisional Conclusion*. University of California, Los Angeles School of Law Research Paper Series No. 03–16, p. 2. http://ssrn.com/abstract-445821 (accessed 2004).

———. 2005. *Human Rights and Rule of Law: What's The Relationship*? UCLA Public Law Series, University of California, Los Angeles, UCLA School of Law, Paper 5–21. http://repositories.cdlib.org/uclalaw/plltwps/5–21(accessed 2007).

Pelikan, Jaroslav. 2004. *Interpreting the Bible and the Constitution*. New Haven, CT: Yale University Press.

Perrin, L. 1989. *L'affaire Lefebvre*. Paris: Cerf.

Perry, Michael J. 1998. *The Idea of Human Rights: Four Inquiries*. New York: Oxford University Press.

Peters, E. N. 2001. *The 1917 or Pio-Benedictine Code of Canon Law in English Translation with Extensive Scholarly Apparatus*. San Francisco: Ignatius Press [unofficial English translation].

Philipse, H. 2007. "Antonin Scalia's Textualism in Philosophy, Theology, and Judicial Interpretation of the Constitution." *Utrecht Law Review* 3(2). http://www.utrechtlawreview.org/publish/articles/000051/article.pdf (accessed June 2007).

Phillips, D. Z. 2001. *Religion and the Hermeneutics of Contemplation*. Cambridge: Cambridge University Press.

Pompe, B. 1988. "Mixed Marriages in Indonesia: Some Comments on the Law and the Literature." *Bijdragen tot de taal-, land-, en volkenkunde* 144:259–75.

Pope John Paul II. 1988. "Motu proprio." *Ecclesia Dei*. July 2. *AAS* 80:1495–98.

———. 1995. Apostolic letter *Tertio Millennio Adveniente*. November 10, 1994. *AAS* 87: 5–41.

Pope John XXIII. 1959. "Allocution to the Cardinals present in Rome." January 25. *AAS* 51: 65–69.

———. 1963. Encyclical *Pacem in terris*. 11 April 1963. *AAS* 55: 257–304.

Pope Leo XIII. 1881. Encyclical *Diuturnum illud*. June 29, 1881. *ASS* 14: 3–14.

———. 1885. Encyclical *Immortale Dei*. November 1, 1885. *ASS* 18: 161–80.

Pope Paul VI. 1971. Apostolic letter *Octogesima adveniens*. May 14, 1971. *AAS* 63: 401–41.

Pope Pius IX. 1991. Encyclical *Quanta cura*. December 8, 1864. In *Enchiridion symbolorum definitionum et declarationum de rebus fidei et morum* by H. Denzinger and P. Hünermann. Freiburg: Herder, 2890–96. [referred to as Denzinger and Hünermann 1991 in text citations].

———. 1991. *Syllabus Pii IX, seu Collectio errorum in diversis*. December 8, 1864. Denzinger and Hünermann, 2901–80.

———. 1937. Encyclical *Divini Redemptoris*. March 19, 1937. *AAS* 29: 79.

———. 1943. Radio Message *Con sempre nuova freschezza* for Christmas 1942. December 24, 1942. *AAS* 35: 9–24.

———. 1945. Radio Message *Benignitas et humanitas*. December 24, 1944. *AAS* 37: 10–33.
Poulton, H., and S. Taji-Farouki, eds. 1997. *Muslim Identity and the Balkan State*. New York: New York University Press in association with the Islamic Council.
Powell, M. A. 1990. *What Is Narrative Criticism?* Minneapolis: Fortress Press.
Power, K. 1995. *Veiled Desire: Augustine on Women*. New York: Continuum.
Ranger, T., and J. Weller. 1975. *Themes in the Christian History of Central Africa*. London: Heinemann.
Ratzinger, J. 1987. *Principles of Catholic Theology: Building Stones for a Fundamental Theology*. San Francisco, CA: Ignatius Press.
Rawls, J. 1972. *A Theory of Justice*. Oxford: Oxford University Press.
Raz, J. 1977. "The Rule of Law and Its Virtue." *Law Quarterly Review* 93(195): 195–96.
———. 1986. *The Morality of Freedom*. Oxford: Clarendon Press.
Raz-Karkotzkin, Amnon. 1993–94. "Exile Within Sovereignty: Towards a Critique of 'Negation of the Diaspora' Within Israeli Culture," in two parts, *Theory and Criticism* (Hebrew), 4:23–56 and 5:113–32.
Rehnquist, W. H. 2001. *The Supreme Court*. 2nd ed. New York: Vintage Books.
Reynolds, P. L. 1994. *Marriage in the Western Church. The Christianization of Marriage During the Patristic and Early Medieval Periods*. Leiden: Brill, p. 214–311.
Rhoads, D. 1999. "Narrative Criticism: Practices and Prospects." In *Characterization in the Gospels: Reconceiving Narrative Criticism*, ed. D. Rhoads and K. Syreeni, 264–85. JSNTSup, 184. Sheffield: Sheffield Academic Press.
———. 2004. *Reading Mark: Engaging the Gospel*. Minneapolis: Fortress Press, p. 202–19.
Rhoads, D., and D. Michie. 1982. *Mark as Story: An Introduction to the Narrative of a Gospel*. Philadelphia: Fortress Press.
Ricoeur, P. 1981. *Hermeneutics and the Human Sciences: Essays on Language, Action and Interpretation*. Trans. and ed. by John B. Thompson. Cambridge: Cambridge University Press.
Rigobon R., and D. Rodrik. 2005. "Rule of Law, Democracy, Openness and Income: Estimating the Interrelationships." *Economics of Transition* 13 (3): 533–64.
Roberts, A., and J. Donaldson, eds. "Fathers of the Third Century: Tertullian, Part Fourth; Minucius Felix; Commodian; Origen, Parts First and Second." In *Ante-Nicene Fathers*, ed. P. Schaff, 4:14. Peabody 1885; Hendrickson 1994.
———, eds. *Ante-Nicene Fathers*, vol. 3. Peabody 1885; Hendrickson 1994.
———, eds. *Ante-Nicene Fathers*, 4:23. Peabody 1885; Hendrickson 1994.
Robertson, A. H. 1950. "The European Convention for the Protection of Human Rights." *British Year Book of International Law* 27:145–63.
Robertson, G. 2005. *The Tyrannicide Brief. The Story of the Man who sent Charles I to the Scaffold*. London: Chatto and Windus.
Rommen, H. 1950. "Church and State." *The Review of Politics* 12:321–40.
Roth, Leon. 1973. "Moralization and Demoralization in Jewish Ethics." *Modern Jewish Thought: Selected Issues, 1889–1966*. New York: Arno Press.
Rowson, E. K. 2002. "Homosexuality." In *Encyclopaedia of the Qurʾān*, vol. II, ed. J. Dammen McAuliffe, 444–45. Leiden: Brill.

Safi, O. 2003. *Progressive Muslims: on Justice, Gender and Pluralism*. Oxford: Oneworld.
Safrai, Zev, and Avi Sagi, eds. 1997. *Between Authority and Autonomy in the Jewish Tradition*. Hebrew, Tel Aviv: s.n.
Said, Edward. 1978. *Orientalism*. New York: Vintage Books.
Salih, M. A. Mohamed. 2004. "The Bible, the Qur'an and the War in South Sudan." In *Scriptural Politics*, ed. N. Kastfelt, 96–120. London: Hurst.
Salvini, G. 2008. "La «Dignitatis Humanae». La libertà religiosa in Paolo VI." *La Civiltà Cattolica* 159(I): 338–48.
Sanders, E. R. 1969. "The Hamitic Hypothesis: Its Origin and Functions in Time Perspective." *Journal of African History* X(4): 521–32.
Sanneh, L. 1989. *Translating the Message. The Missionary Impact on Culture*. Maryknoll, New York: Orbis Books.
———. 1999. *Translating the Message: The Missionary Impact on Culture*. Maryknoll, NY: Orbis Books.
Sarrami, S. 1997. *The Decrees On Apostasy In Islam And Human Rights*. Tehran: Presidency Center for Strategic Research.
Sawyer. D. F. 1996. *Women and Religion in the First Christian Centuries*. London: Routledge, p. 91–116.
Sayeed Abdul A'la Maududi. *Jihad in Islam*. Islamic Publications: Karatchi, p. 9.
Scalia, A. 1997. *A Matter of Interpretation. Federal Courts and the Law*. Princeton: Princeton University Press.
Scatena, S. 2003. *La fatica della libertà. L'elaborazione della dichiarazione "Dignitatis humanae" sulla libertá religiosa del Vaticano II*. Bologna: Il Mulino.
Schacht, J. 1964. *An Introduction to Islamic Law*. Oxford: Clarendon.
Schaffer, E. G. 1991. "Human Rights Protection Under the Council of Europe—The System and Its Documentation." *International Journal of Legal Information* 19:1–10.
Schneiders, S. 1999. *The Revelatory Text: Interpreting the New Testament as Sacred Scripture*. Collegeville: Michael Glazier Books.
Schubeck, Thomas L. 1995. "Ethics and Liberation Theology." *Theological Studies* 56(1).
Schüssler Fiorenza, E. 2001. *Wisdom Ways: Introducing Feminist Biblical Interpretation*. Maryknoll: Orbis.
Schwarz, H. 2004. *Right Wing Justice. The Conservative Campaign to take over the Courts*. New York: Nation Books.
Sen, A. S. 1999. *Development as Freedom*. Oxford: Oxford University Press, p. 227–48.
Sharma, Arvind, and Katherine K. Young, eds. 1999. *Feminism and World Religions* (Albany: State University of New York Press).
Sigmund, P. E. 1987. "The Catholic Tradition and Modern Democracy." *The Review of Politics* 49:530–48.
Simonsen, J. Bæk. 2003. "Sharia and Sunna in the Qur'an and in the Writings of Sayyid Qutb." In *Scriptural Politics. The Bible and the Koran as Political Models in the Middle East and Africa*, ed. N. Kastfelt, 55–65. London: Hurst & Company.

Skinner, Q. 2002. *Visions of Politics, Vol.3, Hobbes and Civil Science*. Cambridge: Cambridge University Press.

Slee, N. 2002. "The Holy Spirit and Spirituality." In *The Cambridge Companion to Feminist Theology*, ed. S. F. Parsons, 171–89. Cambridge: Cambridge University Press.

Soroush, A. 1994. "Ma'refat-e Mo'alefey-e Momtaz-e Modernite-h' [Knowledge: the Primary and Prominent Element of Modernity]." *Kiyan* 20:4–5.

Soskice, M., and J. Martin. 2002. "Trinity and Feminism." In *The Cambridge Companion to Feminist Theology*, ed. S. F. Parsons, 135–50. Cambridge: Cambridge University Press.

Stamatopoulou, E. 1998. "The Development of United Nations Mechanisms for the Protection and Promotion of Human Rights." *Washington and Lee Law Review* 55:687–96.

———. 1998–99. "The Importance of the Universal Declaration of Human Rights in the Past and Future of the United Nation's Human Rights Efforts." *ILSA Journal of International & Comparative Law* 5:281.

Stark, J. C., ed. 2007. *Feminist Interpretations of Augustine*. University Park: Pennsylvania State University Press.

Starr, R. 1967. "International Protection of Human Rights and the United Nations Covenants." *Wisconsin Law Review* 1967:863–90.

Steenbrink, K. 1998. "Qur'anic Guidelines for Economy as a Basis for Interreligious Solidarity in Favor of the Poor? Some Reflections on the Indonesian and Dutch Contexts." *Mission Studies* XV(2): 103–18.

Steiner, H. n.d. "Non-Jews Living in the Land of Israel." www.Yeshiva.org.il.

Stevens, P. Jr. 1973. *The Bachama and their Neighbors: Non-Kin Joking Relationships in Adamawa, Northeastern Nigeria*. Ph.D. thesis, Northwestern University, p. 72–74.

Sulastomo, ed. 1995. *Kontekstualisasi Ajaran Islam: 70 Tahun Prof. Dr. H. Munawir Sjadzali M.A*. Jakarta: Paramadina.

Tabatabaiee, M. H. 1973. *Almizan in Interpretation of Qur'an*. Beirut: A'alami.

Tagle, L. A. G. 2003. "The 'Black Week' of Vatican II (14–21 November 1964)." In *History of Vatican II*, vol. IV, *Church as Communion: Third Period and Intersession September 1964 - September 1965*, ed. G. Alberigo and J. A. Komonchak, 387–452. Leuven: Peeters.

Tahzib, B. G. 1996. *Freedom of Religion or Belief: Ensuring Effective International Legal Protection*. The Hague: Martinus Nijhoff Publishers.

Tamanaha, Z. n.d. *The Rule of Law for Everyone?* St. John's Legal Studies Research Paper. http://ssrn.com/abstract=312622 (accessed June 2007).

Tanner, N. P., ed.1990. *Decrees of the Ecumenical Councils*. Washington: Sheed & Ward and Georgetown University Press, p. 968.

Taylor, C. 1989. *Sources of the Self: The Making of the Modern Identity*. Cambridge, MA: Harvard University Press.

Telford, W. 1999. *The Theology of the Gospel of Mark*. New Testament Theology. Cambridge: Cambridge University Press.

Toope, S. 2003. "Legal and Judicial Reform through Development Assistance: Some Lessons." *McGill Law Journal*, 48(357): 367.

Torfs, R. 1995. "Propria verborum significatio: de l'epistemologie a l'hermeneutique." *Studia Canonica* 19:179–92.

Torjesen, K. J. 1993. *When Women Were Priests: Women's Leadership in the Early Church and the Scandal of Their Subordination in the Rise of Christianity*. San Francisco: Harper Collins.

Treat, James. 1996. *Native and Christian: Indigenous Voices on Religious Identity in the United States and Canada*. London: Routledge.

Troisfontaines, C. 2007. "Mgr De Smedt et la Déclaration *Dignitatis humanae*." *Gregorianum* 88:761–79.

Tuckett, C. M., ed. 1983. *The Messianic Secret*. Issues in Religion and Theology, 1. Philadelphia: Society for Promoting Christian Knowledge (SPCK) Fortress [ten articles by different authors on the "Messianic Secret"].

———. 2002. "The Disciples and the Messianic Secret in Mark." In *Fair Play: Diversity and Conflicts in Early Christianity*, ed. I. Dunderberg, C. M. Tuckett, and K. Syreeni, 131–50. Leiden Brill.

Tully, J. 1988. "The Pen is a Mighty Sword: Quentin Skinner's Analysis of Politics." In *Meaning and Context*, 7–25. Princeton: Princeton University Press.

Turcan, M. 1990. "Être femme selon Tertullien." *Vita Latina* 119:15–21.

Utzschneider, H. 1999. "Text-Leser-Autor. Bestandsaufnahme und Prolegomena zu einer Theorie der Exegese." *Biblische Zeitschrift (BZ)* 43:224–38.

Vail, L. 1989. "Introduction: Ethnicity in Southern African History." In *The Creation of Tribalism in Southern Africa*, ed. L. Vail, 1–19. London: James Currey.

van Dijk, R. 2003. "Pentecostalism and the Politics Prophetic Power: Religious Modernity in Ghana." In *Scriptural Politics. The Bible and the Koran as Political Models in the Middle East and Africa*, ed. N. Kastfelt, 155–84. London: Hurst & Company.

van Iersel, B. M. F. 1998. *Mark. A Reader Response Commentary*. JSNT.S 164; Sheffield.

van Krieken, P. 1993. *Apostasy & Asylum*. Lund: Raoul Wallenberg Institute of Human Rights and Humanitarian Law.

van Oyen, G. 2000. "The Need to Change: Reflections on Characters in the Gospel of Mark." In *In Quest of Humanity in a Globalising World: Dutch Contributions to the Jubilee of Universities in Rome 2000*, ed. W. Derkse, J. van der Lans and S. Waanders, 293–308. Leende: Damon.

van Schaik, T. H. M. 1997. *Alfrink. Een biografie*. Amsterdam: Anthos.

Vatican II. 1964a. Constitution *Sacrosanctum Concilium*. December 4, 1963. *AAS* 56: 97–134.

———. 1964b. Decree *Inter mirifica*. December 4, 1963. *AAS* 56: 145–53.

———. 1965a. Dogmatic Constitution *Lumen gentium*. November 21, 1964. *AAS* 57, 5–67.

———.1965b. Decree *Unitatis redintegratio*. November 21, 1964. *AAS* 57: 90–107.

———. 1965c. Decree *Orientalium Ecclesiarum*. November 21,1964. *AAS* 57: 76–85.

———. 1966a. Dogmatic Constitution *Dei verbum*. November 18, 1965. *AAS* 58: 817–30.

———. 1966b. Pastoral Constitution *Gaudium et spes*. December 7, 1965. *AAS* 58: 1025–1115; hereafter referred to as GS, followed by the paragraph number.

———. 1966c. Decree *Ad gentes*. December 7, 1965. *AAS* 58: 947–90.

———. 1966d. Decree *Presbyterorum Ordinis*. December 7, 1965). *AAS* 58: 991–1024.

———. 1966e. Decree *Apostolicam actuositatem*. November 18, 1965. *AAS* 58: 837–64.

———. 1966f. Decree *Optatam totius*. October 28, 1965. *AAS* 58: 713–27.

———. 1966g. Decree *Perfectae caritatis*. October 28, 1965. *AAS* 58: 702–12.

———. 1966h. Decree *Christus Dominus*. October 28, 1965. *AAS* 58: 673–96.

———. 1966i. Declaration *Gravissimum educationis*. October 28, 1965. *AAS* 58: 728–39.

———. 1966j. Declaration *Nostra aetate*. October 28, 1965. *AAS* 58: 740–44.

———. 1966k. Declaration *Dignitatis humanae*. December 7, 1965. *AAS* 58: 929–41.

Vatican. http://www.vatican.va/.

Vorster, W. S. 1989. "The Reader in the Text: Narrative Material." *Semeia* 48:21–3 9.

Wadud, Amina. 1999. *Qurán and Woman. Rereading the Sacred Text from a Woman's Perspective*. Oxford: Oxford University Press.

Walzer, M. 1985. *Exodus and Revolution*. New York: Basic Books.

Warraq, I. 1995. *Why I am not a Muslim*. Amhurst, New York: Prometheus.

Watt, W. M. 1953. *Muhammad at Mecca*. London: Oxford University Press.

———. 1956. *Muhammad at Medina*. London: Oxford University Press.

———. 1961. *Muhammad, Prophet and Statesman*. London: OUP.

Weissman, D. 2004. "Women's Suffrage: A Halakhic Perspective." In *Men and Women: Gender, Judaism and Democracy*, ed. R. Elior, 70–78. Jerusalem and London: Urim Publications.

Weizer, P. 2004. *The Opinions of Justice Scalia. The Caustic Conservative*. New York: Peter Lang.

Whitaker, C. S. Jr. 1970. *The Politics of Tradition. Continuity and Change in Northern Nigeria 1946–1966*. Princeton: Princeton University Press.

Wilfred, Felix. 1991. *Sunset in the East?* Madras: Chair in Christianity, University of Madras.

Wilson-Kastner, P., ed. 1981. *A Lost Tradition: Women Writers of the Early Church*. Lanham-New York-London: University Press of America.

Wrede, W. 1901, 1969. *Das Messiasgeheimnis in den Evangelien. Zugleich ein Beitrag zum Verständnis des Markusevangeliums*. Göttingen: Vandenhoeck & Ruprecht; English trans. J. C. G. Grieg. 1971. Cambridge: James Clarke & Co.

Yinger, J. Milton. 1946. *Religion in the Struggle for Power: A Study in the Sociology of Religion*. Durham, NC: Duke University Press.

Zakaria, F. 1997. "The Rise of Illiberal Democracy." *Foreign Affairs* 76 (22).

Index

Abeyesekera, S., 26
Abubakar, S., 192
Adamawa, 192
Adamu, M., 192
African Institutes Churches (AICs), 89–90
African Protocol on Human Rights and the Rights of Women in Africa, 246
Agijah, J., 199
Agnon, S., 164, 165
Akiva, Rabbi, 170
A'la Maududi, 30
Al Baqareh, 136
Aleyideino, S., 198
Al Ghazali, 245
Ali, J., 132
Al Irtedad, 136
Aql al Salim, 139
Amar, A. R., 71
American Constitution, 9, 11
Amin, Q., 242
Anderson, J., 18
An-Na'im, A., 135, 140
apostasy, 17, 135, 136
Ascha, G., 85, 98
Attar, Chayim ben, Rabbi, 180
Augustine, 15, 223, 228, 230, 231; *City of God*, 231
Ayodhya Muslims, 24

Babylonian Talmud, 165
Bachama, political community, 193
Bahrain, 41
Barr, J., 186
Beaufort, Father, 27

Beitz, C., 3
Bell, R., 88
Belton, R., 38
Ben Azzai, 170
Bewley, A., 88
Bharatya Janata Party (BJP), 24
Bible, 186
Black-Branch, J., 152
Boff, L., 30
Bosnia Herzegovina, 25
Boswell, J., 219
Botha, P., 102
Boyle, K., 4, 17
Brems, E., 140
Brenner, 24, 187
Brisbin, 70
Brock, P., 7
Brooten, B., 219, 233
Brown, N., 10, 11, 47, 48, 49, 53
Brown's Code, 105
Buddhism, 81
Bulugh, 139
Burrus, V., 219, 220
Burston, B., 179

Caliph, 43
Cameron, A., 222
Canadian International Development Agency (CIDA), 40
Canon, 17, 61
Canon Law, 53
Canon Law Society of America, 53
Carnochan, J., 197
Chakrabarti, A., 24
Chakravorty, P., 18
Chilton, B., 105

Christianity, 81
Clark, E., 219, 220, 221, 225, 229
Gifford, P., 187
Code of Canon Law, 145, 155
Cohen, H., 165
Coleman, J., 190
Commentary Magazine, 167, 168
common humanity, 172
Coriden, J., 10, 53
Crampton, E., 193
cultural politics, 18

Dalactoura, K., 6
Dalli, A., 197
Daniélou, S., 219
Dar al-Harb, 206
Da Vinci Code, The, 103
Dead Sea Scrolls, 121
Declaration on the Elimination of All Forms of Intolerance and of Discrimination Based on Religion or Belief, 127
Declerck, L., 154
Delorme, 106
democracy: definition, 40; Islamic theology, 41
Denzinger, H., 148
Descartes, 57
Diaspora, 179
Dicey, A., 38
Dignitatis Humanae, 143, 151; declaration, 153, 154, 155, 157
Dilthy, W., 5
Donaldson, J., 225
Dudley, B., 193, 194
Dunn, G., 226
Durkheim, E., 31
Duyverman, J., 82
Dworkin, R., 39, 69

Ecclesiastica law, 55
Egypt, 47
Eickelman, D., 187
Eisen, A., 167
El Fadl, K., 42, 43, 44, 45, 46

Elliott, D., 220
Elm, S., 220
Ernstein, R., 2
ethnic reconstruction, 196
European Court of Human Rights, 152
Evans, M., 152
Evans, C., 128, 131, 227
Exodus, 5, 86, 173, 177, 196

Falola, T., 189, 190
Fatemi, S., 6
fatwa, 93
female genital mutilation (FGM), 4, 8, 15, 237, 239
feminist approach to Islam, 239
Fendler, F., 103
Fenton, J., 155
Fiqh, 6, 47, 247
Fortman, B., 8
Foucault, M., 186
Fourth Council of Lateran, 86
Fredriksen, P., 229
Frishman, J., 24
Frithjof, R., 5

Gadamer, H., 7
Galatians, 223
GAMCOTRAP, 245
Garaudy, R., 35
Geertz, C., 11, 14, 81
Genesis, 177
Gentile, in Jewish tradition, 166
Gandhi, 92
Ginsburgh, Rabbi, 170
God's law, 42
Golden Rule, The, 129, 168
Gonnet, D., 155
Gospel of Judas, 121
Gospel of Luke, 86
Gospel of Mark, 12, 101, 111
Gospel of Matthew, 91, 194
Granfield, 146
Greenberg, M., 166, 167, 177
Greinacher, N., 219

Gryson, R., 219
Gustafson, C., 4
Gutmann, A., 24

hadith, 47, 188, 240, 246
Haghighat, S., 30, 205, 215
Halakha, 173
Halbertal, M., 177
Hannum, H., 152
Haq, S., 10, 37
Hasan, R., 140
Hastings, A., 191
Hebrew Bible, 172
Hebrew Homily, 181
Hefner, R., 83
Hendriks, J., 146, 148, 151
hermeneutics, 1, 2, 32, 97, 101; capricious, 81; conciliation, 37; incarnational, 219; Jewish, 14; Lonergan, 56; non-Jewish minorities, 163; of religion, 29; Shi'a, 205; Skinner, 210; spiritual, 16; universality of knowledge, 16
Herzog, Yitzchak HaLevi, Rabbi, 174
hijab, 31, 247
Hill, C., 200
Hinduism, 81, 83
Hindu Nationalism, 24
Hittinger, F., 154
hizb Allah, 188
hizb al-Shaytan, 188
holism, 76, 77
Hong Kong, 41
hudba, 246
human rights, 25
Huysmans, R., 147

Ibn Tamiyya, 206
Ibn Warraq, 85
IDEM, 94
identity construction, 23
identity formation, 23
ijtihad, 47, 48, 239
Ilkaracan, P., 245

Imam, A., 240
Imo, C., 185
individual rights, 38
Indonesia, Majelis Umma, 93, 96
Indonesian, Islam, 92
intifada, 176
interreligious communication, 96
Islamic Eduction, Scientific and Cultural Organization (ISESCO) 241
Islamic texts (Islam), 237
Islamic theology, 41
Israel, 163; Land of, 14; minorities, 163
Izotso, T., 133

Jerusalem, 166, 197
Jewish Economic Ruling of Juilee, 87
Jews, Orthodox, 176
jihad: 14, 15; 2005, 30, 92; definition and typology, 206; Fulbe-led, 192; fundamentalist approach, 208; new reading, 211; offensive, 213; in the Qur'an, 214; Shi'a, 207; by tongue, 212; traditionalist approach, 208
John Chrysostom of Constantinople, Bishop, 225
Judaism, 81; chosenness, 167; classical texts, 163; ethics: moralization and demoralization, 166; minorities, 181; roots of Christianity, 154; traditional culture, 165
judicial textualism, 69
juridical universality, 26
Juviler, P., 4

Kant, I., 56
Kastfelt, N., 8, 193, 190, 194, 197, 198
Kennedy, R., 155
Kimchi, Shlomo (settler rabbi) 180
Kliever, L., 30
Kneal, E., 10, 54
Koby, M., 70

Komonchak, J., 155
Kosovo, 25
Krishnaswami, A., 129
Kronish, R. (founder of ICCI), 164
Kuwait, 41

Laclua, E., 24
Laporte, 219
Last, M., 192
Lauterpacht, 152
law Religious Courts Lay, 92
Levi, W., 30
Levine, S., 2
Leviticus, 94, 169
liberal conception of faith, 129
Linzer, D., 177
Living Constitution, 70, 77
Lombardi, C., 47, 48, 49
Lonergan, B., 56, 57, 58, 59, 60, 62, 63, 64, 65; Blessed Trinity, 67; canon law, 60; method, 58, 60; transcendental concepts, 59
Long, G., 17
Lonsdale, J., 190, 191, 192
Luke, 86
Lutheran Church of Christ in Nigeria (LCCN) 190, 201
Lynch, E., 30

Magaji, A., 197
Mahbubul Islam, 139
Majelis Ulama Indonesia (MUI), 97
Malik bin Anas, Imam, 88
Maodoodi, 18
Margalit, A., 177
Marguerat, D., 108
Markan Code, 12, 103, 106
Mark's code, 105
Marshall, W., 28, 29; Chief Justice, 71
Martens, K., 13, 143
Martin, J., 24
Matthew, 91, 194
Maxwell, D., 188
McGovern, A., 30
McWorld, 82

meaning construction, 33; religion, 27
meek, 198
Meimad, 164
Messiah, 103
Messianic era, 173
Michie, 106
Michiels, G., 54
Mir, M., 88
modern Hebrew, 180
modernist view (apostasy), 140
Monballyu, J., 145
Moneta, P., 53, 54
monogamy, 89
Mosaic Revelation, 168
Moses, 5, 173
Mudzhar, M., 94
Muh, Q., 95
Muqaddimaat, Ibn Rushd, 2006
musawah, 239
Mutahhari, M., 215

Nahas, J., 95
Nahjolbalaqeh, 205
narrative approach, 107
Nasr, H., 209
Netivot Shalom, 164
Neuwirth, A., 88
New Deal legislation, 76
New Testament, 121
Nigeria, 9, 185, 247
Nissen, M., 190
Nkrumah, K., 194
Noether, E., 148
non-Jewish minorities, 181
Northern People's Congress, 194, 195
Nostra aetate, 153, 154
Nowak, M., 3, 4

Old Testament, 172, 195
Oman, 41
Orentlicher, D., 17
Organization of the Islamic Conference (OIC) 89, 241

INDEX

Orientalism, 5
Ormiston, G., 3
Örsy, L., 10, 53, 54
Orthodox Jews, 175
Osaghae, E., 190
Ottaviani, A., 146, 147
Otten, W., 7, 24, 226, 228
Ovey, C., 152
Oz V'Shalom, 164

Palestinians, 178, 179, 180
Parratt, J., 191
Patrick, J., 17
Paul, letter to Galatians, 223
Pavan, P., 154
peace camp, Israel, 174, 175
Peel, J., 191
Peerenboom, R., 41
Perrin, L., 155
Philipse, H., 69
Phillips, D., 3
Pierre Savage (American-Jewish film maker), 174
polygamy, 89
Pompe, B., 94
Pope Benedict XV, 147
Pope Benedict XVI, 151
Pope John Paul II, 91, 144, 145
Pope John XXIII, 145
Pope Leo XIII, 150
Pope Paul VI, 150, 151
Pope Pius IX, 149, 150
Poulton, H., 24
Powell, M., 108
power, 220
public sphere, 24

Qadi, 248
Qur'an, 125, 186, 243; external context, 126; Matthew, 6
Qur'anic (principles for religious freedom) 134
Qur'anic conception of religion, 133
Qutb, S., 188, 189

Rabat Declaration on children's rights, 241
rabbinic homily, 172
Rabbis for Human Rights, 164
Rabin, Prime Minister of Israel, 27
Rawls, J., 31
Raz, J., 39, 128
reddah, 139
reformed churches, 220
Reggio, Rabbi Yitzhak Shemuel, 169
Rehnquist, W., 75
religion: context of revelation, 132; discursive narratives, 32; freedom, 17, 125; intolerance, 28; mobilization, 23; texts, 185
religious freedom, 127, 128, 143, 149; declaration of, 151; justification, 129
religious humanism, 164
religious identity, 7, 22, 25
religious text, construction of meaning, 23
religious tolerance, 149
Reynolds, P., 230
Rhoads, D., 108, 115
Ricoeur, P., 186
Roberts, A., 225
Robertson, A., 143, 152
Roosevelt, F. D. R., 26
Rouwhorst, G., 24
rule of law, 37, 38, 39

Safrai, Z., 173
Sagi, A., 173
Said, E., 5
Salemink, T., 7
Salih, M., 8, 24
Sanneh, L., 191
Sarrami, S., 139
Satanic Verses, The, 8
Scalia, Justice Antonin, 69, 71
Scatena, S., 154
Schaff, P., 228, 230, 232
Schaffer, E., 152

Schneiders, S., 112
Schrift, A., 3
Schubeck, T., 30
scripture: hermeneutics, 33; interpretation of, 185, 198; and politics, 1, 7, 8, 16, 32; Qur'anic, 141
Second Vatican Council, 13, 146
Sen, A., 26
September 11, 1, 5, 21, 27
sex, definitions of, 242
sexuality, 241; female sexuality in religion, 244; in Islam, 243–44
sexual rights, 245
Sha'ria, 13, 47, 49
Shar'ia law, 42
Sharma, A., 237
Sheen, J., 4, 17
shura, 6
Singapore, 41
Simonsen, J., 188
Sisters in Islam (SIS), 240
Skinner, Q.: hermeneutics, 210; procedure, 211
societas perfecta, 147
Sokoto Caliphate, 192
South Africa, 92
Stark, J., 220
Steenbrink, K., 12
Steinsaltz, Adin, Rabbi, 172
Stevens, P., 197
Sudan, 185
Sulastomo, 93
Sunnah, 139, 188
Supreme Constitutional Court (SCC) 31, 47, 49
Syria, 85

Tabatabaiee, M., 133, 134, 138, 212
Tagle, L., 154
Tahzib, B., 128
Taji-Farouki, S., 24
taqlid, 47, 48
Taylor, C., 24

Telford, W., 103
Ten Commandments, 91
Tertio Millennio Adveniente, 144
Tertullian, 15, 227, 228
Tertullian's treatise, 225
theological rationale, 171
Theology, Liberation, 30
Timothy, 224, 231
Toope, S., 38
Torah, 92, 166, 169–72, 178, 180, 182–83
Torfs, R., 53
Touray, I., 237
Treat, J., 7
Trinity, 57; Blessed, 67
Troisfontaines, C., 154
Tuckett, C., 103

Uhud, battle of, 90
UN Resolution 2200A (XXI) 152
United States Constitution, 69
Universal Declaration of Human Rights of 1948 (UDHR), 27, 125, 141
universal responsibility, 35
Uttar Pradesh, 24
Utzscneider, H., 108

van Dijk, 188
van Iersel, B., 108
van Oyen, 12, 101, 116
van Schaik, 152
Vatican, death penalty, 91
Vatican II document, 55

Wadud, A., 240
Walzer, M., 195
Watt, W., 87
Weissman, D., 14, 163, 181
Weizer, P., 69
Weltanschauung, 10, 54
Western European Jewry, 165
Whitaker, C., 193
Wilberforce, King, 199

Wilfred, F., 83
Wilson-Kastner, P., 1981
women: in Early Christianity, 219, 221; as theological prism, 232
Women Living Under Muslim Laws (WLUML) 240
women's rights, 31, 237
World Council of Churches (WCC) 89, 90, 153

Yinger, J., 28
Young, 237
Yugoslavia, 25

Zakaria, F., 41
Zamfara state, Nigeria, 185
Zimbabwe Council of Churches (ZCC) 89, 90
Zionists, 176